Apprehending Love:
Theological and Philosophical Inquiries

Apprehending Love: Theological and Philosophical Inquiries

Edited by
Pekka Kärkkäinen and Olli-Pekka Vainio

WIPF & STOCK · Eugene, Oregon

Wipf and Stock Publishers
199 W 8th Ave, Suite 3
Eugene, OR 97401

Apprehending Love
Theological and Philosophical Inquiries
By Karkkainen, Pekka and Vainio, Olli-Pekka
Copyright © 2019 Luther-Agricola-Seura All rights reserved.
Softcover ISBN-13: 978-1-7252-8279-7
Publication date 6/4/2020
Previously published by Luther-Agricola-Seura, 2019

Risto Saarinen

Tabula gratulatoria

Anneli & Lars Aejmelaeus
Miika Ahola
Jaakko Olavi Antila
Miikka E. Anttila
Hanne Appelqvist
Kenneth Appold
Kaarlo Arffman
Thomas Bremer
Peter De Mey
Theo Dieter
Ismo Dunderberg & Päivi Salmesvuori
Anne-Marit Enroth-Voitila & Anssi Voitila
Sara Gehlin
Hans-Peter Grosshans
Heikki Haara
Raine & Leena Haikarainen
Raimo Hakola
Jaana Hallamaa
Inkeri & Markku Heikkilä
Ida Heikkilä
Simo Heininen
Eija Helander & Gustav Björkstrand
Elina Hellqvist
Christine Helmer & Robert A. Orsi
Minna Hietamäki
Vesa Hirvonen & Markku Laitinen
Bo Kristian Holm
Taina & Toivo Holopainen
Ilkka Huhta
Eero & Anja-Tuulikki Huovinen
Heta Hurskainen
Anna Kaisa & Jouni Inkala
Werner G. Jeanrond
Jutta Jokiranta
Maijastiina Kahlos

Kaarlo Kalliala
Ilmari Karimies
Tuukka Kauhanen
Lauri Kemppainen
Hanna-Maija & Mikko Ketola
Sari Kivistö
Sirpa & Jyrki Knuutila
Simo Knuuttila
Timo Koistinen
Rope Kojonen
Kari Kopperi & Eeva Salo-Kopperi
Päivi Korvajärvi
Heikki J. Koskinen
Pekka Kärkkäinen
Veli-Matti Kärkkäinen
Vera La Mela
Saara Laakkonen
Tuija & Esko M. Laine
Aila & Risto Lauha
Outi Lehtipuu & Olli-Pekka Silfverhuth
Jason Lepojärvi
Volker Leppin
Mikael Lindfelt
Tapio & Pirjo Luoma
Tiina & Petri Luomanen
Antti Marjanen
Hannu Mustakallio
Friederike Nüssel
Isto Peltomäki
Jairzinho Lopes Pereira
Anne Birgitta Pessi
Ted Peters
Anni & Simo Peura
Panu Pihkala
Sami Pihlström
Michael Plathow
Anna-Liisa Rafael

Antti Raunio
Päivi & Matti Repo
Michael Root
Miikka Ruokanen
Jaakko Rusama
Esko & Riikka Ryökäs
Antti Räsänen
Gabriel Salmela OP
Joona Salminen
Markus Siltanen
Teemu Sippo SCJ
Pamela Slotte
Raija & Matti Sollamo
Uwe Swarat
Jouko Talonen
Kati Tervo-Niemelä
Kyllikki Tiensuu & Jari Lampinen
Siiri Toiviainen Rø
Saku & Hanna Toiviainen
Sari Wagner
Olli-Pekka & Salla Vainio
Michael Welker
Elina Vuola
Auli & Mika Vähäkangas
Antti Yli-Opas
Heidi Zitting

Finnsh Ecumenical Council
Helsingin hiippakunta
Institute for Ecumenical Research Strasbourg
Kirkkohallitus
Kirkon koulutuskeskus
Lapuan hiippakunta
Pakilan seurakunta
Studium Catholicum
Teologian Ylioppilaiden Tiedekuntayhdistys
Teologin vid Åbo Akademi, genom Dekanus Mikael Lindfelt

Contents

To Risto 12

Introduction 14

THEODOR DIETER
Über Liebe und Glaube beim frühen Luther 18

WERNER G. JEANROND
Love and Hope 45

VELI-MATTI KÄRKKÄINEN
"ex abundantia caritatis suae": Divine Self-Revelation and
the Abundance of Trinitarian Love 56

MICHAEL WELKER
Bonhoeffer on Love 74

SAMI PIHLSTRÖM & SARI KIVISTÖ
The Limits of Sense and Transcendental Melancholy in the
Philosophy of Love 87

OLLI-PEKKA VAINIO
Locus De Ira et Odio: Hate and Anger as Theological Categories 115

JAANA HALLAMAA
Hate Speech as a Form of Action 127

KENNETH G. APPOLD
The Significance of CA 7 for Lutheran Orthodox Ecclesiologies 145

FRIEDERIKE NÜSSEL
God's Presence in Jesus Christ – Schleiermacher's Transformation
of Luther's Christological Legacy 163

MINNA HIETAMÄKI
"With Love for the Truth, with Charity, with Humility":
Attitudes and Ecumenical Recognition 182

PETER DE MEY
The Love of God as Foundation for Christian Charity in Vatican II
and in the Teaching of Pope Benedict and Pope Francis 209

MICHAEL ROOT
The Individual Theologian and Ecumenical Engagement:
Case Studies on Being, Grace, and Love 228

SIMO KNUUTTILA
Compassion in Medieval Philosophy and Theology 252

ANTTI RAUNIO
Luther on Christian Unanimity in Faith and Love 275

BO KRISTIAN HOLM
Luther, Seneca, and Benevolence in both Creation and Government ... 292

TED PETERS
Is God's Grace Really a Gift? Unraveling a Pseudo-Problem 318

JASON LEPOJÄRVI
"Companions in Shipwreck": J. R. R. Tolkien's Female Friendships ... 344

The list of contributors 371

To Risto

In June 7, 2019 our teacher and colleague, Professor of Ecumenics at the University of Helsinki, Risto Saarinen, turns 60. Professor Saarinen is an internationally renowned scholar, whose work ranges from intellectual history, concentrating especially to the Reformation era, to contemporary themes in systematic theology. To date, his publications include over 300 scholarly articles and over 20 books and edited volumes, including a detective novel – and there seems to be no end in sight.

His major works include the analysis of background assumptions of German Luther scholarship (*Gottes Wirken auf uns: die transzendentale Deutung des Gegenwart-Christi-Motivs in der Lutherforschung*, 1989), two volumes on history of *akrasia* (*Weakness of the Will in Medieval Thought: From Augustine to Buridan*, 1994; *Weakness of Will in Renaissance and Reformation Thought*, 2011) and his recent work on the concept of recognition (*Recognition and Religion: A Historical and Systematic Study*, 2016).

Saarinen began his academic studies in Faculty of Theology at the University of Helsinki and this road led to two PhDs, the first in theology (1988) and the second in philosophy (1994). He served several years as a fellow at the Ecumenical Institute in Strasbourg (2003–2007) before returning to Helsinki first as an acting professor of social ethics and in 2001 he became the full professor in Ecumenics, and successor to his Doktorvater Tuomo Mannermaa (1937–2015). It is largely due to his accomplishments that the University of Helsinki has continued to be one of the main centres in Reformation studies.

During his years in Helsinki he has acted as a central figure in the faculty, among other things as a Vice-Dean for Research. He has led and co-led several major research projects and has trained numerous master's and doctoral students, who have gone on to serve society in various forms, in academia, churches and other communities. Recently, he has been Director of the Academy of Finland's Centre of Excellence "Reason and Religious

Recognition" project (2014–2019). Saarinen has been active in ecumenical dialogues, most importantly in the International Lutheran-Orthodox dialogue. He has been a member of the Finnish Academy of Science and Letters since 1999, and in 2017, he received an honorary doctorate at the University of Copenhagen.

With this volume, we friends, students and colleagues of Risto, express our warm gratitude for his various contributions to many fields of life, and wish him all manner of good things for the coming years.

Helsinki June 7, 2019

Editors and contributors

Introduction

Pekka Kärkkäinen and Olli-Pekka Vainio

This volume collects together Professor Risto Saarinen's friends, students and colleagues, who in their articles engage a variety of themes related to love, broadly understood. The title of this book "apprehending love" employs the notion of *apprehensio* and especially its medieval background. For example, Martin Luther built his understanding of justification around this concept, which, on the one hand, refers to intellectual comprehension but on the other hand means becoming one with the object itself. In faith, Christ becomes not only the outward object of our faith, but its proper subject. In a similar way, when we love someone or something, we are transformed according to the object of our love. Our hope is that these articles are not only intellectually insightful but also transformative to readers.

The outlines of the following fifteen articles are as follows.

Theo Dieter offers an analysis of a text by Luther where he addresses a question how to relate the effectivity of justification, which seeks to direct our loves rightly towards God and one's neighbour, with our state as sinful beings who are never wholly purified in this life. He claims that while the forensic side of justification has a certain primacy for Luther, this is realized in effective *promissio Christi*, so that while the believer's love for God is always fragmentary, in faith the believer apprehends Christ entirely.

Werner Jeanrond investigates the notions of love and hope and explores what it would mean to approach hope from within a horizon of love. He encourages a reconsideration of the virtues of love and hope outside subordination to preconceived or dogmatic notions of faith so that challenging the traditional hierarchy among the three theological virtues might allow us to gain new insights into the dynamics of faith.

Veli-Matti Kärkkäinen highlights the nature and significance of divine revelation through the lens of God's love. He argues that whatever else we might be saying theologically about God's self-revelation and however we define its mode and motif, behind God's voluntary and effectual self-revelation is God's infinitely abundant love. In fact, divine self-revelation is a profound gift of God to humanity.

In his article on Dietrich Bonhoeffer's theology of love, Michael Welker shows how love has both individual and communal effects. Love forms a community that it then keeps active through its own living character, which is shaped by the salvific activity of Christ. Love is a transformative force: God's love overcomes all manifestations of hostility and hate. In gratitude, humility, patience, and in the power of hope, we struggle to be formed according to his divine image of love.

Sami Pihlström and Sari Kivistö examine possible ways of redrawing the boundaries between rationality and irrationality, meaningfulness and meaninglessness, and contingency and necessity in our understanding of love. In dialogue with various literary sources, they argue that we may through love re-examine and re-evaluate everything in our lives, including the meaning morality has for us. This is what it means to speak of love as a "transcendental limit phenomenon".

Olli-Pekka Vainio examines the use of the word hate in the Bible and evaluates the discussion in contemporary moral and cognitive psychology concerning the possible benefits of hate. He offers a systematic and constructive account of hate as a theological category and argues that in some cases hate can be viewed as a moral virtue, and thereby as an act of love.

Jaana Hallamaa assesses and furthers the debate concerning fake news and hate speech with a reference to some recent legal and political cases in Finland. She argues that while there is no easy and simple means to curb hate speech, sound argumentation is the only sustainable alternative to it. However, the problem is that sound argumentation often seems rather powerless in the face of hate speech, which relies on primal psychological and social mechanisms.

Kenneth Appold tackles the ecumenical problem to do with the assumption according to which there are 'fundamental' differences between Lutheran ecclesiology and Roman Catholic, Anglican or Reformed ecclesiologies. Basing his analysis on the Augsburg Confession and its immediate reception and use in early Lutheran communities, he argues that Lutheran ecclesiological theorization were not fully thought through during the Reformation era and contemporary difficulties reflect this origin.

In her article on the relationship between Luther and Schleiermacher, Friederike Nüssel argues that even if Schleiermacher gives up the traditional terminology of incarnational Christology, his theology offers a way to explain the adoption of believers in terms of recognition of their faith. If, however, one takes into account faith as caused by way of communication of the Gospel of Jesus Christ that allows one to recognize Christ as the Redeemer, and if this redemption is granted to recognize Christ's personhood through his ministry in his life, then recognition in justification is a gift mediated through Christ himself.

In her contribution Minna Hietamäki uses the idea of recognition to discuss the movement towards church unity in ecumenism. She focuses especially on love as an attitude which motivates recognition at its very core, namely in the recognition as a person. After the clarification of the concept of recognition in general terms and in theological discourse, Hietamäki analyses different aspects of recognition in ecumenical discussions, culminating with a discussion on the role of love.

In his essay, Peter De Mey continues the discussion on the ecumenical import of the concept of love. His specific topic is the virtue of love (*caritas*) as it is presented in the documents of the Second Vatican Council and later by Popes Benedict XVI and Francis. Already from the discussion of the conciliar documents it becomes evident that the virtue of love is firmly grounded in God's love. Similar ideas are reflected and developed further by the two popes in respect to several theological themes.

Michael Root takes up the discussion on the Catholic theology of love, but at the same time reflects on the modern classic of Protestant theology, Karl Barth. Specifically, Root analyses recent Catholic engagement with Barth's theology of love, which provides critical but constructive insights into the Catholic position. This provides the author a platform for discussing questions about Protestant-Catholic relations on a more general level.

Simo Knuuttila's contribution leads us to another emotion and to another time. Compassion, which is hardly unrelated to love, is examined in the writings of medieval Latin authors. The story begins with Augustine and the Stoics, proceeds with medieval accounts on the conceptual structure of compassion, and ends in discussions on theological formulations of God's mercy.

Antti Raunio in his article again introduces the ecumenical question of Christian unity, providing additional insights from Martin Luther's theology. The key question about unanimity and diversity in the Christian community was not unknown to Luther. Raunio shows how the Reformer discusses the problem with the help of the core concepts of his theology, namely faith and love.

Luther is also discussed in Bo Holm's contribution, this time with regard to Luther's and Melanchthon's reception of Seneca's ideas on benefices. Holm examines Senecan influence in the reformers' theology of creation and in the notions of the benevolence of the creator and the ideal of the benevolent prince.

The Lutheran idea of God's free gift in the justification by faith offers the starting point for Ted Peters's essay. Peters argues that the problem of the pure gift, as it is often described, is misplaced at the outset. He proves this by an analysis of the related concepts of grace, favour, mercy, agape and the gift.

The topic of Jason Lepojärvi's article is J. R. R. Tolkien and women. Lepojärvi discusses Tolkien's views on friendship love between the sexes, but also examines whether Tolkien's relationships with the women in his life actually rose to the level of intimate friendship. In order to answer this question, Lepojärvi provides an overview of Tolkien's interaction with women among his family, his female fandom and in his academic career.

Über Liebe und Glaube beim frühen Luther

Theodor Dieter

Der folgende Text ist der Versuch, eine Frage zu beantworten, die Risto Saarinen mir vor ein paar Jahren gestellt hat. Ich hatte in einem Vortrag Luthers Verständnis der Sünde als In-allem-das-Seine-Suchen (*in omnibus quaerere quae sua sunt*), als universales Aneignungsstreben, entwickelt, das nicht einmal vor Gott als dem *summum bonum* Halt macht.[1] Dementsprechend wird das Haben-Wollen des Menschen äußerst negativ gesehen. Ganz anders dagegen spricht Luther im Freiheitstraktat: "Glaubst du, so hast du. Glaubst du nicht, so hast du nicht."[2] Hier wird das Haben offenbar positiv beurteilt. Wie, so lautete die Frage, verhält sich beides zueinander?[3] Die Antwort wird bestimmte Aspekte des Verhältnisses von Liebe und Glaube beim frühen Luther und die Veränderung ihres Verständnisses im Prozess seiner theologischen Entwicklung erörtern.

I. Die Uneindeutigkeit der Liebe

Menschliches Handeln ist intentional: Es ist auf ein Ziel ausgerichtet; dieses ist als Worumwillen – im Sinn einer Zielursache – ursächlich für das

---

[1] Vgl. Dieter 2016a, 63–67 und Dieter 2001, 80–107. – Im Folgenden wird die männliche Sprachform (Genus) aus Gründen der sprachlichen Korrektheit und der Einfachheit gewählt; der Ausdruck "Sünder" schließt also auch weibliche Personen ein, usw.
[2] Luther 2012, 287.
[3] Dass gerade Risto Saarinen diese Frage stellt, überrascht nicht, denn er hat in seinem umfangreichen Werk das Thema der Gabe höchst perspektivenreich untersucht und unser Verständnis davon wesentlich bereichert. Vgl. zuletzt: Saarinen 2017.

Wollen und Handeln. Dieses Wollen braucht ein letztes Ziel (*finis ultimus*), um nicht haltlos zu sein. Im antiken und mittelalterlichen christlichen Kontext wird dieses letzte Ziel in der Alternative von Liebe zu Gott oder Selbstliebe gesehen. Augustinus hat diese Alternative in der Begründung der *civitas caelestis* und der *civitas terrena* so bestimmt: "Zwei Lieben sind es, die die beiden Staaten schufen: die Selbstliebe bis zur Verachtung Gottes schuf den irdischen, die Liebe zu Gott bis zur Verachtung seiner selbst schuf den himmlischen Staat."[4] In der wirkmächtigen augustinischen Konzeption wird jedes Menschenleben vor eine grundlegende Alternative gestellt. Die beiden Bewegungen der Liebe integrieren die gesamten Aktivitäten eines Menschen in die eine oder die andere Richtung. Da im Christentum der Horizont des Lebens über das irdische Leben hinausreicht in das ewige Leben, haben die Akte des Menschen nicht allein Bedeutung für sein irdisches Leben, sie haben immer auch eine Ewigkeitsbedeutung.

Theologisch wird die Frage der Gottesliebe an zwei Stellen in besonderer Weise zum Thema gemacht. Erstens: Menschen werden – nach dem Sündenfall – in Gottesferne geboren, ohne die theologischen Tugenden Glaube, Hoffnung und Liebe; sie befinden sich nicht im Zustand der Gnade. Darum ist die erste, dringende Frage, wie sie in einen Zustand der Gnade kommen können, denn wenn sie nicht im Stand der Gnade sterben, wird ihre Gottesferne definitiv und endgültig, und das ist die Hölle. Der erste Übergang in den Stand der Gnade geschieht in der Taufe, in der mit der Gnade Glaube, Hoffnung und Liebe den Menschen mitgeteilt werden. Die von Gott gegebene Liebe zu ihm wirkt aber nicht automatisch Akte der Gottesliebe; mit seinem freien Willen kann auch ein Mensch in der Gnade Akte der Selbstliebe bis zur Verachtung Gottes hervorbringen. Hat er eine solche Sünde zum Tode begangen, so zerstört er die von Gott gegebene *caritas*, die ihn gerade auf Gott um Gottes willen ausrichtet. Nun befindet sich ein solcher Mensch wieder in gnadenlosem Zustand.

So stellt sich für den Todsünder die Frage: Wie komme ich wieder in den Stand der Gnade? Wie finde ich einen gnädigen Gott? Die Antwort gibt das Sakrament der Buße, in dem nach scholastischer Auffassung die Reue (*contritio*) des Menschen die entscheidende Rolle spielt. In der Reue aber stellt sich wiederum die Alternative: Gottesliebe oder Selbstliebe?

---

[4] AUGUSTINUS 1955, 451 (XIV, 28).

Bereut ein Sünder aus Angst vor der Hölle oder aus dem Schmerz heraus, Gott verletzt zu haben, also aus Liebe zu Gott? So entsteht ein schwerer Motivationskonflikt: Der Bereuende will etwas Gutes *für sich*, nämlich die Vergebung seiner Sünden und die erneute Verleihung der Gnade. Dazu aber muss er, so die spätmittelalterlichen Theologen, etwa Gabriel Biel, Gott *um Gottes willen*, Gott über alles lieben.[5] Wie soll der Motivationskonflikt zwischen dem eigenen Interesse und dem von allem eigenen Interesse freien Akt der Liebe zu Gott, der zur Erfüllung dieses Interesses notwendig ist, gelöst werden? Was bewegt ("motiviert") den Sünder in der Reue zuletzt, Selbstliebe oder Gottesliebe?

Für Gabriel Biel ist die Auflösung dieses Motivationskonflikts kein Problem, denn ihm zufolge kann der Mensch aufgrund der Freiheit seines Willens Gott über alles lieben, und zwar aus seinem natürlichen Vermögen (*ex suis naturalibus*)[6] – die Gnade kann er ja nicht in Anspruch nehmen; er hat sie als Todsünder verloren und will sie gerade wiedergewinnen. Wahre Reue, die die Verleihung der Gnade erwarten darf, setzt also einen natürlichen Akt der Liebe zu Gott voraus. Dieser Akt ist ein Akt des Willens – "Lieben" und "Wollen" sind hier äquivalent. Die Frage, ob der Todsünder Gott über alles lieben kann, ist eine Frage der Willensfreiheit, und die philosophische Frage der Willensfreiheit hat als ihr höchstes Thema die Liebe zu Gott.

Noch in einer zweiten Grundsituation des Menschen spielt die Liebe zu Gott eine entscheidende Rolle. Wenn menschliche Akte verdienstlich für das ewige Leben sein sollen, müssen sie aus Liebe zu Gott vollzogen werden. "Liebe zu Gott" hat hier eine doppelte Bedeutung. Wird einem Menschen in der Taufe oder im Sakrament der Buße die Sünde vergeben, dann wird ihm die Gnade "eingegossen" und mit ihr, wie schon erwähnt, auch Glaube, Hoffnung und Liebe. Ohne diese eingegossene Liebe oder

---

[5] Vgl. BIEL, *Sent.* II, dist. 27, qu. un., art. 2, concl. 4 K 1–2. 51–54 (BIEL 1984, 517–518). BIEL, *Sent.* III, dist. 27, qu. un., art. 3, dub. 2, prop. 2 Q 70–75 (BIEL 1979, 505–506).

[6] Biel, *Sent.* III, dist. 27, qu. un., art. 3, dub. 2, prop. 1 Q 23–24 (BIEL 1979, 504): "Viatoris voluntas humana ex suis naturalibus potest diligere Deum super omnia." Dass Gott auf einen solchen Akt mit der Vergebung der Sünden und der Verleihung der Gnade antwortet, beruht auf seiner freien, von Ewigkeit her getroffenen Entscheidung zu einem *pactum*, das die Form hat: "Deus dat gratiam facienti quod in se est necessitate immutabilitatis et ex suppositione, quia disposuit dare immutabiliter gratiam facienti quod in se est" (BIEL, *Sent.* II, dist. 27, qu. un., art. 3, dub. 4 O 7–9 [BIEL 1984, 523]).

Gnade kann kein menschlicher Akt verdienstlich sein – so hat Gott das in seiner ewigen Ordnung aus Freiheit festgelegt. Es ist der Wille Gottes, des Gesetzgebers, dass Menschen sein Gesetz nicht nur seinem Inhalt nach (*secundum substantiam*), sondern darüber hinaus in der Gnade erfüllen, damit ihre Werke verdienstlich seien zum ewigen Leben.[7] Aber die eingegossene Liebe bringt keinen Akt hervor; sie ist kein aktives Prinzip, sondern eine Qualität der Seele, also ein naturales Prinzip. Akte des Willens sind freie Akte und werden vom *liberum arbitrium* hervorgebracht. Die eingegossene Liebe zu Gott ist die *Bedingung* für die *Verdienstlichkeit* bestimmter Akte, aber die *Verursachung* der Akte *hinsichtlich ihrer Substanz* liegt beim Willen.[8] Die eingegossene Liebe wird durch ihre Hinneigung (*inclinatio*) den Willen unterstützen; aber es ist der Wille, der bestimmte Akte, zum Beispiel die Willensakte, Almosen zu geben oder in die Kirche zu gehen, auf Gott als ihr Ziel ausrichtet.

Biel betont, dass der Willensakt vor und nach der Verleihung der Gnade von derselben Art ist.[9] Diese Auffassung hat immer wieder Luthers schärfste Kritik gefunden.[10] Hier ist die Gnade kein Mittel, das dem Menschen hilft, mit seiner aktiven Neigung zur Sünde fertig zu werden; nach Biel kann das der Mensch aufgrund der Freiheit seines Willens alleine schaffen, wenn auch mit Mühe. Dass ein Mensch in der Gnade ist, ist nur erfordert für die Verdienstlichkeit eines Aktes, weil eben die göttliche Ordnung diese Bedingung vorgegeben hat. Das In-der-Gnade-Sein ist nach Luthers Urteil dann nur eine *zusätzliche* Bedingung für die volle (nämlich verdienstliche) Erfüllung des Gesetzes.[11]

Weil die Liebe zu Gott die ganze menschliche Existenz betrifft, ist es nicht verwunderlich, dass die Frage nach der Möglichkeit des Menschen

---

[7] Vgl. BIEL, *Sent.* II, qu. un., dist. 28, art. 2, concl. 3 K 16–24 (BIEL 1984, 539).

[8] Vgl. BIEL, *Sent.* II, qu. un., dist. 27, art. 3, dub. 2, vor allem M 17–20; 25–34 (BIEL 1984, 520–521).

[9] BIEL, *Sent.* I, dist. 17, qu. 1, art. 2, concl. 1 C 8–9 (BIEL 1973, 415): "Actus diligendi Deum praecedens talem formam [scil. caritas infusa] et actus diligendi sequens sunt eiusdem rationis."

[10] Vgl. zum Beispiel WA 56; 337, 16–23.

[11] WA 1, 227, 6–11 (*Disputatio contra scholasticam theologiam*): "57. Periculosa est haec oratio: lex praecipit, quod actus praecepti fiat in gratia dei. Contra card. [Pierre d' Ailly] et Gab. [Gabriel Biel] 58. Sequitur ex ea, quod gratiam dei habere sit iam nova ultra legem exactio. 59. Ex eadem sequitur quod actus praecepti possit fieri sine gratia dei. 60. Item sequitur quod odiosior fiat gratia dei quam fuit lex ipsa."

zu dieser Gottesliebe im Zentrum der Auseinandersetzung Luthers mit den scholastischen Theologen steht. Die meisten Thesen der später so genannten "Disputation gegen die scholastische Theologie" beziehen sich auf einen relativ kleinen Textabschnitt aus dem dritten Buch von Gabriel Biels "Collectorium". Es ist ein *dubium*; Luther setzt sich mit vier der fünf *propositiones* dieses *dubiums* auseinander.[12] Das Thema lautet: "Ob der menschliche Wille des Pilgers Gott aus seinen natürlichen Kräften über alles lieben und so das Gebot der Liebe erfüllen kann".[13] Bei dem "Gebot der Liebe" geht es um das Gebot der Liebe zu Gott, das Mk 12,30 so lautet: "Du sollst lieben den Herrn, deinen Gott, von ganzem Herzen [ex toto corde tuo], von ganzer Seele [ex tota anima tua], aus deinem ganzen Verstand [ex tota mente tua] und mit all deiner Kraft [ex tota virtute tua]." In seiner Auslegung dieses Gebots bezieht Biel "cor" auf die "voluntas, quae aliis omnibus imperat", "mens" auf den intellectus, "anima" auf die vis sensitiva und fortitudo (statt "virtus") auf die "vis motiva corporalium membrorum ad opera exsequenda".[14] Biel stimmt Augustins Verständnis des Liebesgebots zu und zitiert wörtlich, was der Kirchenvater über die Ganzheit in der Liebe zu Gott sagt. Gott ist so zu lieben, "dass du alle deine Gedanken, dein ganzes Leben und deinen Verstand auf jenen richtest, von dem du das hast, was du ihm bringst. Wenn er aber sagt 'mit ganzer Seele, mit ganzem Herzen, mit ganzem Verstand', dann lässt er keinen Teil unseres Lebens aus, der leer sein und gewissermaßen Raum geben müsste, um eine andere Sache genießen zu wollen. Vielmehr möge alles andere, was als Liebesobjekt in den Sinn kommen mag, dorthin fortgerissen werden, wohin der ganze Drang [totus dilectionis impetus] der Liebe hingeht."[15] Hat man diese massive Affirmation der Ganzheit des Menschen in der Liebe zu Gott im Sinn, so ist es höchst überraschend, dass Biel ohne weitere

---

[12] Vgl. BIEL, *Sent.* III, dist. 27, qu. un., art. 3, dub. 2 Q–R (BIEL 1979, 503–507). Vgl. zum Folgenden DIETER 2016b.

[13] BIEL, *Sent.* III, dist. 27, qu. un., art. 3, dub. 2 Q 1–2 (BIEL 1979, 503): "Utrum voluntas humana viatoris possit Deum ex suis naturalibus diligere super omnia et ita implere praeceptum dilectionis."

[14] Vgl. BIEL, *Sent.* III, dist. 27, qu. un., art.1, not. 5 H 1–36 (BIEL 1979, 490–491).

[15] BIEL, *Sent.* III, dist. 27, qu. un., art.1, not. 5 H 30–35 (BIEL 1979, 490–491) (zitiert ist AUGUSTINUS, *De doctrina christiana* I, XXII, 21 [AUGUSTINUS 1962, 17-18].). Risto Saarinen hat die Frage der Ganzheit des Willens bei Augustinus wiederholt untersucht; vgl. SAARINEN 1994 und SAARINEN 2011.

Begründung sagt, dieses Gebot der Liebe könne auch so ausgedrückt werden: Gott ist über alles zu lieben (diligere Deum super omnia).[16] Das ist deshalb so verwunderlich, weil "lieben" in dieser Formel für einen Akt des Willens steht, während Biel ja unmittelbar davor dargelegt hat, dass das biblische Liebesgebot die Ganzheit des Menschen in der Liebe zu Gott fordert.

Luther hat diese Engführung des Liebesgebots auf den Willen verworfen, und darin wird man eine entscheidende Differenz Luthers zu beinahe allen scholastischen Lehrern sehen müssen. Die schärfte Invektive gegen die scholastischen Theologen in der Römerbrief-Vorlesung findet sich bezeichnenderweise in einer Erörterung der Frage, ob der Mensch die natürliche Möglichkeit, Gott zu lieben, habe. Darin zeigt sich das andere Verständnis der Gottesliebe bei Luther, und es wird deutlich, dass diese Differenz gerade in der Frage der Ganzheit dieser Liebe zu suchen ist. "Es ist reiner Wahnsinn, wenn gesagt wird, dass der Mensch aus seinen eigenen Kräften Gott über alles lieben und die Werke des Gesetzes tun könne der Substanz nach, wenn auch nicht der Intention des Gebietenden nach, weil ein solcher Mensch nicht in der Gnade ist. Oh ihr Toren! Oh ihr Sautheologen!" Dann appelliert Luther an die Selbsterfahrung dieser Theologen, weil der Beweis für die Freiheit zur Gottesliebe immer in ihrer Verwirklichung liegt. "Sie mögen es wollen oder zurückweisen [nolint], sie fühlen in sich schlechte Begierden. Hier also sage ich: Ei, nun, bitte, bemüht euch! Seid Männer! Bewirkt mit allen euren Kräften, dass diese Begierden nicht in euch sind. Beweist, was ihr sagt, dass Gott natürlicherweise 'mit allen Kräften' geliebt werden kann, und nun sogar ohne Gnade. Wenn ihr ohne Begierden seid, glauben wir euch. Wenn ihr aber mit und in ihnen wohnt, habt ihr das Gesetz schon nicht erfüllt, denn das Gesetz sagt: 'Du sollst nicht begehren', sondern: 'du sollst Gott lieben'."[17]

Luthers Kontrahenten hätten vermutlich die angesprochene Selbsterfahrung bestätigt, ihre Interpretation jedoch verworfen. Ihrer Auffassung nach kann sich die Forderung der Gottesliebe nur auf Willensakte beziehen, weil der Mensch nur Macht hat über seinen Willen, nicht jedoch über seine Emotionen oder nur in beschränktem und indirektem Maß

---

[16] BIEL, Sent. III, dist. 27, qu. un., art.1, not. 5 H 35–36 (BIEL 1979, 491).
[17] WA 56, 274, 11–275, 10. Es gibt kein passendes deutsches Äquivalent zu "nolle"; vgl. unten bei Anm. 27.

(etwa moderierend durch die Tugenden). Sein alternatives Verständnis von Gottesliebe und Sünde begründet Luther an vielen Stellen; besonders klar ist ein Text aus den Materialien der "Heidelberger Disputation"; die Bonner Ausgabe nennt sie "Eine vorbereitende Niederschrift zur Heidelberger Disputation"[18]. Darin findet sich ein Corollarium, in dem Luther die – damals wie heute schockierende – These begründet, dass ein Gerechter auch im guten Handeln sündigt.[19] Es verdient größte Beachtung, dass für Luther die Bestimmung eines Handelns als Sünde *nicht* einschließt, dass dieses Handeln auch böse, also moralisch verwerflich wäre. Luther stellt dies ausdrücklich auch vom im theologischen Sinn Ungerechten – dem Menschen außerhalb der Gnade – fest: "Da es auf der Erde nicht einen Gerechten gibt, der im guten Handeln nicht sündigte, wie viel mehr sündigt der Ungerechte, wenn er Gutes tut."[20] Auch der Sünder kann also moralisch Gutes tun; aber das schließt nicht aus, sondern ein, dass er gleichwohl sündigt. Damit ist klar, dass Luther den moralischen Begriff des Guten und Bösen strikt vom theologischen Begriff der Sünde unterscheidet.

Für seine These präsentiert Luther zwei Arten von Argumenten: erstens argumentiert er mit Hilfe von Schriftstellen ("Probatur auctoritatibus"[21]), sodann beweist er "ratione" ("Ratione probo"[22]).

In der ersten Argumentationsreihe führt Luther drei Schriftbelege an: Koh 7,20[23], Röm 7,19.22f[24] mit Gal 5,17[25], Psalm 143[26]. Luther zitiert Röm 7 nicht nur, er legt die beiden angeführten Verse auch aus mit dem

---

[18] LUTHER 1963 [= BoA], 392, 19–20.
[19] BoA V, 394, 3: "Quod iustus etiam inter bene operandum peccet".
[20] BoA V, 393, 30–31: "Cum non sit iustus in terra, qui benefaciens non peccet, multo magis iniustus peccat, dum bonum facit."
[21] BoA V, 393, 32.
[22] BoA V, 395, 12.
[23] Koh 7, 20 (nach der Zählung der Vulgata ist es Koh 7, 21): "Non est iustus in terra, qui faciat bene et non peccet" (nach BoA V, 394, 4–5).
[24] Röm 7, 19, 22–23: "Quod nolo malum, hoc ago, Quod volo bonum, non ago [...] Condelector legi Dei secundum interiorem hominem, Video autem aliam legem in membris meis, repugnantem legi mentis meae" (nach BoA V, 394, 14-17).
[25] Gal 5,17: "Caro concupiscit adversus spiritum et spiritus adversus carnem. Haec duo enim sibi invicem adversantur, ut non ea quae vultis faciatis" (nach BoA V, 395, 3–5).
[26] Psalm 142 (143), 2: "Non intres in iudicium cum servo tuo, Domine, quia non iustificabitur in conspectu tuo omnis vivens" (nach BoA V, 395, 6–7).

Gegensatzpaar: "voluntas/noluntas" und "velle/nolle". "Nolle" meint nicht die Abwesenheit eines Willensaktes (*non velle*), sondern ein aktives, willentliches Verneinen oder Verwerfen von etwas. "Voluntas" meint hier weder das Willensvermögen im philosophischen Sinn noch genau einen Willensakt, sondern so etwas wie die Bewegtheit des Willens auf etwas hin, während "noluntas" die ebenfalls aktive Bewegtheit des Verwerfens von etwas meint. Luther versteht Paulus so, dass zwei gegensätzliche Bewegtheiten im gerechtfertigten Menschen sind – eine von Gott her und auf Gott hin und eine gegen Gott –, so dass sein Wollen selbstwidersprüchlich ist und er nicht ganz ist in seinem Wollen. In diesem Mangel an Ganzheit des Wollens besteht die Sünde.[27]

In der zweiten Art der Argumentation geht Luther syllogistisch vor; Ziel seiner Argumentation ist es zu zeigen, dass der Gerechte auch im guten Tun sündigt. Der erste Syllogismus:

(I; maior) "Wer weniger tut, als er muss, sündigt."
(II; minor) "Jeder Gerechte, wenn er Gutes tut, tut weniger als er muss."
(III; conclusio) "Also."[28]

Der zweite Syllogismus ist der Beweis für Satz (II):

(II A) "Wer immer mit einer nicht vollständigen und vollkommenen Liebe zu Gott gut handelt, tut weniger, als er muss."
(II B) "Aber jeder Gerechte ist so geartet."[29]
(II C; conclusio nicht erwähnt.)

Beweis für (II A):

(II Aa) "Den Obersatz beweise ich mit jenem Gebot 'Du sollst den Herrn, deinen Gott, mit deinem ganzen Herzen und mit all deinen Kräften usw. lieben.'" Daraus folgt: "Also muss man Gott mit allen Kräften lieben, oder wir sündigen."[30]

---

[27] BoA V, 394, 17–28: "Ecce simul delectatur et displicet in lege Dei, Simul vult bonum secundum spiritum, et tamen hoc non agit, sed contrarium. Hoc itaque contrarium quaedam est noluntas, quae semper est, quando est voluntas [...] Tota autem voluntas in hac vita non est. Ideo semper peccamus, dum benefacimus, licet quandoque minus, quandoque magis. Haec enim est causa, quare 'non sit iustus in terra, qui faciat bene et non peccet.'"

[28] BoA V, 395, 13–14: "Quicunque minus facit quam debet, peccat. Sed omnis iustus bene faciens minus facit quam debet. Ergo."

[29] BoA V, 395, 15–17: "Minorem probo: Quicunque non plena et perfecta Dei dilectione bene facit, minus facit quam debet. Sed omnis Iustus ille est est huiusmodi."

[30] BoA V, 395, 17–21: "Maiorem probo per illud praeceptum: 'Diliges Dominum Deum tuum ex toto corde tuo et totis viribus &c. De quo Dominus Matth. 5. 'Unum iota aut unus

Zum Beweis für (II B) verweist Luther auf schon Gesagtes, das er so zusammenfasst: "Das Nicht-Wollen im Fleisch und in den Gliedern hindert diese Ganzheit, so dass nicht alle Glieder oder Kräfte Gott lieben; vielmehr widersteht das Nicht-Wollen dem inneren Wollen, das Gott liebt."[31] Der Verweis auf "oben Gesagtes" bezieht sich auf die drei Schriftbelege, die er als *auctoritates* genannt hat.[32]

Damit hat Luther in nachvollziehbaren Schritten die These, dass der Gerechte auch im guten Handeln sündigt, bewiesen. Aus dieser Argumentation wird klar, dass Luthers alternatives – biblisches – Verständnis des Gebots der Gottesliebe systematisch im Zentrum seiner Kritik an den scholastischen Theologien steht.

Dadurch, dass Luther die Forderung nach Ganzheit der Liebe zu Gott im biblischen Gebot ernstnimmt, erweist sich die gelebte Liebe zu Gott als ambivalent, gerade für den Menschen in der Gnade. In einem solchen Menschen gibt es tatsächlich ein von Gott gegebenes Wollen (*voluntas*), das auf Gott gerichtet ist, aber eben auch ein Wollen, das das Gegenteil will (*noluntas*). Es gibt ein Wollen (*velle*) aus dem Geist, aber auch ein Wollen des Gegenteils (*nolle*) aus dem Fleisch. Diese Situation ist begrifflich schwer zu fassen, und Luther macht verschiedene Versuche dazu, die alle etwas Unbefriedigendes haben: Es geht nicht um Teile des Menschen, die gegeneinander stehen wie etwa sinnliches und rationales Streben, sondern um Ganzheitsbestimmungen – der Mensch in der Gnade ist als ganzer *caro* und als ganzer *spiritus*, und dennoch ist er nicht ganz *caro* oder ganz *spiritus*.[33] Ganzheit wird hier zweifach verstanden als *totus* und *totaliter*.

Wenn nun der Sünder in allem das Seine sucht und auch der Mensch unter der Gnade davon betroffen ist, dann stellt sich für Luther eine doppelte theologische Aufgabe. Er muss erstens das traditionelle pactum-

---

apex non praeteribit a Lege, donec omnia fiant.' Ergo oportet ex totis viribus diligere Deum, aut peccamus."

[31] BoA V, 395, 21–24: "Sed Minor, quod non ex totis viribus diligamus, supra probata est, Quia noluntas in carne et in membris impedit hanc totalitatem, ut non tota membra seu vires diligant Deum, sed resistit interiori voluntati Deum diligenti."

[32] Luther antizipiert auch den Einwand: Gott ist kein Perfektionist; er verlangt keine Vollkommenheit. Dagegen insistiert Luther darauf, dass das Gesetz Gottes anders lautet und Gott auf die Nicht-Ganzheit des Menschen nicht so reagiert, dass er dessen Halbheit in der Liebe zu Gott nicht mehr als Sünde ansieht, sondern so, dass er die Sünde verzeiht. Vgl. BoA V, 395, 25–396, 4.

[33] Vgl. DIETER 2001, 130–136; SAARINEN 2011, 119–122.

Modell aufgeben, wonach Gott keinem seine Gnade verweigert, der tut, was in seinen Kräften steht, also Gott über alles liebt. Das tut Luther, indem er feststellt, dass ein Akt der Liebe zu Gott um Gottes willen der Verleihung der Gnade nicht vorausgeht, sondern die vollkommene Umkehr durch die Gnade voraussetzt und ihr folgt.[34] Da nun aber auch der Mensch in der Gnade in seiner Liebe zu Gott gespalten ist, kann sein rechtes Verhältnis zu Gott nicht auf diese Liebe gegründet sein. Aber er kann diese Gespaltenheit und also Sünde selbst zum Gegenstand machen, und zwar eines Schuldbekenntnisses. Von diesem gilt das Wort des Paulus, das in der Mönchstradition eine große Rolle gespielt hat: "Wenn wir uns selbst richteten, würden wir vom Herrn nicht gerichtet."[35] Dann ist der Mensch in seinen Augen Sünder, in Gottes Augen hingegen gerecht. Die Gerechtigkeit ist also für den Menschen unter ihrem Gegenteil verborgen.[36]

Weil auch der Mensch in der Gnade Sünder ist, ist auch er davon betroffen, dass in ihm das Streben ist, in allem das Seine zu suchen. Luther vergleicht das Sich-in-allem-selbst-Suchen mit einer Sucht. Er argumentiert:

> "Es ist nämlich unmöglich, dass die Begierde befriedigt wird, wenn sie das erlangt hat, wonach sie begehrt. Wie nämlich die Liebe zum Geld in dem Maß wächst, in dem das Geld selbst wächst, so die Wassersucht der Seele: Je mehr jemand trinkt, umso mehr dürstet er [...] So wird die Ruhmsucht nicht befriedigt, wenn sie Ruhm erlangt hat, auch wird die Begierde zu herrschen nicht befriedigt durch Macht und Herrschaft, und die Ruhmsucht wird nicht befriedigt durch Lob usw. [...] Es bleibt also als Heilmittel, dass die Begierde nicht durch ihre Erfüllung geheilt wird, sondern durch ihre Auslöschung, das heißt: Wer weise werden will, intendiere nicht direkt die Weisheit, vielmehr suche er umgekehrt die Torheit und werde ein Tor."[37]

---

[34] Vgl. BoA V, 322,13–17.
[35] 1 Kor 11, 31. Vgl. etwa WA 56, 393, 29–32. Hier zeigt sich noch ein Rest des pactum-Modells: Der Mensch kann zwar Gott nicht ganzheitlich lieben und so die Gnade erlangen, aber er bekennt sein Unvermögen zu dieser Liebe und wird daraufhin gerechtfertigt.
[36] WA 55/2, 273, 151–153: "*Semper igitur peccatum timendum*, semper nos accusandum et Iudicandum in conspectu Dei. Quia si nos ipsos Iudicamus, non vtique a Domino Iudicabimur." WA 1, 359, 29–30: "quantum nos accusamus, tantum Deus excusat." In der Resolution zur fünften Ablassthese erläutert Luther, was er unter "evangelischer Strafe" versteht: Danach ist die poenitentia spiritualis, die von Christus geboten und heilsnotwendig (*de necessitate salutis*) ist: "secundum illud i. Cor: xi. Si nos ipsos iudicaremus, non utique iudicaremur a domino. Haec est crux [...] et mortificatio passionum [...]" (WA 1, 534, 32–34).
[37] BoA V, 389, 16–29: "Impossibile est enim, quod cupiditas satietur his quae cupit

Darum entwickelt Luther den Gedanken, der Mensch könne etwas Gutes nur so haben, dass er es unter seinem Gegenteil hat und dass auch Gott dem Menschen unter dem Gegenteil verborgen begegnet und sich so dem menschlichen Aneignungsstreben entzieht.

> "Unser Gutes ist nämlich verborgen, und zwar so tief, dass es unter dem Gegenteil verborgen ist. So ist unser Leben unter dem Tod, die Liebe zu uns unter dem Hass auf uns, die Ehre unter der Schande, das Heil unter dem Verderben, das Reich unter der Fremde, der Himmel unter der Hölle, die Weisheit unter der Torheit, die Gerechtigkeit unter der Sünde, die Kraft unter der Schwachheit. Und allgemein: Wenn wir irgendetwas als etwas Gutes bejahen, dann vollzieht sich das unter seiner Verneinung, so dass der Glaube seinen Ort hat in Gott, der eine negative Wesenheit ist, und seine Gutheit und Weisheit und Gerechtigkeit können nicht besessen oder erreicht werden, es sei denn unter Verneinung aller unserer affirmativen Bestimmungen."[38]

Diese Auffassung wird programmatisch in der theologia crucis der "Heidelberger Disputation". Hier widerspricht Luther einem Grundzug des mittelalterlichen Denkens. Biel hat das so ausgedrückt: Wenn Gottes unsichtbare Eigenschaften aus der Schöpfung erkannt werden und der Intellekt Gott, den Schöpfer, als etwas Gutes für uns erkennt, kann er von da aus auch weitergehen zu der Erkenntnis, dass Gott gut in sich selbst ist, dass er in sich selbst das höchste Gut ist. Nun ist aber der Wille in der Lage, dem Urteil der Vernunft zu folgen und darum die anfängliche Liebe zu Gott, die Gott als Gut für den Menschen liebt, zu übersteigen in die Liebe zu Gott um Gottes willen, also zu wollen, dass Gott Gott ist, dass er gut, gerecht, weise usw. ist. Biel entwickelt diesen Gedanken

---

acquisitis. Sicut enim crescit amor nummi, quantum ipsa pecunia crescit, Sic hydropisis animae, quo plus bibit, plus sitit [...] Sic cupiditas gloriae non saturatur acquisita gloria, Nec cupido dominandi saturatur potestate et imperio, Nec cupido laudis saturatur laude &c. [...] Restat ergo remedium, ut non explendo curedur, sed extinguendo, id est, ut qui vult fieri sapiens non quaerat sapientiam procedendo, sed fiat stultus quaerendo stulticiam retrocedendo."

[38] WA 56, 392, 29–393, 3: "Bonum enim nostrum absconditum est et ita profunde, Vt sub contrario absconditum sit. Sic Vita nostra sub morte, dilectio nostri sub odio nostri, gloria sub ignominia, salus sub perditione, regnum sub exilio, celum sub inferno, Sapientia sub stultitia, Iustitia sub peccato, virtus sub infirmitate. Et vniversaliter omnis nostra affirmatio boni cuiuscunque sub negatione eiusdem, Vt fides locum habeat in Deo, *Qui Est Negatiua Essentia et bonitas et Sapientia et Iustitia Nec potest possideri aut attingi nisi negatis omnibus affirmatiuis nostris.*"

mit Bezug auf Röm 1, 19–20. In diesem Aufstieg soll die Selbstliebe aufgehoben werden in die Gottesliebe.[39] Luther erkennt aber, dass Paulus betont, dass die Menschen in ihrem Willen dieser Erkenntnis gerade nicht gefolgt sind, denn im folgenden Vers (V. 21) stellt er fest: Obwohl die Menschen Gott erkannten, haben sie ihn nicht als Gott geehrt und haben ihm nicht gedankt. Darum betont Luther in der berühmt gewordenen 19. und 20. These der "Heidelberger Disputation", dass "nicht der mit Recht Theologe genannt wird, der das Unsichtbare Gottes erblickt, erkannt durch das, was geschaffen ist, [...] sondern der, der das Sichtbare und die 'Rückseite' Gottes erkennt, erblickt durch Leiden und Kreuz."[40] Luther beruft sich in der *probatio* auf Paulus, der in 1 Kor 1 und 2 die universale heilsgeschichtliche Umkehrung so beschrieben hat: "Weil die Welt mit ihrer Weisheit Gott in seiner Weisheit nicht erkannt hat, hat es Gott gefallen, die Glaubenden durch die Torheit der Predigt [vom Kreuz] zu retten."[41] Paulus bestätigt, dass der Aufstieg zur Erkenntnis Gottes nicht zur Überwindung der Selbstliebe durch eine reine Gottesliebe geführt hat; die Erkenntnis Gottes als des *summum bonum* hat nicht dazu geführt, dass die Menschen Gott über alles geliebt hätten. Darum begegnet Gott dem universalen Aneignungsstreben des Sünders damit, dass er ihm in dem Gekreuzigten begegnet. Das *summum bonum* am Kreuz! Entweder wenden sich Menschen angewidert von diesem "Gut" ab, oder jenes Aneignungsstreben zerbricht. Dann können sie als Kreuzestheologen nachvollziehen: "[I]n Christo crucifixo est vera Theologia et cognitio Dei."[42]

---

[39] Vgl. BIEL, *Sent*. III, dist. 26, qu. un., art. 3, dub. 2, N 21–25 (BIEL 1979, 476).
[40] BoA V, 388, 5–6, 12–13.
[41] BoA V, 388, 20–22; vgl. 1 Kor 1, 21. – Laut einer Nachschrift von Oskar Becker ist Martin Heidegger in einer Vorlesung im Sommersemester 1921 ("Augustinus und der Neuplatonismus") auch auf Luthers "Heidelberger Disputation" und darin gerade die Thesen zur theologia crucis eingegangen. Zu Röm 1, 19-20 bemerkt Heidegger: "Das Unsichtbare Gottes wird seit der Schätzung [lies: Erschaffung] der Welt an seinen Werken durch das Denken gesehen. Dieser Satz kehrt in den patristischen Schriften ständig wieder, er gibt die Richtung auf den (platonischen) Aufstieg aus der sinnlichen Welt zur übersinnlichen. Er ist (oder wird aufgefasst als) die aus Paulus genommene Bestätigung des Platonismus. Aber darin liegt ein Missverständnis dieser Paulus-Stelle. Erst *Luther* hat sie zum ersten Male eigentlich verstanden. Luther hat in seinen ersten Werken ein neues Verständnis des Urchristentums eröffnet." (HEIDEGGER 1995, 281–282).
[42] BoA V, 388, 29–30.

Kreuzestheologie ist nicht nur eine Erkenntnis, sondern zugleich ein Existenzvollzug. Darin wird die *passio* (das Erleiden) der *actio* vorgezogen. Das ist gemeint, wenn es in der 21. These heißt: "Der Theologe der Herrlichkeit nennt das Übel gut und das Gute übel, der Theologe des Kreuzes sagt, wie es sich in Wahrheit verhält."[43] Leiden ist für einen Kreuzestheologen ein *bonum*, die Werke hingegen erscheinen als *malum*: "Die Freunde des Kreuzes nennen das Kreuz gut und die Werke schlecht, weil durch das Kreuz die Werke zerstört werden und Adam gekreuzigt wird, während er durch die Werke eher aufgebaut wird."[44] Das ist Passivität beim frühen Luther! Sie ist in wörtlichem Sinn zu verstehen als Leiden und Kreuz, durch die der um sich kreisende Mensch destruiert wird. Eine *actio* setzt eine Intention voraus, zu der die Frage nach dem letzten Worumwillen gehört; das menschliche Tun kann ohne jene Passivität – das "Kreuz" – nicht der Selbstbezüglichkeit allen Wollens entkommen.[45]

Weil der Mensch ohne die Theologie des Kreuzes das Beste auf das Schlimmste missbraucht,[46] kann alles, was Gott dem Menschen an Gutem gibt, nur unter der Gestalt des Gegenteils gegenwärtig sein, um seine missbräuchliche Aneignung zu verhindern. Diese Auffassung hat als ihre Grundvoraussetzung, dass es die Liebe als strebende Bewegung des Menschen ist, die sein Verhältnis zu Gott bestimmt. Die Liebe aber ist durch die Sünde ambivalent geworden, und zwar so tief, dass auch die Gnade diese Liebe nicht zur Eindeutigkeit bringen kann. Dieser Mangel an Eindeutigkeit und damit auch an Gewissheit hat Luther bewegt, nicht bei diesem Stand seiner theologischen Erkenntnis stehenzubleiben.

Die Liebe des Menschen zu Gott ist als zweideutig erschienen, als Luther das biblische Liebesgebot mit seiner Ganzheitsforderung ernstgenommen hat. Luther hat damit einen transmoralischen Sündenbegriff gewonnen, der die Dimension des moralisch Guten zwar voraussetzt und einschließt, aber bei weitem überbietet. Weil auch der Mensch in der Gnade dieses Gebot nicht im vollen Sinn erfüllen kann, muss Luther urteilen, dass der

---

[43] BoA V, 388, 33–34.
[44] BoA V, 389, 6–8.
[45] BoA V, 389, 8–10: "Impossibile est enim, ut non infletur operibus suis bonis, qui non prius exinanitus et destructus est passionibus et malis, donec sciat seipsum esse nihil et opera non sua sed Dei esse."
[46] BoA V, 390, 8–9: "homo sine Theologia crucis optimis pessime abutitur."

Gerechte auch im Tun des Guten sündigt. Wegen der Zweideutigkeit, in die die Liebe des Menschen durch die Sünde geraten ist, kann die heilvolle Beziehung des Menschen zu Gott nicht primär in dieser Liebe bestehen oder auf sie gegründet sein. Wie der Glaube bei Luther in seine Zentralstellung einrückt, soll nun an einem Text aus dem Jahr 1518 untersucht werden, an dem man diesen Prozess in seiner entscheidenden Phase im Detail beobachten kann: seinen "Resolutiones" zu den 95 Ablassthesen.[47]

II. Die Eindeutigkeit des Glaubens

In seiner sechsten Ablassthese behauptet Luther, dass der Papst die Schuld der Sünde nicht anders vergeben kann als indem er erklärt, dass sie von Gott bereits vergeben ist.[48] Was zunächst wie eine kritische Einschränkung der Macht des Papstes erscheinen könnte, ist tatsächlich das im Mittelalter weit verbreitete Verständnis, dass Gott auf die Reue des Menschen über seine Sünde mit der Vergebung der Sünde antwortet, die der Priester im Bußsakrament nur bestätigen, nicht aber bewirken kann. In der dazu gehörenden probatio betont Luther: "Der erste Teil [der These] ist so offensichtlich, dass etliche auch zugegeben haben, es sei eine uneigentliche Redeweise, wenn man sagt, dass der Papst Vergebung der Schuld erteilt. Andere aber sagen, sie verstünden das nicht. Alle geben nämlich zu, dass die Schuld allein von Gott vergeben wird [...]"[49], und dann verweist Luther auf eine Reihe von Bibelstellen und auf Augustinus. Luther merkt aber selbstkritisch an, dass der zitierte erste Teil der These nicht in Übereinstimmung mit dem Evangelientext Mt 16,19 steht. Dort heiße

---

[47] Das sind die beiden Resolutionen 7 und 38 (WA 1, 539, 32–545, 8; 593, 39–596, 39). – Natürlich spricht auch der frühe Luther vor 1518 sehr oft vom Glauben, aber die Bedeutung dessen, was mit "Glauben" gemeint ist, verändert sich in diesen Jahren tiefgreifend. Dazu ist die scharfsichtige Untersuchung "PROMISSIO" von Oswald Bayer (BAYER 1989) zu vergleichen. Bayer hat insbesondere die Bedeutung der beiden erwähnten Resolutionen wie auch der Disputatio "Pro veritate inquirenda et timoratis conscientiis consolandis" (WA 1, 630, 1–633, 12) für das Verständnis der Entwicklung Luthers erkannt und diese Texte minutiös und bis heute unübertroffen untersucht: BAYER 1989, 164–202.

[48] WA 1, 233, 20–21: "Papa non potest remittere ullam culpam nisi declarando et approbando remissam a deo [...]."

[49] WA 1, 538, 40–539, 1.

es nämlich nicht: "Was ich im Himmel löse, sollst du auf Erden lösen", sondern: "Was du auf Erden löst, werde ich lösen oder es wird im Himmel gelöst sein". Darunter verstehe man eher, dass Gott die Vergebung des Priesters bestätigt als umgekehrt.[50]

Dieses Problem wird dann ausführlich in der Resolutio 7 erörtert. Die siebte These lautet: "Gott vergibt überhaupt keinem die Schuld, ohne ihn zugleich, in allem gedemütigt, dem Priester als seinem Stellvertreter zu unterwerfen."[51] Wenn nun in dieser These angedeutet wird, dass die Vergebung durch den Priester der Vergebung durch Gott vorausgeht, dann entsteht die Frage, wie dies geschehen kann, bevor die Gnade und also die Vergebung eingegossen worden ist, wo doch ein Mensch ohne die Gnade, die zuerst die Schuld vergibt, gar nicht den Wunsch haben kann, die Vergebung zu suchen.[52] Luther schlägt eine Lösung vor, indem er zwei Ebenen unterscheidet: erstens die der Wirklichkeit der Vergebung und zweitens die des Bewusstseins oder der Gewissheit der Vergebung.

> "Wenn Gott beginnt, den Menschen zu rechtfertigen, verdammt er ihn zuvor, und wen er aufbauen will, den reißt er nieder, wen er heilen will, den schlägt er, wen er lebendig machen will, den tötet er." Dazu verweist Luther auf eine Reihe von Bibelstellen (unter anderem 1 Sam 2, 6; Dtn 32, 39; Ps 38,4; Ps 18,15-16; Ps 111,10). "Mit einem Wort, hier wirkt Gott ein fremdes Werk, um sein eigenes Werk zu wirken. Das ist die wahre Reue des Herzens und die Demütigung des Geistes, das Opfer, das Gott am meisten gefällt [Ps 51,19] [...] Aber dann weiß der Mensch so wenig um seine Rechtfertigung, dass er sich ganz nahe der Verdammung wähnt und meint, dies sei nicht die Eingießung der Gnade, sondern die Ausgießung des Zornes Gottes über ihn. [...] Solange aber diese elende Verwirrung seines Gewissens währt, hat er keinen Frieden und keinen Trost, wenn er nicht zur Vollmacht der Kirche Zuflucht nimmt und, nachdem seine Sünden und sein Elend durch sein

---

[50] WA 1, 539, 17–23: "Primo circa primam partem videtur esse ista oratio vel sententia impropria et euangelico textui incongrua, quando dicitur summum Pontificem solvere, id est declarare solutam, culpam seu approbare. Textus enim non dicit 'Quodcunque ego solvero in caelis, tu solves super terram', Sed contra 'Quodcunque tu solveris super terram, ego solvam seu solutum erit in caelis', ubi magis intelligitur deus approbare solutionem sacerdotis quam econtra."
[51] WA 1, 233, 23-24: "Nulli prorsus remittit deus culpam, quin simul eum subiiciat humiliatum in omnibus sacerdoti suo vicario."
[52] WA 1, 540, 4-7: "In quibus omnibus omnino prior remisiso in terra significatur quam ea quae est in caelis, merito quaeritur, quomodo ante gratiam infusam, id est ante remissionem dei, haec fieri possint, cum sine gratia dei primo remittente culpam nec votum remissionis quaerendae habere possit homo."

Bekenntnis aufgedeckt sind, Trost und Heilmittel begehrt. Denn nicht durch eigene Klugheit oder Hilfe wird er sich Ruhe verschaffen können, vielmehr würde die Traurigkeit zuletzt in Verzweiflung münden. Wenn hier der Priester eine solche Demütigung und Zerknirschung sieht, soll er im Vertrauen auf die Vollmacht, die ihm verliehen ist, um Barmherzigkeit zu üben, diese voll und ganz in Anspruch nehmen und ihn lösen und als gelöst erklären, und so soll er ihm den Frieden des Gewissens schenken. Der Loszusprechende aber soll sich mit allem Eifer davor hüten, daran zu zweifeln, dass ihm seine Sünden bei Gott vergeben sind, und er soll beruhigt sein in seinem Herzen."[53]

Die Selbsterfahrung eines Menschen in einer solchen Situation, ein verlorener Sünder zu sein, und die Wirklichkeit der Vergebung seiner Sünden sind die zwei Seiten einer Sache, das fremde und das eigene Werk Gottes. Das entspricht dem, was oben gesagt wurde, dass das Gute Gottes, hier die Gerechtigkeit Christi, nur unter ihrem Gegenteil gegenwärtig sind. Diese Erfahrung ist für einen Menschen unerträglich, aber der Priester kann dem Menschen das verborgene Werk Gottes in der Vergebung verkünden. Das ist immer noch ein deklaratives Verständnis der Vergebung: "Non ergo prius solvit Petrus quam Christus, sed declarat et ostendit solutionem."[54] Die Vergebung vollzieht sich in der unmittelbaren, inneren Beziehung Gottes und des Menschen und geht dem, was der Priester sagt, voraus. "Zwar geschieht die Vergebung der Schuld durch die Eingießung der Gnade vor der Vergebung durch den Priester, aber die Eingießung der Gnade ist derart und so unter der Gestalt des Zornes verborgen [...], dass der Mensch hinsichtlich der Gnade ungewisser ist, wenn sie da ist, als wenn sie nicht da ist. Daher ist uns in aller Regel die Vergebung der Schuld nur durch das Urteil des Priesters gewiss."[55] Das Wort des Priesters bewirkt also etwas, nämlich den Frieden des Gewissens des Beichtenden angesichts und trotz seiner Selbsterfahrung. "Du hast so viel an Frieden, wie du dem Wort dessen, der verspricht: 'Was du auf Erden lösen wirst ...', glaubst. Unser Friede nämlich ist Christus, aber im Glauben. Wenn einer diesem Wort nicht glaubt, wird er, auch wenn er millionenmal vom Papst persönlich losgesprochen würde und der ganzen Welt beichtete, niemals

---

[53] WA 1, 540, 8–42.
[54] WA 1, 542, 14–15.
[55] WA 1, 541, 16–21.

Ruhe finden."⁵⁶ Der Ehebrecherin von Joh 8 war schon vergeben, bevor Jesus sie aufrichtete, aber im Angesicht der vielen Ankläger erkannte sie das nicht. Dazu bedurfte es des Wortes Jesu.⁵⁷ Luther sieht darin den Sinn der theologischen Rede von der Effektivität der Sakramente: Sie haben eine kognitive Funktion, die aber tiefgehende Folgen hat: *pax* und *quies* des Gewissens.⁵⁸

Wenn es in Joh 20,23 heißt: "Wem ihr die Sünden erlasst, denen sind sie erlassen", dann versteht Luther das so, dass im ersten Teil dieses Satzes dem Priester die Vollmacht zugeteilt wird, während im zweiten Teil der Sünder zum Glauben an die Vergebung aufgefordert wird.⁵⁹ Luther urteilt: "Es genügt nämlich nicht die Vergebung der Sünden und das Geben (*donatio*) der Gnade, sondern man muss glauben, dass sie vergeben ist."⁶⁰

Das Problem des deklarativen Verständnisses ist es, dass der Priester sich irren kann, wenn er die Zeichen der Reue (*signa contritionis*) im Beichtenden erforscht. Der Beichtende kann den Priester täuschen, er kann sich selbst täuschen. Dieses Moment der Ungewissheit kann prinzipiell nicht überwunden werden, auch wenn es in der Praxis durch einsichtige Beichtväter (wie Johann von Staupitz) abgemildert werden konnte. Luther betont sogleich, dass der Beichtende "mit allem Eifer" verhindern müsse, an der Vergebung zu zweifeln, die ihm der Priester verkündigt hat.⁶¹ Das Argument, mit dem Luther eine Irrtumsmöglichkeit des Priesters abweist, ist der Hinweis, dass "jene Vergebung" – die *declaratio* der Vergebung – sich nicht auf den Priester und sein Urteil stütze, sondern auf das Wort Christi, das der Priester sagt.⁶² Streng genommen kann man das aber nur sagen, wenn das Wort Christi durch den Priester auch das bewirkt, was es sagt; hier aber setzt der Priester die Sündenvergebung als von Gott her

---

⁵⁶ WA 1, 541, 7–11. Vgl. 543, 8–9.
⁵⁷ Vgl. WA 1, 541, 30–33.
⁵⁸ Vgl. WA 1, 542, 9–19.
⁵⁹ WA 1, 543, 16–19: "Ideo in verbo 'Quorum remiseritis peccata' confertur potestas, sed in verbo 'remittuntur eis' provocatur peccator ad fidem remissionis, Sicut et in verbo 'Quodcunque solveris' potestas datur, in verbo 'soluta erunt' fides nostra excitatur."
⁶⁰ WA 1, 543, 23–24.
⁶¹ WA 1, 540, 41–42.
⁶² WA 1, 543, 35–544, 1: "Nec hic oportet cogitare 'quid, si sacerdos erraret?' quia non in sacerdote, sed in verbo Christi nititur remissio illa. ideo […] si ex levitate [sacerdos] absolveret, adhuc obtineres pacem ex fide tua, sicut baptismum seu eucharistiam dat, sive ille lucrum quaerat sive levis ac ludens sit, tua fides plenum accipit. Tanta res est verbum Christi et fides eius."

geschehen bereits voraus. Die Gewissheit der Vergebung ist noch nicht mit ihrer Wirklichkeit vermittelt. Damit ist klar, dass die in Resolutio 7 vorgestellte Lösung nur eine Zwischenlösung sein kann und der hier entwickelte Gedanke weiter treibt zu einer endgültigen Lösung.

Luther erläutert, dass er mit der sechsten These nicht vollständig einverstanden ist; sie drücke nicht seine Meinung aus, sondern er habe sie aufgestellt, weil andere so denken; er betont aber, dass alle seine Gegner zusammen mit ihren Magistri nicht in der Lage seien zu erklären, wie der Priester die Schuld vergibt. Er kennt natürlich die Auffassung, dass die Sakramente des neuen Bundes allen die Gnade geben, die dem keinen Riegel vorschieben. Diese gewöhnliche Meinung nennt er häretisch, weil man mit Glauben zum Sakrament hinzutreten müsse.[63] Man kann Luthers Ringen erkennen: Mit Augustin betont er: Nicht das Sakrament, sondern der Glaube an das Sakrament rechtfertigt, aber dieser Satz hat hier noch eine andere Bedeutung als später; er bezieht sich auf das Bewusstsein und die Gewissheit der Vergebung. Denn sogleich stellt er – erkennbar unsicher – fest: "Es ist wahrscheinlicher (!), dass der Priester des neuen Bundes nur die Vergebung Gottes erklärt [declarat] und bestätigt [approbat] (das heißt: auf sie hinweist) und durch diesen Hinweis und sein Urteil das Gewissen des Sünders zur Ruhe bringt, der dessen Urteil glauben und Frieden haben muss."[64]

In den Resolutionen 37 und 38 geht Luther den skizzierten Denkweg weiter und kommt zum Durchbruch, zu einem neuen Verständnis der Sündenvergebung. Die beiden Thesen haben eine analoge Struktur wie die Thesen 6 und 7. These 37 lautet: "Jeder wahre Christ, sei er lebend oder tot, hat Teil an allen Gütern Christi und der Kirche, die ihm von Gott auch ohne Ablassbriefe gegeben werden."[65] Diese These bezieht sich auf die *Instructio Summaria* des Erzbischofs Albrecht von Brandenburg, an der Luther so schweren Anstoß genommen hatte. Darin werden vier Hauptgnaden des Ablasses genannt. Die dritte ist eben die Teilhabe an

---

[63] Vgl. WA 1, 544, 33–41.
[64] WA 1, 545, 1–4.
[65] WA 1, 235, 9–11: "Quilibet verus christianus, sive vivus sive mortuus, habet participationem omnium bonorum Christi et Ecclesie etiam sine literis veniarum a deo sibi datam."

allen Gütern der universalen Kirche.⁶⁶ Luther hat ergänzt: Teilhabe an den Gütern *Christi* und der Kirche und argumentiert: Wer Christus hat, hat auch alle seine Güter. Er schließt die Resolution so: "Diese Teilhabe wird nicht durch die Kraft der Schlüssel oder durch die Wohltat der Ablassbriefe gegeben, sie wird vielmehr vor und ohne jene gegeben von Gott allein, wie die Vergebung vor der Vergebung, die Absolution vor der Absolution, so auch die Teilhabe vor der Teilhabe."⁶⁷

Die 38. These lautet: "Dennoch sind die Vergebung und das Anteilgeben des Papstes in keiner Weise zu verachten, weil, wie ich gesagt habe, sie die göttliche Vergebung bekunden."⁶⁸ In der Resolution teilt nun Luther mit, dass ihm die Redeweise, der Papst bekunde nur die göttliche Vergebung ("declarando" wie in These 6) oder das Anteilgeben ("declaratio" wie in These 38), nicht gefalle. Sie unterschätze die Schlüssel der Kirche und mache das Wort Jesu aus Mt 16,19 gewissermaßen unwirksam. Das deklarative Verständnis sei zu schwach. Außerdem bleibe für den, der nur eine declaratio hört, alles im Ungewissen.⁶⁹ Hier ist Luther dabei, zwei Thesen aus den 95 Thesen ausdrücklich zurückzunehmen. Zwar argumentiert Luther zunächst wie in Resolutio 7, dass der unter der Last seiner Sünde Leidende das Urteil des Priesters braucht, um der Vergebung und der Teilhabe an den Gütern Christi trauen zu können. Aber dann bringt er unvermittelt einen überraschenden Gedanken:

> "Denn nicht wegen des Priesters und nicht wegen seiner Vollmacht, sondern wegen des Wortes dessen, der gesagt hat und nicht lügt: 'Alles, was du lösen wirst' usw. [glaube ich]. Bei denen nämlich, die an dieses Wort glauben, kann der Schlüssel nicht irren. Er irrt aber allein bei denen, die nicht glauben, dass diese Lossprechung gültig ist. Denn stelle dir vor (es sei unmöglich oder möglich): Wenn jemand keine

---

⁶⁶ KÖHLER 1934, 115: "*Tertia principalis gratia* est participatio omnium bonorum ecclesiae universalis [...]."

⁶⁷ WA 1, 593, 32–34.

⁶⁸ WA 1, 235, 12–13.

⁶⁹ WA 1, 594, 5–13: "Verum, licet hanc conclusionem ab omnibus (ut puto) acceptam non negem, dixi tamen supra conclusione vi. [siehe WA 1; 539, 17–23; 542, 20–21] mihi non placere hunc modum loquendi, quod Papa nihil aliud faciat quam quod declaret aut approbet remissionem divinam seu participationem. Nam id primo nimis viles reddit Ecclesiae claves, immo verbum Christi facit irritum quodammodo, ubi dixit: Quodcunque &c. Declaratio enim nimis modicum est. Secundo, Quia incerta erunt omnia ei, cui fit declaratio, licet aliis seu Ecclesiae foris in facie certa fiat illius remissio et reconciliatio."

hinreichende Reue hat oder zu haben meint und dennoch dem, der ihn losspricht, mit voller Zuversicht glaubt, er sei losgesprochen (so meine ich zuversichtlich), macht ebendieser Glaube, dass er in Wahrheit losgesprochen ist, weil er an den glaubt, der gesagt hat: 'Alles, was' usw. Der Glaube an Christus aber rechtfertigt immer, genau so, wie wenn dich ein ungeschickter, leichtfertiger, einfältiger Priester tauft. Nimm noch hinzu, auch wenn du meinst, du hättest keine hinreichende Reue (denn dir kannst und darfst du nicht trauen), aber gleichwohl dem glaubst, der gesagt hat: Wer glaubt und sich taufen lässt, wird gerettet werden [Mk 16,16], ich sage dir, dieser Glaube an sein Wort macht, dass du in Wahrheit getauft wirst, wie es auch immer um deine Reue bestellt sein mag. Deshalb ist der Glaube überall vonnöten. So viel hast du, wie viel du glaubst."[70]

Den letzten Satz "So viel hast du, wie viel du glaubst" hat Luther schon in Resolutio 7 gebraucht,[71] dort aber charakteristischerweise mit Bezug auf den Frieden des Gewissens *nach* der Vergebung der Schuld *unmittelbar* durch Gott, aber er ist dort noch nicht auf die Vergebung der Schuld selbst bezogen, auch wenn die Formulierungen in beiden Resolutionen beinahe gleichlautend sind. Aber am Ende von Resolutio 7 erklärt Luther, wie oben gesagt, ausdrücklich, dass der Priester des neuen Bundes die Vergebung Gottes "bekundet und bekräftigt (das heißt: darauf zeigt)".[72] Luther hat in Resolutio 7 bereits Formulierungen, deren voller Sinn ihm offenbar erst wenig später aufgeht.

Die Struktur der Vergebung ist gegenüber der Tradition neuartig und komplex, und Luther hat sie hier und wohl auch später nicht vollständig begrifflich aufgeklärt. Wieder geht es um die Frage der Irrtumsmöglichkeit des Priesters, wenn er das "Absolvo te" im Namen Jesu Christi spricht, also das Wort von Mt 16,19 in die konkrete Situation des einzelnen Beichtenden umsetzt. Nach Luther gibt es bei denen, die diesem Wort glauben, keine Irrtumsmöglichkeit, bei denen hingegen, die diesem Wort nicht glauben, irrt der "Schlüssel", das heißt der Priester. Ist das nun analog zu der von Luther kritisierten Situation zu verstehen, dass der Priester annimmt, der Beichtende habe echte Zeichen der Reue und *daraufhin* könne dieser losgesprochen werden? Dann wäre nur ein innerseelischer Zustand im Beichtenden (die Reue) durch einen anderen (den Glauben)

---

[70] WA 1, 594, 33–595, 5.
[71] WA 1, 541, 7–8; 543, 8–9; siehe oben bei Anm. 56.
[72] WA 1, 545,1–2.

ersetzt. Luther sagt sogar: "Der Glaube an Christus rechtfertigt immer", so dass man annehmen könnte, die *Gabe* der Sündenvergebung sei die *Frucht ihres Empfangens* im Sinn einer self-fulfilling prophecy. Das wäre ein schreckliches Missverständnis, denn dann würde der Glaube an sich selbst glauben; er glaubt aber an das Wort Christi, das durch den Mund des Priesters zu ihm kommt. Der Satz "Der Glaube an Christus rechtfertigt immer" wird durch die Aussage weitergeführt, dass das nicht weniger zutrifft, als wenn ein ungeeigneter Priester tauft. Gemeint ist wohl, dass ein Priester einen Erwachsenen tauft, ohne dass dieser einen ernsthaften Willen zur Taufe hat und also nicht getauft werden sollte. Wenn dieser aber später auf die sakramentale Promissio der Taufe zurückkommt, kann er sich unbedingt auf diese verlassen. Die Irrtumsmöglichkeit beim deklarativen Verständnis kommt daher, dass die Reue eine Bedingung oder gar Teilursache für die Vergebung ist und in deren Wahrnehmung durch den Priester Fehler passieren können. Nun setzt Luther zwar die Reue bei der Sündenvergebung als Gegebenheit voraus; es sind Menschen mit einem zitternden Gewissen, die zur Beichte kommen, während Luther sagen muss, dass die, die solche Gewissensqualen nicht haben, mit der Absolution nichts anfangen können. Aber niemand darf die Vergebung auf seine Reue stützen noch die Vergebung für zweifelhaft halten, weil die Reue möglicherweise halbherzig war. Das Wort Christi in Mt 16, das zum "Absolvo te" im Mund des Priesters wird, ist eine Promissio Christi, die als schöpferisches Wort *Christi* verlässlich ist und der der Mensch *darum* im Glauben entsprechen kann und soll. Luther zitiert Psalm 119, um das deutlich zu machen: "die Hoffnung soll nach dem Propheten [Verfasser des Psalms] nicht auf unsere Reue, sondern auf gottes Wort gesetzt werden. Der Prophet sagt nämlich nicht: 'Denk an die Reue deines Knechtes, durch die du mir Hoffnung gegeben hast', sondern: Denk an dein Wort, durch das du mir Hoffnung gabst [Ps 119,49]."[73]

Das Wort Jesu nennt keine Bedingung, die erfüllt sein müsste, auch nicht den Glauben. Es ist eindeutig als Zusage. Gerade deshalb fordert es den Glauben und ruft ihn hervor; der Glaube hat seine Eindeutigkeit, weil er durch und durch intentional ist, vertrauende Intention, so dass der Mensch im Glauben allein auf das Wort Christi blickt und gerade nicht fragen kann,

---

[73] WA 1, 595, 27–30.

wie es um sein Herz steht. In solcher Selbstreflexion würde der Glaube sich untreu, weil er Glaube nur als Glaube allein an das Wort Christi sein kann, ja, er würde Christi Wort untreu. Der Glaube ist eindeutig und gewiss, weil er sich allein an das Wort Christi hängt und den Seitenblick der Reflexion auf sich selbst als Verletzung der Vertrauenswürdigkeit Christi versteht.

Aber die Frage sei noch einmal gestellt: Warum spricht Luther dann so vom Glauben: *fides facit absolutum verissime*? Hier muss man zwei Hinsichten unterscheiden: *In intentione recta* sagt der Glaubende: 'Ich glaube, dass mir meine Sünden vergeben *sind*, weil das Wort Jesu, das der Priester mir zugesprochen hat, gewiss ist.' Es geschieht etwas, wenn der Priester dieses Wort sagt, sonst hätte der Glaube keinen Gegenstand. Darum kann man dieses Wortverständnis "sakramental" nennen. Etwas anderes ist es, wenn in der theologischen Reflexion – *in intentione obliqua* – auf das Geschehen der Vergebung geblickt wird; dann muss sagen: 'Es ist gewiss, dass die Sünden vergeben sind, wenn geglaubt wird, dass sie vergeben sind.'[74] Weil die Vergebung durch etwas Worthaft-Sakramentales geschieht, ist sie nur im Glauben präsent und wirklich im Menschen. Luther macht die Leser darauf aufmerksam, dass sie nicht auf ihre Reue, aus welcher Liebe diese auch kommen mag, schauen sollen, sondern auf das Wort Christi. Das ist dann auch die Hauptaufgabe des Priesters, das schöpferische Wort "*Dir* sind deine Sünden vergeben" im Namen Christi Menschen so zuzusprechen und in der Predigt so darüber zu reden, dass Vertrauen in dieses Wort "provoziert" wird. Wo ein Mensch diesem Wort nicht Vertrauen schenkt, nimmt seine Seele Schaden.[75] Das setzt voraus, dass durch das Wort etwas geschieht, dem der Unglaube widerspricht. Luther schließt die Resolutio 38 damit, dass er These 38 nicht als ganze aufrechterhält, ja, dass er sie zum großen Teil bestreitet.[76]

In der Disputation "Pro veritate inquirenda et timoratis conscientiis consolandis" stellt Luther sein neues Verständnis der Absolution in

---

[74] Vgl. dazu die 15. These der "Disputatio pro veritate inquirenda et timoratis conscientiis consolandis", in der Luther intentio recta und intentio obliqua miteinander verbindet, was an dem doppelten "certum/certa" gut zu erkennen ist: "Certum est ergo, remissa esse peccata si credis remissa, quia certa est Christi salvatoris promissio" (WA 1, 631, 17–18).

[75] Vgl. WA 1, 595, 15–18.

[76] WA 1, 596, 38–39: "Itaque istam conclusionem, ut iacet, non omnino teneo, sed ex magna parte nego."

systematischer Weise vor.⁷⁷ Der innere Kern der Thesen lautet, negativ formuliert: "Christus wollte nicht, dass das Heil der Menschen in der Hand des Menschen oder seinem Willen liegt"⁷⁸, also weder in der Reue des Sünders noch in einer Vollmacht des Priesters, sofern sie als persönliches Vermögen gedacht ist. Das folgt aus dem, worin positiv das Heil gründet: "Sondern, wie geschrieben steht: 'er trägt alles mit seinem starken Wort' [Hebr 1,3], und: 'mit dem Glauben reinigt er ihre Herzen' [Apg 15,9]."⁷⁹ In der Vergebung wird eine Relation hergestellt zwischen Christus und seinem Wort einerseits und dem Glauben an dieses Wort, der die Herzen reinigt, andererseits. Diese Relation ist asymmetrisch, weil Christus "alles trägt", also auch das andere Relatum, den Glauben und das, was Inhalt des Wortes Christi ist. Dieses Wort ist also ein in höchstem Maß schöpferisches Wort, so sehr, dass Luther sagen kann, die Vollmacht der Schlüssel wirke ein unfehlbares Werk.⁸⁰ Hier kommt bei Luther eine Infallibilität ins Spiel! "Die Schlüssel" sind nicht einfach der Priester, sondern das Wort der Promissio Christi und das Mandat, diese Promissio Menschen zuzusprechen. Das allerdings ist die Aufgabe des Priesters, der "Diener des Wortes ist, um Glauben an die Vergebung zu wecken".⁸¹ Der Heilige Geist ist Subjekt dieses unfehlbaren Werks, und doch wirken Heiliger Geist und Priester untrennbar zusammen: "Wie der Priester wirklich (*vere*) lehrt, tauft, das Abendmahl erteilt und dies dennoch allein (*solius*) Werk des innerlich wirkenden Geistes ist, so vergibt er wirklich (*vere*) die Sünden und löst von der Schuld, und dennoch ist das allein (*solius*) Werk des innerlich wirkenden Geistes."⁸² Dass Sündenvergebung

---

⁷⁷ WA 1, 630, 1–633, 12.

⁷⁸ WA 1, 631, 9–10: "Non voluit Christus, in manu vel arbitrio hominis consistere salutem hominum" (These 11).

⁷⁹ WA 1, 631, 11–12: "Sed sicut scriptum est: portans omnia verbo virtutis sue, et: fide purificans corda eorum" (These 12).

⁸⁰ WA 1, 631, 35–36: "Potestas Clavium operatur verbo et mandato dei firmum et infallibile opus, nisi sis dolosus" (These 24).

⁸¹ WA 1, 631, 33–34: "Sacerdotes non sunt authores remissionis, sed ministratores verbi in fidem remissionis" (These 23).

⁸² WA 1, 632, 9–12: "Sicut sacerdos docet, baptisat, communicat vere, et tamen hec solius sunt spiritus intus operantis, Ita vere peccata remittit et absolvit a culpa, et tamen hec solius sunt spiritus intus operantis"(Thesen 30-31). Man beachte die überraschende Struktur des "solus": Es schließt die menschliche cooperatio des Priesters nicht aus, sondern ein, betont aber in diesem Zusammenwirken das uneingeschränkte Subjektsein des Heiligen Geistes! Man beachte: Es geht hier *nicht* um die cooperatio des Beichtenden, sondern um die des Priesters!

und Rechtfertigung allein Sache des Heiligen Geistes ist, muss mit dem folgenden Satz zusammengedacht werden: "Nichts [...] rechtfertigt als allein der Glaube an Christus, für den der Dienst am Wort durch den Priester notwendig ist."[83] Auch der Glaube, also die Relation des Menschen zum Wort Christi, ist Werk des Heiligen Geistes.

Freilich, auch die in der scholastischen Theologie mit der gratia infusa mitgeteilte Liebe zu Gott ist Werk des Heiligen Geistes. Aber der Glaube an Christus hat eine Eindeutigkeit, die die Liebe zu Gott *post lapsum* nicht hat. Etwas Gutes will geliebt werden, eine Promissio will geglaubt werden. Bei der Liebe stellt sich die Alternative "Selbstliebe oder Gottesliebe", beim Vertrauen gibt es diese Alternative nicht. Weil der Mensch als Sünder in allem das Seine sucht, sieht Luther das Haben-Wollen ablehnend, und weil selbst die von Gott geschenkte Gottesliebe jenes Um-sich-selbst-Kreisen nicht völlig überwinden kann, kann auch die Rechtfertigung des Menschen nur unter ihrem Gegenteil der Selbstanklage gehabt werden. Das heißt, dass Anklage und Freispruch, Gesetz und Evangelium so ineinander liegen, dass der Glaube als Übernahme des Urteils Gottes, also als Selbstanklage, den Menschen rechtfertigt. Erstaunlicherweise ist es das Wort Jesu an Petrus (Mt 16,19) – gleichlautend in Mt 18,18 an alle Jünger gerichtet –, das Luther weiterhilft, dieses Ineinander zu entwirren. Durch die Promissio nach Mt 16,19 wird das Evangelium eindeutig und unterscheidet sich vom anklagenden Gesetz als ein anderes Wort. Die Anklage durch das Gesetz Gottes hört nicht auf; Gott nimmt die Forderung des Gebots der Gottesliebe nicht zurück. Aber Gesetz und Evangelium sind zwei Worte; diese Unterscheidung erst macht das Evangelium eindeutig.[84] Damit kann

---

[83] WA 1, 632, 13–16: "In iis [den in der vorigen Anm. genannten Vollzügen] omnibus, dum ministrat verbum Christi, simul fidem exercet, qua intus iustificatur peccator. Nihil enim iustificat, nisi sola fides Christi, ad quam necessaria est verbi per sacerdotem ministratio." (Thesen 32–33).

[84] Vgl. oben Anm. 32. In seiner Schrift "Von der Freiheit eines Christenmenschen" betont Luther, dass der Mensch aus den Geboten sein Unvermögen zur Gesetzeserfüllung erkennt; das setzt Luthers Verständnis der Gottesliebe voraus. Und Luther insistiert: Das Gebot muss erfüllt sein, oder der Mensch muss verdammt sein. Vgl. LUTHER 2012, 287. Aber wenn der Mensch nichts in sich findet, wodurch er gerecht werden könnte: "Dann jedoch kommt das *andere* Wort, die göttliche Verheißung und Zusage, und spricht: Willst du alle Gebote erfüllen, deine böse Begierde und Sünde los werden, wie die Gebote erzwingen und fordern, siehe da, glaube an Christus, in welchem ich dir alle Gnade, Gerechtigkeit, Frieden und Freiheit zusage. Glaubst du. So hast du. Glaubst du nicht, so hast du nicht." (ebd.; Hervorhebung T.D.)

der Glaube an die Promissio Christi als Haben Christi der Falle jenes Aneignungsstrebens, das alles Gute für den Menschen schlecht macht, entgehen. Dieser Glaube beruht nicht auf einem Streben des Menschen. Das Wort Christi konstituiert eine Relation zum Menschen, und es schafft zugleich die Relation des Menschen zu Gott, den Glauben an eben dieses Wort. Wenn nun der Glaube bei Luther die Zentralstellung einnimmt, dann schließt dies auch ein, dass das, was mit "Glauben" gemeint ist, sich verändert hat. Der Glaube, der der Promissio Christi glaubt, ist ein anderer als der Glaube als Selbstanklage und Sündenbekenntnis. Also ändern sich sowohl der Inhalt dessen, was "Glaube" bedeutet, wie auch seine Rolle in der Rechtfertigung.

In der finnischen Lutherforschung wird mit Recht der enge Zusammenhang von forensischer und effektiver Rechtfertigung bei Luther betont. Die verbreitete Auffassung der forensischen Rechtfertigung, wonach der Mensch nur von außen anders angesehen wird, gleichwohl aber in sich derselbe bleibt, lässt außer Acht, dass es sich hier um das Forum *Gottes* handelt. Wen Gott gnädig ansieht, der bleibt nicht derselbe, denn er wird im Glauben an die Promissio Christi ein Anderer! Es ist gerade die Relation von Promissio Christi und Glauben an diese Promissio, die das Forensische effektiv sein lässt. Freilich, das, was man in der Regel mit der Effektivität der Rechtfertigung verbindet, ist die Veränderung im komplexen Strebevermögen des Menschen, sein Verhältnis zu den Geboten Gottes, das Wachsen in der Liebe zu Gott. Gott hört ja nicht auf, vom Menschen diese Liebe von ganzem Herzen und mit allen Kräften zu erwarten. Dennoch wird die Veränderung des Menschen hin zu dieser Ganzheit nie vollkommen sein. Das war der Antrieb für die theologische Entwicklung Luthers, die hier skizziert worden ist. Darum hat in der Rechtfertigung das Forensische ein Prae gegenüber dem Effektiven (im zuletzt genannten Sinn). Die *Liebe* des Glaubenden zu Gott ist immer *bruchstückhaft*, aber im *Glauben* hat der Mensch die Promissio Christi *ganz*, das heißt: Er hat Christus ganz! "In ipsa *fide* Christus adest."[85]

---

[85] WA 40/1, 229, 15 (Hervorhebung T. D.).

Bibliographie

AUGUSTINUS, Aurelius
1955   *De civitate Dei libri XI–XXII*. Eds. Berhard Dombart / Alfons Kalb. Corpus Christianorum. Series Latina XLVIII. Turnhout: Brepols.
1962   *De doctrina christiana. De vera religione*. Corpus Christianorum Series Latina XXXII. Ed. Joseph Martin. Turnhout: Brepols.

BAYER, Oswald
1989   *PROMISSIO. Geschichte der reformatorischen Wende in Luthers Theologie*. Darmstadt: Wissenschaftliche Buchgesellschaft.

BIEL, Gabriel
1973   *Collectorium circa quattuor libros Sententiarum. Prologus et liber primus*. Eds. Wilfried Werbeck / Udo Hofmann, Tübingen: Mohr Siebeck.
1979   *Collectorium circa quattuor libros Sententiarum. Liber tertius*. Eds. Wilfried Werbeck / Udo Hofmann. Tübingen: Mohr Siebeck.
1984   *Collectorium circa quattuor libros Sententiarum. Liber secundus*. Eds. Wilfried Werbeck / Udo Hofmann. Tübingen: Mohr Siebeck.

DIETER, Theodor
2001   *Der junge Luther und Aristoteles. Eine historisch-systematische Untersuchung zum Verhältnis von Theologie und Philosophie*. Theologische Bibliothek Töpelmann 105. Berlin / New York: de Gruyter.
2016a   Luther und die Philosophie. – *Luther: Katholizität & Reform*. Eds. Wolfgang Thönissen / Josef Freitag / Augustinus Sander. Leipzig / Paderborn: Evangelische Verlagsanstalt / Bonifatius. 60–88.
2016b   Martin Luthers kritische Wahrnehmung "der" Scholastik in seiner so genannten "Disputatio contra scholasticam theologiam". – *Die Reformation und ihr Mittelalter*. Eds. Günter Frank/Volker Leppin. Stuttgart-Bad Cannstatt: frommann-holzboog. 153–188.

HEIDEGGER, Martin
1995   *Phänomenologie des religiösen Lebens*. Martin Heidegger Gesamtausgabe. Vol. 60. Eds. Matthias Jung / Thomas Regehly / Claudius Strube. Frankfurt am Main: Vittorio Klostermann.

KÖHLER, Walther
1934   Ed. *Dokumente zum Ablassstreit von 1517*. Tübingen: Mohr Siebeck.

LUTHER, Martin
1883–2009 *D. Martin Luthers Werke. Kritische Gesamtausgabe*. Weimar: Böhlau [= WA].
1963   Luthers Werke in Auswahl [= BoA], Vol. V. Ed. Erich Vogelsang. Berlin: de Gruyter.
2012   Deutsch-deutsche Studienausgabe. Vol. 1. Ed. Dietrich Korsch. Leipzig: Evangelische Verlagsanstalt.

SAARINEN, Risto
1994   *Weakness of the Will in Medieval Thought. From Augustine to Buridan*. Leiden / New York / Köln: E.J.B. Brill.
2011   *Weakness of Will in Renaissance and Reformation Thought*. Oxford / New York: Oxford University Press.
2017   *Luther and the Gift*. Tübingen: Mohr Siebeck.

Love and Hope

Werner G. Jeanrond

In the past, theological treatises of the three so-called theological virtues of faith, hope and love gave instant priority to faith. The dimensions of faith, including the dynamic relationship between human beings and God (*fides qua*) and the doctrinal deposit of faith (*fides quae*) to which believers were meant to assent, dominated discussions of hope and love. Martin Luther argued that love ought to be subordinated or even controlled by faith.[1] However, is this right? Should we not also pay attention to the Apostle Paul's insight into the predominance of love? Paul lifted love above both faith and hope when he wrote to the Corinthians: "And now faith, hope and love abide, these three; and the greatest of these is love." (1 Cor. 13:13)[2]

In this essay, I wish to consider love and hope and to explore what it would mean to approach hope from within a horizon of love. I do not intend to undermine the virtue of faith; rather I wish to encourage a reconsideration of the virtues of love and hope outside any narrow subordination to preconceived or dogmatic notions of faith. Challenging the traditional hierarchy among the three theological virtues might even allow us to gain new insights into the dynamics of faith.

---

[1] For a discussion of the subordination of love to faith in Martin Luther, see JEANROND 2010, 100–101. – Luther was not primarily concerned with the theological virtues as such, but with Christ's presence in each believer that allowed faith, hope and love to flourish. For a thorough study of Luther's christology, see ZACHHUBER 2017.

[2] All biblical quotations are from *The Holy Bible* (NRSV), New York/Oxford: Oxford University Press, 1989.

Love

There can be no doubt that love is at the centre of Christian discipleship.[3] Not love as a romantic sentiment, but love as the hard work of recognising and respecting the other as other and God as the radical other, and as the desire to relate to the respective other in mutual openness and expectation. Mutual does not need to mean symmetrical. Many forms of love are not symmetrical, for instance the love between parents and children, teachers and pupils, God and human beings etc.

Not every experience of love is explicitly linked to an experience of God. However, the Jewish, Christian and Muslim traditions of experiencing God's self-disclosure in our world point to the possibility of transcendence and transformation in every genuine encounter of love. Love is creative, dynamic and transformative. Hence, love can only be realised in the process of loving and of being loved: love is praxis.[4] Its consequences cannot be calculated in advance. Therefore, it is not advisable to subject love completely to rules, doctrines and regulations. Love and teaching or dogma always remain in tension since love (as openness to and engagement with concrete others) represents a continuous and dynamic challenge to any system of doctrines and beliefs. For in the loving relationship with God and with human beings emerges first a constantly changing encounter which allows mutual recognition and in-depth knowledge (and possibly a union of selves) to develop.[5]

It is also important not to confuse *love* with *like*. Love is not the same as like. Nobody can command me to like my neighbour. Rather the biblical love command asks of me to love even the neighbour whom I do not like, even my enemy. Or, to put it differently, I am called to become a neighbour to others. Thus, the difference between love and like concerns the affects, emotions and attitudes to the respective other. Love may well include these, but it goes further in so far as it respects and accepts the other in all her relational potential, including her relationship to God. Through the loving eye, the other is seen not as closed, static and calculable,

---

[3] For a more comprehensive discussion of the significance of love for Christian life and theology, see Jeanrond 2010.
[4] For a defence of a unitary concept of love, see JEANROND 2010, 135–171.
[5] Cf. SAARINEN 2016, 8.

but as open for a potentially transformative interpersonal praxis in an emerging communion. Love, thus, remains always open for new relational discoveries. In this sense, love is revolutionary.

According to the gospels, Jesus's proclamation and celebration of the coming reign of God centres around *love* and not around *like*.[6] Jesus makes every effort to reach even those people who conventionally were disliked and excluded by the ruling religious and civic authorities. He thus renews God's covenant with all human beings – with Israel first but then also with all people. The conflict between love and law eventually kills Jesus, though, surprisingly for his disciples, it does not kill God's relationship with Jesus, his followers, Israel, and God's creation. Therefore, it cannot be appropriate to let the praxis of love be dominated by a new doctrinal system, established by church and theology now in the name of Jesus Christ. That is why, agreeing with the Apostle Paul, I place love first and propose to consider both hope and faith in the light of love.[7]

God's initiative to establish a reign of love, then, requires thorough reflection. In which way can Christians participate in God's creative and reconciling project? How can they identify and deal with the problems that impede this project in this world? How should they relate to other religious and social initiatives in this world? How should they relate to differing Christian interpretations of the demands of this divine-human project? How can they benefit from the theological insight and wisdom of previous generations without, therefore, being limited in their own imagination and in their own responsible, critical and self-critical praxis of love? Neither appeals to Christian passivity in some Protestant traditions nor references to a totally coherent doctrinal system in Roman Catholic tradition must be allowed to undermine the continuous reflection on the implications of the gratuity of the gift of divine grace in our lives.[8] Moreover, the point of a critical and self-critical systematic theology is not to limit Christian imagination and praxis but, at best, to inspire its dynamics and to enrich its journey through constructive and critical retrievals of Christian origins,

---

[6] See, for instance, Luke 10: 25–37.

[7] Cf. also Thomas Aquinas, *Summa Theologiæ*, vol. 34: *Charity*, trans. R. J. Batten, OP, London: Eyre & Spottiswoode, 1975, 77: "Charity denotes union with God, whereas faith and hope do not" (2a.2æ.24, 12).

[8] Cf. SAARINEN 2017, 226–241.

wisdom and memory. Thus, more than a new *Glaubenslehre* we today may need a new *Liebeslehre*.

The context for such a systematic theological endeavour today is global, pluralist, polycentric and dynamic. Hence, however understandable and useful a clearly defined theological self-understanding may be for Christian churches and movements, the desire to appreciate the full implications of the dynamic relationship between God and humanity will always encourage the questioning and transcending of confessional, national and other external boundaries. Therefore, a systematic theology today must consider its global trajectory and dynamic publics in church, society and the academy.

At present, we can observe a vogue of nationalist movements that seek to instrumentalise religion for their own purposes of adding a "soul" to their view of the world in order to legitimise and foster their respective autocratic political goals. Against this background, it is important to articulate a theology of resistance in the name of God's gift of love.[9] An argument for a homogeneous society of like-minded people remains an argument that favours *like* over *love*. Here, otherness remains a threat and not an invitation to develop a culture of love. However, a genuine culture of love can never recognise national and confessional limits. If we are unable to relate to human otherness, how much less will we be able to relate to God's radical otherness? Efforts to reduce God, who is love (1 John 4:8 and 16), to a national God and to privilege love to one's nation at the expense of the universal vocation of all women, men and children to co-operate with God in the building of God's coming reign contradict the biblical love command.

Hope

Hope and love are closely related. Love is concerned with the direct relationship to and possible communion and union with the respective other, while hope opens the future perspective of our human relationships.

---

[9] For an instructive discussion of nationalist efforts to instrumentalise Christian faith in today's Europe, see Byström, 2017. For a demythologisation of the idea of a European "soul", see Jeanrond 2012a, 151–170.

In both hope and love, trust plays a major role. Hence, there is a considerable overlap between the praxis of love and the praxis of hope.

However, we must not confuse hope with optimism. Anthony Kelly offers the following clarification:

> Optimism is no bad thing in itself. It is a kind of implicit confidence that things are going well in the present situation. Optimism may be simply a feature of temperament expressing itself in a spontaneous logic: we can manage and cope in a world that is reasonably predictable. Optimism is happy enough with the system. In contrast, genuine hope is always "against hope." It begins where optimism reaches the end of its tether. Hope stirs when the secure system shows signs of breaking down. Hope is at home in the world of the unpredictable where no human logic or expectation is in control.[10]

Whereas optimism builds on trust into the calculability of the system, hope builds on trust in and relationship with other persons and with God. In that sense, mere trust into dogmatics could be said to be more optimistic, while the praxis of love is more hope-full. Hope, in my understanding, is always relational, including human hope in God's gift of persistent love.

In spite of much agreement otherwise, my approach differs somewhat from Ingolf Dalferth's understanding of hope. He approaches hope as the mode of being open to the possibility of the good, which comes to us from outside without our own doing.[11] While I agree that hoping is a mode of orientation in the world, I see this mode exclusively in personal terms, i.e. in the horizon of love. Loving relationships make hope possible and realistic.

Hope in God could also take the shape of *radical hope*, particularly then when all our human support structures, such as church, family, school, culture etc., lose their effectivity and power, and we are left with nothing other than mere trust in the constancy of God's love.[12]

Hope provides time-space to our human acts and expressions of love. Moreover, it opens the eschatological horizon from the present experience of love, transcendence, conversion and transformation toward the eternal quality of God's gift of relationship. God's love and God's gift open up

---

[10] KELLY 2006, 5.
[11] DALFERTH 2016, esp. 170–171.
[12] For an exploration of the dimensions of radical hope, see LEAR 2008.

eternal dimensions for us human beings already here and now. Eternity does not mean endless life as we know it. Rather it means a new quality of life as God knows, creates and sustains it.[13]

Such an approach to theology might be criticised for starting with the gift of love rather than with the experience and awareness of human sin and sinfulness, which God confronts with his soteriological initiative in Jesus Christ, especially his cross and resurrection. Such a criticism would show its dependence on one form of doing systematic theology, namely one which prefers as its starting point the more or less total depravation of humankind and the world. While I grant that some biblical readings and some theological discourses inspired by such readings suggest such a default position, this is not the only hermeneutical perspective possible when dealing with the Jewish and Christian Scriptures and with the experiences of past and present Christian disciples. Moreover, the dualistic dimensions associated with such a starting point have led generations of Christians to ignore the creative and imaginative possibilities disclosed by an ever-deepening love relationship between God and human beings. The Scriptures witness to this graceful relationship and to the radical hope which it discloses. God's love story does neither begin with nor culminate in the cross and resurrection of Jesus Christ; rather it has begun with creation, is continuing with creation and with reconciliation, as embodied by Jesus Christ, and will culminate in the fulfilment of God's reign of love which Jesus Christ has proclaimed in God's name.

Hence, the attraction of God's creative and reconciling project does not lie primarily in the insight into human fallenness and sinfulness, but in the insight into the gift of God's gracious and faithful love of his creation in spite of human sinfulness and persistent acts of evil. Appeals to salvation would thus need to include a response to God's ongoing offer of reconciliation within a dynamic culture of love in which human beings are not only recipients, but subjects, agents, and "friends".[14]

---

[13] See DALFERTH 2016, 167–168: "Deshalb ist die christliche Hoffnung keine Sonntagshaltung, sondern ein Modus, in dem das ganze Leben gelebt wird: Wer liebend lebt, lebt hoffend, und wer hoffend lebt, hofft nicht primär für sich, sondern darauf, dass Gott auch für andere das will und tut, was für sie gut ist. Christliche Hoffnung ist deshalb kein eigenständiges Phänomen, sondern ein Modus der christlichen Liebe, und christliche Liebe gibt es nur, indem sie als Gottes- und Nächstenliebe gelebt wird."

[14] Cf. CARMICHAEL 2004; and JEANROND 2010, 205–215.

Once again, my point here is not to downgrade faith; rather it is to link both faith and hope ever more intimately with love. I continue to be inspired by Martin Luther's insight into the relational nature of faith and resulting liberation of faith from a once desiccated dogmatics that had reduced faith to an attitude of mere assent to a list of church doctrines. *Fides qua* witnesses to God's grace, *fides quae* can become a dangerous liability when it limits rather than supports *fides qua*. However, I consider Luther's monist form of defending his own particular rationality of faith against all those *others*, i.e. Jews, Romans, and Turks, as deeply problematic.[15] It discloses an approach to faith that lacks love. Moreover, it reduces the divine gift of love to a confessional praxis that is no longer open to the divine dynamics of transcendence, conversion and transformation.

This is one of the tragedies of the sixteenth century Reformation: the promising process of liberating *fides qua* from a limited version of *fides quae* sadly turned soon into promoting the emergence of a newly closed orthodoxy, which, like the Catholic Counter-Reformation, now defined itself against the respective other(s) instead of engaging in a culture of mutually critical understanding, love and justice. Doctrinal exclusion, appeals to theological homogeneity, and confessional vilification can never be adequate ways of meeting the Christian (or religious) other and her human, religious and cultural experiences and expectations. This is not to deny the validity of theological debate, genuine disagreement and confessional pursuits. Rather, this is to call for a culture of love as the most appropriate horizon in which to conduct theological arguments and conversations.

There is no such thing as Christian, Jewish or Muslim love; there is no Anglican, Lutheran, Orthodox or Catholic love. Rather, there is God's universal gift of love, which Christians share with all people on earth – living, dead and not yet born – and in response to which they try to live their lives. Once again, the biblical command is not to *like* other religious movements and spiritual pilgrimages. The command is not to *like* God, either. Rather, the biblical command urges treating all human beings and God with respect for their distinctive otherness and to move towards an

---

[15] Cf. Martin Luther's approach to the Jews in his second treatise on the Jews of 1543. "Von den Juden und ihren Lügen", in *D. Martin Luthers Werke: Kritische Gesamtausgabe*, vol. 53, Weimar: Hermann Böhlaus Nachfolger, 1920, 417–552.

ever-closer relationship and communion with the other and with God, the radical other. Doctrine can never replace experience, though it may well be able to guide and encourage human experience of otherness and of divine radical otherness.

Karl Rahner repeatedly insisted that the devout Christians of the future will either be "mystics", that means people who have experienced something, or they will cease to be anything at all.[16] Rahner's point here is not to reduce Christian faith to mysticism, but to stress the link between faith and experience (*fides qua*). The interesting question resulting from Rahner's observation touches on the spectrum, location and context of Christian experience today. What kind of experiences might disclose God's love and God's creative and reconciling presence in our time, place and language?

Love, hope and transformation

A critical and self-critical praxis of Christian hope is both relational and political – in the non-partisan sense of the word. For it remains open to be transformed in the creative and reconciling love relationship, which God has been offering to all human beings. At the same time, it longs for the transformation of the world into a realm of love, hope, peace and justice.[17] While nationalist agendas often promise to defend so-called Christian values, they usually fail to promote the love of otherness and of radical otherness, and they tend to lift their own political agenda above the hard and messy work of facing otherness in the various contexts of our lives. However, only by relating to and struggling with the otherness of concrete persons and of God in love can hope unfold its transformative dynamics.

Moreover, the social, political and emancipatory power of hope necessarily transcends expectations of merely individual salvation.[18] However, rather than playing out the concern for individual salvation against the concern for the emergence of a new heaven and a new earth, we may wish to consider that both aspects of a Christian praxis of hope

---

[16] RAHNER 1973, 15; and RAHNER 1981, 149.
[17] For a discussion of the relationship between love and peace, see JEANROND 2012a, 57–70.
[18] Cf. here also JEANROND 2012b, 217–237.

are in need of being freshly coordinated in the differing contexts of our world. Hence, it would be inappropriate to seek to construct a theology that would fit all and every single theological experience and desire in our pluralist, varied and complex context. Hope is relational and thus particular to persons and communities. Therefore, I wish to argue in favour of abandoning work on a "one shape fits all" type of a universal Christian theology. However, this is not to argue against comparing notes on hope as they originate in the different relational experiences of Christians and non-Christians past and present.

In this context, Anthony Kelly calls for an inter-hope dialogue. "Inter-hope dialogue would highlight the unimaginable 'otherness' of eschatological fulfillment. It looks beyond what is, to what is to come."[19] Kelly argues that the future is what we human beings have in common and that this is the point where Christians, among others, must demonstrate what they hope for and how they engage in hope.[20] "If Christians must never give up hope even for their enemies and persecutors, there is surely a lot that can be said – or left unsaid in the necessary darkness of our present perceptions – regarding the ultimate reconciliation of all in eternal life."[21] Hope, inspired by and cultivated in the praxis of divine-human love, can never be satisfied with only partial fulfilment. "Inter-hope dialogue is more a matter of all looking toward a promised future of communion in eternal life."[22]

The collapse of much Christian eschatological imagination in recent decades need not necessarily be a bad thing. Until not long ago, Christians nurtured a hope to remain among themselves in heaven. There were few, if any, images of the possibility of a shared future with others. Hence the joke that when a Protestant comes to heaven and hears voices in some corner he asks Peter what was going on behind these heavenly walls. Peter replies: Lower your voice so as not to disturb the Catholics over there, because they think they are alone in heaven. And when, not long before his death, Karl Barth was asked whether or not he expected to see his loved

---

[19] KELLY 2006, 16.
[20] Cf. 1 Peter 3:15b: "Always be ready to make your defense to anyone who demands from you an accounting for the hope that is in you".
[21] KELLY 2006, 16.
[22] KELLY 2006, 17.

ones again on the other side of death, he replied, "I am afraid not only my loved ones".[23] It would seem that we not only have a problem with otherness during our lives, but even with regard to our expectations of the God-given eternity. We have often harboured rather tribal views of God and God's transformative love.[24]

The challenge of radical hope is to free ourselves from such restrictive views and for a personal and communal relationship with God and God's people beyond bourgeois calculations, individualist expectations, and confessionalist and nationalist projections. Radical hope might thus be able to liberate Christian eschatology for a deeper understanding of human otherness and of God's radical otherness.

Radical hope denies any closure by whatever systems of hope. Even when all our personal and communal hopes and our trust in the continuation and substance of our religion and culture and their respective institutions are shattered, this does not necessarily signify the end of hope. Rather it implies the challenge to face up to radical hope which comes to us without our own doing from God's love. Radical hope confronts us with radical transcendence. Radical hope, encouraged by the example of Jesus Christ, inspires a life of discipleship in trust, love, communion and anticipation, however without absolute certainty and total control.

The praxis of hope continues to remind us that the history of transformation of each person, of the churches, of other religious traditions, and of the universe as a whole is not a linear process upwards, but a complex process including neglect, injustice, hatred, limitation, interruption, forgetfulness, suffering and death. Only when all of these aspects of human life are gathered into the critical orbit of hope can the praxis of love appropriately unfold – God's love for us and our love for God, for God's creation, for our fellow human beings, and for our own fragile and emerging selves. In hope, human love can face death and ultimate truth through divine judgement. In hope, human beings can explore God's gift of eternal life, a gift that at once affirms human death and transcends it.

---

[23] One version of this often-narrated anecdote is cited by Eberhard Busch, "Eine Reformierte Stimme", *Letter from the Karl Barth-Archives*, 10 December 2002 (Nr. 4), 6–7, here 7.

[24] See, for further examples, CASEY 2009.

Bibliography

Byström, Gabriel
2017   *Med Guds hjälp: Om religion och politik i Ryssland, Ungern och Polen*. Stockholm: Ordfront.

Carmichael, E. D. H. (Liz)
2004   *Friendship: Interpreting Christian Love*. London: T&T Clark.

Casey, John
2009   *After Lives: A Guide to Heaven, Hell, and Purgatory*. Oxford: Oxford University Press.

Dalferth, Ingolf U.
2016   *Hoffnung*. Grundthemen Philosophie. Berlin: De Gruyter.

Jeanrond, Werner G
2010   *A Theology of Love*. London/New York: T&T Clark.
2012a   *Kyrkans framtid: Teologiska reflexioner III*. Lund: Arcus.
2012b   Individuum und Gemeinschaft: Eschatologische Positionen in der gegenwärtigen Dogmatik – Hermann Deuser and Saskia Wendel, eds., *Dialektik der Freiheit: Religiöse Individualisierung und theologische Dogmatik*. Tübingen: Mohr Siebeck.

Kelly, Antony
2006   *Eschatology and Hope*. Maryknoll: Orbis.

Lear, Jonathan
2008   *Radical Hope: Ethics in the Face of Cultural Devastation*. Cambridge, Mass./London: Harvard University Press.

Rahner, Karl
1973   *Theological Investigations*. vol. 7, trans. David Bourke, London: Darton, Longman & Todd.
1981   *Theological Investigations*, vol. 20, trans. Edward Quinn, London: Darton, Longman & Todd.

Saarinen, Risto
2016   *Recognition and Religion: A Historical and Systematic Study*. Oxford: Oxford University Press.
2017   *Luther and the Gift*. Tübingen: Mohr Siebeck.

Zachhuber, Johannes
2017   *Luther's Christological Legacy: Christocentrism and the Chalcedonian Tradition*. The Père Marquette Lecture in Theology 2017. Milwaukee: Marquette University Press.

"ex abundantia caritatis suae":
Divine Self-Revelation and the Abundance of Trinitarian Love[1]

Veli-Matti Kärkkäinen

For orientation: divine self-revelation springing from the shared love of Father, Son and Spirit

Latest since Protestant Reformation, the doctrine of revelation has been at the center of theological and ecumenical disputes. To clarify – or: to confuse –, a number of "models" of revelation[2] has been devised with the hope of being able to explain as to why and how the Sovereign God chose to reveal God's own self to the humanity. Engaging those debates is not in the interest of this essay. Rather, the present discussion seeks to highlight the nature and significance of divine revelation through the lens of God's love. The essay sets forth a simple and profound thesis: whatever else we could be saying theologically of God's self-revelation and however define its mode and motif, behind God's voluntary and effectual self-revelation is God's infinitely abundant love. We can also put it this way: divine self-revelation is a profound gift[3] of God to humanity.

Linking the divine self-revelation with God's love is to speak of revelation in trinitarian terms. Similarly to all divine works *ad extra*, from creation

---

[1] The present essay is based on and draws directly from Kärkkäinen 2014, chap. 2. Published with permission.
[2] For a classic recent study, see Dulles 1992.
[3] I am using the term "gift" and related terms such as "hospitality" in their everyday sense and do not engage the complex philosophical and theological debates, headed by the late French philosopher J. Derrida, on the (im-) possibility and conditions thereof. For a fine study, see Saarinen 2005.

to providence to salvation to consummation, the work of revelation is a joint work of Father, Son, and Spirit. The Reformed Karl Barth saw this clearly as both methodologically and materially he began the exposition of Christian dogmatics with a trinitarian notion of divine self-revelation. For him, Trinity was of such central importance that even before getting into the discussion of the dogmatics, Trinity had to be established as the overarching context and goal of systematic argumentation. In keeping with this trinitarian orientation, Barth defined self-revelation of God famously: "*God* reveals Himself. He reveals Himself *through Himself*. He reveals *Himself*".⁴ While this *formal* trinitarian statement of revelation may be liable to the critique of Pannenberg⁵ that it is *formal* and thus not successful in keeping with the biblical narrative which ascends from the concrete history of salvation onto the knowledge of the Father, Son, and Spirit, its basic intuition is still valid.

Importantly, later Barth had an occasion to correct and clarify his standpoint as he reminded us that the Bible points to "the life of God Himself turned to us, the Word of God coming to us by the Holy Spirit, Jesus Christ".⁶ Here he is not speaking the Idealist philosophy of an abstract, contents-less *self*-revelation of God but rather the economic language of the Bible in which the loving Father sends his Son, the incarnate Word, to live with us, in the power of the Holy Spirit, to redeem and perfect the world which has been created by the Father through the Son in the life-giving power of the Spirit. This same trinitarian truth is finely expressed in the common ecumenical statement by Roman Catholics and Lutherans: "What God has done for the salvation of the world in Jesus Christ is transmitted in the gospel and made present in the Holy Spirit. The gospel as proclamation of God's saving action is therefore itself a saving event".⁷ This central Christian statement calls for further elucidation and amplification.⁸

---

⁴ BARTH 1956–1975, I/1, 296 [hereafter: *CD*].
⁵ For discussion and critique of revelation as divine "self-revelation" in BARTH, see PANNENBERG 1968, 3–8 particularly.
⁶ *CD*, I/ 2, 483, see also, 512–13.
⁷ *The Gospel and the Church – The Malta Report* (1972), # 16 (available at Centro Pro Unione website: http://www.pro.urbe.it/dia-int/l-rc/doc/e_l-rc_malta.html); also, KASPER 2009, 12.
⁸ For an important ecumenical trinitarian statement on revelation, see KINNAMON & BRIAN 1997, 139–144. For a fine theological discussion of the implications of Trinitarian view of revelation, see METZGER 2005, 21–34.

Building on this "foundational" idea of divine self-revelation springing from the shared love of Father, Son, and Spirit, let us zoom in on the distinct, although unified, tasks of each of the trinitarian persons in the unfolding of this infinitely abundant love. This concrete, particular observation of the economy of salvation in the process of revelation avoids the danger of a formal, abstract doctrine and instead, helps us appreciate the ways Father, Son, and Spirit love the world through the divine self-revelation. In this task, we can learn from across the ecumenical spectrum, particularly from Roman Catholic and Lutheran sources.

Loving Father and the cruciform revelation

Vatican II's *Dei Verbum* represents a dramatic shift in traditional theology of revelation in general and Roman Catholic tradition in particular as it turns to personalist, relational, and dynamic notion of revelation. Citing the words of St. John from the beginning of his first Epistle, the *Dogmatic Constitution on Divine Revelation* – a most inappropriate and misleading title as it has! – begins with this proclamation (#1): "We announce to you the eternal life which dwelt with the Father and was made visible to us. What we have seen and heard we announce to you, so that you may have fellowship with us and our common fellowship be with the Father and His Son Jesus Christ (1 John 1:2–3)". This turn to the economy of salvation is one of the theologically most pregnant statements on the meaning of revelation in the biblical narrative (#2):[9]

> In His goodness and wisdom God chose to reveal Himself and to make known to us the hidden purpose of His will (see Eph. 1:9) by which through Christ, the Word made flesh, man might in the Holy Spirit have access to the Father and come to share in the divine nature (see Eph. 2:18; 2 Peter 1:4). Through this revelation, therefore, the invisible God (see Col. 1;15, 1 Tim. 1:17) out of the abundance of His love speaks to men as friends (see Ex. 33:11; John 15:14–15) and lives among them (see Bar. 3:38), so that He may invite and take them into fellowship with Himself. This plan of revelation is realized by deeds and words having in inner unity: the deeds wrought by God in the history of salvation manifest and confirm

---

[9] All Vatican II documents can be found (in various languages) at www.vatican.va (all citations in this essay come from there).

the teaching and realities signified by the words, while the words proclaim the deeds and clarify the mystery contained in them. By this revelation then, the deepest truth about God and the salvation of man shines out for our sake in Christ, who is both the mediator and the fullness of all revelation.[10]

To say that Father out of his love reaches out to and communicates with his creatures is to find the "source" and "reason" for revelation, namely the overflowing and infinite love. However, that is not yet to say what kind of love this is. Here we are guided by no one else but Martin Luther himself. While routinely named as the theologian of justification, Luther might be more appropriately named as the theologian of love. His theology of divine love, linked with his theology of the cross, makes a profound contribution in this respect to the trinitarian nature of God's revelation as well.

The last thesis of Luther's *Heidelberg Disputation* (1518),[11] formulated on the eve of Protestant Reformation, outlines the basic vision of not only of his "theology of the cross",[12] but also of love. He makes an important distinction between two kinds of love, namely *amor Dei* and *amor hominis,*

---

[10] "Placuit Deo in sua bonitate et sapientia Seipsum revelare et notum facere sacramentum voluntatis suae (cf. *Eph* 1,9), quo homines per Christum, Verbum carnem factum, in Spiritu Sancto accessum habent ad Patrem et divinae naturae consortes efficiuntur (cf. *Eph* 2,18; 2 *Petr* 1,4). Hac itaque revelatione Deus invisibilis (cf. *Col* 1,15; 1 *Tim* 1,17) *ex abundantia caritatis suae* homines tamquam amicos alloquitur (cf. *Ex* 33,11; *Io* 15,14–15) et cum eis conversatur (cf. *Bar* 3,38), ut eos ad societatem Secum invitet in eamque suscipiat. Haec revelationis oeconomia fit gestis verbisque intrinsece inter se connexis, ita ut opera, in historia salutis a Deo patrata, doctrinam et res verbis significatas manifestent ac corroborent, verba autem opera proclament et mysterium in eis contentum elucident. Intima autem per hanc revelationem tam de Deo quam de hominis salute veritas nobis in Christo illucescit, qui mediator simul et plenitudo totius revelationis exsistit." (emphasis added)

[11] In April 1518, Martin Luther presided over the opening disputation of the chapter of his Augustinian Order at Heidelberg. The disputation concerned a series of theses which Luther had drawn up for the occasion at the invitation of Johannes von Staupitz. In the previous year (1517) Luther had posted the Theses on Indulgences at Wittenberg, and in 1519, the year following the Heidelberg Disputation, he had the historic Leipzig Disputation with Johannes Eck.

[12] Although Luther's theology of the cross is a topic that has drawn much interest since the beginning of the twentieth century, only recently has a major monograph on the Heidelberg Disputation been written by a Finnish Lutheran scholar Kari KOPPERI, titled *Paradoksien teologia: Lutherin disputaatio Heidelbergissä 1518 [Theology of Paradoxes: Luther's Disputation in Heidelberg 1518]*. Suomalaisen Teologisen Kirjallisuusseuran julkaisuja 208 (Saarijärvi: Gummerus, 1997). Unfortunately the work is written in Finnish, and so inaccessible to a wider audience. A brief but helpful outline can be found in MANNERMAA, 2010, chap. 3. More widely, consult McGRATH 1985. For a discussion, see KÄRKKÄINEN 2002.

God's love and human love, respectively: "The love of God does not find, but creates, that which is pleasing to it. The love of man comes into being through that which is pleasing to it."[13] Human love is always basically selfish and looks for its own good. Human love is oriented towards objects which are inherently good, where self-love defines the content and the object of the love.[14] Men and women love something that they believe they can enjoy. For Luther, love as defined by medieval scholastic theology provided an example of this kind of love. Luther sometimes calls God's love *amor crucis:* "This is the love of the cross, born of the cross, which turns in the direction where it does not find good which it may enjoy, but where it may confer good upon the bad and needy person."[15]

Human mind believes it can discover this loving God in his majesty, power, and glory. Luther categorically denies this and instead, argues that the only way to know the God is to become the theologian of the cross, instead of the theologian of glory. Namely, God reveals himself exactly where he is not supposed to be, hence reveals himself through concealing his "godly" attributes and manifesting himself in the opposites. This is the theology of the cross, of the crucified and humiliated Christ as the true – and only way – to the knowledge of God. This is the cruciform doctrine of revelation.

Why, then, might the human mind be so easily fooled? The human mind naturally follows the logic of "knowledge is of like by like,"[16] and that rule was followed in early Christian theology with its idea of analogy in the knowledge of God. "God is known in the analogies to him in the order of creation or in acts of history which point to him, or else he is

---

[13] LUTHER 2002, 31:41. *Heidelberg Disputation*, # 28 [hereafter: *HDT*]. The 28 theses are first listed and thereafter (under a longer heading beginning with "Proofs – – ") discussed in some detail. A groundbreaking study of Luther's theology of love is MANNERMAA 2010 (which appeared first in Finnish in 1983).

[14] MANNERMAA 2010, uses Thomas Aquinas as the template for human love (see particularly chap. 2). Mannermaa considers Luther's view as a corrective to Thomas's understanding of love according to which love in the most general sense means the inclination and desire of all beings toward the specific and attainable good of that being. In contemporary language, the essence of Thomas's conception of love would then be self-fulfillment, realization of one's full potential to its maximum.

[15] *LW* 31, 57; *HDT,* # 28. See further BORNKAMM 1975, 130–146.

[16] ARISTOTLE 1908, III, 4.10.

known in his self-revelation, or only in the Holy Spirit of God."[17] There is of course no denying the granting of some knowledge of God to humanity in this analogous way. The problem is that if the "principle of likeness is applied strictly, God is only known by God."[18] Apart from this logical problem, the material problem with one-sided application of the analogical principle is that according to the biblical testimonies, God has also chosen to reveal himself in means not only different from but totally opposed to the principle of analogy. This is the rule of the opposites, so to speak. Hence, the analogical rule must be supplemented and at times corrected with the dialogical rule according to which "God is only revealed as 'God' in his opposite: godlessness and abandonment by God. In concrete terms, God is revealed in the cross of Christ who was abandoned by God. His grace is revealed in sinner. His righteousness is revealed in the unrighteous and those without rights, and his gracious election in the damned."[19] Hence the Johannine Jesus' saying, "He who has seen me has seen the Father" (John 14:9) applies as much to the suffering and humiliated Jesus as the victorious and glorious one. Herein the leading Reformed Moltmann is speaking the language of Luther!

Indeed, according to Luther, God not only reveals himself but also works in the opposite way from the human expectations: God conceals Godself in lowliness to reveal the greatness of God's love. Whereas the natural mind imagines the works of God to be beautiful, fine and attractive, the opposite is the case. God's works "are always unattractive and appear evil, (but) they are nevertheless really eternal merits," insofar as they are in accordance with his true love.[20] Here Luther introduces one major aspect of his "theology of paradoxes": God's alien work *(opus alienum Dei)* and God's proper work *(opus proprium Dei)*. God's alien work means putting down, killing, taking away hope, leading to desperation, and so on. God's proper work means the opposite: forgiving, giving mercy, taking up, saving, encouraging, and so on.[21] The alien works Luther sometimes calls "the works of the left hand" and the proper works "the works of the right hand." As Luther puts

---

[17] MOLTMANN 1993, 26.
[18] MOLTMANN 1993, 26.
[19] MOLTMANN 1993, 27.
[20] *HDT* 4; *LW* 31, 44.
[21] Just consult for example Luther's vivid exposition in *LW* 14, 95.

it in his typical manner: "To be born anew, one must consequently first die and then be raised up with the Son of Man. To die, I say, means to feel death at hand."[22] It is important to understand that, while these two kinds of works seem to be the opposite of each other, they result from the same love of God. God's proper work is veiled in his alien work and takes place simultaneously with it.

These reflections take us to the most profound manifestation of Father's love in sending his Son to live and die for us, one among us – and so also offer a word of hope not only to men and women but the whole of creation.

Incarnated Son and embodied revelation

According to the formula of Irenaeus, "the Father is the invisible of the Son, but the Son the visible of the Father."[23] Father's reaching out in abundant love to his creatures keeps the theology of revelation solidly grounded in the economy of salvation. Sending his Son as the divine revelation not only speaks of the cross but also incarnation, which is the clue to the Christian understanding of the revelation of God. In his *On the Incarnation of the Word of God*, St. Athanasius offers the classic reasoning of the way the Loving Father, "[w]ho by nature is invisible and not to be beheld," has made it possible for humans to know and see him by virtue of incarnation: "He, indeed, assumed humanity that we might become God. He manifested Himself by means of a body in order that we might perceive the Mind of the unseen Father." In a most remarkable statement, Athanasius summarizes the significance of incarnation: "For this purpose, then, the incorporeal and incorruptible and immaterial Word of God comes to our realm, howbeit he was not far from us before. For no part of Creation is left void of Him: He has filled all things everywhere, remaining present with His own Father."[24]

While few theologians would object to the claim that Jesus Christ is *the* divine revelation, that is not to say that all agree in contemporary theology what that means. Richard Bauckham outlines helpfully three important

---

[22] *HDT* 24; *LW* 31, 55.
[23] IRENAEUS, *Against Heresies*, 4.6.6 ANF, 1:489.
[24] ATHANASIUS, *On the Incarnation of the Word* 8:1.

paradigms for understanding the claim that Jesus is the revelation of God.[25] One such he describes as that in which "Jesus illustrates the moral character of God." As it is put sometimes, Jesus is a "parable" of God and as moral attributes, inclusively understood are such that they can be communicated to humanity, it makes sense to think that in his person Jesus reveals us the compassionate, loving, righteous, and holy nature of God. This paradigm seems to imply that while preciously valuable, revelation in Christ does not have to be unique – or be unique only in degree. Similar kinds of "attributes" of God can be discerned in other human lives. The second paradigm is that "Jesus reveals the universal possibility of Divine-human union." Linked with the first one, this view also can be distinct and often is since it goes beyond the mere possibility of knowing the God, to union with God. Jesus then of course represents the culmination of that union. The possibility of union calls for incarnation, the coming of the Divine in the human form. As to what kind of incarnation that is, is still negotiable as evident in the theology of the late Anglican John Macquarrie.[26] While he speaks of incarnation as "unique" in Jesus Christ, he is not thereby limiting incarnation totally to one human person.[27]

Bauckham's third paradigm is one in which "Jesus reveals the unique presence and action of God which is Jesus' own history." In this view, "Jesus does not merely illustrate what God is like, nor is he merely the representatively fullest instantiation of humanity united with God. His unique human life, death, and resurrection are at the same time uniquely God's human history, in which God's unique act of self-giving love for all humanity took place."[28] It is clear without saying that this third paradigm materially represents classical Christian tradition. This is where tradition's focus on Logos, the Word-made-flesh comes to the fore, as the uniquely Christian way of understanding salvation.

The incarnated, embodied nature of Christian revelation is, indeed, its most distinctive feature and its significance among religions cannot be overemphasized. In Christian revelation, rather than being a matter of God telling us what the divine is like or how to live in order to live rightly, or

---

[25] BAUCKHAM 2004, 174–200.
[26] MACQUARRIE 1990.
[27] BAUCKHAM 2004, 179.
[28] BAUCKHAM 2004, 180.

even God showing us what the nature of divine is like, "God makes the Divine reality itself present in a particular historical form. The life of Jesus, for a fully incarnational form of Christian faith, is the self-expression of the Eternal in time."[29] Rightly then, it can be said that

> This is not, as in Islam, the revelation of a set of propositions, as though God were dictating laws of doctrines to be carefully written down. It is not, as in Hinduism, an inner experience of a supreme Self, as though someone had a particularly vivid of intense sense of the Supremely real. It is not, as in Buddhism, an experience of release from sorrow, desire, and attachment. It is not, as in Judaism, Divine disclosure through the control of historical events, as though God were causing water, wind, or earth to act in extraordinary of miraculous ways. It is the unlimited Divine Life taking form in a particular human life. It is the realization of the Eternal in a particular historical individual.[30]

Rightly, then, my Reformed colleague, the American theologian William A. Dyrness speaks of embodiment as one of the "normative categories" in the articulation of the theological reality of our life in the world which also correspond to the trinitarian approach to life, faith, and theology. Having created a world in which human life and life in general is physical, embodied, God's loving reaching out to the world takes the shape of embodiment, incarnation.[31] In this sense, the divine revelational embodiment in Christian tradition thus is a "home-coming," "God's being at home in the world, a situation which even the sin cannot efface, leads to God's full identification with creation in the incarnation of Jesus."[32] As Irenaeus pointedly put it, "And vain likewise are those who say that God came to those things which did not belong to Him." Indeed, God's home-coming was triggered with abundant love as the Bishop further explains so beautifully: For we have given nothing to Him previously, nor does He desire anything from us, as if He stood in need of it; but we do stand in need of fellowship with Him. And for this reason it was that He graciously poured Himself out, that He might gather us into the bosom of the Father."[33]

---

[29] WARD 1994, 193.
[30] WARD 1994, 193.
[31] DYRNESS 1997, chap. 1 particularly.
[32] DYRNESS 1997, 22.
[33] IRENAEUS, *Against Heresies*, 5.2.1; *ANF* 1:528.

This observation may help Christian theology make more sense of the obviously scandalous claim in the religiously pluralistic world that the final and ultimate revelation has come in the coming of this one Man, Jesus the Christ. This is not a claim about the superiority of Jesus, "considered in the abstract as a person of such-and-such intelligence, moral character, and temperament. It is rather that God is manifesting the Divine Being decisively in his one historical life; so that this life becomes for ever the image of God, as a historically purposing and redemptive power and value."[34] Whereas Irenaeus, Athanasius, and many later theologians, most brilliantly St. Thomas Aquinas, reflected deeply on the aptness of divine embodiment, contemporary theology and religious studies is vested with the interest in this "scandal of particularity," in other words, in what sense can it be said that it is in this one particular human person that the Divine became embodied and manifested. Mainline Christian tradition has never claimed that the incarnation of the Word would express everything that there is to be known of the Divine – or else creation and history would be void of meaning. What Christian theology is saying "is that a particular, limited point of time and space, the Divine Life transforms a particular human life by uniting it to itself. The particular is taken into God, as a foreshadowing of the destiny that awaits all finite things."[35]

Recall that the thesis of this essay is: out of the abundance of divine love, the Father reaches out to men and women under the disguise of the cross, the Son embodies this divine love both in his righteous life and glorious resurrection from the shameful death on the cross; and the divine, life-giving Spirit brings about and makes alive this revelation.

Life-Giving Spirit and living revelation

In a healthy trinitarian grammar, the loving Father sends his Son, the word-made-flesh, in the power and energies of the Holy Spirit. Hence, the linking of revelation and Scripture to the Spirit of God has always

---

[34] WARD 1994, 195.
[35] WARD 1994, 194. See also 196: "Christ does not narrow the Jewish vocation to just one person; he expands it until it spreads throughout the world, by internalizing and universalizing its teaching."

been part of Christian theological intuitions. The late Canadian Baptist theologian Stanley J. Grenz forges this link in a robust way by locating in his presentation of dogmatics the discussion of Revelation under pneumatology.[36] Appropriately he begins the discussion with citation from 1 Corinthians 2:9–14:[37]

> But, as it is written, "What no eye has seen, nor ear heard, nor the heart of man conceived, what God has prepared for those who love him," God has revealed to us through the Spirit. For the Spirit searches everything, even the depths of God. For what person knows a man's thoughts except the spirit of the man which is in him? So also no one comprehends the thoughts of God except the Spirit of God. Now we have received not the spirit of the world, but the Spirit which is from God, that we might understand the gifts bestowed on us by God. And we impart this in words not taught by human wisdom but taught by the Spirit, interpreting spiritual truths to those who possess the Spirit. The unspiritual man does not receive the gifts of the Spirit of God, for they are folly to him, and he is not able to understand them because they are spiritually discerned.

Where tradition has usually failed is to jump directly from this biblical statement and similar passages to the consideration of the Spirit's role in inspiration and illumination of Scripture to the reader without considering the wider horizon of the Spirit's ministry. Moltmann rightly remarks that to "see the Spirit at work only in the verbal inspiration of scripture is a reduction of the mighty efficacy of God the Spirit – –"[38] Without any way diminishing this important ministry, there is a wider, more inclusive trinitarian linking of the Spirit with the process of revelation, not only its medium, the Scripture. Here again, Grenz got it right:[39]

> The Spirit's mission is to complete the program of the triune God in the world. To this end, he is the Creator Spirit. Not only is he the source of life, the Spirit is the power of the eschatological renewal of life. He is the agent who brings into being the new creation (2 Cor. 5:17). He effects the union of believers with Christ and Christ's community, the reconciled people of God. At the consummation, the Spirit's mission will reach its ultimate goal as he establishes the glorious fellowship of the redeemed people living in a redeemed word and enjoying the presence of their Redeemer God. En route to that day, the Spirit nourishes the spiritual life he creates.

---

[36] GRENZ 2000, ch. 14 (in part 4: "Pneumatology: The Doctrine of the Holy Spirit.")
[37] GRENZ 2000, only cites vv. 12–13.
[38] MOLTMANN 2000, 136.
[39] GRENZ 2000, 379.

In order to set in a wider trinitarian framework the more specific ministry of the Spirit with regard to the inspiration and illumination, we should remind us of the foundational role of the Spirit in the world as the Spirit of Life. From the beginning of the biblical narrative, the Spirit's role in creation, as the principle of life, comes to the fore. The same Spirit of God that participated in creation over the chaotic primal waters (Gen. 1:2) is the principle of human life as well (Gen. 2:7). This very same divine energy also sustains all life in the cosmos: "When you [Yahweh] send your Spirit [*ruach*], they are created, and you renew the face of the earth" (Ps. 104:30). Similarly, when Yahweh "take[s] away their breath [*ruach*], they die and return to the dust" (v. 29). Furthermore, this creative life-force is also the eschatological Spirit of God (Joel 2:28–32; Acts 2). In this framework, Moltmann brilliantly argues, we can perceive

> the function of scripture *in the trinitarian history of God*, into which human beings are integrated through baptism and the rebirth to a living hope. In the perspective of the eschatological finality of the death and resurrection of Christ, scripture is *closed* and complete. Christ "died to sin once for all, but the life he lives he lives to God" (Rom 6.10). The christological *ephapax* – the once for all – applies to the christological witness of scripture too, as Heb. 1.2 intimates. But in the perspective of the Pentecostal beginning of the eschatological experiences of the Spirit, scripture is *open*. The eschatological experience of the Spirit is itself the *future* of scripture – – With this future 'the fulfillment of scripture' in the kingdom of God being. In this respect we have to understand "what is written" in the great framework of God's economy of the Spirit.[40]

While joint work, there is also a divine *taxis* in the trinitarian economy. The Spirit comes as the Son, the incarnated One, exits. The *Paraclete*, the Spirit of truth, takes from Jesus' words and conveys them to us (John 16:13). "Just as no one knows the Father except the Son (Matt. 11.27), so no one confesses Jesus as Lord except *in* the Holy Spirit (I cor. 12.4)."[41]

In the trinitarian joint work, the Father in his infinite love reaches out to men and women by sending his eternal Son, the Word-made-flesh, in the power and energies of the Holy Spirit. If God is the "author" of Scripture in general, then "the Bible is the Spirit's book"[42] in particular, both in its

---

[40] MOLTMANN 2000, 144–45.
[41] MOLTMANN 2000, 145.
[42] GRENZ 2000, 379.

inspiration and appropriation in daily life by the people of God, the body of Christ, the temple of the Holy Spirit. Of this part of the Spirit's ministry *Dei Verbum* (# 5) says this:

> "The obedience of faith" (Rom. 13:26; see 1:5; 2 Cor 10:5–6) "is to be given to God who reveals, an obedience by which man commits his whole self freely to God, offering the full submission of intellect and will to God who reveals," and freely assenting to the truth revealed by Him. To make this act of faith, the grace of God and the interior help of the Holy Spirit must precede and assist, moving the heart and turning it to God, opening the eyes of the mind and giving "joy and ease to everyone in assenting to the truth and believing it." To bring about an ever deeper understanding of revelation the same Holy Spirit constantly brings faith to completion by His gifts.

The Spirit's illuminating work of revelation and Scripture, should never be made external to the truth the message carries as has happened at times in the well-meant Pietistic turn to subjective certainty as a response to alleged lack of certainty of truth. Nor can it be made a merely subjective, individual experience. Reacting against Classical Liberalism's conception of the inspiration of Scripture as the function of our faith, Barth rightly warned that "it is not our faith but the power of God that underlies the inspiration of the Bible."[43] A remedy against this kind of danger is what has been recently named as Barth's "objective pneumatology," his conviction that the Spirit in speaking to us cannot be collapsed into human subjectivity or experience.[44] As Barth wrote, "[t]he witness of Holy Scripture is therefore the witness of the Holy Spirit."[45] In this unified witness of Spirit and text, we are not just speaking of our *experience* of the divine Word, "but its actual presence."[46] What governs the voice of Scripture is the divine self-giving in Christ and not our experience of this: "[t]he presence of the Word of God is not an experience, precisely because and as it is the divine decision concerning us."[47] Of course, our reception of the Spirit's witness is always colored by human subjectivity and our interpretations of the Bible always threaten to take the Bible captive, but Barth is confident that the Spirit's

---

[43] *CD*, I/2, 534.
[44] See Thompson 1991.
[45] *CD*, I/2, 538.
[46] Ibid., 533.
[47] Ibid., 532.

speaking through the text "is objective enough to emerge victorious from all the inbreaks and outbreaks of man's subjectivity."[48]

The pneumatological framing of revelation in a healthy trinitarian framework helps us see the wideness of God's love towards all men and women, created in God's image, and indeed, toward the whole of creation. Rightly another Canadian Baptist theologian, the late Clark Pinnock remarks: "There is a cosmic range to the operations of the Spirit, the Lord and giver of life – – Spirit is the ecstasy that implements God's abundance and triggers the overflow of divine self-giving – – The universe in its entirety is the field of its operations – –"[49] Hence, we should not make "God's leading into the truth to be a matter of only parochial interest. It should be placed in a global setting, because God's interests are much wider than the church. God is self-revealed in creation and history as well as in the experiences of Israel and the story of Jesus. God does not leave himself without witness among the nations – – The Spirit is guiding, luring, wooing, influencing, drawing all humanity, not just the church – – Not every one listens, but God speaks to all."[50]

Because revelation is a triune event, the word-made-flesh, indeed, it is an *event* rather than an *idea*, it links revelation in the history of this world. It makes revelation *historical*, a most unique feature among religions of the distinctively Christian view of divine revelation.

Last words: revelation pointing into the future consummation

This essay has sought to highlight the significance to contemporary faith and theology of Triune God's love as manifested in God's gracious and free gift of revelation. It has built on this foundational Christian conviction that in all works *ad extra*, there is an integral co-operation among Father, Son, and Spirit. Whether we look at creation or reconciliation or consummation, the same rule holds. In the revelation of the Father through the Son in the Spirit, the triune God not only makes Godself known to humanity but also graciously invites men and women into eternal fellowship.

---

[48] Ibid., 534.
[49] Pinnock 1996, 50.
[50] Pinnock 1996, 216.

That triune revelation, in the form of promise, is anchored in the history of this world in the expectation of the final manifestation of the God of the Bible. An essential task for contemporary Christian theology of revelation is to seek to discern the gracious way the Father gathers men and women from all contexts into the body of Christ, which in the power of the Spirit participates in the coming of God's righteous rule that encompasses the whole of creation, in the eager anticipation of the coming of the new creation. Only then will the love of God shown us in the face of his Son and poured out in our hearts through the Holy Spirit be experienced face-to-face. Only then can this eternal love make complete and transcend faith and hope (1 Cor. 13:13) in the eternal communion of creatures with their Creator.

Hence, divine revelation springing forth from the abundance of the shared love of the Father, Son, and Spirit is also an eschatological event. While deeply embedded in the long and winding history of the people of God and God's dealings with the world God has created, revelation points to future. Revelation is, as Moltmann already decades ago put it, a profound "promise" of God.[51] Christian revelation is neither a box dropped down from heaven containing fixed doctrinal formulae, nor an abstract, elusive collection of human thoughts about eternal truths. It is God-with-us; it is divine love poured on all flesh; it is a living power leading us into the eternal destiny for which we were created. "Through this revelation, therefore, the invisible God *out of the abundance of His love* speaks to men as friends and lives among them, so that He may invite and take them into fellowship with Himself."[52]

---

[51] MOLTMANN first developed his idea of revelation as promise in his inaugural international monograph titled *Theology of Hope: On the Ground and the Implications of a Christian Eschatology*, tr. James W. Leitch (London: SCM, 1967 [1964]).

[52] *Dei Verbum*, # 2 (emphasis added; biblical references deleted in the text).

Bibliography

ARISTOTLE
1908   *Metaphysics*. Trans. W. D. Ross. The Classic Library. Available at http://www.classicallibrary.org/aristotle/metaphysics/book03.htm

ATHANASIUS
            On the Incarnation of the Word. Christian Classics Ethereal Library, Grand Rapids, MI. Available at https://www.ccel.org/ccel/athanasius/incarnation.pdf.

BARTH, Karl
1956–1975   *Church Dogmatics*. Eds. Geoffrey William Bromiley & Thomas Forsyth Torrance. Trans. G. W. Bromiley. 14 vols. Edinburgh: T. & T. Clark.

BAUCKHAM, Richard
2004   Jesus the Revelation of God. – *Divine Revelation*. Ed. Paul Avis. Eugene, OR: Wipf and Stock.

BORNKAMM, Heinrich
1975   Die theologischen Thesen Luthers bei der Heidelberger Disputation 1518 und seine theologia crucis. – *Luther, Gestalt und Wirkugen*. Ed. Heinrich Bornkamm. Gütersloh: Gütersloher Verlagshaus.

DULLES, Avery, S.J.
1992 [1983] *Models of Revelation*. Maryknoll, NY: Orbis.

DYRNESS, William A.
1997   *The Earth is God's. A Theology of American Culture*. Maryknoll, NY: Orbis.

GRENZ, Stanley J.
2000   *Theology for the Community of God*. Grand Rapids, MI.: Eerdmans.

IRENAEUS
1885–1897   *Against Heresies*. – The Ante-Nicene Fathers. Translations of the Writings of the Fathers down to a.d. 325. Eds. Alexander Roberts & James Donaldson et al. 9 vols. Edinburgh. Public domain. Available at www.ccel.org.

KÄRKKÄINEN, Veli-Matti
2002   'Evil, Love and the Left Hand of God'. The Contribution of Luther's Theology of the Cross to an Evangelical Theology of Evil. – *Evangelical Quarterly* 74:3. 215–34.
2014   *Trinity and Revelation. A Constructive Christian Theology for the Pluralistic World*. 5 vols. Vol. 2. Grand Rapids, MI: Eerdmans.

KASPER, Walter
2009   *Harvesting the Fruits. Basic Aspects of Christian Faith in Ecumenical Dialogue*. London/New York: Continuum.

KINNAMON, Michael & COPE, Brian E. Eds.
1997   *The Ecumenical Movement. An Anthology of Key Texts and Voices.* Grand Rapids, MI: Eerdmans.

KOPPERI, Kari
1997   *Paradoksien teologia. Lutherin disputaatio Heidelbergissä 1518.* Suomalaisen Teologisen Kirjallisuusseuran julkaisuja. Saarijärvi: Gummerus.

LUTHER, Martin
2002   *Luther's Works.* American ed. Libronix Digital Library. Eds. Jaroslav Pelikan & Helmut T. Lehman. 55 vols. Minneapolis: Fortress Press.

MACQUARRIE, John
1990   *Jesus Christ in Modern Thought.* London: SCM Press.

MANNERMAA, Tuomo
2010   *Two Kinds of Love: Martin Luther's Religious World.* Transl. Kirsi Stjerna. Minneapolis: Fortress Press.

MCGRATH, Alistair E.
1985   *Luther's Theology of the Cross: Martin Luther's Theological Breakthrough.* Oxford, U.K./New York: Oxford Press.

METZGER, Paul Louis
2005   The Relational Dynamic of Revelation. A Trinitarian Perspective. – *Trinitarian Soundings in Systematic Theology.* Ed. Paul Louis Metzger. London/New York: Continuum.

MOLTMANN, Jürgen
1993   *The Crucified God. The Cross of Christ as the Foundation and Criticism of Christian Theology.* Transl. R.A. Wilson and John Bowden. Minneapolis: Fortress Press.
1967 [1964] *Theology of Hope. On the Ground and the Implications of a Christian Eschatology.* Trans. James W. Leitch. London: SCM.
2000   *Experiences in Theology.* Trans. Margaret Kohl. Minneapolis: Fortress Press.

PANNENBERG, Wolfhart
1968 [1961] Introduction. – *Revelation as History. A Proposal for a More Open, Less Authoritarian View of an Important Theological Concept.* Ed. W. Pannenberg. Trans. David Gransko. London: Collier-Macmillan.

PINNOCK, Clark H.
1996   *Flame of Love. A Theology of the Holy Spirit.* Downers Grove, IL: InterVarsity Press.

SAARINEN, Risto
2005   *God and Gift. An Ecumenical Theology of Giving.* Unitas Books. Collegeville, MN: Liturgical Press.

THOMPSON, John
1991   *The Holy Spirit in the Theology of Karl Barth.* Princeton Theological Monograph Series. Eugene, OR: Pickwick.

WARD, Keith
1994   *Religion and Revelation. A Theology of Revelation in the World's Religions.* Oxford: Clarendon.

Shorthands

ANF   *The Ante-Nicene Fathers. Translations of the Writings of the Fathers down to a.d. 325.* Eds. Alexander Roberts & James Donaldson et al. 9 vols. Edinburgh. Public domain; available at www.ccel.org.

CD   BARTH, Karl. *Church Dogmatics.* Eds. Geoffrey William Bromiley & Thomas Forsyth Torrance. Trans. G. W. Bromiley. 14 vols. Edinburgh: T. & T. Clark. 1967–1975.

HDT   *Heidelberg Disputation*

LW   *Luther's Works.* American ed. Libronix Digital Library. Eds. Jaroslav Pelikan & Helmut T. Lehman. 55 vols. Minneapolis: Fortress Press, 2002.

Bonhoeffer on Love

MICHAEL WELKER

The creative scholarship of Risto Saarinen concerning the broader phenomenon of "love" has provided welcome assistance to the theological, religious, and academic world's attempts to illuminate this intriguing field,[1] an undertaking in which I myself feel a profound connection with him.[2] The following discussion will consider the understanding of love from one of the classic partners in this theological undertaking, namely, Dietrich Bonhoeffer.[3]

I. Love in the power of the Spirit – the young Bonhoeffer's ingenious reflections 1926–1927 (DBWE 9 and DBWE 1)

At 7:00 a.m. on September 21, 1925, Dietrich Bonhoeffer accompanied his professor Reinhold Seeberg to the Berlin train station, who had offered the young student this opportunity to speak with him about plans for a doctoral dissertation. Just two years later, Bonhoeffer submitted his inspired piece *Sanctorum communio. A Theological Study of the Sociology of the Church* (DBWE I) at the university of Berlin. After his acceptance as a doctoral candidate during his third year at the university, probably in early 1926, Bonhoeffer delivered a paper in Seeberg's seminar with the title "The Church and the Kingdom of God," which Seeberg corrected on January 22, 1926. Picking up on texts by Reinhold Seeberg, Johannes Weiß, and Emanuel Hirsch, Bonhoeffer works out an understanding of love that far

---

[1] Picking up on Phil 4:2f: SAARINEN 2011; 2012; 2014.
[2] WELKER 2001; 2014; 2015.
[3] The references in the following text refer to Dietrich BONHOEFFER Works = DBWE.

surpasses not only the prevalent philosophical and theological notions of his own time, but much in our time as well, an understanding, moreover, that shapes the enduringly exemplary theological and sociological impulses in his doctoral dissertation.

Whenever what is known as healthy human understanding reflects and speaks about love, it generally thinks of bi-personal relationships, relationships involving I and You, at most perhaps God and the individual, in which case God, however, is often conceived merely as a "counterpart," a "reference point." Nineteen-year-old Dietrich Bonhoeffer, however, inspired as he was by great theological-academic models, speaks instead about love in fundamentally more complex contexts, to wit, about the "entity that has been predetermined by the Father in eternal election, the church community of believers that has been established by the saving action of Christ in history as the spiritual body of the spiritual head. It is kept active by the Holy Spirit by means of living, community-building love" (DBWE 9:314).

In this context, Bonhoeffer is thus understanding love christologically and as being shaped and determined by the Holy Spirit. Love forms a community that it then keeps active through its own living character. In turn, it is shaped within history by the salvific activity of Christ, who is the spiritual head of a spiritual body. Just as breath and blood stimulate and pulsate through our own bodies, so also does love stimulate and pulsate through, and indeed animate the community of believers. The twenty-year-old Bonhoeffer maintains this lofty perspective during the following semester in a seminar paper on John 15 and Paul. Human beings are to abide in the love that is God the Father's love for the Son and the Son's love for humankind. They abide in this love by keeping the commandments of Jesus Christ. Keeping these commandments, however, rather than being a burden, is instead a tremendous joy. Human beings do what brings joy to Jesus, and precisely in that love come to share his joy (DBWE 9:400).

It is against this background that the young Bonhoeffer can speak repeatedly about love's goal being "to overcome evil" (DBWE 9:538, picking up on Rom 12:21). Here he is particularly inclined to use the expression "alluring love" (DBWE 9:542, 547 ["alluring spirit"], 551), though the question remains whether these references are not incorporating certain romantic notions of incipient partner love back into his understanding.

Bonhoeffer will in any case hardly mention such references to "alluring love" in later texts. That his early reflections and conception of love do occasionally revert to rather vague notions and simplistic personal evocations can be seen in his "Catechetical Outline concerning the Second Article of Faith," which he presented on July 21, 1926, in which he asserts that "God is love; God is joy; God is holy seriousness" before concluding, however, with the wish that he might "walk hand in hand with my Lord Jesus on my life's path" and "be allowed to delight in being a child of God forever" (DBWE 9:501). It is, of course, difficult to avoid the impression that Bonhoeffer the student has not yet quite taken entirely seriously the kind of practical theology that will later become so profoundly important for him.

In his dissertation, however, Bonhoeffer merges into a single context God's dominion in his kingdom and God's love, maintaining that "God's will to rule is the will to love God's church community. This is how intimately the concepts of God's rule and of God's kingdom are interconnected; and yet they must be distinguished logically, materially, and, as we can now add, sociologically" (DBWE 1:177). Bonhoeffer can then join Luther in stating that those who share God's love in Christ will also practice this love towards each other. "We are God through the love that makes us charitable toward our neighbor" (DBWE 1:178). That is, it is in love itself that a person becomes God for another person—a rather steep assertion that Bonhoeffer explicates as follows: "One person bears the other in active love, intercession, and forgiveness of sins, acting completely vicariously. This is possible only in the church community of Christ, and that itself rests . . . on the love of God" (DBWE 1:191). In Bonhoeffer's view, "the unity of the Christian church is *not based on human unanimity of spirit*, but on *divine unity of Spirit*" (DBWE 1:198). He speaks repeatedly about the *sanctorum communio* as a community of love, about love as the living principle of the community, and about the kingdom of God as the victory of God's love. Here, however, one cannot so easily distinguish between the church, on the one hand, and God's kingdom, on the other.

II. Jesus Christ and the love that is "stronger than death" (DBWE 10, 2, 11, 12, 3) 1928–1933

In his doctoral dissertation, *Sanctorum communio*, Bonhoeffer speaks about how God's dominion in the form of his love is to be understood as God's "service" to humanity. In his writings in Barcelona during 1928/29, especially in presentations and lectures for his church there, he cultivates this position further especially from the perspective of christology and a theology of the cross: "In Jesus of Nazareth, the bearer of God's revelation, God inclines toward the sinner. Jesus seeks the company of sinners, follows them with limitless love . . . God's love is wherever Jesus is... Jesus's death on the cross of the criminal, however, shows that divine love extends even to the death of the criminal." Picking up on the Song of Solomon 8:6, Bonhoeffer maintains that love is stronger than death; that is "the meaning of Good Friday and of Easter Sunday" (DBWE 10:356; see also the sermon on Remembrance Sunday, November 25, 1928, DBWE 10:537–38).

On the basis of the confession and recognition that "God is love," Bonhoeffer is then able, in his Habilitationsschrift, to level trenchant criticisms at various metaphysical concepts of God (e.g., as "divine continuity of being," the "sheer 'is,'" or the "eternal 'is,'" DBWE 2:75).

In his baptism sermon on Pentecost Sunday 1932 (DBWE 11:440–42), Bonhoeffer develops the assertion from 1 John 4:16 that "God is love, and those who abide in love abide in God, and God abides in them." Klaus and Paula Bonhoeffer's son Thomas, Bonhoeffer's nephew, is being baptized, and the ceremony takes place at the home of the grandparents, Karl and Paula Bonhoeffer. Bonhoeffer maintains that "God is love—from today on in the life of this child that is no longer a general word of wisdom... but is the real, only indestructible basis on which his whole life is built. It is truth, and it is reality. That is the meaning of baptism." Although the assertion "God is love" may come across as merely a well-intentioned exaggeration, or at least as something religiously self-evident in any case, Bonhoeffer emphasizes that "when the love of God is spoken about, we are speaking about something that simply cannot at all be taken for granted, something improbable, unbelievable . . . The laws of human life are broken through when God's love comes over a person" (DBWE 11:440–441). "When God's love comes over a person"—Bonhoeffer can also say, "God's love stands over a person"—then that person's life "has been stripped of its last selfish inclination and has been won for God." "Whoever abides in love takes not the prescribed path of excellence in the world but his own, often incomprehensible, often foolish paths. He lacks the last bit of worldly cleverness that is called selfishness. But in these foolish, strange paths the one who has eyes to see will see some of the glow from the glory of God himself" (DBWE 11:442).

Jesus Christ brought this essentially revolutionary love onto the cross, and it is through precisely this love that human beings are truly liberated, sinners saved, and evil disempowered (DBWE 11, e.g., 426–27; 470–71). And it is also with precisely this miraculous love that God repeatedly jolts and rouses us. In a sermon on Psalm 63:3[4], "Your steadfast love is better than life," Bonhoeffer explicates this miracle even more precisely, speaking first about the meagerness of our love, both of our love for God as well as that for our neighbor. "God asks us how much his love is worth to us, and we answer him: certainly less than our own. In doing this we banish God's loving kindness from our life" (DBWE 11:407). And now the miracle happens through which God penetrates through to us in his revolutionary and beneficent love, seizes us, transforms us, and thereby wins us for true freedom and indeed for true life.

Bonhoeffer, however, is unable to maintain this lofty level in his theology consistently during the years 1932 and 1933. And although he does courageously address various ideological developments and misanthropic tendencies emerging within his political and ecclesiastical surroundings, his work nonetheless occasionally exhibits views and statements that can cause difficulty for those who are familiar with his work and appreciate his theology. In the memorandum "The Social Gospel" from the winter semester 1932/33, he remarks with some distancing himself that "Jesus is God's revelation, to the extent that he embodied his teaching in his life. His cross is the symbol for his complete devotion to the ideal of brotherly love" (DBWE 12:239). In an essay written during this same semester, "Thy Kingdom Come! The Prayer of the Church Community for God's Kingdom on Earth" (DBWE 12:285–97), he writes that only those "who love the Earth and God *as one*, can believe in God's kingdom" (DBWE 12:286, my italics). He repeatedly speaks about how God's kingdom acquires form within the state, to wit, how "the form in which the kingdom of God is attested as order we call—the *state*" (DBWE 12:293; see also 293ff). He deals extensively with the relationship between state authority and love (in critical discussion with Wilhelm Lütgert, the successor of Bonhoeffer's dissertation advisor, Seeberg, in Berlin), as well as with that between a people's *nomos*, on the one hand, and the *nomos* of love, on the other (DBWE 12:206–9). Several documents dating to these years involving critical readings of publications by his colleagues and church leaders have come down to us (DBWE 12:260ff), as well as attempts to articulate his independent scholarly and intellectual relationship with them. Although Bonhoeffer's reflections on the topic of love still remain relatively imprecise and undeveloped in his 1933 book *Creation and Fall*, he does nonetheless strongly emphasize there the polarity between "love and hate" that will remain an important component of his thinking on this subject during the following years. Otherwise he articulates these reflections on the love between man and woman in starkly personalistic figures and various negative statements concerning sexuality (DBWE 3:98ff).

III. "God is love" and interpersonal love (1933–1937/39) (DBWE 13, 14, 5)

On October 17, 1933, Dietrich Bonhoeffer begins his parish ministry in London, and on April 15, 1935, he returns to Germany. In numerous sermons during this London period, Bonhoeffer continues to develop his understanding of the relationship between, on the one hand, the love that, as he puts it, comes "from God's self," (DBWE 13:388) and for just that reason never ends (1 Cor 13:4-7), and, on the other hand, human love. Of particular importance in this context are several sermons on 1 Cor 13 (DBWE 13:375ff) that culminate in a sermon on 1 Cor 13:13 on Reformation Sunday 1934: "And now faith, hope, and love abide, these three; and the greatest of these is love."

Bonhoeffer continues to maintain during these years that God's love is a revolutionary power that can quickly confront us with enormous challenges: "Where people say something is despicable God calls it blessed"; "Where people turn their eyes away in indifference or arrogance, God gazes with a love that glows warmer there than anywhere else" (DBWE 13:344). Such statements can give the rather frightening impression that God's love "hurts so much, that your grace is so stern" (DBWE 13:351). At the same time, Bonhoeffer ardently emphasizes the efficacious power of love among human beings without which no person can live and in which the very meaning of life itself is fulfilled. He repeatedly emphasizes the power of love characterizing every kindness and every truth, the love through which even the most difficult adversaries are overcome and which always accompanies perfect truth (DBWE 13:375f, 378f, 389, et passim). Whereas hate fails to recognize one's neighbor, and indifference misses that person altogether, love leads us to know a person fully and completely (DBWE 13:389). Finally, Bonhoeffer similarly highlights the significance even of properly understood self-love, the necessity, that is, of also nurturing "compassion for our own poor souls" (DBWE 13:396).

After Bonhoeffer's return to Berlin, the christological focus of his understanding and articulation of love moves increasingly to the forefront, finally coming to expression in 1939 in his book *Life Together* (DBWE 5). Jesus Christ, in whom is "all truth, all righteousness, all freedom, and all love" (DBWE 14:911; cf. also 602 on 2 John 16), not only speaks the commandment: "love one another," but also demonstrates this very love. Bonhoeffer now connects this "love among one another" with the notion of "living in peace." Jesus Christ brings peace, and "spiritual love creates the *freedom* of Christians under the Word" (DBWE 5:32).

In general during these years, and especially in his book *Life Together*, Bonhoeffer makes a discernible effort to differentiate between the various types of love—emotional and spiritual love, Eros and Agape, Eros as both pious and impious urge, etc. (see DBWE 5:42f, 44f, 38f). He similarly repeatedly addresses the relationship between love, mercy, and justice (DBWE 5:33f, 99f, 115f, 170f). One insight that eventually acquires central significance is that of God's love as "forgiveness of one's enemies," a topic that has concerned Bonhoeffer since his work on the 1937 volume *Discipleship* and which derives from his exegesis of the Sermon on the Mount; this love is revealed with unmistakable clarity on the cross of Jesus Christ (DBWE 5:175f).

IV. Merciful love and love for one's enemies (1937–1940) (DBWE 4, 15)

"God's merciful love lives in the midst of its foes." Bonhoeffer writes this sentence in the preface to his book *Discipleship* (DBWE 4:40) with reference to Psalm 110:2: "The Lord sends out from Zion your mighty scepter. Rule in the midst of your foes" (NRSV). God rules through God's love. And God's love is directed especially to the poor and lowly (DBWE 4:106 et passim). Yet it is directed in an equally focused fashion to sinners and even to God's adversaries. Bonhoeffer continues in the preface to *Discipleship*: "It is the same Jesus Christ who by grace calls us to follow him and whose grace saves the thief on the cross in his last hour"; "Jesus died on the cross alone, abandoned by his disciples. It was not two of his faithful followers who hung beside him, but two murderers. But they all stood beneath the cross: enemies and the faithful, doubters and the fearful, the scornful and the converted, and all of them and their sin were included in this hour in Jesus' prayer for forgiveness. God's merciful love lives in the midst of its foes" (DBWE 4:40).

In his book *Discipleship*, just as repeatedly elsewhere in his work, Bonhoeffer intimately associates the theology of the cross with the ethos of love: "Service to sisters and brothers... is... the path to the cross" (DBWE 4:125), a statement that may well appear rather bold or even objectionable, especially when taken out of context. Although the phenomenon of devoted, self-sacrificial, "kenotic" love is familiar enough, people tend to associate love much more strongly either with the rapture of romantic love or with the faithful love of family and friendship, the kind of faithful (covenantal) love that is willing to go "though thick and thin," through the "highs and lows" of life. Such love is, of course, quite prepared to endure suffering and indeed does not hesitate to confront situations that may well involve suffering. At the same time, however, in most cases it is sustained by a wealth of experiences of joy both given and received. And even the general love of neighbor of the sort Paul insists we owe to all human beings at all times (Rom 13:8), the general disposition of philanthropy with all its myriad manifestations of helpfulness and charitable consideration—such love can nonetheless not really be characterized as a "path to the cross" in any general or universal sense. Here Bonhoeffer seems to focus and dramatize his understanding of divine love and the love of Jesus Christ in a way that renders access to his theology somewhat difficult.

One must see that what Bonhoeffer is trying to do here is lay out clearly and unequivocally before us the seriousness and profundity and creativity of God's love. In the process, he criticizes the cozier and more hackneyed notions of God's love, and especially notions or references to

God's "cheap grace" (DBWE 4:43). God's intention is nothing less than to overcome evil in this world through God's love, and yet at the same time to recognize human beings as wholly worthy of active participation in precisely this loving struggle with evil. "The passion of Jesus as the overcoming of evil by divine love is the only solid foundation for the disciples' obedience... Participation in the cross is given to the disciples by the call into discipleship. They are blessed in this visible community" (DBWE 4:136f). Such assertions, however, can easily alienate some people, for are suffering and the willingness to suffer not being glorified here in an almost dangerous fashion?

In order to comprehend fully the essence of Bonhoeffer's articulation of the unity of the theology of the cross, on the one hand, and the ethos of love, on the other, one must understand Jesus's entire path as a single journey to the cross, must take utterly seriously the suffering of the world under the power of sin, and must profoundly perceive the breadth of hatred among human beings. Reflections on the Heidelberg Catechism concerning hate as the counterforce to love have helped me personally come to a deeper understanding here. For many years, I found the answer to the fifth question extremely offensive, even repugnant. That answer is: I cannot keep God's law "for I am prone by nature to hate God and my neighbor." How can one seriously maintain that I am somehow prone by nature to "hate God and my neighbor"? Does such an assertion not portray human beings in an utterly exaggerated fashion as bad and evil?

If we associate "hate" solely with aggressive rage and violence, with persecution, malediction, and combat, then the catechism's statement here does indeed sound shrill and exorbitant. The semantic field of "hate," however, is considerably broader, especially in the biblical languages. According to the most important reference work in German (*Duden der sinnverwandten Wörter*), it also encompasses the much more extensive range of "not being able to love" and "not wanting to love." That is to say, "hate" does not refer merely to hostility, revulsion, resentfulness, and aggression. "Hate" also stands for "no longer being able to bear," "not having time for," "attaching little value to." "Hate" stands for "not finding personable," "having no time for or interest in," "not wanting to have anything to do with," "not being able to stand," or simply "not liking." That the Heidelberg Catechism is sensitive to the nuances inhering within the considerable breadth of the concept "hate" is evident when it castigates as "hate toward

God" even our "silence and connivance" in the face of profanation of the name of God (question 99). With respect to our neighbor, it admonishes us to "defend and promote my neighbor's good name" (question 112)—as a way of respecting that person's human dignity, we might say today.

Bonhoeffer is drawing in this context from a correspondingly broad image of love in the thirteenth chapter of Paul's letter to the Romans. "Love does no wrong to a neighbor" (Rom. 13:10). Love avoids hate and combats hate in all its variations, all the way to that of cold indifference toward God and one's neighbor. And yet this circumspect and farseeing love as a counterforce against evil in the world can neither be taken seriously nor rigorously and consistently practiced without a willingness to endure suffering. This love needs infinite patience, yet also makes a person sensitive and gives true sight, whereas human judging and quick condemnation make us blind, as Bonhoeffer puts it (DBWE 4:17–72).

Finally, Bonhoeffer associates the gift of the power of love with the theologically difficult and challenging reference to justification and sanctification:

"Justification liberates believers from their sinful past. Sanctification makes it possible for them to stay close to Christ, to persevere in their faith, and to grow in love… Justification is the new creation of the new human being. Sanctification is their preservation and safekeeping unto the day of Jesus Christ" (DBWE 4:259–60)

Here we encounter a wonderful variant to the oft-cited statement in 1 John 4:16: "Those who abide in love abide in God, and God abides in them." It is not until one adds to this grand statement not only love for the weak and poor, but also the merciful love of one's enemies does it reach its full depth and at the same time a remarkable proximity to real life.

Bonhoeffer remains focused on this understanding of love during the period of the illegal pastoral seminary (DBWE 15, 1937–1940). We cannot, he maintains, esteem too highly the patience of God's love, nor also the patience of love expected of those in discipleship to Jesus (DBWE 15:357, picking up on 1 Cor 13:7), nor God's love for his enemies—despite the hatred with which God is confronted, nor liberation from the power of sin through this love: "Christ wants to win his victory among the enemies" (DBWE 15:467ff; cf. 558f).

V. God's love and love for the world 1940–1945 (DBWE 16, 7, 6, 8)

In his notes and writings during his imprisonment (DBWE 16 and 7), in his *Ethics* (DBWE 6), and in the collected papers published under the title *Letters and Papers from Prison* (DBWE 8), Bonhoeffer develops and deepens several other ideas concerning the relationship between God's love and the love between human beings or love for the world. While Bonhoeffer's earlier understanding of God's love as love for one's enemies remains constant (e.g., DBWE 6:241ff), he now also emphasizes how gratitude and humility can emerge from experiences of received love (DBWE 16:489f) and how through love, God reveals truth, and through that same truth judges creation (DBWE 16:604f).

Picking up on John 2:15, John 4:4, and other biblical mediations, Bonhoeffer tries to articulate the distinction between good and bad "love of the world." "There is a love of the world that is enmity toward God… because it arises from the essence of the world in itself and not from God's love for the world" (DBWE 6:66). He exhaustively analyzes the so-called "tyrant's love for humanity" and unmasks it as tyrannical contempt for humanity ("the tyrannical despiser of humanity"); so-called "good-natured human love" that is inclined to excuse and repress everything is similarly shown to be nothing more than contempt for humanity (DBWE 6:85ff). He praises the "openness to the world" in Christian love over against "trite worldly wisdom" in the form of radicalism and an all-too-eager inclination to compromise (DBWE 6:156f).

In addition to Bonhoeffer's earlier explications concerning the relationship between love and peace, he now also brings to expression as the root of freedom: God's love for humanity that has been revealed in Jesus Christ the incarnate human being (DBWE 6:232f). Bonhoeffer now turns an unflinchingly critical eye on the liberating power of the cross in an examination of the idolization of death (DBWE 6:91ff). And one might devote an entirely separate treatise to the reflections in his *Ethics* on the topic of "God's Love and the Disintegration of the World" (DBWE 6:299–38), which pick up earlier ideas concerning the loving and judging interaction of human beings among one another. This text, distinguishing between an "examination" or "testing" that seeks truth, and one that disguises it, tries to clarify what it means to live from a reception of God's love. The riches of God's love in this sense, however, are disclosed only if we gratefully accept the fullness of all that God has revealed and bequeathed to us in Jesus Christ (DBWE 6:334ff).

In Bonhoeffer's letters from prison, the notion of the "polyphony of life," of the divine life and of human life, now acquires central significance. He also emphasizes this polyphony, however, with respect to love—in this case over against its widespread reduction to erotic love (DBWE 8:393f), which is invariably accompanied by a loss of precisely such polyphony. We can, however, learn to love life and honor God at the same time by acquiring through faith in Jesus Christ the proper relationship with this polyphony of life (DBWE 8:266).

Unfortunately, Dietrich Bonhoeffer never quite succeeded in reinforcing and cultivating these ideas further from the perspective of the Holy Spirit. His early writings are dominated by an understanding of the spirit shaped by Hegel and a more popularized form of Hegelianism. Although Bonhoeffer was indeed able to move past this particular understanding, he, like most of the theologians of his generation, never entirely succeeded in working out a christologically and biblically based pneumatology. Indeed, in his later writings he says almost nothing about the spirit or the Holy Spirit, and any future theological study of "Bonhoeffer and love" will likely have to commence with a look at precisely this problem.

Conclusion

Even as early as his student days, Bonhoeffer was already developing a christologically and pneumatologically shaped understanding of love. Love, rather than being active merely between two individuals, instead establishes a community and, even more, then animates and maintains that community as an active, living entity. Divine love is determined by Christ's salvific activity within history and is characterized by what is essentially a revolutionary power, for through it human beings are truly liberated, sinners saved, and evil disempowered. The cross and resurrection of Jesus Christ reveal that this love is in fact stronger than death itself, and at the same time it becomes quite clear here that God's love is meant not just for the poor and weak, but for sinners as well, and indeed is to be understood essentially as love for one's enemies.

That said, it is nonetheless not at all so easy for human beings to accept this love and to allow themselves to be seized and shaped by its power. Notwithstanding that this love overcomes even the most resolute adversaries, and even though it bequeaths knowledge of truth, as well as freedom and peace, human beings shrink from the seriousness and power of this love, or even oppose it outright. Yet "God's merciful love lives in the midst of its foes" (DBWE 4:40).

At the same time, Bonhoeffer criticizes various cozy, trite notions of God's love. With respect to Christ's cross, it becomes clear that God's love intends to overcome all manifestations of the world's hostility and hate. In gratitude, humility, patience, and in the power of hope, we accept this love and try to implement and practice it each in our own way, for it is knowledge of Christ that discloses for us the rich polyphony of this love. And it is Christ's person and life that reveal for us the paths this love can take along with the freedom and profound joy it bequeaths—even or especially in the dark and distressing periods of our earthly life.

Bibliography

BONHOEFFER, Dietrich
2015   Dietrich Bonhoeffer Works. Vols 1–17. Minneapolis, MI: Fortress Press.

SAARINEN, Risto
2011   Syzygy: Love Made Strange. – *Dialog. A Journal of Theology*, Vol. 50/1.
2012   Love from afar: distance, intimacy and the theology of love. – *International Journal of Systematic Theology*, Vol. 14.
2014   Liebe, Anerkennung und die Bibel. Die Gabetheorien der heutigen Theologie. – *Liebe. Jahrbuch für Biblische Theologie* 29. Eds. M. Welker & G. Oberhänsli-Widmer. Neukirchen: Neukirchener Verlag. 321–38.

WELKER, Michael
2001   Romantic Love, Covenantal Love, Kenotic Love. – *The Work of Love: Creation as Kenosis*. Ed. John Polkinghorne. Grand Rapids: Eerdmans and London: SPCK. 127–36.
2014   Geist und Liebe. – *Liebe. Jahrbuch für Biblische Theologie* 29. Eds. M. Welker & G. Oberhänsli-Widmer. Neukirchen: Neukirchener Verlag. 271–81.
2015   'Rooted and Established in Love': The Holy Spirit and Salvation. – *Spirit of God: Christian Renewal in the Community of Faith*. Eds. Jeffrey W. Barbeau & Beth Felker Jones. Downers Grove, IL: InterVarsity Press. 183–93.

The Limits of Sense and Transcendental Melancholy in the Philosophy of Love

SAMI PIHLSTRÖM & SARI KIVISTÖ

1. Introduction: bestowal, appraisal, and recognition

This essay examines – in the very special context of the philosophy of (romantic) love – some possible ways of redrawing the boundaries between *rationality and irrationality, meaningfulness and meaninglessness*, as well as *contingency and necessity*. The philosophy of love will be investigated in dialogue with literary sources, especially some classical depictions of love and lovers. We will, as we focus on conceptual boundaries, study the nature of love from a *transcendental* philosophical point of view,[1] but this discussion will be crucially enriched by literary readings.[2] We will in this introductory section begin with some conceptual preliminaries and in the next section move on to literary explorations focusing on tragic lover characters in classical literature. We will then turn to our transcendental analysis based on Wittgensteinian considerations, in particular.

In his now classical philosophical study of the history of love, Irving Singer makes a conceptual distinction that is useful for any philosophical

---

[1] The concept of transcendentality ought to be understood in its *Kantian* sense: here the transcendental denotes, roughly, the necessary conditions for the possibility of something that is actually given to or whose reality must be presupposed by us (e.g., cognitive experience, linguistic meaning). We will not, however, discuss Immanuel Kant's own philosophical views on love. It might be supposed that Kant, given his rigorous apriorism and general philosophical rationalism, might not have had much to say about such a human phenomenon as love, but Pärttyli Rinne has examined Kant's philosophy of love in interesting detail (see RINNE 2018).

[2] In this sense, our methodology here resembles the interplay of literary and philosophical perspectives in our earlier joint work, especially our study of evil, suffering, and (anti)theodicy (KIVISTÖ & PIHLSTRÖM 2016) – topics arguably not irrelevant to the study of love.

analysis of love. This is the distinction between two types of valuing – *appraisal* and *bestowal* – based on the general idea that love is "a way of valuing something", "a positive response *toward* the 'object of love'".³ Love goes beyond the mere ascribing of objective value (on some scale) to the beloved, amounting to a response to another "as something that cannot be reduced to *any* system of appraisal", because the lover has an interest in the beloved "as a *person*" and thereby "bestows importance upon *her* needs and *her* desires, even when they do not further the satisfaction of his own".⁴ The beloved would not have this bestowed value independently of the lover's attitude of bestowal, and it is through bestowal that the lovers "have 'a life' together".⁵

This response to another – the beloved – as the particular person s/he is and the related bestowal of unique value on her/him can be clarified by means of the concept of *recognition*, extensively studied in the context of religion by Risto Saarinen. Saarinen particularly emphasizes the relevance of Marsilio Ficino's Renaissance work *De amore*, which involves a theory of loving recognition and heavily uses the verb *recognosco*.⁶ From the point of view of the history of recognition, Ficino is important as the first thinker to articulate an essentially horizontal conception of recognition between equals.⁷ He also reminds us about the significance of the act of *self*-recognition inherent in the relation between lovers (who in a way recognize their ideal archetypes in and through each other) and the identity-constitutive features of such recognition acts.⁸ "Through the beloved", Saarinen explains, "the lover can connect himself with his own inner archetype so that a new and deeper self-recognition emerges".⁹

---

³ SINGER 1984, 3.
⁴ SINGER 1984, 6.
⁵ SINGER 1984, 7. Note that Singer refers to the lover in the masculine and to the beloved in the feminine. We, of course, will not continue this habit but will have to stick to it when quoting his work. It should also be noted that we can here only provide a barest outline of Singer's theory, let alone its detailed historical applications. For a careful analysis of love as an intentional attitude directed toward a unique individual, see KRAUT 1986.
⁶ See SAARINEN 2016, 79–87; 2014, 139–149.
⁷ SAARINEN 2016, 86.
⁸ SAARINEN 2016, 86–87; see also 188, 235; 2014, 145–146.
⁹ SAARINEN 2016, 193. Obviously, love should not be reduced to serve self-recognition only. We won't here dwell on the intricacies of the theory of recognition, while we do recognize the obvious relevance of the concept of recognition to any analysis of love. Indeed, theorists

It might be suggested, admittedly somewhat speculatively, that the kind of bestowal of value upon the beloved that Singer finds crucial to the relation of love can also go not only beyond mere appraisal but also beyond the "mere" recognition of the other as uniquely valuable, even if that recognition were based on a Ficino-like Platonic account of ideal archetypes. Of course there are clear elements of recognition in the lovers' relation to each other – love is a matter of accepting the other as s/he is and of responding to what s/he is[10] – but love is not merely recognition (even the kind of recognition fundamental to all other modes of recognition) because it cannot be reduced to responding to the other, even to responding to the other as the uniquely precious individual s/he is, but involves the element of gratuitously creating new value in the other.[11] Due to bestowal, there is also an essentially imaginative element in love.[12]

What is particularly significant in Singer's analysis for our purposes in this essay is that he notes a potential tension between love and morality:

> Love and morality need not diverge, but they often do. For love is not *inherently* moral. There is no guarantee that it will bestow value properly, at the right time, in the right way. Through love we enjoy another person as he is, including his moral condition; yet this enjoyment may itself violate the demands of morality.[13]

Moreover, it is not only the bounds of morality that may be transgressed by love – as literature also teaches us – but also many (or even all) other practical purposes of human life may simply be of secondary value when love comes to the picture:

> Purposive attitudes are safe, secure, like money in the bank; the loving attitude is speculative and always dangerous. Love is not *practical*, and sometimes borders on madness. We take our life in our hands when we allow love to tamper with

---

of recognition usually follow HONNETH (2005) in regarding love as "both genetically and conceptually prior to other modes of recognition" (SAARINEN 2016, 8). In addition to Saarinen's extensive work, see HONNETH 2005 for the paradigm of the contemporary theory of recognition, as well as KOSKINEN 2017 for more recent systematic conceptual articulations. In his historical study, SINGER (1984, 347, 365) comments on Ficino only relatively briefly in passing and does not explicitly take up the concept of recognition.

[10] Cf. SINGER 1984, 9.
[11] See SINGER 1984, 14–15.
[12] SINGER 1984, 16–17.
[13] SINGER 1984, 11.

our purposive habits. Without love, life might not be worth living; but without purposiveness, there would be no life.[14]

Love, then, is "always a threat to the status quo"[15] – whether, we might add, we are talking about the status quo of our life arrangements or the status quo of our conceptual categorizations of the world we live in. It is potentially overwhelming in its capacity to change our lives. Love may lead us to, or even beyond, the boundaries of reason and irrationality, or even morality and immorality, and it is precisely for this reason that the concept of love (we suggest) plays a transcendental role in our lives – arguably analogously to the way in which concepts such as death and mortality may be seen as playing a transcendental role in coloring our entire lives and challenging their structures of meaning.[16]

Love, like death, challenges us to re-examine the ways in which we operate in terms of the distinctions between rationality and irrationality, meaning and meaninglessness, or even necessity, possibility, and impossibility. Love is transcendental precisely in its ability to fundamentally structure, and restructure, the schemes and categories through which we encounter reality in general.

2. *Tragic female characters*

It is of great significance to our understanding of love that the bestowal of value fundamental to the loving relation can, as we just learned from Singer, exceed all ordinary boundaries of prudence, rationality, and even morality. This phenomenon can be, and has been, investigated both artistically and philosophically. Let us first turn to some literary examples.

In particular, tragic women heroes in classical epic poems and ancient tragedies are often taken to represent irrationality, mindlessness, and excess in contrast to reasonable moderation. Although there are also "good" wives in Greek tragedy (such as Alcestis or Euadne), their conjugal love is usually overshadowed by such tragic women as Medea or Phaedra who

---

[14] SINGER 1984, 14.
[15] SINGER 1984, 21.
[16] Cf. PIHLSTRÖM 2016.

are possessed by desire that takes a grip on them, leading them towards disruption and catastrophe.[17] Medea traditionally epitomizes excessive female desire and a form of madness that disrupts reasoning and leads to a loss of control, but what is less often noted is that Medea's revenge may not have been affected by her passionate love as much as by her husband Jason's violation of their conjugal loyalty. Medea herself relies on a certain form of trust and lovers' oaths that she expects Jason to obey, and it is thus her idea of justice and her dishonored pride that ignite her rage. Nevertheless, the example of tragic women does not redraw the boundaries of proper love; on the contrary, they have always functioned as warning examples of transgressive love that goes beyond all suitable limits. Thus, their love has served the purposes confirming social norms rather than redrawing the areas of acceptable conjugal love and mad desire. The social condemnation of their erotic desire is visible in the way the tragic plot usually develops; they remain solitary figures in their bewildering emotion that separates them from the rest of the community and brings inevitable destruction.

In tragedies, excessive passion is reproachable not only for threatening the identity of the woman but because it endangers the whole community. Change is one of the major threats following incontrollable female desire, and tragic women are examples of such irrational seduction that menaces the status quo and the established order of the whole society. The violent individual emotion is frequently contrasted with the stability of the community. Dido's example in particular encompasses both personal and political dimensions, and demonstrates how violent passions are capable of destroying entire kingdoms. Vergil equates Dido's excessive love and loss of self-control with the destruction it brings to her kingdom as she forgets her duties as ruler and gives herself to the stranger. Aeneas and Dido even start to build an empire together as an indication of their mutual love and symmetry. The value that Vergil bestows on Dido is depicted in terms of superficial wealth and outward glitter. Dido shines in her purple garment and gold, alluring Aeneas to the extent that he forgets his patriotic duties. Aeneas is never as ridiculous as he is when he has fallen under Dido's "spell", as if he had become her property:

---

[17] The erotic experiences of "good" wives are examined, for example, in KAIMIO 2002.

> When first his [Mercury's] winged feet
> came nigh the clay-built Punic huts, he saw
> Aeneas building at a citadel,
> and founding walls and towers; at his side
> was girt a blade with yellow jaspers starred,
> his mantle with the stain of Tyrian shell
> flowed purple from his shoulder, broidered fair
> by opulent Dido with fine threads of gold,
> her gift of love ...[18]

Aeneas' momentary lapse is depicted here in terms of changed behavior and outward glamour – he wears a Tyrian mantle that is broidered with golden threats, called Dido's gift of love, but this wealth merely underlines the futility of their affair. The passage shows that love has the power of changing identities, as is noted in Aeneas' figure, but this change is not welcome to the gods. Ultimately, Dido's dangerous wealth and alluring gold turn out to be minor attractions to Aeneas when Mercury reminds him of his duties to establish Rome in Latium and he travels away without hesitation. The lovers' passion is not mutual or equally strong, since Dido's love far surpasses Aeneas' temporary lapse that is described here as a kind of spell from which Mercury awakens him.

However, what should be noted is that Dido's love is not mere madness, but it is tied with her sense of justice that is crucial to love as a form of mutual and symmetric give and take. Her apparent irrationality lies on her ideas of justice and order that the man of Troy fails to share. Dido accuses Aeneas of breaking his promise of marriage that also entails the forthcoming enmity between the two kingdoms, since a failure in personal trustworthiness equals lack of trust and reliability in political relationships. Dido claims that Aeneas forgets his oath of fidelity symbolized in the figure of the right hand, but as Richard C. Monti has shown, swearing with the right hand refers to political relationships and was not used to symbolize marriage vows in Roman literature.[19] Dido's claim on trustworthiness thus entails that her marriage to Aeneas would also have been a political alliance. She claims that Aeneas failed to exhibit the agreed loyalty to her, although she offered him a share in her royal glory. Dido complains that

---

[18] *Aeneid*, 4.259–264; trans. Theodore C. Williams.
[19] See MONTI 1981.

"no trusting heart is safe in all this world" (*nusquam tuta fides*).[20] For Dido, personal love was supposed to manifest itself in the objective order of the world, in their reciprocal loyalty. Thus, Aeneas is in fact less rational than Dido here, since he clearly fails to show gratitude to the queen for her favors and benefactions. Still, for the Romans Dido's passion epitomized her political failure as a queen whereas Aeneas never gave up his piety and duty, although he did give up his obligations to the queen. For the Romans, political relationships were far more important than personal ones. Although Dido clearly relies on the rational principles of trust and symmetry in her relationship with Aeneas, her irrational desire is at the same time represented as reproachable precisely because it is a political threat.

Similar exhortations to rationalize love and desire frequently appear in our own age. In his book on the conditions of love, John Armstrong has called disturbing tragic love as immature, since in his view love can become the source of happiness only when the lover reduces his or her expectations from the romantic heights and "judges not by what is desired but by what it is possible to obtain".[21] Undoubtedly, such love is more rational and more easily obtained, but in ancient thinking, love and desire always had some untamable force, and still one would not call such love immature. Although the tragic woman's identity is bound to erotic mania and the inevitable misery and death it results in, it would be unwise to tell her to rationalize and control her emotions or to condemn her for failing to do so. The tragic heroes show us the force of strong emotions to blur identities and to test the limits of human life. Likewise, ancient tragic women – and tragedy in general – point out that everything does not make sense in the world, and the world is not a safe and ordered place, or as it ought to be. The confused and enraged tragic women bring this dark side of life to the foreground, while deep in their hearts they may nurture such human ideals as justice, trust, and genuinely mutual love.

---

[20] *Aeneid*, 4.373.
[21] ARMSTRONG 2003, 157.

3. The limits of meaning and the contingency of necessity

One of the paradoxes of love is that it may challenge us to revisit our most fundamental conceptual categorizations and structures of world-articulation – even schemes we, at least in "normal" circumstances, find *necessary* for the structuring of any contingent facts and processes of the world we live in – but it does this entirely *contingently*. This is because it is highly contingent that we have in our lives so much as ever encountered the person(s) we love, or have loved. Let us therefore continue our analysis by drawing attention to what has, especially in the context of Wittgenstein scholarship, been called the *contingency of necessity*. We may here use this phrase to describe the fact, examined by Wittgenstein, that the limits of language (or of linguistic meaning and expressibility) are based on our form of life, on which thoughts and what kind of life we (or even I) contingently have.[22] In Vergil's epic, Aeneas' arrival to the shores of Carthage represented such contingency. Aeneas was brought there by stormy winds, a fierce Boreas that changed Dido's life, and again, when Aeneas leaves, Dido complains that despite their mutual love he compels his ships off to sea through the stormy skies and forgets the promise he once gave to her. Love is in ancient lyrics often compared to a cruel north wind that shakes the heart.

These issues are not unrelated to the conceptual groundwork of section 1 above. We might say that what (who) we are able to recognize in the sense of loving recognition, or how we are able to appraise and bestow value in the sense relevant to love, largely *defines us*: our identities as lovers and as beloved depend on our contingent relations of love. Our having entered into just those relations we have de facto entered into is highly contingent, yet it defines who we are and what is possible or impossible for us. This may seem paradoxical, because there is a sense in which our identities are necessarily what they are; if we didn't have the particular identity we do have, we wouldn't be "us" at all but something different, but love reminds us of the striking contingency of such necessities.

---

[22] We should realize that it may be problematic to call this phenomenon a "fact" of any kind. If it is a fact, it is, perhaps a transcendental fact comparable, for instance, to the "facts" (analyzed by Kant) that human cognitive experience requires both sensibility and understanding or that human intuition (*Anschauung*) is sensible and we lack "intellectual intuition". These are deep facts about constitutive features of human experience.

In brief, what is at issue here is that, to put it in Wittgensteinian terms, while the limits of language grounded in the rules and grammar of a language-game set conditions for what is possible and impossible for us to express within that language-game (i.e., by making "moves" within it according to its grammatical rules), it seems that, given the contingent historical variability of such rules – or the historical changes in how language-games are played – there is a sense in which we have, at least potentially, a variety of different limits of language that are contingently drawn in the ways they are based on the life (with language) we lead. Our contingent form of life, including its contingent features such as relations of love, determines (albeit not immutably but always in a historically contextualized and therefore potentially changing manner) how we are "minded",[23] or how we draw the limits of expressibility – and this "we" may itself change and be reinterpreted along with such transformations of the structures of the language we use, to the extent that Jonathan Lear speaks about the "disappearing 'we'" in this context.[24]

We may here briefly examine some of Wittgenstein's formulations, as they appear in his pupils' notes in "Lectures on Religious Belief", thus implicitly proposing an analogy between love and religious faith. In those lecture notes from the early 1930s, Wittgenstein is, among other things, concerned with "*[w]hat we call* believing in a Judgement Day or not believing in a Judgement Day".[25] He says he "can't contradict" the person who believes. The following passage is crucial:

> In one sense, I understand all he says – the English words "God", "separate", etc. I understand. I could say: "I don't believe in this," and this would be true, meaning *I haven't got these thoughts or anything that hangs together with them.* But not that I could contradict the thing. [...] My normal technique of language leaves me.[26]

That is, the thoughts that we (or you) have (or haven't) contingently "got" determine the limits of language for us, at least regarding this particular matter at the moment. Necessity is, then, grounded in contingency. Whether you *can* contradict someone or not (i.e., what the logic or grammar of your

---

[23] Cf. LEAR 1998.
[24] See LEAR 1998, chapter 12.
[25] WITTGENSTEIN 1967, 55; our emphasis.
[26] WITTGENSTEIN 1967, 55; our emphasis; see also, e.g., PUTNAM 2012, 490.

language is like, or what you can do, logically speaking, by using your language) depends on your contingently "having got" certain thoughts, or your leading a life that "hangs together with them". The distinction between modalities (necessity, possibility) and factual contingencies is not necessarily drawn in the way we draw it; it could be drawn in a different way. The ways in which we contingently do draw this distinction reflexively influence our understanding of the notions of contingency and modality themselves – and contingently emerging love can shake the ways in which we have drawn such distinctions, and point out new ways of drawing them.

Another interesting example Wittgenstein discusses is this: "'Seeing a dead friend,' again means nothing much to me at all. I don't think in these terms. I don't say to myself: 'I shall see so and so again' ever."[27] Again, what is essential here is whether we contingently think in certain terms or say certain things to ourselves (or not). At this point we may return to the famous remark in the *Investigations*: "If I have exhausted the justifications, I have reached bedrock and my spade is turned. Then I am inclined to say: 'This is simply what I do.'"[28] What we *are able to do* – what our grammar and rules enable us to do or say – depends on what we *actually do*, and it is in this sense that necessities and possibilities are ultimately grounded in contingency. Or so Wittgenstein seems to be arguing – and this has the greatest relevance to our understanding of love that may shatter the status quo of necessities of reason and morality by leading us to revise our conception of, and commitment to, the grammar and rules structuring our world-experience.

The fact (though, again, it sounds strange to call it a "fact" in any sense) that the necessities of linguistic meaning and its limits are grounded in contingencies of our life-practices – and even in the contingent relations of love that may lead us to fundamentally revise those practices – leads us to appreciate the commonplace that love is very difficult or even impossible to properly express. It is an understatement to note that linguistic expression often encounters its limits when love enters the picture. But it is more interesting to see that this is part of why love is transcendental (or that the relevant kind of inexpressibility is itself a transcendental feature of love).

---

[27] WITTGENSTEIN 1967, 63.
[28] WITTGENSTEIN 1953, I, §217.

Clearly, lovers often feel that they do not have the proper means to express their love to each other. If they tried to do this by, e.g., using Singer's concepts of appraisal and bestowal or Honneth's and Saarinen's vocabulary of recognition, they might still find that something remains unexpressed and indeed inexpressible. This phenomenon itself arguably plays not only an ironic but also a transcendental role here. *Inexpressibility (or ineffability) is itself an expression of love*, just as (to borrow a phrase from Wittgensteinian philosopher D.Z. Phillips) one's saying that one's words cannot describe one's gratitude is itself an expression of gratitude.

One delightfully ironic account of the inexpressibility of love is Aldous Huxley's short story "Cynthia"[29] in which the main character Lykeham has fallen in love with the goddess of the moon. He uses (to quote the narrator's words) "an awful novelist's expressions"[30] to describe his beloved who is "incredibly beautiful", "simply perfect", "made of a sort of burning ice", and, paradoxically, "virginally passionate".[31] In the woman's eyes, "the whole soul seemed to burn in their depths, like fire under the sea", and during their moments of togetherness the memory of Lykeham becomes "a sort of burning mist".[32] The lovers confess – the spirit of confession is crucial to love – their mutual feelings by amusing parallelisms: "I was sure she was a goddess, and she said she was certain that I was a god".[33]

These limping metaphors and platitudes parody the incommunicable character of love and passion that has frequently recourse to clichés, idealizing the beloved and lifting her up to the Platonic heavens. Metaphors are used here as a bridge between the material and the spiritual world; they refer to the universal characteristics of the beloved who is literally deprived of her humanity and individuality while becoming the goddess of the moon. The attributes of divinity that are often attached to the loved one while one desperately tries to give an expression to the totality of the emotion become concrete and literal at the end of the short story. Lykeham stares as if bewitched at the thin crescent of the moon and runs to the hills to embrace something that remains invisible to the narrator, until finally in

---

[29] The story is included in HUXLEY 1920.
[30] HUXLEY 1920, 250.
[31] HUXLEY 1920, 252.
[32] HUXLEY 1920, 253.
[33] HUXLEY 1920, 251.

the moonlight he holds in his arms a figure of a woman, as if reaching out to the conceptual world. At that stage, the metaphor of divinity materializes: the woman becomes a goddess and the narrator (clearly an outsider in the exclusiveness of love) walks away, since "it is not for a mere mortal to look on at the embracements of the gods".[34]

In its parodical intensity, Huxley's short story depicts all the four elements of passionate and idealizing love that John Armstrong mentions in his book on the conditions of love.[35] Armstrong's example of such love is Goethe's Werther, another well-known figure of romantic love that brings only destruction. Like Werther, Lykeham is longing to be continually with his beloved. He is enraptured by contact with her, tormented by doubt about her true feelings and, bestowing to his loved one all the value and beauty in the world, even heightening her to a goddess, without which everything is barren. For Armstrong, Lykeham would undoubtedly represent a parodically exaggerated and ridiculous version of immature love that seeks union with the loved one in some idealized sphere. But still, if there is something in the human life that can even try to challenge and transgress the boundaries of individual isolation, it might well be love.

The redrawing of established limits and the emergence of new openings are multifarious in lovers' lives: there can, for instance, be not only the recognition of the inexpressible but also a widening of some previously taken-for-granted limits of expression and expressibility, just as there can be new ways of speaking and living that make new kinds of thought possible and, importantly, shareable (see below). Love may have a *strangefying* effect on our lives and, like art, it can *defamiliarize* our perceptions of the world, help us recover the sensation of life and feel anew. Love offers a possibility for new openings and perhaps also for fuller self-fulfillment in the lovers' lives. This all becomes possible for the lovers through their commitment to sharing their lives in totality and living differently, to changing their lives – or simply through letting them change: there is a tension between activity and passivity here, because it must also be acknowledged that the lovers may not always be fully in control of the changes in their lives. They may also have to reconsider to what extent their autonomous subjectivity itself remains in place.

---

[34] HUXLEY 1920, 257.
[35] See again ARMSTRONG 2003.

The dialectics and perspectivalness of contingency and necessity are fundamental here in another way, too. It is of course highly contingent that we have the loved one(s) we do in our lives, both in the case of romantic love and in the case of, say, loved children or some other significant others. Yet at the same time it may very strongly seem to be necessary for our lives as the unique personal lives they are that we do have precisely those unique individual loved one(s) we do (if we ever do); having precisely them, and not some other individuals, in our lives defines who *we* are.[36] This may be one way of bestowing special unique value to just those beloved individual(s).

In a literary context, this could be compared to the notions of fate and tragedy, which enable a tragic hero's life-story to constitute a coherent whole in which everything, including the tragic mistakes, fall in their place in a totality that is uniquely what it must be. The tragic hero would not be himself or herself without his or her tragic errors that highlight the sense of contingency; hamartia, the tragic error, can be understood in the non-moral sense as a mistaken act that for some reason ends in catastrophic failure. It has been argued that the tragic identity is particularly strong. This does not merely mean that it is dominated by such powerful emotions as erotic love, but it consists of unexpected turns and tragic mistakes and would not be the same without them; these contingencies are integral to the tragic identities. What we have here is an interplay between the empirical and the transcendental – or an acknowledgment of the perspectival character of this distinction itself. Love can thus bring about a fundamental enrichment in our understanding of how we view that crucial philosophical distinction.

The profound significance of the necessity we attach to our relation(s) of love to our individual and unique beloved depends on our ability to also see them – both those individuals and those relations – under the perspective or aspect of radical contingency. Now, *whose* ability is this? Ours? But how can it be "ours" if it also at the same time defines and redefines us? One option is to suggest that what is at work here is really a conceptual shift available to what philosophers in the Kantian tradition call the *transcendental self*. As we are challenged to view our lives in terms of both

---

[36] Raimond GAITA (2004) draws attention to parents' typically seeing their children as the children they necessarily have, while usually being (reasonably) fully aware of the deep contingency of their having just those unique children instead of some other genetic recombinations (this is briefly discussed in PIHLSTRÖM 2016).

necessity and contingency, or to understand our necessities as contingent, we must, at the transcendental level, be able to switch perspectives, to genuinely view our lives (in general) under both aspects. Thus, contingency in a way wins at the meta-level. Both mere (tragic) fate and unlimited (e.g., Sartrean) freedom are one-sided conceptualizations of the picture at the transcendental level. Neither is possible without the phenomenon we have, in a Wittgenstein-inspired way, here called the contingency of necessity.

The appreciation of this meta-level contingency may also help us combine a transcendental analysis of love with the recognition of both fully "natural" and embodied (specifically sexual) and cultural-historical contexts for romantic love. Even as transcendental lovers we never engage in love outside the natural and cultural contexts that we, as historical beings, contingently find ourselves in and that we through our own activities constantly shape. The notion of romantic love, in particular, is strongly culturally and historically embedded, to a great extent constructed through literary and other artistic representations of love throughout human history, and continuously reconstructed through historical changes in our natural and social conditions of life. The transcendental limits of meanings, categorizations, and life-structures that love challenges and restructures are, even *qua* transcendental, realized and instantiated in empirical and historical contexts, and a sufficiently rich transcendental philosophical approach should acknowledge this.

4. Transcendental shareability and melancholy

Lovers sometimes conceptualize the depth of their relationship by speaking (at least to each other if not to outsiders) about the possibility of *sharing everything* in their lives, that is, not just sharing a house or pieces of property or dinners or political views, but in some sense sharing each experience, thought, mood, etc. – which presumably amounts to a sharing of life. This possibility, or perhaps (again) the transcendental necessity of such shareability, may be seen as a characteristic of genuine love. Lovers are often said to share their whole lives together, but this does not mean that two separate creatures would become one when united; rather, it is through the lovers' sharing their whole lives that their individual lives can become full. Love offers a possibility of sharing everything in one's life with another and contributes to all kinds of new openings that otherwise would not have been possible. There are also obvious dangers in such mutual connectedness, if we fail to appreciate the otherness of the beloved and merely long for a perfect union. Woody Allen has amusingly caricatured such longing in his *Husbands and Wives*, saying that "Spencer was searching for a woman interested in golf, inorganic chemistry, outdoor sex and the music of Bach. In short he was looking for himself, only female."[37]

One problem here resembles the famous paradox of love discussed by Jean-Paul Sartre: how can the *otherness of the other* – of the beloved other – be maintained if everything is, or can be, shared by the lovers?[38] For Sartre this is a problem because the lover wants the beloved other as a free subject, but already by the act of love the other is in a sense objectified into something that lacks such existential freedom. Analogously, somehow the lovers must view their lives as entirely shareable while also appreciating the genuine otherness of the beloved, which seems to preclude such radical shareability.[39] Armstrong suggests that instead of elusive fantasies of the perfect union lovers should acknowledge that loving includes constant adaptations of oneself to another, and compatibility is the achievement of love, not its precondition.[40]

Our paradoxical situation of pursuing all-encompassing shareability, or even seeing it as transcendentally necessary for the possibility of love as the special kind of value-bestowing activity we take it to be, may lead to a kind of resignation. Perhaps we cannot, for conceptual reasons, ultimately

---

[37] Quoted in ARMSTRONG 2003, 33.

[38] It could also be suggested that the genuine otherness of the other remains unarticulated in Ficino's Platonic theory of love in terms of ideal archetypes and self-recognition (as analyzed by SAARINEN 2016; see above). For Sartre's existentialist reflections on love as a "conflict", see SARTRE 1956, 474–493.

[39] *Can* everything (anything whatsoever) even in principle really be shared? Is there, for instance, a tension between the lovers' transcendental shareability and transcendental guilt (cf. PIHLSTRÖM 2011), which could be regarded as *per definitionem* personal, even solipsistic – because, as GAITA (2004) aptly notes, shared guilt is corrupted guilt. Can lovers share even guilt – share it genuinely, unlike a collective shared guilt for a historical atrocity, for instance – while maintaining its fundamentally personal character? Or is there a sense in which they would be able to share the unshareability of such personal traits and experiences as guilt (and in *this* sense be able to share "everything", including even the unshareable)? This is one example of a further philosophical paradox of love that deserves to be examined.

[40] ARMSTRONG 2003, 26.

engage in true love in this sense. Perhaps love in the strong transcendental sense we have analyzed here is too much for human beings. However, rather than resignation, we might approach this situation in terms of melancholy.

Love, we may suggest, is fundamentally melancholic in the sense that true happiness and joy are possible only against the background of a kind of *transcendental melancholy*, a fundamental seriousness characterizing one's (or the lovers') attitude toward life as fragile and uniquely valuable (fragile because dependent on the value-bestowing attitudes of the lovers). A melancholic attitude can even be a crucial connecting bond between lovers if they share the basic recognition of life as incomprehensible and even tragic – if they are willing to face vulnerable humanity with its weaknesses instead of trying to transcend it or bypass our confusion and limited vision. Melancholic lovers, if they share the view of reality as it reveals itself to them in its tragic and melancholic mood, may be able to form an exceptionally strong link between each other. As Christopher Hamilton has noted in his philosophy of tragedy, the tragic mood is even in its opacity "experienced as deeply revelatory".[41]

In this sense, melancholic love also aims to see through life permeated by illusion and thus view the world as it is. It does not aim at a "happy valley", to use Hamilton's term,[42] where all our desires are satisfied; nor does it aim to be at home in the world in the sense of some kind of full engagement with the presence and stability in our lives. Instead, being melancholic together means that lovers can share a certain "ill-health", a feeling that they are not immersed in the world in the same way as others are, since there is a different relationship between themselves and the world, a relationship that includes hesitation, doubt, and perhaps even an incapacity to live a full life.

Hamilton uses Italo Svevo's novel *La coscienza di Zeno* (1923) as an example of this particular disenchantment. In the novel, the main character Zeno suffers from an incapacity to live a transparent and full life unlike his wife Augusta who has "the ability to be at home in the world, to accept the world and things in it for what they are".[43] Augusta arranges everything so that things have their comfortable places in the house; even Zeno's little

---

[41] HAMILTON 2016, 32.
[42] HAMILTON 2016, 40–41.
[43] HAMILTON 2016, 52.

study undergoes alterations. Augusta is a healthy-minded soul who could take shelter and keep warm in the present reality, whereas Zeno, although he craves similar health, is fully conscious of his mental disability: for him, the world is available only in an agonizing state.[44] As Hamilton further puts it, for Zeno "to seek to live without illusion is inevitably to be confronted by the tragedy of the human condition".[45] Zeno illustrates his and his wife's attitudes to life by the images of sickness and health: "… in my spirit a hope was formed, the great hope finally to come to resemble Augusta, who was the personification of health."[46] A passage that describes their differing notions of life deserves a longer quote:

> Still it amazed me; her every word, her every action made it clear that, deep in her heart, she believed in eternal life. Not that she called it that: indeed, she was surprised when, on one occasion, I, who was repelled by errors until I began to love hers, felt obliged to remind her of life's brevity. What?! She knew everyone had to die, but all the same, now that we were married, we would remain together, together, together. She was thus unaware that when two are joined in this world, the union lasts for a period so very, very short that we cannot comprehend how we arrived at intimacy after an infinite time when we hadn't known each other, and we were now prepared never to see each other again for an equally infinite time. I understood finally what perfect human health was when I realized that for her the present was a tangible truth within which one could curl up and be warm. I sought admission and I tried to remain there, resolved not to make fun of myself and her, because this attack could only be my old sickness and I should at least take care not to infect anyone entrusted to my charge. Also for this reason, in my effort to protect her, for a while I was capable of acting like a healthy man.[47]

Although Zeno believes that because of his marriage he is on his way to his convalescence and for a moment his wounds are less infected, ultimately he realizes that he can never become fully sober or be immersed in the world. His ill-health is crucial to his self-understanding. Zeno claims that "health

---

[44] William JAMES's (1902) well-known contrast between the "healthy-minded" and the "sick soul" would undoubtedly be relevant here. See our discussion of the notion of the sick soul from the point of view of the (anti)theodicy debate in KIVISTÖ & PIHLSTRÖM 2016, chapter 6. On the image of the sick soul of the sinner in satirical literature, see KIVISTÖ 2009.
[45] HAMILTON 2016, 53.
[46] SVEVO 2003, 156.
[47] SVEVO 2003, 157.

doesn't analyze itself, nor does it look at itself in the mirror. Only we sick people know something about ourselves."[48]

Unlike with sick Zeno and healthy Augusta who is at ease in the world and for whom things have their proper places there, it might be argued that melancholic lovers can perhaps share the feelings of dislocation and ill-health. Their shared life may even rest on the founding idea that it would be *immoral* to be too much at home in the world. Precisely their not accepting life as it is, or as it is seen through illusions, can bind them together, as the tragic condition of humanity is momentarily revealed to them and the evil aspects of life – including, in particular, meaningless human suffering – are shown to be among its very essence. Shared melancholic love means that the lovers do not turn their gaze away from the meaningless evils, disorder and afflictions of the world, and thus they share the same critical and melancholic insight into the messy reality they live in.[49]

We might also say, perhaps extending the concept of melancholy beyond its standard scope, that the constantly perspective-switching transcendental self is also melancholic precisely in its inability to remain fixed in any single perspective or standpoint; this is a kind of *existential restlessness*. One dimension of the broader philosophical relevance of the philosophy of love can be seen here: we need the concept of the transcendental self/subject in order to be able to characterize the subject of switching the perspective between necessity (fate) and contingency (free individual existential choice). It is this restlessness that may manifest itself in a melancholy that constitutively colors the lovers' being in, and concern with, the world (and life) they share.

The *Song of Songs* reminds us that love is only as strong as death, not stronger.[50] It (its actuality) will end with death, though its human meaningfulness – that is, its transcendental horizons of meaning, including shareability, that make it possible for us to structure and restructure our lives in terms of love – may in a sense transcend mortality. Can *this* basic

---

[48] Svevo 2003, 163.

[49] This indicates the close relation between our exploration of the philosophy of love (in this essay) and our more comprehensive treatment of the problem of evil and suffering (in Kivistö & Pihlström 2016).

[50] "… for love is as strong as death…" (*Song of Songs* 8:6). This is a major point in Vladimir Jankélévitch's (2005) analysis of the concept of forgiveness, also discussed in Kivistö & Pihlström 2016, chapter 3.

melancholy, the experience of one's intimately personal finitude and vulnerability, genuinely be shared by the lovers (at the meta-level)? Could, then, even the transcendentality of the self be shared, too? Transcendental shareability inevitably conflicts with the kind of transcendental solipsism that may be an inherent feature of the very concept of the transcendental self,[51] and the irresolvability of this tension may itself be a major source of melancholy.

Melancholy is, however, compatible with *happiness*, perhaps particularly with the kind of special happiness related to love, and it must in any case be carefully distinguished from backwards-looking nostalgia. The melancholic lover, while never fully "at home" in the world (as suggested), is constantly prepared to move on to the future, yet remaining conscious of the irrevocability of the past. The transcendental melancholy constitutive (we claim) of true love is, moreover, comparable to what we have elsewhere called *antitheodicy*, understood as the refusal to explain away meaningless suffering or interpret experiences of such suffering in terms of any coherent theodicy narratives.[52] Genuine love does not explain away suffering, either. Rather it acknowledges the tragic condition of life; our instability and vulnerability are manifested in suffering. Theodicies are, arguably, based on a misunderstanding of religious language and on misrecognitions of both suffering and God (regardless of whether we actually believe in God or not); as Andrew Gleeson interestingly argues, divine love is "frightening", because it is beyond human moral principles and judgment, and thus it may be horrible, too.[53] This can be readily compared to the above-mentioned view, emphasized by Singer (and Vergil), that love is always dangerous and a challenge to the status quo. Those who wish to maintain the status quo at any cost may seriously misrecognize both love and their relation to the divinity.

---

[51] Cf. PIHLSTRÖM 2016.
[52] See again KIVISTÖ & PIHLSTRÖM 2016.
[53] GLEESON 2012.

5. The love of the good

We have here mainly discussed romantic love, the love between individuals who bestow upon each other very special and unique value and who may thus share their lives with each other even in their fundamental melancholy and being unable to find themselves "at home" in the world. We have also occasionally referred to the love between a parent and a child, for instance. While other types of love mostly fall beyond the scope of this essay, it is important to recognize the analogies between the transcendentality of the kind of romantic love we have examined here and some features of, say, more explicitly theological (and ethical) notions of love.

Let us consider, first, the kind of love that has been labeled "the love of the good". Citing Wittgenstein's cryptic remarks on happiness and harmony, Ilham Dilman maintains that happiness in this sense is an "inward" attitude belonging to one's "inner life" – such as a "genuine love of the good" which would be better described as something like the state of one's "soul" rather than as (for example) mere conformity to some objective moral standards.[54] Dilman suggests a plausible reading of the *Notebooks 1914–1916* passage where Wittgenstein claims that it is only "through the life of knowledge" that even a person who cannot ward off the misery of the world can be happy.[55] Here, Dilman says, "knowledge" is close to what Plato meant by "knowledge" or "wisdom", a necessary condition of which is "detachment", "renouncing [*verzichten*] the amenities [*Annehmlichkeiten*] of the world".[56] He continues:

> This [detachment] does not mean indifference to the pain of others. Quite the contrary. For a man who is immersed in a life of worldliness will be relatively deaf to other people's cries of pain. Detachment is a positive renunciation of such a life which allows the soul to turn to the good, to become sensitive to moral considerations. [...] The condition of such renunciation is love – the kind of love that is present in pity for the afflicted, forgiveness of those who wrong one, gratitude for those who help one, and remorse for the wrong one has done to others. It is this love which both Plato and Wittgenstein see as a form of knowledge – this love which for Wittgenstein is an attitude of the will towards the world as a whole.

---

[54] DILMAN 1974, 179–180.
[55] WITTGENSTEIN 1961; remark on August 13, 1916. Dilman analyzes carefully both the *Notebooks* and the *Tractatus* (WITTGENSTEIN 1921) remarks on happiness and harmony.
[56] DILMAN 1974, 180.

> It may be called love of the good, and the kind of pity which Dostoyevsky portrays in Sonia is a concrete manifestation of it. In that form it is what usually goes under the name 'love of one's neighbour'. The relation between such selfless love and the kind of knowledge in question is internal.[57]

Therefore, Dilman tells us, the kind of happiness Wittgenstein is thinking of in the *Notebooks* (and, presumably, the *Tractatus*) is not "indifferent to the misery of the world, though it is one which that misery need not and even, perhaps, cannot destroy".[58] Arguably, it is, above all, the task of recognizing and being attentive to others' suffering that is necessary for living rightly in Wittgenstein's pregnant ethical sense – and thus for happiness – but it is this same task that, when taken seriously, deprives us from happiness. We may perhaps join Dilman in concluding that the view of happiness of Wittgenstein's *Notebooks* invokes "a state of soul which contains its own reward".[59] There is nothing external or "outward" in this transcendental happiness. Perhaps this kind of happiness is what is available to lovers in romantic love as well, though in a different way. It also has its "inward" reward, if we may say so – or at least nothing external to such a relation of love can be seen as the reason why the lovers engage in the relation in the first place (or otherwise it is no genuine love at all). Such an internal "reward" may, however, be a complex one.

Dilman is right in perceiving an important link with the internal happiness of a morally engaged soul and the concept of love; after all, Wittgenstein himself declares love to be the greatest happiness of a human being.[60] *This* kind of "love", however, must presumably be the kind that is usually denoted by the Greek word *agape*, instead of *eros*, although Wittgenstein's own words may be deliberately ambiguous here. In any event, this (quasi-)Wittgensteinian transcendental picture of happiness and love (of the good) is in striking contrast with the various banalizing

---

[57] DILMAN 1974, 180–181.
[58] DILMAN 1974, 182.
[59] DILMAN 1974, 182. Dilman thus also sees Wittgenstein (as well as, among others, Simone Weil) as returning to the Socratic view that the evil person is necessarily unhappy, while the one who "dedicates his life to justice" is by necessity happy, "no matter how the world treats him" (DILMAN 1974, 183–184). For some alternative views of virtue as being rather insignificant to one's happiness, see HAMILTON 2016, chapter 4.
[60] See WITTGENSTEIN 1980, remark in 1948.

treatments of these notions that surround us in contemporary popular culture. Dostoevsky's Sonia (in *Crime and Punishment*) may indeed be full of love, but she does not boast about her love, or her moral character, in the way our narcissistic culture today may encourage us to do, and hence her love (unlike, perhaps, most real-life individuals') remains genuine and uncorrupted.[61]

Moreover, the kind of detachment from the world we saw Dilman describe in his characterization of the love of the good can be regarded as integral to the way in which the melancholic lovers who can never find themselves fully "at home" in the world may, as was suggested above, even find it immoral to be too completely "immersed" in the world around them. A more comprehensive philosophy of love would have to contain a critical (transcendental) examination of (as we might put it) the limits of immersion.

6. Love as a limit phenomenon

Love is in many ways like religious faith. Potentially it claims to provide *the* overall perspective for evaluating all other perspectives one may take on the world – and for seeing the world and life "rightly". Therefore it opens up fundamental issues of world-comprehension, just like death and evil and suffering do. Hence, love can, like religion, run into conflict with morality.[62] But it can also crucially enrich morality, because it can lead us to consider the morality and immorality of our being "at home" or "immersed in" the world. In seeking to better understand love, we must appreciate it as one of the "limit phenomena" defining and conditioning our lives, contingently yet with their own peculiar kind of necessity, as analyzed above.

---

[61] Wittgenstein is known for his high appreciation of Dostoevsky (as well as Tolstoy). *The Brothers Karamazov* is, of course, a standard reference in moral antitheodicies protesting against any allegedly harmonious reconciliation with pain and suffering. See, e.g., GLEESON 2012 as well as KIVISTÖ & PIHLSTRÖM 2016. For a more detailed investigation of happiness, harmony, and disharmony in the context of Wittgenstein's philosophy, see PIHLSTRÖM 2019.

[62] As recognized by SINGER 1984, as we saw above.

In love, the very comprehensibility of the world is at issue, just like it is in the problem of evil and (anti)theodicy.[63] Everything changes when the world is seen through the lens of love – or in terms of antitheodicy, for that matter. This transcendental feature of love establishes a clear analogy to our earlier analyses of transcendental antitheodicy as a constitutive feature of our ethical relations to other human beings. It is for these transcendental reasons that the very distinctions between rationality and irrationality as well as between meaningfulness and meaninglessness become redrawn and rearticulated in and through love. While love, as we saw Singer remind us, is not necessarily moral, we may through love re-examine and re-evaluate everything in our lives, including the meaning(s) morality has for us. This is precisely what it means to speak of love as a transcendental limit phenomenon. Our appreciation of love draws and redraws our world-structuring and meaning-bestowing conceptual boundaries and categories in new ways, focusing on the conditions for the possibility of practices such as morality (or, basically, any other practices we engage in) and their actual or potential meaning-bestowals.[64]

In Vergil's *Aeneid*, this fundamental change in the structures of the world caused by love is clearly visible in the ways the surroundings are described to reflect the love affair. In Book 1, Dido walks serenely among her people, sanctions laws and divides tasks in equal portions while building her kingdom:

> Dido not less fair
> amid her subjects passed, and not less bright
> her glow of gracious joy, while she approved
> her future kingdom's pomp and vast emprise.[65]

The passage underlines that justice is clearly important to her, and the rising city is full of promise and unlimited possibility. Then, when Aeneas arrives, everything changes, and the construction work literally stops:

---

[63] Cf. NEIMAN 2002.
[64] Still, as the discussion of the "love of the good" in the previous section indicates, love may also be an element of morality. Such ethical (and/or religious) love may also be transcendental, defining and redefining our ways of viewing the world we live in.
[65] *Aeneid*, 1.503–504; trans. Theodore C. Williams.

> Her enterprise
> of tower and rampart stops: her martial host
> no longer she reviews, nor fashions now
> defensive haven and defiant wall;
> but idly all her half-built bastions frown,
> and enginery of sieges, high as heaven.[66]

The sense of the precious totality of love is carried in the images of the changing city. The world's fragility becomes evident when Dido desperately ranges up and down the spaces of her city and sets her entire world on flame. The loud lament spreads around Carthage that has turned from a construction site to a dying city, as if "a besieging host should break the walls of Carthage or old Tyre, and wrathful flames o'er towers of kings and worshipped altars roll".[67] The metaphorical destruction of the mighty empire underlines the devastating effects that love can have on one's life and the world.[68]

7. Conclusion

There is a sense in which our transcendental reflections on love in its various dimensions lead us to explore such meta-level conceptual anomalies as the rationality of irrationality or the sense of senselessness (absurdity). These may be comparable to the senselessness of evil and suffering, or the specific kind of meaningfulness based on the meaninglessness we may associate with human mortality.[69] Here we cannot examine such transcendental topics further. We will conclude with one reflexive problem that needs to be raised.

---

[66] *Aeneid*, 4.86–89.

[67] *Aeneid*, 4.669–671.

[68] Also in more everyday contexts love can of course take extreme and even pathological forms that might lead to destructive personal and social results, despite – or perhaps rather due to – the lovers' genuine and total devotion to each other and their acquiescence in their own "bubble" sealed off from the wider world. Precisely for this reason, the specific ways in which the lovers' transcendental melancholy manifests an impossibility of being fully "at home" in the world in general (as analyzed above) may be ethically relevant for their distinctive loving relation. Their turning toward each other always takes place in a human world whose ethical structures their love may deeply challenge.

[69] Cf. again KIVISTÖ & PIHLSTRÖM 2016; PIHLSTRÖM 2016.

Our philosophical and literary examination of love has of course offered a kind of objectifying intellectual perspective on the phenomenon of love. It might be suggested, however, that love is one of those elements of life that make all kinds of detachment, especially ironic detachment, impossible. Is love, or the attachment integral to love, then *necessarily naïve* in the sense of being unreflective and non-ironic? If so, does this mean that a serious philosophical-cum-literary study of love is in some sense impossible?

Here, again, a distinction can be drawn between the "first-order" level of naïve, irrational, senseless, and thus in some sense necessarily non-reflective love, on the one hand, and reflective, transcendentally articulable, meta-level love which makes those "first-order" attitudes rational and meaningful in their contexts. It is thanks to the (ironic, philosophical, literary) detachment from naively lived love that we may, paradoxically, both understand and live that kind of love more fully. By truly understanding why it may be morally and existentially problematic, or even impossible, for melancholic lovers to be immersed in the world we may be able to appreciate the unique and highly special nature of such love in its striking contingency.[70]

Bibliography

Armstrong, John
2003   *Conditions of Love: Philosophy of Intimacy*. London: Penguin.

Dilman, Ilham
1974   Wittgenstein on the Soul. – Godfrey Vesey (ed.), *Understanding Wittgenstein*. Royal Institute of Philosophy Lectures 7. London and Basingstoke: Macmillan. 162–192.

Gaita, Raimond
2004   *Good and Evil: An Absolute Conception*. New York and London: Routledge. 2nd ed. (1st ed. 1991.)

---

[70] We thank the editors for the kind invitation to submit this article to the Festschrift. We are also grateful to two anonymous referees for useful comments. Having learned immensely from Risto Saarinen's work over the years, it is our great pleasure and honor to congratulate him with this essay.

GLEESON, ANDREW
2012   *A Frightening Love: Recasting the Problem of Evil.* Basingstoke: Palgrave Macmillan.

HAMILTON, CHRISTOPHER
2016   *A Philosophy of Tragedy.* London: Reaktion Books.

HONNETH, AXEL
2005   *Kampf um Anerkennung.* Frankfurt am Main: Suhrkamp. 2nd ed. (1st ed. 1992.)

HUXLEY, ALDOUS
1920   *Limbo.* London: Chatto & Windus.

JAMES, WILLIAM
1902   *The Varieties of Religious Experience: A Study in Human Nature.* Eds. Frederick H. Burkhardt, Fredson Bowers, and Ignas K. Skrupskelis. Cambridge, MA and London: Harvard University Press, 1985.

JANKÉLÉVITCH, VLADIMIR
2005   *Forgiveness.* Trans. Andrew Kelly. Chicago: The University of Chicago Press. (French original 1967.)

KAIMIO, MAARIT
2002   Erotic Experience in the Conjugal Bed: Good Wives in Greek Tragedy. – Martha Nussbaum and Juha Sihvola (eds.), *The Sleep of Reason: Erotic Experience and Sexual Ethics in Ancient Greece and Rome.* Chicago: The University of Chicago Press. 95–119.

KIVISTÖ, SARI
2009   *Medical Analogy in Latin Satire.* Basingstoke: Palgrave Macmillan.

KIVISTÖ, SARI AND PIHLSTRÖM, SAMI
2016   *Kantian Antitheodicy: Philosophical and Literary Varieties.* Basingstoke: Palgrave Macmillan.

KOSKINEN, HEIKKI J.
2017   Mediated Recognition and the Categorial Stance. – *Journal of Social Ontology* 3. 67–87.

KRAUT, ROBERT
1986   Love *De Re.* – *Midwest Studies in Philosophy* 10. 413–430.

LEAR, JONATHAN
1998   *Open Minded: Working Out the Logic of the Soul.* Cambridge, MA and London: Harvard University Press.

MONTI, RICHARD C.
1981   *The Dido Episode and the Aeneid: Roman Social and Political Values in the Epic.* Mnemosyne, Supplementum sexagesimum sextum. Leiden: Brill.

NEIMAN, SUSAN
2002 *Evil in Modern Thought: An Alternative History of Philosophy.* Princeton, NJ: Princeton University Press.

PIHLSTRÖM, SAMI
2011 *Transcendental Guilt: Reflections on Ethical Finitude.* Lanham, MD: Lexington Books.
2016 *Death and Finitude: Toward a Pragmatic Transcendental Anthropology of Human Limits and Mortality.* Lanham, MD: Lexington Books.
2019 Wittgenstein on Happiness: Harmony, Disharmony, and Antitheodicy. – *Philosophical Investigations* 42. 15–39.

PUTNAM, HILARY
2012 *Philosophy in an Age of Science.* Eds. Mario De Caro and David Macarthur. Cambridge, MA and London: Harvard University Press.

RINNE, PÄRTTYLI
2018 *Kant on Love.* Berlin: de Gruyter.

SAARINEN, RISTO
2014 Love and Death in Ficino's *De amore.* – Outi Hakola & Sari Kivistö (eds.), *Death in Literature.* Newcastle upon Tyne: Cambridge Scholars Publishing. 139–149.
2016 *Recognition and Religion: A Historical and Systematic Study.* Oxford: Oxford University Press.

SARTRE, JEAN-PAUL
1956 *Being and Nothingness: A Phenomenological Essay on Ontology.* Trans. Hazel E. Barnes. New York: Washington Square Press. (French original 1943.)

SINGER, IRVING
1984 *The Nature of Love 1: From Plato to Luther.* Chicago and London: The University of Chicago Press. 2nd ed. (1st ed. 1966; paperback reprint 1987.)

SVEVO, ITALO
2003 *Zeno's Conscience: A Novel.* Trans. William Weaver. New York: Vintage. (Italian original 1923.)

VERGIL
Aeneid. Trans. Theodore C. Williams. Available online at the Perseus Digital Library: http://www.perseus.tufts.edu/hopper/text?doc=Perseus%3Atext%3A1999.02.0054%3Abook%3D1%3Acard%3D1. (The translation originally published 1910.)

WITTGENSTEIN, LUDWIG
1921   *Tractatus Logico-Philosophicus.* Trans. D.F. Pears and B.F. McGuinness. London: Routledge and Kegan Paul, 1974.
1953   *Philosophische Untersuchungen / Philosophical Investigations.* Eds. G.E.M. Anscombe and G.H. von Wright. Trans. G.E.M. Anscombe. Oxford: Basil Blackwell, 1958.
1961   *Tagebücher / Notebooks 1914–1916.* Ed. G.E.M. Anscombe and G.H. von Wright. Trans. G.E.M. Anscombe. Oxford: Basil Blackwell. 2nd ed., 1973.
1967   *Lectures and Conversations on Aesthetics, Psychology, and Religious Belief.* Ed. Cyril Barrett. Berkeley: University of California Press.
1980   *Vermischte Bemerkungen / Culture and Value.* Ed. G.H. von Wright. Trans. Peter Winch. Oxford: Blackwell.

Locus De Ira et Odio: Hate and Anger as Theological Categories

Olli-Pekka Vainio

I am writing this article in New Jersey after the unforeseen rise, and even more bewildering victory, of Donald Trump. His presidential campaign could tap into the current discontentment among the working-class people who had suddenly found themselves to be on the losing side of globalization. On my way to work, I see signs on well-kept lawns asserting, "Hate has no home here" and bumper stickers declaring, "Love trumps hate." After the election, the polarization between different groups in the USA has increased, and although the country has always been polarized, the anger is now visible for all to see.[1] Both sides have attacked each other verbally and physically.[2]

These remarks serve as an ad hoc introduction to the wider and more common phenomenon of hate and anger we humans feel towards our neighbors when we disagree about the things that matter to us. Hate and anger are common human emotions, but defining and analyzing them is not that easy. Sometimes, these concepts are used almost as synonyms that on closer inspection reveal that this is not always so. Sometimes they go hand in hand and appear as mutually enforcing attitudes. My hate

---

[1] Campbell 2016.
[2] Perhaps unsurprisingly, Americans have found ways to turn hate into money. For example, at least some post-election left-wing attacks against centrists and conservatives are based on a well-functioning business model that is dependent on the ever-deepening societal polarization. This is the business model of, for example, the Southern Poverty Law Center, which started after the election to list alleged hate crimes. Cannon 2017. Post-election chaos led to a bewildering phenomenon of hateful fake news. In spring 2017, the fact-checking site Snopes reported that while both the left and right produced fake news that supported their own narrative, anti-right fake news outweighed anti-left fake news. See BBC 2017.

towards something can make me angry, and being angry may strengthen my feelings of hate. But this is not necessarily so as it is also possible to be angry with someone without hating him or her, and it is likewise possible to hate someone without feeling anger.[3]

Later in this paper, I will offer a more nuanced account, but for now it suffices to note that I will treat 'hate' as a moral species term. In other words, to label a reaction as a form of 'anger' is not yet to have made a moral judgment. Some forms of anger are justified, others are not. Hate, by contrast, could be considered a moral species term that has two different manifestations. In both cases to call something 'hate' is to render a negative moral judgment, simply by applying the term. But like anger, hate can also be justified or unjustified. Unjustified hate or anger can also be called wrath. Justified forms, on the other hand, include cases when someone is said to hate something that is evil.

This article focuses on hate and anger viewed from the viewpoint of Christian theology. First, I will examine the use of the words hate in the Bible, focusing on the New Testament, and then evaluate the discussion in contemporary moral and cognitive psychology. In conclusion, I will offer a systematic and constructive account of hate and anger as theological categories and ask whether they can be viewed as virtues and, if so, by what kind of criteria should they be evaluated.

Theological dictionaries do not typically list hate and anger in their own loci. I believe that the concepts deserve some attention not only due to recent socio-(theo)political developments but also because they have been widely discussed in the past by both philosophers and theologians.[4] The question and method relate to Professor Risto Saarinen's work in multiple ways. Among other things, he has published extensively on the nature of love, emotions and other movements of the soul, written a biblical commentary with a special attention to human psychology and

---

[3] An example of the first case, would be a parent who gets furious with a disobedient child. However, the parent does not hate the child, even if the parent hates what the child has done. The latter case is depicted in the opening scene of Quentin TARANTINO's *Inglourious Basterds* (2009), where SS Colonel Hans Landa explains his attitude towards Jews in this manner to Monsieur LaPadite.

[4] The earliest and still influential terminological distinctions appear, for example, in PLATO, *Laws*, Book II, ARISTOTLE, *Rhet*. II.3 (1382a); PLUTARCH, *De invidia et odio* and SENECA, *De Ira*.

the regulation of emotions, and translated Philip Melanchthon's *Loci Communes* (1521) into Finnish. In following his scholarly example, I hope to offer here a concise *locus de ira et odio*.

Hate and anger in the Bible

There are dozens of references to hate (Gr. *miseoo, misos, miseetos*) in the New Testament.[5] Here I focus only on cases where the concept is mentioned, excluding instances that might appear as potentially hateful or where God appears to be angry.[6] Perhaps the most obvious passage on hate in the Bible is Matthew 5: 43–48 (NIV):

> You have heard that it was said, 'Love your neighbor and hate your enemy.' But I tell you, love your enemies and pray for those who persecute you, that you may be children of your Father in heaven. He causes his sun to rise on the evil and the good, and sends rain on the righteous and the unrighteous. If you love those who love you, what reward will you get? Are not even the tax collectors doing that? And if you greet only your own people, what are you doing more than others? Do not even pagans do that? Be perfect, therefore, as your heavenly Father is perfect.

The Old Testament does not command one to hate one's enemy. It is not clear therefore what teaching Jesus is referring to here. However, the Dead Sea Scrolls include a passage where the author commands the believers to "love all the sons of light, each according to his lot among the council of God, but to hate all the sons of darkness, each according to his guilt in the vengeance of God."[7] It can be concluded that the boundaries of love and hate were discussed publicly in Jesus's time. Jesus challenges this apparently popular teaching by extending the love from neighbors to enemies, who are not just to be loved but persuaded to become brothers and sisters in Christ (Mt. 28:19).

Hate is typically depicted as a grave sin. In 1. John 3:15, hate is as serious as murder: "Anyone who hates a brother or sister is a murderer, and you

---

[5] MICHEL 1979; BARRETT 2017.
[6] One of these instances is the fate of the Canaanites in the Book of Joshua. For the discussion of this event and others like it, see BERGMANN, MURRAY & REA 2010.
[7] OGLETREE 2016, 30.

know that no murderer has eternal life residing in him." In Johannine theology, hate and love are connected to darkness and light. A hater is like Gollum in *The Lord of the Rings*, who shies away from the light because he cannot bear the light of truth (John 3:20). Consequently, Gollum "loves to hate" the light.

But there are also cases when hate is portrayed as a good thing, for example in Rev. 2:6, "But you have this in your favor: You hate the practices of the Nicolaitans, which I also hate." Christians are commanded to hate evil in Rm. 12:9, "Love must be sincere. Hate what is evil; cling to what is good." In many passages, God is also said to hate: "You must not worship the LORD your God in their way, because in worshiping their gods, they do all kinds of detestable things the LORD hates. They even burn their sons and daughters in the fire as sacrifices to their gods." (Dt. 12:31). God's hate is typically deserved for various kinds of injustices and idolatry, which are often portrayed as going hand in hand (e.g., Dt. 16:22; Jer. 44:4; Ez. 23:38). Even though English translations may use the word wrath (Gr. *thymos,* Rev. 16:1) in relation to God's coming judgment, it clearly refers to justified anger that is passionate.[8]

One perplexing passage concerns the election of Jacob and Esau (Rm 9:13): "I have loved Jacob, but I have hated Esau." However, this must be understood against the antonymic relation between love and hate in the Bible. Hating often means rejection, renunciation, and disavowal. Instead of speaking about God's emotions, the passage refers to God judging Jacob as righteous, while condemning Esau.[9]

The world hates believers. In the Psalms, prayers address the plight of being hated by one's enemies (Ps. 25:19; 69:14) In the New Testament, it is often underlined how Christians should expect that they will be persecuted and hated, but they cannot answer hate with hate (Lk. 6:22, 27; Mt. 10:22; 24:9).

The proper response needs to be carefully managed. In the pastoral epistles, harmful desires (*epithymia*) are often listed among the causes

---

[8] David Bentley HART (2017, 62) defines God's anger thus: "Even the wrath of God in Scripture is a metaphor, suitable to our feeble understanding, one which describes not the action of God towards us, but what happens when the inextinguishable fervency of God's love toward us is rejected." See also SCRUTTON 2013.

[9] See also GRISLIS 1961.

of all kinds of bad things (2. Tim. 2:22; 3:6). Proper Christian conduct requires *metriopatheia*, the moderation of emotions. This does not mean *apathaeia*, a state that is totally passionless. Instead, Christians are called to express contentment, self-discipline, sound judgment, and steadfastness.[10] Ephesians 4:26 advises "In your anger (Gr. *orgisthee*), do not sin," offering support for understanding anger as such, not as a moral species term. However, being angry in an uncontrolled way leads to harmful and irrational behavior (e.g. Mt. 22:7; Lk. 15:28; Rev. 12:17).

Augustine states something similar when he quotes Cicero's *Tusculae Disputationes*, stating "chronic anger becomes hatred" (*Ira inveterata fit odium*) (Sermo 49, 7 [CCL 41, 619]), Cicero borrowing this idea from Stoicism. It seems therefore that Christian moral theory here builds strongly upon older philosophical traditions.[11]

Based on this quick overview of the canonical texts, we can conclude the following. Having unchastised feelings of hate and anger is dangerous. However, Christians can hate things and deeds that are evil, but never persons *per se*, even if they perpetuated evil actions.

Hate in moral psychology

The Merriam-Webster Dictionary defines hate as "intense hostility and aversion usually deriving from fear, anger, or sense of injury" or "extreme dislike or disgust." Therefore, it is apt to broaden our vocabulary to include the various psychological states that humans naturally connect with hate. Hate and anger are as natural to humans as breathing. Every one of us has felt these feelings, and we have little reason to believe that we can reach a state where we are free from hate and anger any time soon. In contemporary moral psychology, among the basic responses to injustice are anger and disgust. Jonathan Haidt, for example, has distinguished five basic moral modules that are connected to emotions:[12]

---

[10] SAARINEN 2008, 136, 233–241. For a substantial treatment of the management of the feeling of anger, see NUSSBAUM 2016.
[11] GILLETTE 2010, 129. See also BYERS 2012.
[12] HAIDT 2012, 124.

1 Care/harm	compassion
2 Fairness/cheating	anger, gratitude, guilt
3 Loyalty/betrayal	group pride, rage at traitors
4 Authority/subversion	respect, fear
5 Sanctity/degradation	disgust

If the value on the left is violated, the emotion on the right follows almost automatically. This reaction is often unconscious and beyond our control. If one looks at the list of emotions on the right, almost all of them are negative. This partly explains the naturalness of anger; it is an ordinary, quick and cost-effective reaction to something that we perceive as a moral violation.[13] Moreover, moral violations have a group enhancing function (3), which helps to understand why anger is often displayed communally so that "us" are set against "them." This consequently has further morally and societally harmful consequences.[14] Anger, therefore, has a paradoxical nature. On the one hand, it seems to be a reasonable reaction to moral violations, but on the other hand, it seems to aggravate moral conflicts.[15]

Psychologists differ on how they see the value of anger. Some see it more as a generally negative force with no beneficial consequences, while some see a value in it if it is managed properly. According to the former, contentious human situations should be dealt with nonemotionally, and anger can only harm the situation, making resolution more difficult. The latter typically underline the motivating force of anger that can help people to change their situations for the better.

Among the harmful consequences of anger are, for example, the following.[16] More generally, anger leads to biased thinking and acting.[17] Angry persons are prone to attribute malicious intent to those who disagree with them. This creates an escalating cycle, where attitudes can quickly become more extreme. Anger hinders one's cognitive capabilities to assess cases so that one is typically is too optimistic about one's own point of view. When the issue is not properly analyzed, this leads to quick and impulsive

---

[13] In antiquity, anger was linked to a sense of justice. See, e.g., AUGUSTINE, *De civitate Dei* 14, 19.
[14] On the harmful consequences of moral grandstanding, see TOSI & WARMKE 2016.
[15] On this effect in American politics, see, e.g., LILLA 2017.
[16] I am using here the studies listed in COGLEY 2014; LITVAK ET AL. 2010.
[17] On cognitive biases in general, see KAHNEMAN 2011; STANOVICH 2011.

decisions and one is biased towards choosing procedures that have a very low chance of bringing about the desired state of affairs.

However, Aristotle is among the optimists who see some value in anger even if he remains cautious about being angry in a successful manner: "Anybody can become angry – that is easy, but to be angry with the right person and to the right degree and at the right time and for the right purpose, and in the right way – that is not within everybody's power and is not easy." (NE 1109a27–29). As already noted, the positive element in anger is related to its motivational force; it makes people act to end injustices. While anger and hate can cause aggression, they are neither necessary or sufficient conditions for aggression.[18] As already noted, one can harm another person without feeling anger, and most of the time angry people do not act aggressively towards others. Anger can motivate people to act for a change in ways that do not involve aggression. A mother of a bullied child can get angry but can channel this anger through a calm phone call to the principal. Even some extreme reactions made in a state of anger are not necessarily irrational or evil. If someone attacks me physically and I defend myself so that the attacker gets hurt, I have not necessarily done anything wrong. Moreover, getting angry has probably helped me to overcome the threatening situation.

Hate and anger as virtues

Mundane uses of the word 'hate' portray a wide range of meanings. For example, Dylan Roof, who killed nine people in a Charleston church on June 17, 2015, stated after hearing his death sentence that "Wouldn't it be fair to say that the prosecution hates me because they're trying to give me the death penalty?"[19] Atheist Christopher Hitchens has criticized infringements on the freedom of speech that have been argued for because criticism may appear to be hateful.[20] If a court pronounces a death sentence

---

[18] COGLEY, 2014, 207; TAVRIS 1989.
[19] http://www.foxnews.com/us/2017/01/10/charleston-church-shooter-to-face-death-sentence.html
[20] http://blog.skepticallibertarian.com/2014/09/30/christopher-hitchens-freedom-of-speech-means-freedom-to-hate/

on someone, does it mean that it hates him? It is possible, but not necessary. Does freedom of speech give a permission to hate? It depends on what we mean by hate, and this is where I turn next.

Aquinas in *Summa Theologiae* (ST II.2.Q. 158, resp.) offers a useful discussion of anger. Anger is a passion, and passions can be evil in two ways. First, the object, or species, of the passion can be evil if it wills something that is evil. Anger does not necessarily qualify as a vice in this first sense because if anger is understood as a desire for revenge, it can also be a good thing if revenge is here understood as the fulfillment of justice. Obviously, there are cases where the desire for revenge can take a vicious form.

Second, passions can be evil with regard to their magnitude if the reaction is too powerful or not powerful enough. Anger is vicious if one is too angry. For example, hitting a child because he spilled his milk, is obviously wrong. On the other hand, not being angry can also be a vice if, for example, when hearing about, say, genocide we remain totally emotionless. For anger to be a virtue it needs a proper measure and a proper aim, namely justice.

Earlier, Aquinas (ST II.2.Q.43. resp.) explains how it is allowed to hate something that a person has done, but one is never allowed to hate the person: "it is lawful to hate the sin in one's brother, and whatever pertains to the defect of Divine justice, but we cannot hate our brother's nature and grace without sin. Now it is part of our love for our brother that we hate the fault and the lack of good in him, since desire for another's good is equivalent to hatred of his evil. Consequently, the hatred of one's brother, if we consider it simply, is always sinful."

In Christian monastic culture, there has been a long tradition of "internal" hate and anger that is directed towards one's own sin and the evil within oneself. Gregory of Nyssa, for example, explains how even negative emotions and movements of the mind can be beneficial in this respect if they are properly managed by reason:

> ...if reason instead assumes sway over such emotions, each of them is transmuted into a form of virtue. For anger produces courage, cowardice caution, fear obedience, hatred aversion from vice, the power of love the desire for what is truly beautiful. High spirit in our character raises our thought above the passions, and keeps it from bondage to what is base. The great apostle, too, praises such a form of mental elevation when he bids us constantly to 'set our minds on things that are

above' (Col. 3:2) and so we find that every such motion, when elevated by loftiness of mind, is conformed to the beauty after the divine image.[21]

Based on what has been said above, we can conclude the following.

1. Hate is unavoidable as a human feeling.
2. There are cases when hate is the wrong reaction.
3. There are cases when hate is the right reaction.

We can deepen our analysis by including Aquinas's analysis of anger and hatred, and by distinguishing between two types of hate. In contemporary virtue theory, it is common to distinguish between anger and wrath, anger being a justified response to wrongdoing, whereas wrath is a vengeful attitude that seeks to harm someone. An angry person only wants to right wrongs (that is, to hate the sin but love the sinner), but the wrathful person wants to harm the wrongdoer.[22]

Zac Cogley extends his analysis of virtuous anger to three additional points: (1) anger is an appraisal of wrongdoing, (2) it is a motivating force, and (3) it has a communicative function.[23] The first point means that emotions entail an epistemic judgment. Feeling angry means that one has, consciously or unconsciously, made a value evaluation about something that has turned out to be negative. Of course, our judgments are not always right and we can get angry when in fact we shouldn't. Leaving the question about the legitimacy of the death penalty as such aside, Dylan Roof's assessment of his sentence seems to be such a case. Mere feeling of anger as such is not an indication that it is in fact warranted.

Secondly, if one gets angry but does nothing about the things that would be in one's power to change, then the person does not act virtuously. If a person encounters racist behavior at his workplace, let's say he sees

---

[21] GREGORY OF NYSSA, *On the Creation of the Human* 18. 3-5. Translation from LOUTH 2013, 77. See also BASIL OF CAESAREA, *Homilia adversus eos qui irascuntur*, Patrologia Graeca 31.356.

[22] According to NUSSBAUM (2016, 22), this desire for payback is the crucial issue that needs to be managed when one confronts the anger within oneself.

[23] I understand Cogley to refer here to anger in a stronger sense, as a moral species term, which I earlier reserved for 'hate.' Virtuous anger is a form of hate that is justifiably directed against something that is judged to be evil.

a worker bullied by a co-worker and gets angry about it, but does not do anything about it, then this anger does not express virtue as it falls short of excellence.[24]

Third, anger can have a beneficial communicative function. This broadens one's reactions to include other people outside one's immediate sphere. Showing anger can display and make manifest a social wrong. In this way public anger may contribute toward beneficial social change. Cogley uses as an example Martin Luther King's "I have a dream" speech, where some lines can be read as angry but where the overall text displays a range of virtues.[25]

Therefore, we can conclude with the following account of hate and anger that displays virtuous ideals.

4. Hate and anger is the right reaction if:
   a. It seeks justice and harmony, not revenge.
   b. It is expressed in the right measure.
   c. It offers an epistemically correct appraisal of the situation.
   d. It motivates one to act to change the situation.
   e. It involves a virtuous mode of communal communication.

In conclusion, we can never reach a state that is free from hate and anger. Humans continue to value things differently and they choose different stories to live by. This difference will always cause tension and disagreement, which sometimes surface as negative emotions. Attempts to eradicate these passions are likely only to make them stronger, and less than virtuous. Managing anger is not easy, but it is nevertheless demanded of Christians.[26]

---

[24] However, this is often easier said than done. A recent study found that messaging that tries to force people to adopt certain values can easily backfire and increase prejudice towards outsiders. LEGAULT, GUTSELL & INZLICHT 2011.

[25] Cogley refers to the beginning of the speech, which lists things that were promised but never given ("bad check"). Later King mentions the Governor of Alabama in relation to "vicious racists," but ends the sentence with a hopeful note that, "one day right there in Alabama little black boys and black girls will be able to join hands with little white boys and white girls as sisters and brothers."

[26] I thank Timo Nisula and two anonymous reviewers for their valuable comments on this paper.

Bibliography

BARRETT, Rob
2017   Hate, Hatred. – *Encyclopedia of the Bible and Its Reception*. Berlin: De Gruyter.

BERGMANN, Michael, MURRAY, Michael & REA, Michael C. (eds.)
2010   *Divine evil?: the moral character of the God of Abraham*. Oxford: Oxford University Press.

BBC
2017   *The rise of left-wing, anti-Trump fake news*. Available at: http://www.bbc.com/news/blogs-trending-39592010 (Accessed: 8 June 2017).

BYERS, Sarah Catherine
2012   *Perception, Sensibility, and Moral Motivation in Augustine: A Stoic-Platonic Synthesis*. Cambridge: Cambridge University Press.

CAMPBELL, James E.
2016   *Polarized: Making Sense of a Divided America*. Princeton: Princeton University Press.

CANNON, Carl
2017   *The Hate Group That Incited the Middlebury Melee. RealClearPolitics*. Available at: https://www.realclearpolitics.com/articles/2017/03/19/the_hate_group_that_incited_the_middlebury_melee_133377.html (Accessed: 8 June 2017).

COGLEY, Zac
2014   A study in virtuous and vicious anger. – *Virtues and Their Vices*. Timpe, K. and Boyd, C. A. (eds.) Oxford: Oxford University Press. 199–225.

GILLETTE, Gertrude
2010   *Four Faces of Anger: Seneca, Evagrius Ponticus, Cassian, and Augustine*. Lanham: University Press of America.

GRISLIS, Egil
1961   Luther's Understanding of the Wrath of God. *The Journal of Religion*, 41(4).

HAIDT, Jonathan
2012   *The Righteous Mind: Why Good People Are Divided by Politics and Religion*. London: Allen Lane.

HART, David Bentley
2017   *The Hidden and the Manifest*. Grand Rapids: Eerdmans.

KAHNEMAN, Daniel
2011   *Thinking, Fast and Slow*. London: Allen Lane.

LEGAULT, Lisa, GUTSELL, Jennifer N. & INZLICHT, Michael
2011   Ironic effects of antiprejudice messages: How motivational interventions can reduce (but also increase) prejudice. *Psychological Science*, 22(12).

LILLA, Mark
2017   *The Once and Future Liberal: After Identity Politics*. New York: Harper.

LITVAK, P. M. *et al.*
2010   Fuel in the Fire: How Anger Impacts Judgment and Decision-Making. – *International Handbook of Anger*. Potegal, M. (ed.) New York: Springer. 287–310.

LOUTH, Andrew
2013   *Introducing Eastern Orthodox Theology*. Downer's Grove: IVP Academic.

MICHEL, O.
1979   miseoo. – *Theological Dictionary of the New Testament*. Eerdmans.

NUSSBAUM, Martha
2016   *Anger and Forgiveness: Resentment, Generosity, Justice*. Oxford: Oxford University Press.

OGLETREE, Thomas W.
2016   Interpreting the Love Commands in Social Context: Deuteronomy and Jesus's Sermon on the Mount. – *Love and Christian Ethics. Tradition, Theory, and Society*. SIMMONS, F. V. and SORRELLES, B. C. (eds.). Washington, D.C.: Georgetown University Press. 19–35.

SAARINEN, Risto
2008   *The Pastoral Epistles with Philemon and Jude*. Grand Rapids: Brazos.

SCRUTTON, Anastasia
2013   Divine passibility: God and emotion. *Philosophy Compass*, 8(9).

STANOVICH, Keith
2011   *Rationality and the Reflective Mind*. Oxford: Oxford University Press.

TAVRIS, Carol
1989   *Anger: The Misunderstood Emotion*. New York: Simon & Schuster.

TOSI, Justin & WARMKE, Brandon
2016   Moral Grandstanding. *Philosophy & Public Affairs*, 44(3).

Hate Speech as a Form of Action

Jaana Hallamaa

Fake news and hate speech appear to have become the new norm of public discourse. In his tweets, President Donald Trump has adopted the habit of labelling every piece of information that does not support his views or flatter him, his statements, or policies as 'fake news'. His political opponents, for their part, have used the term hate speech to describe the President's statements of people and groups whose presence in the US President Trump finds somehow detrimental. Both fake news and hate speech are written in a negative tone. A world in which people and groups communicate through fake news and hate speech has little to offer for mutual trust and understanding.

Traditional news media have established a number of mechanisms to verify and fact-check in hopes of combatting fake news. The results have not been encouraging thus far. Those who most likely consume fake news are the least likely to read the fact-checking reports. To these consumers, the various verification processes constitute yet another plot by the establishment against the people. For basic psychological reasons, most of us tend to read the types of news that do not conflict with our adopted views. We tend to seek confirmation of our solid convictions rather than expose ourselves to information that could contradict them. In other words, there is a strong human tendency to believe what one wants to believe.[1]

Attempts to eradicate hate speech have also not been highly successful. Several countries throughout the world have passed laws to combat forms of public discourse that utilise features of hate speech.[2] Nonetheless, it is difficult to prosecute and sentence people of deeds that fulfil the hate

---

[1] Plous 1993, 233.
[2] For the most up-to-date list, see https://en.wikipedia.org/wiki/Hate_speech

speech clauses as defining sufficient criteria for such offences depends on interpretation. In addition, guilty verdicts seldom have a generally favourable effect for forming a unanimous opinion against hate speech. Offenders may be viewed as martyrs whose only fault is their boldness to articulate ideas that everyone knows to be true but that the elite has labelled as politically incorrect.

Fake news and hate speech pose a problem because they threaten to erode the basis of public discourse. There is an obvious need to do something. In the following, I will concentrate on discussing hate speech. As a departure point, I will adopt the analysis proposed by Risto Saarinen. He examined Finnish theological discussion during the past decades to recognise forms of discourse that bear the marks of hate speech.[3] I begin by briefly introducing Saarinen's main ideas and then continue with an attempt to find new ways to solve problems posed by hate speech.

Analyzing the malady – hate speech as eristic

Saarinen's starting point for understanding the nature of hate speech is to contrast it with argumentation. He therefore defines the main characteristics of hate speech through the features that differentiate it from argumentation. According to Saarinen, hate speech is essentially a form of rhetoric known since Antiquity as eristic.

The eristic is a rhetoric technique that relates to how orators construct their claims. Here, the soundness of inferences that lead to a conclusion matters less than the goal to defeat the adversary. In this way, Saarinen finds the focal difference between hate speech and fair communication based on argumentation in the orator's motive. The speaker's motive in argumentation is to determine the truth of the matter at hand, whereas in eristic, the motivating force behind the orator's discourse is the will to crush an adversary.

Saarinen's analysis is particularly compelling and useful because he suggests stages that occur in formulating hate speech. For example, prior to full-scale defamation, Saarinen maintains that the target is repeatedly placed in a negative light. By applying Saarinen's ideas, the process towards

---

[3] SAARINEN 2015.

full-scale hate speech proceeds as follows: the first step is to raise suspicion of the person or group of people by associating them with negative characteristics or some type of action that the speaker considers detrimental or condemnatory. Thus, the target is labelled as an adversary whose aims and deeds must be opposed.

The second step toward full-scale hate speech involves spreading suspicion concerning the adversary. Here the orator can rely on previously accomplished work: repeated hints of the suspicion regarding the target gradually create a basis for further negative attribution. By combining these characterisations, a description or profile of the target is created that begins to resemble a collection of facts. This contributes to the impression that the adversary has not only morally questionable characteristics but also acts to achieve detrimental goals that clearly pose a threat to the common good. Therefore, it is only reasonable and justified to reveal further – negative – details about them. Eventually, it is only natural that people begin to lose patience. At this stage, the demand that something should be done to curb the contagion, is expressed through different channels in angry statements and expressions of rage.[4]

Another advantage of Saarinen's analysis is that it covers various types of communicative feedback. In this way, Saarinen succeeds in revealing the parallels between fair estimation based on argumentation and unfair estimation as eristic. Table 1 summarises Saarinen's classification concerning different types of feedback:

	Negative feedback	Neutral feedback	Positive feedback	Purpose of estimation
Fair estimation, argumentation	sound criticism	describing	pointing out merits, encouraging	(common) truth
Unfair estimation, eristic	raising suspicion, spreading suspicion, defaming	indifference, ignoring	flattery, brown-nosing	defeat of the adversary

Table 1[5]

---

[4] Richard EVANS (2004, 118–129) describes the process in Nazi Germany in his *The coming of the Third Reich*. Penguin Books, London.
[5] SAARINEN 2015, 401.

By classifying different stages of hate speech as estimations, Saarinen avoids labelling all forms of negative feedback as hate speech. It is crucial for sound public and political discourse that we can discern legitimate means of providing negative feedback from the forms of discourse we wish to restrain. It is important to see that the criterion of fair feedback is not its friendliness. Sound criticism may be harsh and it may offend the recipient even when it is justified and well-grounded.

The classification proposed by Saarinen also reveals the other, non-negative forms of eristic. It is interesting that even if we can define a neutral form of eristic, it does not actually exist as a speech form. Since it is eristic, it is by definition unfair and has no neutral forms. Positive forms of eristic aim to make the object of speech an ally or supporter by using the unfair means involving groundless attribution of positive characteristics through sycophancy and flattery.

The vicious cycle of hate speech

Before continuing, I wish to point out one more typical feature of eristic. Forms of hate speech – unlike arguments – are not based on the *logos* means of presentation, such as claims based on facts and sound steps of inference. For this reason, eristic must utilise the *pathos* and *ethos* type of rhetorical strategies to make a point. In eristic, colourful attributes, defaming comparisons and insulting metaphors are used to persuade listeners. Hate speech is consequently laden with emotion and designed to arouse emotion in others.

Argumentation is basically a truth-finding method. Its correct use leads to well-justified claims about reality. For this reason, argumentation as a technique is not tied to the arguer's motives. A sound argument is independent of its origin. However eristic is different in that the link between the orator and the target is crucial and eristic derives its emotive force from that relationship. The hate speaker wants an adversary to feel bad. There is, however, more to the dynamics. Slandering the object is not sufficient to constitute hate speech. It must defeat the enemy in front of an audience. Defaming language is supposed to contaminate the audience with the orator's emotive fervour.

Negative emotionality often spreads. For example, a group of hate speakers may give rise to a parallel group that receives its energy from the original defamers. The driving force of the parallel group is their moral indignation towards the hate speakers. Initiating a dispute with them seems – and often is – futile. The combination of an aggressive tone and the negative content soon drives away those who do not agree, as their attempts to protest or to make a different point are silenced with angry *ad hominem* attacks or red herring tactics. Their anger then finds an outlet in morally horrified reactions and condemnatory comments about the hate speaker's stupidity and ignorance.

What these lamentations have in common with hate speech is that they also shun argumentation. They are emotive in style and their purpose is to negatively label the hate speakers, even if the vocabulary may differ from theirs. As a result, the similarly minded remain in their own bubbles where they mutually intensify each other's aggression and this unifies each like-minded group.

In this manner, hate speech is prone to invoke parallel forms of non-argumentative statements that are often interpreted as hate speech by their target groups. This creates a vicious cycle that incites different groups to label each other as adversaries who make it impossible to conduct reasonable discussions. The only means of dealing with them is to clarify how impossible those people are and how action should be taken against them.

A different view of hate speech

Saarinen states that his definitions are preliminary and he has invited others to continue his work. In the following, I focus on two main points. Firstly, hate speech is not based on sound argumentation and may therefore be criticised as unreasonable because there are better forms of communication. Such criticism does not make hate speech irrational per se. I suggest that we could better understand the phenomenon of hate speech by examining it as a form of intentional action adopted by actors to achieve something meaningful and important – at least to them. Analysing forms of hate speech as intentional action offers a means to formulate criteria for successful hate speech. What does successful hate speech accomplish? Could defining such criteria offer a better understanding of the nature of hate speech and assist in finding means to combat it?

Another topic that deserves further attention is the social nature of hate speech. Whom do the hate speakers address when they defile their target? Pursuing these lines of inquiry, we can ask in what sense hate speech is a form of action and what makes, or fails to make, it successful.

To answer these types of questions, it is useful to examine definitions of hate speech. Even if there is no consensus as to what constitutes this speech, we can discern some of its basic features in different forms. Legislative attempts to curb unfair communication provides useful reference points for analysis.

A general definition of hate speech is "… usually thought to include communications of animosity or disparagement of an individual or a group on account of a group characteristic such as race, color, national origin, sex, disability, religion, or sexual orientation".[6] Prohibiting hate speech has a strong international precedent in the United Nations' treaty of International Covenant on Civil and Political Rights[7] and the United Nations' International Convention on the Elimination of All Forms of Racial Discrimination.[8] To summarise the basis for human rights regarding this matter, the right for protection from discrimination limits freedom of speech.

During the past decades, the need to identify and define new types of discrimination connected to hate speech which has surfaced on social media has become acute. It is clear that the traditional UN definition of basic human rights is insufficient to combat such violations of human dignity. Furthermore, the UN declarations no longer appear to command the authority they once had. Referring to human rights now is associated with ill-famed political liberalism. What is especially depressing is that the moral weight of the UN treaties can be undone by the indifference of simple comments such 'So what?' and 'Who cares?'.

---

[6] NOCKLEBY 2000; see also http://www.dictionary.com/browse/hate-speech, retrieved 23 January, 2018.

[7] Generally known by the acronym ICCPR. The covenant was adopted by the United Nations General Assembly in 1966 and has been in effect from 23 March 1976.

[8] Referred to as ICERD from 1965 (in force since 4 January 1969).

Central features of hate speech

Even the most general definition should include two central aspects of hate speech. Hate speech projects negative characterisations onto a person who represents a specific group or onto these groups themselves and it does so to defame its target. These two focal points of hate speech are highlighted in legal acts designed to curb it. Hate speech is detrimental to society, and may be considered a crime for two reasons. Firstly, hate speech may threaten public order. It poses such a threat by often implicitly recommending some type of violence as a justified reaction towards the target of hate speech. Secondly, hate speech offends the personal dignity of its target because it consists of insulting expressions.[9]

Both public justifications for curbing hate speech by law – maintaining public order and protecting personal dignity – are connected to the orator's willful intention, or motive, as Saarinen calls it, to denigrate the target. It is difficult, or even impossible, to verify what a person's intention or motive is, which is why an assessment of a given expression as hate speech must rely on the social uses of language. The public proof of a detrimental motive is when an orator attaches a negative label to a group of people or a member of that group.[10] These features can be highlighted by citing an example of the best-known Finnish court case concerning hate speech.

The politician Jussi Halla-aho, leader of the Finns Party since June 2017, has a website called *Scripta* where he has published several hundred lengthy blog posts since 2003.[11] As his posts began to gain popularity, his readers wanted to comment on them and continue discussing their themes. To enable this, a guest book (vieraskirja) was added to the *Scripta* website in 2005. As time passed, the popularity of this comment section rendered it impossible to moderate, prompting the creation of a new website in 2008, Hommaforum, or simply Homma ('Job Forum' or 'Job'). This new blog became the forum for discussions on Halla-aho's favourite political themes.

Today, Homma claims to be the leading forum for critical discussion concerning asylum and immigration policies in Finland. It has more than

---

[9] BELL 2009.
[10] Not all hate speech meets these criteria, as the orators learn to use expressions to avoid detection in social media, see BROWN-SICA AND BEALL 2008.
[11] http://www.halla-aho.com/scripta/

10 000 registered participants and over the years, its various subjects of discussion have received more than 2 million contributions from its readers. According to its critics, the site spreads hostility against foreigners and the contributions often adopt an offensive style toward those of differing opinions.[12]

Halla-aho's posts generated such popularity and admiration towards their author that his supporters began to call him 'the Master' (Mestari). As is typical of extreme opinions, Halla-aho's views divided the public and his writings evoked not only admiration but also indignation to the extent that two of his blog posts were reported to the police. In one of them, Halla-aho's discussion of the growing numbers of asylum seekers led him to state that this trend will most likely result in an increase in sexual assaults and rapes. After this statement, he expressed a wish that the sexual predators immigrating to Finland would target the right types of women, namely environmentally conscious leftist do-gooders and their political supporters.[13] The prosecutor did not find the wording sufficiently strong to press charges against Halla-aho.

In the other post, Halla-aho stated that Islam is a religion of pedophiles and that the Finnish Somali minority's livelihood is robbing others and enjoying social security services. Reporting this post to the police was successful in the sense that it resulted in Halla-aho being charged with incitement of ethnic agitation. After two acquittals in the lower courts, the Supreme Court of Finland closed the case by delivering a guilty verdict. Halla-aho was ordered to pay a fine and remove the offensive post from his web site.[14] After this verdict, others have published the same text on the

---

[12] https://fi.wikipedia.org/wiki/Homma

[13] "Koska näin ollen yhä useampi nainen tulee joka tapauksessa raiskatuksi, toivon hartaasti, että uhrinsa sattumanvaraisesti valitsevien saalistajien kynsiin jäisivät oikeat naisihmiset. Vihervasemmistolaiset maailmanparantajat ja heidän äänestäjänsä." http://www.iltalehti.fi/politiikka/201706092200198784_pi.shtml

[14] https://korkeinoikeus.fi/fi/index/ajankohtaista/tiedotteet/2012/06/tiedote8.6.2012-poliitikolletu.html. 25.2.2019. According to the Supreme Court, Halla-aho claimed that Islam is a pedophilic religion and that robbing and living as parasites on tax payers' money is a national, if not a genetic, feature of Somalis. Their verdict was that Halla-aho's claims about Islam constituted slander and denigration both in content and style. His characterisations of Somalis were vilifying and insulting. Halla-aho's statements were prone to evoke intolerance, contempt and possibly anger towards these groups. As a whole Halla-aho's expressions resembled hate speech and thus were not covered by the right to freedom of speech.

Internet where it is easily detectable. These publications have not lead to any further legal action.

Criteria for successful hate speech

Halla-aho's case is enlightening because it provides clues for examining both our questions on the criteria for successful hate speech and its social nature. According to the Supreme Court's verdict, Halla-aho's writings incited ethnic hatred against Muslims and people of Somali origin by defaming them. Let us interpret this as Halla-aho succeeding in creating hate speech against Muslims and Somalis as groups of people.

What are the criteria for hate speech as successful action? We refer to a person's action as successful if that person succeeds in achieving the goal he or she intends to attain and that person accomplishes this by means of his or her action. Not all actions fulfill these criteria without qualifications.

Most goals are complex in that we require different types of action to achieve them, or our actions only partially realise our goals. Moreover, not all goals are as concrete and well-defined such as eating an apple or catching a bus. I have reached my goal of eating an apple when I have succeeded in eating an (or a particular) apple and I have achieved my goal to catch a (certain) bus when I have caught the bus. If my aim is to learn French, the criteria for successful action are far more difficult to define. Learning French requires time and involves performing several different actions. Assessing whether the goal was achieved also depends on the level of language skills one is trying to master.

Modern language education has sophisticated methods of estimating one's skill level. One standard method is to assess how well the students understand spoken language and written texts and how accurately they can express themselves when speaking and writing in various communicative contexts. The level of their skills serves as a basis for placing people in categories that indicate how likely they are able to successfully communicate in different types of situations.[15]

---

[15] *Council of Europe (2011). Common European Framework of Reference for Languages: Learning, Teaching, Assessment,* https://www.coe.int/en/web/common-european-framework-reference-languages/level-descriptions. 25.2.2019.

Setting criteria for successful action is often even more difficult than assessing language skill levels. A lover may promise to make his or her loved one happy. In this case, there is no standard set of actions that will lead to achieving that goal and even if the lover does everything in his or her power – as the song by Leonard Cohen, 'I'm your man'[16] promises – it would still be uncertain whether we consider the actions an achievement and deem them successful. It is unclear if happiness is a goal, and even if we accept it as one to pursue, being happy does not solely depend on external factors or on others' actions but also on personal attitude, the ability to be grateful and how high expectations have been set. Acting to make someone else happy is an even more complicated goal. These actions must have the desired effect on the recipient so that he or she identifies them as contributing to his or her happiness.

What about successful hate speech? As a type of action, it is not as simple as eating an apple or catching a bus. Can we say that it is more similar to mastering a language than trying to make someone happy? Hate speech requires mastering a certain level of language skills. As it is a form of eristic, it is clear that linguistic inventiveness and wittiness enhance the desired effects of hate speech. Hate speech also resembles actions involved in trying to make someone happy. Success in both depends not only on a person's actions, but also how they affect the target and the target's willingness to play along.

Double standards?

Expressions such as those adopted by Halla-aho in his posts result in heated discussions on what was stated and how it was formulated. Part of the discourse focusses on the nature of the expressions used. There are those who wish to weaken the debate by understating the offensiveness of words and expressions. Others observe that the actual problem concerning what is labelled as hate speech is the existence and application of double standards. These refer to the derogatory characterisations of certain groups which remain systematically unpunished, while similar or more benign

---

[16] https://www.azlyrics.com/lyrics/leonardcohen/imyourman.html

talk about others is judged as reprehensible or even punishable.[17] This has been considered to be evidence of widespread hypocrisy and a politically maintained systemic bias. The critics connect this partiality to the liberal toleration ideology that purportedly idealises other cultures and religions and devalues one's own religious tradition and national heritage.[18]

The usual answer to such criticism is to refer to differences in social position. Those socially and economically affluent as well as those in power positions and public offices must be prepared to receive harsh criticism and even more assaults directed at them personally than ordinary people or members of religious and ethnic minorities.[19] The situation appears different if rather than focussing on the phrases and expressions used or who the target group of such statements is, we consider hate speech as action. This enables us to compare how the criteria of success vary according to the target group. Let us consider two examples concerning hostile statements against a religious figure and against a group of people.

During recent years, caricatures that insult and defile the Prophet Muhammad have led to widespread protests. A similarly denigrating claim was implicit in the aforementioned post by Halla-aho: when he referred to Islam as a pedophilic religion, Halla-aho refers to the tradition that allowed Muhammad to marry one of his wives when she was a very young girl. As Muhammad and his life are considered to be exemplary, marrying a child paves the way for sexual abuse in the form of child marriage.

Is there bias in how different convictions are treated? For example, it is not difficult to find negative statements concerning Jesus Christ, the central figure of Christianity. Would writing 'Jesus Christ was homosexual – therefore he was a pedophile'[20] lead to prosecution and a guilty verdict? As the critics have pointed out, it is unlikely, but perhaps not for the reason they think it is. In our context, criticising the majority religion and attributing negative characteristics to its central figures has a long tradition. Calling Jesus homosexual and a pedophile may offend believers but most people, even devout Christians, would probably find such disparaging talk largely meaningless. These are merely empty words that are highly unlikely

---

[17] http://keronen.blogspot.fi/2012/06/jussi-halla-ahon-tuomioon-johtanut.html
[18] See, e.g., http://www.halla-aho.com/scripta/oikeudenkaynti.html. 25.2.2019
[19] SAARINEN 2015, 389.
[20] https://groups.google.com/forum/#!topic/alt.atheism/GRYXPQJIabU 22.2.2018

to incite hostility against Christians. If there is a harmful effect, its target is not Jesus Christ or the Christian community, but rather the one who spreads such statements. Propagating statements that defame the central figure of Christianity do not seem to have a genuine chance of succeeding as hate speech.

This talk also fails as hate speech because it has become the customary view that profane law can only protect humans and human institutions. Transcendental matters lie beyond the protection of law but also beyond the human capacity to defile them. If Jesus is the risen Christ and the Second Person of the Trinity, nothing humans say can affect him or his position. The anger that Muslim believers harbour for the caricatures of the Prophet may reflect that they have a far stronger belief in the power of words and images than people who have been raised in Western culture.

How can Halla-aho's statement that the Somali minority earn their livelihood by robbing and living on social security be interpreted as insulting and slandering against the Somali as a group of people? What are the grounds for the Supreme Court to state that these types of statements were likely to evoke intolerance, contempt and even hatred towards members of the Somali community?[21]

Halla-aho contrasts his characterisations of Muslims and the Somalis with a newspaper editorial he finds offensive to ethnic Finns. The editor discussed a type of violence considerably more common in Finland than in other Nordic or Western countries, i.e. the relatively high frequency manslaughter cases where both the victim and the killer are intoxicated. The editor suggested that this phenomenon may be best explained by the hypothesis that Finnish males have certain hereditary characteristics that make them genetically prone to violent behaviour connected with alcoholism.

A reader who was annoyed by the editor's claim, filed a complaint about the hostile nature of the text to the Council for Mass Media in Finland. This complaint was rejected without a full handling by the Council, accompanied only by a soothing comment from the Council secretary. The whole incident demonstrates, according to Halla-aho, that the media

---

[21] https://yle.fi/uutiset/3-6171365 22.2.2018

maintains double standards that place the national majority, especially men, at a disadvantage in comparison to ethnic minorities.[22]

By finding Halla-aho guilty, the Supreme Court has stated that Halla-aho defiled Muslims and Somalis and that he invoked intolerance, contempt and even hatred towards these groups. A guilty sentence was passed to protect Muslims and Somalis, human dignity, and peace of practicing religion. The judicial decision appears to be a double-edged sword. It cannot protect human dignity without simultaneously acknowledging that Halla-aho's writing was a successful piece of hate speech that defiled its object. Halla-aho's formulations are condemnatory because they are socially effective and can therefore cause concrete, societal changes. His words are harmful. Hence, the court sentence offers protection to a minority group by accentuating the vulnerability of its members.

In contrast, if someone claimed that Finnish drinking habits and relatively high numbers of certain types of manslaughter can be best explained by hereditary characteristics. This claim does not amount to hate speech within the Finnish context.[23] Even if taken as a fact, it is difficult to see how these characteristics could effectively evoke intolerance, hostility or hatred towards Finnish men. It is merely something someone said – perhaps as a resigned joke – and it is difficult to see how it could seriously harm anyone. Here, protecting the target group – ethnic Finnish males – from negative speech by court orders or condemnatory statements would remain as ineffective as the claims themselves.

These examples clarified important features of hate speech. The two legal aims for making hate speech punishable – maintaining public order and protecting personal dignity – are connected. Threats to public order occur as violations of personal dignity, and violations of personal dignity pose a threat to public order. In short, there is a social connection between public order and personal dignity.

---

[22] http://keronen.blogspot.fi/2012/06/jussi-halla-ahon-tuomioon-johtanut.html
[23] If presented by a Swede in Sweden during the 1970s when hundreds of thousands of Finns moved to Sweden in search for work and a better life, the claim could have been successful as hate speech.

The performative nature of hate speech

The meanings of hateful utterances are determined by the social context in which they are used. As I attempted to illustrate above, the meaning of the claims does not sufficiently determine the limits of hate speech. The meaning plays or fails to play its designated role within the social setting which dictates all human actions. As hate speech is intended for an adversary the orator wishes to defeat, this may obscure the fact that the target of hate speech is not its only recipient.

The hate speakers are often not familiar with the target group of their slanderous statements and hate groups are also not usually willing to become familiar with anyone from the group they vilify. It may also be irrelevant to them whether members of target groups receive their message. What certainly matters are the reactions of the audience when the orator addresses them and whether the orator convinces them. Hate speech is rendered weak without an audience and the audience's reactions are decisive for this type of discourse to succeed. Without its excited response and emotional reactions, hate speech is merely words. Halla-aho's *Scripta* would be of little importance or relevance without its active followers, their comments and heated discussions.

Hate speech requires a social arena because the adversary who has negative characteristics and the label as someone who plots for detrimental goals has to be defeated in front of an audience. Thus, the target of hate speech begins to resemble a social scapegoat. For a scapegoat to fulfil its social purpose, it requires that an audience witnesses the scapegoating.

Hate speech is thus inherently performative because it requires an audience. This is yet another feature that differentiates hate speech and argumentation. Anyone can construct an argument for personal or public purposes, as a tool for reasoning and reaching conclusions. The aim of argumentation remains the same irrespective of whether there is an audience to receive it or not. By contrast, for hate speech to function, an audience is necessary.

What does the performative nature of hate speech contribute to its criteria of successful action? Any performance begins with a script: there must be utterances that count as hate speech. The example of linking the excessive drinking habits of Finnish males and their proneness to violence with their typical genetic features shows that having a script is not a sufficient condition for something to be considered as hate speech. Furthermore, it is necessary that a performance achieves the intended impact on the audience.

The goal of eristic, defeating the adversary, is a zero-sum game such that my victory is your loss and only my failure will secure that your position does not worsen. For this reason, the aim of the eristic is necessarily negative. Defeating an adversary is by definition something detrimental to the one who is defeated. The intended good in these actions is only revealed if the target's defeat profits the speaker and their supporters.

Not even successful hate speech offers anything substantially positive per se. The object group is defiled, the audience is smitten by negative emotionality and ready to act (violently if need be) against the target. None of this solves any problems at hand but further complicates them.

Hate speech creates interest groups according a division between 'us' and 'them'. The nature of hate speech as a zero-sum-game also impacts how the interests of the in-group are constructed. For us to achieve our vital goals, it is necessary that they do not succeed in achieving theirs. Presented in this way, denigrating the out-group 'other' is a precondition for the strivings of the in-group 'us'. It also serves as a morally coloured fake-argument, as is apparent in the wordings that Halla-aho used in his blog. His characterisations include a condemnatory description of the target groups, Muslims and Somalis. This type of labelling implicitly entails a warning against any type of co-operation with such people. Pedophiles should be isolated from the community and free riders should be forced to do their share before permitting their participation in any joint activity. Anecdotes and single experiences count as evidence that supports the conviction.

Hate speech that often gains more impetus from fake news has rapidly become an ill that not only targets individuals and groups, but also has a detrimental impact on our political systems and democratic election processes. Traditional print media as well as governments have begun to realise the need to take action against this phenomenon. Fact-checking agencies aim to stem the flow of false information. Sound argumentation still seems to be the only sustainable alternative to hate speech. The problem is that an unyielding pursuit of facts and cherishing the ideals of sound argumentation often seem rather powerless in the face of hate speech. It is much faster to invent fake news than to research and test the facts. The formulation of hate speech is simple and definite, whereas sound argumentation often contains reservations and qualifications. Facts and sound argumentation also lack the emotive and moral fervour of fake news and hate speech that arouses indignation and creates the pressing need to take action. And hate speech appeals to certain sectors of society because when personal prospects are limited, it is invigorating to feel almost any strong group emotion.[24]

Hate speech as social action

There are no easy and simple means to diminish hate speech. It is a mass phenomenon that derives its power from deep-rooted socio-psychological mechanisms that sound argumentation alone cannot defeat. Yet analytic thinking is on the frontline to combat this epidemic. Hate speech also differs from many other types of criminal action. For example, a thief's description of their action differs from that of their victim and the judiciary system. So a thief's main objective is his or her own gain but is convicted for the unlawful deed based on the loss that the theft causes to the victim. For hate speakers, their goal to harm the target and incite (possibly violent) action against them – is equal to the grounds of the punishability of their deed. A thief may assess the gains and the risks of their venture and extract the effects of their deed – getting the loot – from the effects the theft has on the victim – whatever material, emotional and physical loss. A hate speaker's reasoning is different because the aim of the deed is to cause the loss that they intend the victim to suffer.

For both a thief and a hate speaker, moral reform would involve a change in how they construct their social setting. An ex-thief prefers lawful work to stealing as a means of living and wishes to engage with others in his or her social life as equals who are under the obligations and protection of the judiciary system. The reform involves a wish to become part of the 'we' and 'us' that comprise society. For hate speakers, a shift in their mindset would involve including 'them' as part of the 'we' and 'us'. This step requires broadening worldviews that can be difficult if gaining and losing are perceived as social zero-sum games.

---

[24] STAUB 1989, 35–50.

Part of the appeal of hate speech evidently resides in the presuppositions concerning the nature of favourable in-groups. The human tendency to bond with those who are most similar to ourselves requires us to expend extra effort to tolerate, accept or even welcome members who are different in some respect. For the same reason, dissidents and critics are often accused of spoiling the good atmosphere in a group and everything would be so much more comfortable without them. As all types of differences are easily identified as sources of dispute, we are driven to seek the company of those who resemble us. Differences are also connected with diverging interests which complicates the situation.

Broadening the 'we' group is likely to increase group heterogeneity. Differing likes, dislikes, needs and desires lead to divergent aims. When all wishes cannot be fulfilled, problems arise. The simplest way to inhibit such difficulties is to reserve the in-group for the like-minded. This calculation misses the new opportunities both in terms of new goals and different types of co-operation that conflicts bring forth when people must negotiate with others, find compromises and struggle to find ways to recognise each other as agents who are bound to living together.[25]

Bibliography

BELL, Jeannine
2009   Restraining the heartless: racist speech and minority rights -- *Indiana Law Journal* 84. 966–7, 973, 976–977. https://www.repository.law.indiana.edu/cgi/viewcontent.cgi?referer=https://www.bing.com/&httpsredir=1&article=1132&context=ilj Retrieved 23 January2018.

EVANS, Richard
2004   *The coming of the Third Reich*. Penguin Books, London.

HALLAMAA, Jaana
2017   *Yhdessä toimimisen etiikka*. Gaudeamus. Helsinki.

---

[25] HALLAMAA 2017, 277–284.

NOCKLEBY, John T.
2000 Hate Speech – *Encyclopedia of the American Constitution*. Ed. Leonard W. Levy and Kenneth L. Karst. Vol. 3. 2nd ed. Detroit: Macmillan Reference USA, 2000. 1277–1279.

PLOUS, Scott
1993 *The Psychology of Judgment and Decision Making*. New York, NY: Mcgraw-Hill Book Company.

SAARINEN, RISTO
2015 Vihapuhe ja mustamaalaus teologian kysymyksenä. – *Teologinen Aikakauskirja* 5–6. 387–402.

BROWN-SICA, Margaret and BEALL, Jeffrey
2008 Library 2.0 and the Problem of Hate Speech – *Electronic Journal of Academic and Special Librarianship*, vol. 9 no. 2 (Summer 2008). http://southernlibrarianship.icaap.org/content/v09n02/brown-sica_m01.html#_edn2 Retrieved 23 Jan 2018.

STAUB, Erwin
1989 *The Roots of Evil. The Origins of Genocide and other Group Violence*. Cambridge: Cambridge University Press.

The Significance of CA 7 for Lutheran Orthodox Ecclesiologies

KENNETH G. APPOLD

Many Lutherans have observed that ecclesiology acts as something of a "bottom line" in ecumenical dialogue. Whatever else one begins discussing, one soons finds oneself talking about ecclesiology. In recent years, many Lutherans have also maintained that ecclesiological positions separate them in a serious way from other churches, suggesting that there are "fundamental" differences between Lutheran ecclesiology and Roman Catholic, Anglican or Reformed ecclesiologies. I would agree that there is a need for serious discussion—but I cannot help wondering at the definitive tone of some of those commentaries. What is its basis? Do Lutherans really have a distinct and fully defined confessional ecclesiology? I must admit, I see little evidence of this. In fact, the wide variety of polity structures that call themselves "Lutheran"—from the strongly episcopal systems of Scandinavia to the more synodal-presbyterial forms used in parts of Germany and North America to the modified congregationalism of the Lutheran Church-Missouri Synod—seem to speak against such a notion, unless we are willing to argue that variety itself is a hallmark of Lutheran ecclesiology (as some do). More than a few studies in Lutheran systematic theology, however, seem to suggest that such a diversity is not entirely welcome and represents something of a deficit—an area of Lutheran theology that is comparatively under-developed. I do not know how many times I have heard the complaint, "What we really need is a Lutheran ecclesiology". I will not provide one in this paper. In fact, I will not offer an assessment of whether such complaints are accurate or not. Instead, I would like to focus on what the Augsburg Confession, in its Seventh Article, says about the church and, in particular, on how CA 7 served as a foundation for the ecclesiologies of early Lutheranism. Drawing heavily upon research done for my recent book on disputations in Lutheran Orthodoxy[1], I will offer a survey of how theologians of this period worked with CA 7 and of how the article affected—both positively and negatively—this foundational period in the development of Lutheran ecclesiology. In that sense, my paper offers not a remedy, but rather something of a diagnosis of the problems I mentioned above.

In a formal sense, CA 7 had a direct influence on most accounts of ecclesiology during the Orthodox era. This is because most of those treatments took place within the context of academic disputation. Defending and explaining the Augsburg Confession was a principle task of Lutheran disputation during the late-16th and 17th centuries, and theological faculties produced countless *collegia* of disputations that went sequentially through the (generally first 21) articles of the CA. The Confession, by the way, enjoyed a pre-eminent position in such enterprises. There are far more disputations on the CA than on any of the other confessional writings, such as the Formula of Concord, or on the creeds. Based on their day-to-day teaching, it seems that Lutheran Orthodox theologians identified much more closely with the CA than with the remaining Lutheran confessions. Because of the importance of disputation for academic theology and for the formulation of doctrine, that means that CA 7 was without a doubt the most significant direct source of Lutheran ecclesiology during the Orthodox period. One would therefore expect CA 7's conceptuality and language to exert an enormous influence upon early Lutheran ecclesiologies. As we shall see, however, these expectations are not entirely met. For as it turned out, the things that CA 7 *does not* say were at least as significant as what it does.

Article Seven of the Augsburg Confession reads:

> Item docent, quod una sancta ecclesia perpetuo mansura sit. Est autem ecclesia congregatio sanctorum, in qua evangelium pure docetur et recte administrantur sacramenta. Et ad veram unitatem ecclesiae satis est consentire de doctrina evangelii et de administratione sacramentorum. Nec necesse est ubique similes esse traditiones humanas seu ritus aut ceremonias ab hominibus institutas; sicut inquit Paulus: Una fides, unum baptisma, unus Deus et pater omnium etc.[2]

---

[1] Appold 2004.
[2] BSLK[10], 61. Engl. transl.: "Likewise, they teach that one holy church will remain forever. The church is the assembly of saints in which the gospel is taught purely and the sacraments are administered rightly. And it is enough for the true unity of the church to agree concerning the

The church, in this account, is defined as a congregation of saints in which the Gospel is purely taught and the Sacraments are properly administered. This one and holy church remains perpetually. For the true unity of the church, it is sufficient to have consensus on the teaching of the Gospel and on the administration of the Sacraments. It is not necessary that humanly instituted rites, ceremonies or traditions be the same everywhere.

Defining the church as a congregation in which the Gospel is taught and Sacraments administered lies at the heart of Article Seven. Reading that sentence in light of the subsequent conditions for unity implies that it is the Word—audible in the Gospel and visible in the Sacraments—that causes the saints to congregate and to become church. One could say that "congregation", in this sense, is one of the perlocutionary effects of the Word. The Word causes its hearers to come together as church.

One of the strengths of Lutheran Orthodox theology, in my view, is its appreciation of this point and of the performative dimension of the Word in general. It was this appreciation that led many theologians of the period to place an analysis of the Word's effects—described as "the Holy Spirit's application of grace"—into the conceptual center of their dogmatic systems. Both the Word of the Gospel and the Sacraments are, as for example Abraham Calov puts it, effective in calling, converting, justifying, conserving in righteousness, and glorifying the person to whom they are applied—i.e. the person who hears and receives them.[3] One readily recognizes the classic components of what later came to be known as the "ordo salutis", or order of salvation.[4] Expositions of this doctrine are powerful descriptions, from the perspective of the human recipient, of how saving grace is applied. While, at first glance, terms such

---

teaching of the gospel and the administration of the sacraments. It is not necessary that human traditions, rites, or ceremonies instituted by human beings be alike everywhere. As Paul says [Eph. 4:5,6]: 'One faith, one baptism, one God and Father of all…" (The Book of Concord, ed. by R. Kolb and T. Wengert, Minneapolis 2000, 43).

[3] "Acquisitionem salutis a Christo factam excepit subjectum, cui ea est applicanda, quod sunt fideles: Ideoque superest, ut de applicatione ipsa nunc agamus, tum qua medium, quod est Verbum, & ακουστον & ορατον: tum qua modum, per vocationem, conversionem, justificationem, justitiae conservationem, & glorificationem, eamque non modo quatenus hic in praesenti vita inchoative, & in spe, sed etiam quatenus in altera vita consummate, & in actu ipso obtinenda, quo nos perducunt τα εσχατα vel Novissima." ABRAHAM CALOV, *Systema locorum theologicorum*, tom. IX: *ΜΥΣΤΗΡΙΟΣΟΦΙΑ divina, de verbo Dei et sacramentis divinis*, 1–2.

[4] For a study of Calov's *ordo salutis*, cf. APPOLD 1998.

as vocation, illumination, conversion, or mystical union appear highly individualistic, they also contain a strong ecclesial component that is often overlooked by later commentators. Not only are the means of grace—Word and Sacrament—administered by the church, their effects on the human subject, too, are tied to the church. When Calov defines the "call to faith", he describes it as a "Vocatio divina *ad Ecclesiam* [italics added]", by which those located outside the church are brought into the church through the Word and Sacraments.[5] Calling's *terminus a quo* is the realm of darkness, its *terminus ad quem* is the church. Conceptually, that move is significant because it grounds the spiritual experience of calling and conversion—and justification—in an external, public and ecclesial process rather than leaving it entirely internal and private, as would be the case in later, more one-sided, appropriations of this terminology by pietist strains of Lutheranism.

That pattern even holds true for the notion of mystical union, which signifies the most intensive form of intimacy between humans and God. Read retrospectively and from the standpoint of later, more subject-oriented philosophies, this theologoumenon seems to describe the apex of an individual's personal communion with God. Such a reading would miss much of the notion's original intent, however. For one thing, the doctrine of "mystical union" has its *Sitz im Leben* not in mystical practices or spiritual exercises of the individual, but in the sacramental practice of the church. As Theodor Mahlmann has shown, the *unio-mystica*-terminology emerged from reflections on the Eucharist, as is evident in early-17th-century disputations chaired by the Wittenberg theologian Friedrich Balduin.[6] A parallel preoccupation of Orthodox theologians centered on how to describe the church as a "koinonia", as a union of believers with Christ and—by extension—with each other. Here, they frequently anticipate the conceptuality of mystical union developed more fully by their successors, again revealing an explicit ecclesial and communal

---

[5] "Vocatio divina ad Ecclesiam est infidelium, extra Ecclesiam positorum, ad Ecclesiam per Verbum & Sacramenta a DEO ex gratia dispensata efficax adductio." CALOV, *Systema, tom. X: De ΣΩTHPIOΠOIIA, sive salutis consequendae modo*, 1.

[6] Cf. FRIEDRICH BALDUIN, *Disputationes tres de pane vitae...*, Wittenberg 1619; and MAHLMANN 1996.

grounding to the doctrine.[7] When later Lutherans such as Abraham Calov began to include a *locus* on mystical union in their theological systems, they retained that ecclesial focus. Calov makes this particularly clear when he describes mystical union as a *desponsatio mystica*—and in so doing repeats the language and biblical references used by his predecessors in their ecclesiologies; union is a kind of betrothal, and in this case the bride is the church:

> Sponsa est Ecclesia, et anima quaevis fidelis, casta, et sancta. Vinculum est fides. Forma est unitas Christi cum fidelibus, qui sunt unus spiritus, quemadmodum mas et foemina sunt in unam carnem [...] conjugii indissolubilitas.[8]

In this context, Calov clearly speaks of a "conjugi[um] Christi cum Ecclesia" that may also be described as an "unio mystica Christi capitis cum membris suis fidelibus"[9], thereby highlighting the doctrine's conceptual origins. One should also note that Calov almost always refers to the human "subject" of mystical union in the plural, describing it as an *unio fidelium cum Christo mystica*,[10] or, as in the corresponding heading: "De unione mystica cum

---

[7] Especially clear evidence along these lines comes from an early disputation by Leonhard Hutter on CA 7 and 8: HUTTER, *De ecclesia, ex septimo et octavo Confeßionis Augustanae articulis/ Resp. Casparus Rigeman* [held on March 18, 1598] (Wittenberg 1598). Hutter, writing before the development of an explicit *unio-mystica*-doctrine, anticipates that doctrine by describing a "spiritual conjunction of souls in faith and in the Spirit". Significantly, it is his definition of "congregation" and comes as an answer to the question: "Quid sit ecclesia?":

"Congregatio, quae Generis locum obtinet, denotat et externam illam societatem sive conventum piorum in templis: et inernam illam fidelium communionem, sive spiritualem animorum conjunctionem, in fide et Spiritu." (Hutter, *De ecclesia*, th. 151)

Other Lutheran theologians of this period showed similar interests. One notable example comes with DAVID RUNGE, *De societate et participatione ecclesiae illi catholicae communi, ex verbis sanctorum communionem / Resp. Bernhard Textorius* [held on May 9, 1601] (Wittenberg, 1601). Runge asks what, exactly holds the *koinonia* together, and mentions, among other things, a spiritual union of Christ with his believers that also effects a union of the believers with each other:

"Huius corporis spiritualis caput est Christus. Eph. 1, v. 22; Coll. 1, v. 18. Fideles omnes in toto terrarum orbe, sunt ejus membra, Eph. 1, v. 23. Inter se autem commembra. Unio illa Christi cum membris suis et membrorum inter se confirmatur etiam Ioh. 15, 5; 1. Cor. 6, 17; 1. Ioh. 4, 13." (Runge, op. cit., th. 8)

[8] CALOV, *Systema*, tom. X, 572–573.
[9] CALOV, *Systema*, tom. X, 573.
[10] CALOV, *Systema*, tom. X, 568.

fidelibus".[11] The "subject" of mystical union and divine inhabitation is not an individual, but believers in plural: "Subjectum inhabitationis divina, et unionis cum Deo sunt credentes."[12] And finally, the point of mystical union, according to Calov, involves in general terms sanctification and conservation of the believers[13], but more specifically results in an empowering of the believers to act as spiritual "prophets, priests and kings"[14]—i.e. in making them more effective servants to the church and to their fellow human beings.

As these examples illustrate, Calov and his orthodox contemporaries were certainly sensitive to more individual aspects of spiritual experience. But they were also careful to place such experience in an ecclesial context; they define the church as the place in which such experience comes to fruition—and where those fruits are put to use. This is evident not only in their doctrines of applied grace, but also in their descriptions of the *media salutis*. Word and Sacraments effect an experience of being one with other believers in the body of Christ—an experience of "church." In that sense, one may say that a central theme of CA 7, namely the power of an efficacious Word to assemble human beings in—and as—church, not only is retained by Orthodoxy's dogmatic systems, but remains fundamental to the conceptuality of those systems as a whole.

CA 7 exerted more specific influences on early Lutheran ecclesiologies, too. At the level of language, most disputations on ecclesiology contained either direct quotes of CA 7 or at least some reference to the words of that text. Interestingly, though, Article Seven's basic definition of the church as "congregatio sanctorum" was rarely used by later Lutherans in their own definitions. This may be a consequence of criticisms that had been voiced

---

[11] Calov, *Systema*, tom. X, 505. When Calov does use the singular, as in the definition on this same page, he does so to denote a collective noun, as in "mystical union, by which God conjoins himself with believing *man* in faith... (Unio mystica est, qua Deus cum homine credente per fidem conjungitur)".

[12] Calov, *Systema*, tom. X, 506.

[13] "Finis est, ut impleat nos gratiae plenitudine, et conservat nos usque ad gloriae impletionem." (Calov, *Systema*, tom. X, 507)

[14] Calov spells out this dimension of the mystical union in a corresponding doctrine of mystical or spiritual unction, which he regards as a consequence of *unio mystica*: "Unctio mystica est, qua renati virtute Unctionis Christi Spiritu Sancto delibuti, donis ejus instructi sunt, ut spirituales Prophetae, Sacerdotes, et Reges." (Calov, *Systema*, tom. X, 568)

in the Confutatio[15] and were taken up by Melanchthon's Apology[16]. Critics had read "congregation of saints" in a Hussite sense, charging that the church, so understood, includes only the elect and exludes all the rest.[17] After defending the definition extensively in the Apology[18], Melanchthon dropped it from his own writings; by the 1535 edition of his *Loci theologici* he had replaced it with "congregatio iustorum"[19], and in the *Loci* of 1559 he uses a thoroughly re-worked definition:

> Ecclesia visibilis est coetus amplectentium Evangelium Christi et recte utentium Sacramentis, in quo Deus per ministerium Evangelii est efficax et multos ad vitam aeternam regenerat, in quo coetu tamen multi sunt non renati, sed de vera doctrina consentientes.[20]

While Melanchthon does not, as far as I know, comment on his motives for making these changes, the final definition appears influenced by the exchange with the Confutatio. His emphasis on the *visible* nature of the church and his mentioning of members who are "not reborn" addresses the dangers of perfectionism and spiritualism in ways that the language of CA 7 did not. Certainly, his insistence that the church is "visible" responds to charges leveled by Johann Eck, among others, that Lutherans understood the church as a spiritualised "mathematical" or "Platonic"

---

[15] Cf. CR 27, 105; also: *Die Confutatio der Confessio Augustana vom 3. August 1530*, ed. by Herbert Immenkötter, Münster 1979 (Corpus Catholicorum 33), 95–96.

[16] Cf. BSLK[10], 233–246.

[17] The Confutatio begins with the following point, rejecting what it takes to be CA 7's description of the church as a congregation of only saints:
Septimus confessionis articulus, quo affirmatur ecclesiam esse congregatio sanctorum, non potest citra fidei praeiudicium admitti, si per hoc segregentur mali et peccatores. Nam articulus ille in Constantiensi condemnatus est concilio inter errores damnatae memoriae Joannis Huss et plane contradicit evangelio. Nam ibi legitur Johannem Baptistam comparasse ecclesiam areae, quam Christus permundabit ventilabro suo *et congregabit triticum in horreum suum, paleas autem comburet igni inextinguibili*, Mat. 3. Quid autem paleae significant, nisi malos sicuti triticum bonos? Et Christus ecclesiam comparavit saganae, in qua sunt pisces boni et mali, Matth. 13. Christus item comparat ecclesiam decem virginibus, quarum quinque erant prudentes et quinque fatuae, Matth. 25. Quapropter hic articulus confessionis omnino non acceptatur. (*Confutatio* 95f).

[18] BSLK[10], 233–246, especially 233–241.

[19] CR 21, 506.

[20] CR 21, 826.

idea devoid of visible marks.[21] Melanchthon retained this emphasis on the Church's visibility—and a rejection of an *ecclesia invisibilis*—in all of his writings.

As some scholars have observed, the 1559 definition contains an ambiguity that had already been present in the different wording of CA 7: it leaves open whether the church is an assembly constituted 1) by the preached Gospel and utilized Sacraments, or 2) by preaching the Gospel and using the Sacraments. In Melanchthon's definition, the church is both. It is at once the place where saved humans are and the mediating agency through which they are saved. If modern scholars have difficulty reconciling these points, Lutheran Orthodox theologians seem not to have been troubled by, or even aware of the distinction. That characteristic may stem from their emphasis on the efficacy of the Word. Preaching, while generally mediated by human beings as *causa instrumentalis*, nonetheless remains an act of God—whether it is involved in constituting the church or being done by persons already in the constituted church. Proclamation through Word and Sacrament, then, belongs to the nature of the church in such a basic way that engaging in that—divine—activity is what humans do as a result of being called to the church. The Word not only causes people to come together as church, it also causes them to proclaim it as church. While they did not state the conceptual problem in the terms above, Lutheran Orthodox theologians could also have responded by pointing to their widely used notions of *inhabitatio Dei* or *unio cum Christo*: As God applies grace to the believer, God also "enters" and "takes up residence in" the believer. As a consequence, the same activity that God had used

---

[21] Johannes Eck, *Enchiridion locorum communium adversus Lutherum et alios hostes ecclesiae (1525–1543)*. Ed. Pierre Fraenkel. Aschendorff: Münster, 1979 [Corpus Catholicorum 34], 33f: "Si ecclesia est occulta, quomodo Christus praecepit 'dicendum ecclesiae, et si ecclesiam non audierit', etc.? Si autem esset [ecclesia] occulta, quod posset ei dici, aut quomodo audierit? Similiter ecclesia corpus Christi, et Christiani membra: Rom. 12, 4.5; 1Cor 1 [10, 17]; et 12, 12–30. Eph. 1, 23; 5, 22–32; Col. 1, 18. Dicat Lutherus an illi fuerunt occulti et solum mathematice [dt. 'fantaseisch'] ecclesia, quando dixit Paulus: 'Vos autem estis corpus Christi et membra de membro'. Haereticorum est habere criptas, speluncas et latebras; ecclesia 'ponit lucernam super candelabrum': Monstratur tibi ecclesia in conciliis, in Sede apostolica, in episcopis et praepositis singularum ecclesiarum. Nam si solum mathematica esset ecclesia, frater Pauli non haberet 'laudem per omnes ecclesias'; non diceret David: 'Apud te laus mea in ecclesia plebis, et in cathedra seniorum laudent eum'. Pro hoc vide Augustinum, Super Canonica Ioannis, tractatu primo, in fine."

to call and convert the believer is now continued "in" the believer—i.e. using the believer as mediating agent. Against that light, one may say that, to early Lutherans, the church was both an object and agent of grace simultaneously.

Most Lutheran Orthodox theologians adopted Melanchthon's definition of the 1559 *Loci* rather than that of CA 7—even when commenting directly on CA 7. Those who stay closer to the Confession's language tend to replace *congregatio sanctorum* with *congregatio vocatorum*.[22] Those few who do quote CA 7's definition directly, do so with specific reasons in mind. Leonhard Hutter, for example, begins his 1598 disputation on Articles Seven and Eight of the Confession[23] by describing the visible church as a *coetus vocatorum*,[24] but goes on later to answer the question "quid sit Ecclesia?" with language quoted from CA 7.[25] He then continues by defining both *congregatio* and its specification as *congregatio sanctorum*—something which the Confession had not done, but which allows Hutter to reiterate a theme he sounded at other points in the disputation: aside from being an external assembly of pious people in church, a congregation is also an internal communion of the faithful, a spiritual conjoining of souls in faith and the Holy Spirit. This "internal" aspect is particularly important because it allows the congregation to exist even when tyrants prohibit its "external" assembly, as Hutter goes on to observe.[26] In making this point, Hutter echoes a theme of the Apology, which had described the church

---

[22] Cf. ÄGIDIUS HUNNIUS, *De ecclesia, ex septimo articulo Augustanae Confessionis / Resp. Andreas Schafmann* (Wittenberg, 1593), th. 3: Hunnius defines the visible church as a "congregatio vocatorum, amplectentium verbum Dei, et utentium Sacramentis". Other theologians using the *congregatio/coetus vocatorum* terminology include GEORG MYLIUS, "De ecclesia disputatio contra Pontificis, ad cuius positiones"/ Resp. Paulus Laurentius (Jena 1595); JOHANN GEORG VOLCKMAR, *De vera Christi in terris ecclesia,et num ea in fide errare et deficere possit, contra Pontificios / Prop. Hermann Wolf, Resp. Georg Schwegler* (Wittenberg, 1596); HUTTER, *De ecclesia*; DAVID RUNGE, *De ecclesia, ex verbis sanctam ecclesiam catholicam / Resp. Axel Oxenstierna* (Wittenberg 1601); and others.

[23] HUTTER, *De ecclesia* (cf. n. 6, above).

[24] HUTTER, *De ecclesia*, th. 8.

[25] HUTTER, *De ecclesia*, th. 149: "Confessio nostra, his ita praemissis, definit Ecclesiam, *Quod sit Congregatio sanctorum, in qua Evangelium recte docetur, & Sacramenta recte administrantur*."

[26] HUTTER, *De ecclesia*, th. 151: "Congregatio, quae Generis locum obtinet, denotat & externam illam societatem sive conventum piorum in templis: & internam illam fidelium communionem, sive spiritualem animorum conjunctionem, in fide & Spiritu: Qua sola interdum pii contenti esse debent, prohibente externum illum conventum Tyrannorum crudelitate."

principally as a "societas fidei et spiritus sancti in cordibus"—to which certain "external" marks do, of course, adhere, but which remains first and foremost a spiritual body.²⁷

Like many of his contemporaries, Hutter shows an interest in defining the nature of that spiritual fellowship further. His description of the congregation as a spiritual conjoining of souls in faith continues a line of thought he had opened earlier in the disputation while speaking about the unity of the church. Here he had anchored that spiritual unity in the Eucharist—those who partake of the Sacrament are conjoined in a unity that transcends space, time and all other external conditions.²⁸ This is certainly a viable interpretation of CA 7's insistence that unity of the church is predicated upon agreement in doctrine and in the administration of the sacraments, but in interpreting the text, Hutter has shifted its focus. Unity of the church, in his view, comes to be not by a second-order consensus on the Sacraments, but is effected by the Sacraments themselves (specifically the Eucharist). All who participate in the Sacraments are bonded together by the Spirit into one transcendent body.²⁹

What constitutes—and marks—true unity of the church is a question that most of Hutter's contemporaries had also addressed. Surveying their treatments of the issue quickly gives one the impression that CA 7's

---

²⁷ BSLK¹⁰, 234,5: "At ecclesia non est tantum societas externarum rerum ac rituum sicut aliae politiae, sed principaliter est societas fidei et spiritus sancti in cordibus, quae tamen habet externas notas, ut agnosci possit, videlicet puram evangelii doctrinam et administrationem sacramentorum consentaneam evangelio Christi." Cf. BSLK¹⁰, 236,16ff: "At sic Paulus discernit ecclesiam a populo legis, quod ecclesia sit populus spiritualis, hoc est, non civilibus ritibus distinctus a gentibus, sed verus populus Dei, renatus per spiritum sanctum."

²⁸ HUTTER, *De ecclesia*, th. 51–55.

²⁹ Explaining why it is that there can be many *ecclesiae particulares* and at the same time one *catholica ecclesia*, Hutter writes: "[Th. 51] Porro unitatem Ecclesiae non labefactat, quod multae particulares sive Topicae dicuntur esse Ecclesiae, locis, regionibus, provinciis, quin et regnis orbis Christiani distinctae. [Th. 52] Manet enim nihilominus una tantum Catholica Ecclesia, particulares illas omnes, ceu mater filias suo ambitu complectens. Una enim est columba mea, una est perfecta mea, Cant. 6.8. [Th. 53] Ratio affirmati est isthaec, Quia unitas Ecclesiae non consistit in loci, temporis, corporum, aut ulla cujusquam rei externa conditione: sed in conjunctione fidei, & Spiritus ipsius vinculo. [Th. 54] Hinc adeo fit, ut quotquot fide ista participant, & ubicunque Sacramenta ex institutione Christi dispensantur: unitate ista omnes quantumvis etiam locorum intervallis disjuncti ac dissiti, contineantur. [Th. 55] Ab hac unitatis Ecclesiae forma & societatis sive communionis universalis complexu Symbolum Apostolicum Catholicam appellitare voluit Ecclesiam."

"satis est" was anything but sufficient. Ägidius Hunnius spells out three conditions for church unity: communion as a mystical body with Christ as head[30]; consensus in doctrine[31]; and a bond of mutual love and support (*nexus charitatis*)[32]. Only the second is mentioned directly by CA 7. What motivated Hunnius to depart in such an obvious way from the text of the Confession remains unclear. In any case, his move raised no eyebrows at the time—and he did not remain alone. Hutter ennumerates the same factors as Hunnius but distinguishes between communion with Christ and unity in the Spirit, thereby creating four conditions.[33] Later theologians continued this line of thought, occasionally substituting "faith in the fundamental articles" for "consensus in doctrine"[34], or, more frequently, elaborating on the notion of mutual charity. Clearly, the "satis est" formula of CA 7 was far less important to early Lutherans than to many of their contemporary successors.

One of the most eloquent exponents of Christian charity and its ecclesiological signficance was the Wittenberg theologian Andreas Kunad. Writing in 1655, Kunad largely follows his predecessors—but not CA 7—in naming three conditions for church unity: unity in faith, consensus in the doctrine of salvation, and a band of charity (*unitas fidei, consensus*

---

[30] HUNNIUS, *De ecclesia* (cf. n. 14), th. 9: "Et primoquidem, ad constituendam eam unitatem, communio capitis requiritur, quod est Christus Iesus, Eph. 1 & 5. [Th. 10] Unitas quoque Spiritus, per quem in societatem corporis mystici sub uno capite Iesu Christo copulamur."

[31] HUNNIUS, *De ecclesia*, th. 11: "Requiritur et consensus in doctrina, seu fidei unitas, qua sumus unum in Christo, unum in veritate, Ioan. 17, eadem mente eademque sententia 1. Cor. 1."

[32] HUNNIUS, *De ecclesia*, th. 12: "Requiritur et charitatis nexus, haec namque vinculum est perfectionis, Coloß. 1. Christianos simul omnes in unum perfectum corpus devinciens, ut tanquam unius eiusdemque corporis membra in mutuam sui conservationem et aedificationem pulcherrime conspirent."

[33] HUTTER, *De ecclesia.*, th. 33–36: "[Th. 33] Caeterum ad constituendam Ecclesiae unitatem, ex descriptione Apostolica quatuor potissimum προσκείμενα requiruntur: I. Communio capitis, quod est Christus. Ephes. 1,22 et cap. 5,23. [Th. 34] II. Consensus in doctrina, sive fidei unitas, qua unum sumus in Christo, unum in veritate. Ioh. 17,11 et 19 eadem mente, eademque sententia 1. Cor. 1,10. [Th. 35] III. Charitatis mutuae nexus: haec siquidem perfectionis vinculum, in unum perfectum Corpus Christianos devincit. [Th. 36] IV. Unitas Spiritus, per quem in societatem Corporis mystici, quod est Ecclesia, sub uno capite Iesu Christo copulamur."

[34] E.g. JOHANNES MEISNER, Disputatio XVIII. De ecclesia et ministerio ecclesiastico / Resp. Georg Werckmeister – J. MEISNER, *Compendium theologiae* (Wittenberg, 1652).

in doctrina salutis, vinculum charitatis).³⁵ Kunad then goes on to describe that unity more closely. Church unity, he argues, is an "inner" unity, consisting formally in faith in Christ, by which the faithful are connected to Christ and through him participate in the life of the Holy Spirit which makes them "co-members" of one body. This "inner unity" lets the various members cohere and communicate with each other, obliterating all distinctions of rank, sex and race (referring to Gal. 3, 26–28)³⁶. It finds expression in mutual charity, praying for and serving one another, and a sharing of spiritual goods and hardships. In this vein, Kunad exchanges the traditional definitions of the church as "congregatio sanctorum" or "coetus vocatorum" for something entirely new: he defines the church as a "coetus renatorum".³⁷

That kind of pastoral idealism has a counterpart in Kunad's comparatively irenical attitude toward doctrine. While some theologians of this period appear to treat doctrinal consensus as if it were an end to itself, expanding the list of fundamental articles whenever a new group or confession needed to be excluded, Kunad keeps this criterion focused narrowly on doctrine as foundation of preaching and as means to salvific faith: Since saving faith is born of the preaching of the Gospel, agreement on the doctrine of salvation, which is the basis of that preaching, is required. Specifically, such doctrine teaches what we need to know and believe about the Triune God, about Christ as Theanthropos, and everything relating to our salvation³⁸; other (in his opinion: most) doctrinal matters are non-fundamental and do not need to be agreed upon.³⁹ Clearly, Kunad is more concerned with moving beyond such "external" matters and on to the inner unity characterized by mystical union with Christ and mutual charity

---

³⁵ ANDREAS KUNAD, *Disputatio theologica de ecclesiae unitate, Jodoco Keddio Jesuitapotiss. opposita / Resp. Matthias Eber* (Wittenberg, 1655), th. 7.

³⁶ KUNAD, *Disputatio theologica*, th. 7.

³⁷ KUNAD, *Disputatio theologica*, th. 25. He makes more explicit use of this definition in another ecclesiological disputation: A. KUNAD, Disputatio XV. De ecclesia / Resp. Heinrich Henning – KUNAD, *Locorum theologicorum compendium* (Wittenberg, 1659), th. 6.

³⁸ A. KUNAD, Disputatio XV, th. 8: "Cum autem Fides salvifica ex praedicatione Evangelii nascatur, eadem opera etiam requiritur Consensus in doctrina salutis, & necesse est, ut omnes idem sentiant & credant. Nam Evangelium proponit Nobis verum Objectum Fidei, quid sciri ac credi oporteat de Deo Trinuno, de Christo Θεανθρωπω, adeoque de toto negotio nostrae salutis. ..."

³⁹ A. KUNAD, Disputatio XV, th. 9.

among the believers.⁴⁰ This shapes his assessment of public agreements of doctrine and of oaths sworn to the confessions: these kinds of "external testimony" are useful only insofar as they foster public peace and harmony; they say nothing at all about a "communio spiritualis sanctorum interna". Therefore, Kunad concludes, freedom of conscience should be granted in matters of doctrine.⁴¹ As this brief description suggests, Kunad has adopted a remarkably loose interpretation of CA 7's conditions of unity and seems, in general, to focus on ecclesiological concerns that have little to do with those of the Augsburg Confession.

While Kunad's conceptuality is fairly unique within mid-century Orthodoxy, his detachment from the language of CA 7 is characteristic of most Lutheran theologians of this age. Abraham Calov makes virtually no use at all of the Augsburg Confession in his own ecclesiology, as spelled out in Book Eight of his *Systema*, entitled "Ekklesiometria". The only point of contact lies in Calov's commitment to demonstrating the church's perpetuity. This is a concern he shares with several other 17th-century Lutherans, and it is precipated by controversies with the Socinians, a unitarian group active in Eastern Europe. The Socinians rejected the notion that there was a church during the time of the Old Testament, and theologians like Wolfgang Franz⁴² and his successor in Wittenberg, Calov, took pains to demonstrate the opposite. Calov unfolds a monumental, 14-chapter salvation-historical account of the Church Before the Flood, the Patriarchal Church after the Flood, the Israelitic Church under Theurgic and Mosaic Rule, and so on up to the Reformation; from thence he offers a glimpse ahead to the End of the World. While, theoretically, one could regard this account as a defense of the first sentence of CA 7, the relationship is rather tenuous.

On many of the 17-century's important ecclesiological issues, CA 7 was

---

⁴⁰ A. KUNAD, Disputatio XV, th. 10. KUNAD addresses the "unio fidelium cum Christo" and "unio fidelium inter se" more explicitly in De ecclesia, th. 10–11. For quotes and analysis, cf. APPOLD 2004, 288-289.

⁴¹ KUNAD, *Disputatio theologica*, th. 12–13. In invoking freedom of conscience in this manner, Kunad has in mind the practice of requiring oaths of allegiance to the CA or the Book of Concord in use at many German universities at this time. His criticism anticipates similar arguments by Pietists toward the end of the 17th century.

⁴² Cf. especially WOLFGANG FRANZ, *De ecclesia, pro Aug. Conf. art. Septimo/ Resp. Johannes Moshauer* (Wittenberg, 1609). For an analysis, cf. APPOLD 2004, 236–241.

simply not much help. Ecclesiological discussion focused much more on controversialist exchanges than on the Confession itself; for Lutherans, this meant, above all, extended disputes with Roberto Bellarmine and later members of his Jesuit order. One of the biggest battles concerned the question of defining—and recognizing—the true church. It centered on the issue of *notae ecclesiae*. The Augsburg Confession does not mention these marks of the true church explicitly, but one could derive two without too much trouble: preaching of the Gospel and administration of the Sacraments. Indeed, many Lutherans of the time pointed to those two. More than a few, including Melanchthon in an early disputation and in the *Examen ordinandorum*[43], added a third: obedience to the ministry, or, in other words, church discipline. There seemed little agreement—or controversy—within post-Reformation Lutheranism on this point. What did unite Lutherans was their rejection of Bellarmine's list of thirteen, of which submission to the pope and episcopal succession were considered the most odious.

Another central concern of post-Reformation ecclesiology lay in distinguishing between a visible and an invisible church. Melanchthon, as mentioned earlier, strenuously rejected the notion of an *ecclesia invisibilis* and his reasons for doing so are spelled out clearly in the Apology. Luther, on the other hand, had mentioned something like an invisible church[44], preferring instead the notion of an "inner" church, but these references were oblique when compared to the teachings of Zwingli or the Württemberg Reformer Johannes Brenz. Both took up a traditional Hussite theme and described the true church, consisting only of the predestined, as something distinct from the one that was visible and contained far more. Critics accused Zwingli, in particular, of positing a "twofold" church, and Lutherans sought to avoid that charge. They argued that while the body of true believers remains invisible to human eyes, it is inseparable from the visible church that administers the only ordinary means of grace: Word and Sacrament. No one who is not in the visible church, so the Lutheran argument, could be in the invisible church. Melanchthon's influence kept the doctrine of an *ecclesia invisibilis* out of Lutheran circulation for a while,

---

[43] Cf. CR 12, 488; CR 23, 37.
[44] Cf. WA 3, 183; WA 4, 107; WA 7, 709f; WA 39^{II}, 161.

but one of Brenz's compatriots, the Tübingen theologian Jacob Heerbrand, reinstated it in his influential theological compendium of the 1570s.[45] Most Lutherans (with the notable exception of Johann Andreas Quenstedt) now included an account of the *ecclesia invisibilis* in their ecclesiologies, always careful to refute the charge of a "twofold church". What Lutherans of this period could not agree upon, however, was how to relate the distinction of a visible and invisible church to the various attributes applied to the church, especially those of unity, sanctity, apostolicity and catholicity. CA 7 gave them little guidance. That fact, in turn, meant that, whatever option they chose, it would not be in explicit conflict with the Confession. Some, like Polycarp Leyser and Johann Gerhard, attributed unity and catholicity to the invisible church; most others, however, applied these attributes to the *ecclesia visibilis*. This last move was problematic, for if the church's catholicity and unity belong to the visible church, then catholicity and unity themselves must, by extension, be visible. There were many strategies for dealing with this problem; most appealed to the above-described conditions of unity: communion with Christ and corporate unity with the Holy Spirit (particulary when mediated by Word and Sacraments), agreement in doctrine, and the bands of mutual charity. Orthodoxy's attempt to describe visible unity and visible catholicity is laudable from a contemporary ecumenical perspective—and generally unknown to contemporary Lutherans—but none of the conceptualities employed proved very durable. Still, Orthodoxy's concern highlights a perennial deficit in Lutheran ecclesiology: how to define the external aspects of the church which are so patently indispensable. No one was satisfied with defining the church simply in spiritual or "inner" terms; but there was less unanimity on defining the external conditions and marks of unity. The requirements stipulated by a "minimal reading" of CA 7 were clearly inadequate in meeting that challenge—and that may be why such a reading would have been completely foreign to early Lutheranism. Lutheran theologians of the 16th and 17th centuries were not at all interested in minimizing requirements for unity; they expanded them constantly. But

---

[45] JACOB HEERBRAND, *Compendium theologiae* (Tübingen, 1576); Heebrand expanded the doctrine in a reworked version of the *Compendium theologiae* (Tübingen, 1578). Cf. APPOLD 2004, 171–176.

they were unable to agree on a doctrinal formula that brought together the external characteristics they saw as necessary consequences of the spiritual unity they cherished.[46]

As I observed at the outset of this paper, the Augsburg Confession occupied a place of central importance for the doctrinal reflection of Lutheran Orthodoxy. The CA's authority was so great that some Orthodox theologians even attributed a kind of indirect *theopneustia* to the document. Nonetheless, their attitude toward the Confession was in many ways less reserved or deferential than that of many "confessional" Lutherans today. For one thing, few Lutherans of the 17th century viewed the process of writing confessions as something that had come to an end with the Book of Concord. In that sense, they fully believed that issues not treated with sufficient clarity or breadth by the CA could be addressed by future confessional statements. An example of such an attempt to amend the CA came at mid-century and was occasioned by inner-Lutheran conflicts between exponents of Orthodoxy and the so-called Syncretists gathered around Georg Calixt. A coalition of theologians in Wittenberg, Leipzig and Jena drafted a document known as the *Consensus repetitus fidei vere lutheranae* (1666) and sought to have it ratified by other faculties. That attempt failed, but it reveals the areas where this group of conservative Lutherans thought the Confession—and its Seventh Article—should be improved. Most of these changes reflect the particular historical circumstances surrounding the *Consensus*; they call for a clear rejection of all who would count Papists and Calvinists as part of the one true church (the Greeks, by the way, do belong to the true church, according to the *Consensus*[47]); they affirm the condemnations of the Augsburg Confession—what was condemned then, is condemned now.[48] One addition to CA 7 appears more neutral and takes up the often-heard theme of an "inner unity" in the church: the text begins by defining the church as being principally a society of faith and of the Holy Spirit in the [believers'] hearts. This church may be recognized by (two) external marks: its pure doctrine of the Gospel and its administration of the

---

[46] The reasons for this need to be studied further and cannot be elaborated in the space provided here.

[47] *Consensus repetitus fidei vere lutheranae* (Wittenberg, 1666), p. 75–76.

[48] *Consensus repetitus fidei vere lutheranae*, 79–80.

Sacraments.[49] It is worth noting the precise formulation of the first *nota*: rather than using the verb "docetur" to signify the fact that the Gospel "is taught" in true churches, the *Consensus* shifts to the substantive "doctrina"; in this light, the church is true because it *has* pure doctrine, not because of what it *does* with that doctrine.[50] As if to underscore that point, the authors of the *Consensus* continue by defining the church as a "column of truth that retains the pure Gospel and foundation, that is, true knowledge of Christ and faith."[51] The authors point out that their adversaries, the Papists and Calvinists, destroy that foundation and cannot, in this sense, be part of the "true church".[52] Whether those changes may considered "improvements" to CA 7 need not be decided here. Certainly, the focus on cognitive possession of pure doctrine marks a reduction of the Confession's ecclesiological scope; it is, one should also say, not representative of Lutheran Orthodoxy as a whole—not even of the Wittenberg school. In fact, even Abraham Calov, who was involved in preparing the *Consensus* and promoted it energetically, spells out a much more comprehensive—and much more interesting—ecclesiology in his Systema.

The *Consensus repetitus fidei* is representative in one sense, however: like most ecclesiologies of the Orthodox era, it upholds the authority of CA 7 while at the same time moving beyond that text. CA 7 provided a point of departure for Lutheran ecclesiologies of this era, but not much more. Its main themes—the centrality of Word and Sacrament to the life and definition of the church, the church's perpetuity—are retained, but are no longer in the forefront of the theological effort. New concerns have emerged and eclipsed those of 1530. Nowhere is that more evident than in discussions of church unity. Here Lutheran Orthodox theologians pay no

---

[49] "Profitemur & docemus, Ecclesiam veram principaliter esse societatem fidei & Spiritus S. in cordibus. Quae tamen habet externas notas, ut agnosci possit, videlicet puram Evangelii Doctrinam, & administrationem Sacramentorum, consentaneam Evangelio Christi." (*Consensus repetitus fidei vere lutheranae*, 75)

[50] It may be worth comparing this shift to the much different language of Andreas Kunad, above. Kunad was a member of the Wittenberg faculty during the preparation of the Consensus, but does not appear to have played a significant role; he died before the text was published.

[51] "Quare Ecclesia proprie est columna veritatis, retinetque purum Evangelium, &, ut Paulus inquit, fundamentum, hoc est, veram Christi cognitionem, & fidem." *Consensus repetitus fidei vere lutheranae*, 75.

[52] *Consensus repetitus fidei vere lutheranae*.

heed to CA 7's "satis est" and liberally add conditions of their own. "Satis est" was not "satis" to early Lutherans.

Bibliography

APPOLD, Kenneth
1998   *Abraham Calov's Doctrine of Vocatio in Its Systematic Context.* BHTh 103. Tübingen.
2004   *Orthodoxie als Konsensbildung. Das theologische Disputationswesen an der Universität Wittenberg zwischen 1570 und 1710.* BHTh 127. Tübingen.

MAHLMANN, Theodor
1996   Die Stellung der unio cum Christo in der lutherischen Theologie des 17. Jahrhunderts– *Unio. Gott und Mensch in der nachreformatorischen Theologie*, ed. Matti Repo and Rainer Vinke. SLAG 35. Helsinki: Luther-Agricola-Society. 72–199.

God's Presence in Jesus Christ – Schleiermacher's Transformation of Luther's Christological Legacy

FRIEDERIKE NÜSSEL

Introduction

In historical research on the development and overall profile of Protestant thought, one intriguing and difficult question regards the relationship between Luther and Schleiermacher. On the occasion of the 150th anniversary of Friedrich Schleiermacher's death in March 1984, the International Schleiermacher Congress, held at Freie Universität in Berlin (Germany was still divided), the systematic theologian and Luther expert, Gerhard Ebeling, gave a keynote lecture on 'Luther and Schleiermacher.'[1] Drawing on earlier debates, Ebeling framed the importance of the relationship between Luther and Schleiermacher for the profile of Protestant theology and its future construction as such: "Luther und Schleiermacher—das ist, verschlüsselt in zwei Namen, seither immer noch, immer wieder die Konstellation protestantischer Theologie."[2]

While this statement still holds true for leading strands of German speaking Protestant Systematic Theology today, it is certainly not applicable to the plurality of Protestant theologies across the globe. Luther's theology is formative in many different contexts and regions, but this is not the case with Schleiermacher's theology. Nevertheless, in a European and North

---

[1] EBELING 1984, 21–38. Interestingly, in the section on 'The Notion of Protestantism – Schleiermacher as Politician, Church-Politician and Theologian of the Union,' Oswald BAYER contributed a paper with a complementary title to Ebeling's paper: 'Schleiermacher and Luther.'
[2] EBELING 1984, 22.

American context, especially in theological conversations between Finland and Germany, the reflection on discontinuity and continuity between the theologies of Luther and Schleiermacher can still serve as one (although not the only) heuristic lens by which to view the profile and future formation of protestant theology. This procedure necessitates one to ask fundamental methodological questions and make critical decisions.

Gerhard Ebeling's fundamental methodological decision in his Berlin lecture was not to compare Luther and Schleiermacher in their explanation of certain *dogmatic topoi*.[3] Instead, he proposed to concentrate on the distinctive character and role of religion in Luther and Schleiermacher which he, at his time, conceived to be a key question of modern Protestant theology. Ebeling identified structural analogies between Luther's understanding of reason and faith and Schleiermacher's understanding of religion. Additionally, he found that both authors, in their respective ways, criticize philosophical metaphysics and ethics. According to Ebeling's analysis, the remarkable continuity between Luther and Schleiermacher culminates in a similar understanding of theology as a practical discipline.[4] In line with one dominant strand of Schleiermacher research, Ebeling sees Schleiermacher's central contribution to post-Enlightenment theology in the development of the concept of religion by which Schleiermacher was able to develop a philosophy of religion that would take up Luther's emphasis on the salvific importance of individual certainty and trust in God's salvation and grace. Thus, Schleiermacher's notion of 'religion,' or later 'piety' (*Frömmigkeit*), translates and defends Luther's soteriological insight in the context of Enlightenment criticism of religion and Kantian epistemology. While Luther took the articles of faith to be speaking about God's redemptive and revelatory activity through Jesus Christ and the Holy Spirit, Schleiermacher, in response to the epistemological challenge of Kantian epistemology, concedes that a scholarly explanation

---

[3] In Ebeling's view, a comparison of dogmatic topoi would actually miss the real theological question involved in the relationship between Luther's and Schleiermacher's theologies. See EBELING 1984, 24.

[4] In a first step, Ebeling compares Luther's and Schleiermacher's critique of the theological role of metaphysics. Secondly, he demonstrates the convergence between Schleiermacher's understanding of 'feeling' and Luther's notion of 'conscience.' Thirdly, he shows a correlation in the practical character of theology that has to serve religion.

of the Christian faith can no longer take the articles of faith as referring to objective facts of divine revelation (*Offenbarungstatsachen*), but has to make clear that their status is to express the convictions of faith that are constitutive for the explicit pious Christian self-consciousness. In light of this significant change in the understanding of the articles of faith, it may seem appropriate that Ebeling did not attempt to explore the continuity between Luther and Schleiermacher with regard to dogmatic loci.

In spite of the different understandings of the articles of faith and the subject of dogmatics, there are certainly a number of significant dogmatic convergences between Luther and Schleiermacher. Five of such convergences deserve mention here. First, both theologians understood the Christian religion to be grounded in and centered on the person and redemptive work of Jesus Christ. Second, they were both convinced that divine redemption from sin and a renewal of the human relationship with God through Jesus Christ was necessary for human salvation and eternal beatitude and was caused by God's grace alone (*sola gratia*). Third, they were convinced that the only source of redemption[5] was the revelation of God's love in Jesus Christ for the sake of redemption and salvation (*solo Christo*). Fourth, each theologian was convinced that divine grace and redemption is communicated through the proclamation of the word in preaching and administration of sacraments (*solo verbo*). Lastly, both theologians understood human faith and trust in God to be the just and adequate relation towards God (*sola fide*). When it comes to Christology, however, the convergences come to an end. While Luther takes the Chalcedonian formula regarding the two natures of Jesus Christ and the one personhood of Jesus Christ as an adequate and theologically constitutive interpretation of the New Testament,[6] Schleiermacher offers a profound and detailed critique of this dogma and all its aspects in his dogmatics, *The Christian Faith*.[7] Unlike Luther and the old-Protestant teachings, Schleiermacher explains the salvific work and singularity of Christ's personhood in terms of extraordinary pious self-consciousness which was a perfect and uninterrupted God-consciousness. In this way, Schleiermacher gives up the traditional terminology of incarnational Christology. In his view, Christ's

---

[5] SCHLEIERMACHER 1999, § 93, 377–385.
[6] LUTHER 1966, 106ff.
[7] SCHLEIERMACHER 1999, § 95–98, 389–417.

perfect God-consciousness is the reason for Christ's singular personhood and for his being the cause of a new communal life that overcomes and replaces the old reign of sin which allows human beings to experience rebirth in conversion, justification, and sanctification.

Luther's Christological principle

Luther developed his Christology in different stages of his theological work in response to changing contexts and challenges. Before 1520, his Christological reflections focused on the salvific character of Christ's suffering death on the cross, especially in the Heidelberg disputations and sermons on scholastic theology (both in 1518 in his sermon on the true contemplation on the sacred suffering of Jesus Christ and in the sermon on the preparation to die (both in 1519). Only later, in the controversy with Zwingli, Karlstadt, and Oekolampad, was Luther driven to unpack the implications of his theology of the cross for the theology of incarnation and the understanding of the personhood of Jesus Christ in his comprehensive study *On the Lord's Supper* that ends with his own confession (1528). Here, Luther explores the particular unity of the person of Christ as constituted in the incarnation of the Logos, which, for him, is the backbone to understanding Christ's promise in the words of institution as a promise of his presence in, with, and under the elements of bread and wine in the Lord's Supper. Luther contradicts Zwingli's symbolic understanding of Christ's presence on the basis of three particular distinctions. First, the symbolic interpretation misses the literal meaning of the words of institution and denies the effective character of Christ's own promise.[8] Second, Zwingli's argument that the human nature can only be present at one place at a time, which leads him to deny the bodily presence of the risen Christ in the Lord's Supper, ignores the communication of divine omnipresence to human nature.[9] Third, and most importantly, Zwingli's

---

[8] FC SD VII, nr. 75–77. Cf. LUTHER 1909, 492,17–26.
[9] The argument builds on a distinction between different understandings of presence and omnipresence and is quoted in the Formula of Concord. In a first sense omnipresence involves comprehensible bodily (locally circumscribed) presence (FC SD VII, nr. 99, cf. Luther 1909, 335, 29–38). In a second sense, it involves incomprehensible spiritual presence, "according to which

symbolic understanding of the presence of Christ undercuts the unity of the person of Jesus Christ that is taught in the dogma of Chalcedon according to which "there are not [in Christ] two separate persons, but only one person." From the third point in particular, one can see Luther not only acknowledges, but builds on the theological impact of the old church's dogmatic decree. He argues against Zwingli:

> There it is the one undivided person; and wherever you can say, 'here is God,' there you must also say, 'then Christ the man is also there.' And if you would point out a place where God is, and not the man, the person would already be divided, because I could then say with truth: Here is God who is not man, and who never as yet has become man. However, no such a God for me! For it would follow hence that space and place separated the two natures from one another, and divided the person, and yet even death and all devils could not divide or rend them from one another. And there would remain to me a poor sort of Christ [a Christ of how much value, pray?], who would be a divine and human person at the same time in no more than in only one place, while in all other places He must be only a mere separate God and divine person without humanity. No, friend, wherever you place God, there you must also place with Him humanity; they do not allow themselves to be separated or divided from one another. There has been made [in Christ] one person, and it [the Son of God] does not separate from itself the [assumed] humanity.[10]

He neither occupies nor vacates space, but penetrates all creatures wherever He pleases [according to His most free will] ...This mode He used when He rose from the closed [and sealed] sepulcher, and passed through the closed door [to His disciples], and in the bread and wine in the Holy Supper, and, as it is believed, when He was born of His mother [the most holy Virgin Mary]" (FC SC VII, nr. 100, cf. Luther 1909, 335, 38–336, 7). In a third sense, the omnipresence transcends both the comprehensible bodily omnipresence and the incomprehensible spiritual form of presence in a sublime way: "For if, according to that second mode, He can be in and with creatures in such a manner that they do not feel, touch, circumscribe, or comprehend Him, how much more wonderfully will He be in all creatures according to this sublime third mode, so that they do not circumscribe nor comprehend Him, but rather that He has them present before Himself, circumscribes and comprehends them! For you must place this being of Christ, who is one person with God...far outside of the creatures, as far as God is outside of them; and again, as deep and near within all creatures as God is within them. For He is one inseparable person with God; where God is, there must He also be, or our faith is false. But who will say or think how this occurs? We know indeed that it is so, that He is in God outside of all creatures, and one person with God, but how it occurs we do not know; it [this mystery] is above nature and reason, even above the reason of all the angels in heaven; it is understood and known only by God. Now, since it is unknown to us, and yet true, we should not deny His words before we know how to prove to a certainty that the body of Christ can by no means be where God is, and that this mode of being [presence] is false." (FC SD VII, nr. 101–102, cf. LUTHER 1909, 336, 8–337, 26).

[10] FC SD VIII, nr. 82–83. Cf. LUTHER 1909, 332, 28–333, 8.

The pronounced phrase "wherever you place God, there you must also place with Him humanity" can be taken as a maxim of Luther's Christological thinking which he further interprets by drawing on the patristic teaching of *communicatio idiomatum*. His claim is that the unity of the two natures in Christ must not be perceived in analogy to two boards that are glued together — "so that they realiter, that is, in deed and truth, have no communion whatever with one another"[11] — but as a real communion that entails communication between the two natures. Thus, the Logos permeates the human nature and allows the human nature to participate in the divine presence.[12]

This communication also has implications for the understanding of the death of Jesus Christ. In line with his Christological maxim, Luther emphasizes in *Of the Councils and the Church* (1539) that Christ had not suffered on the cross only by his human nature:

> We Christians must know that if God is not also in the balance, and gives the weight, we sink to the bottom with our scale. By this I mean: If it were not to be said [if these things were not true], God has died for us, but only a man, we would be lost. But if 'God's death' and 'God died' lie in the scale of the balance, then He sinks down, and we rise up as a light, empty scale. But indeed, He can also rise again or leap out of the scale; yet He could not sit in the scale unless He became a man like us, so that it could be said: 'God died,' 'God's passion,' 'God's blood,' 'God's death.' For in His nature God cannot die; but now that God and man are united in one person, it is correctly called God's death, when the man dies who is one thing or one person with God.[13]

Thus, Luther explores the intimate communion that constitutes Christ's personhood in two directions. On the one hand, the human nature participates in the ubiquitous presence of the divine nature that renders real presence of Christ in the Sacrament of the Altar according to his promise. On the other hand, God shares in the life and suffering of the human nature and in this way overcomes the power of sin and death. If one had to say that only the human nature suffers (as Anselm of Canterbury did), this would in Luther's view dissolve the real unity of the person. This account cannot explain the salvific power of Christ's death on the cross.

---

[11] FC SD VIII, nr. 14. Cf. LUTHER 1914, 589, 21–33; 595, 18–34.
[12] FD SD VIII, nr. 27–30. Cf. LUTHER 1914, 598, 21–33; LUTHER 1909, 336, 8–337, 26.
[13] FD SD VIII, nr. 44. Cf. LUTHER 1914, 590, 11–22.

The discovery of mutuality and reciprocity in the reception of Luther's Christology

Luther's Christological interpretation of the real sacramental presence of Christ was a matter of debate among Lutherans already during Luther's lifetime, but even more so after his death. Even though the so-called gnesio-Lutheran debates between 1550 and 1577 centered on the doctrine of justification, the role of the law and of good works, a coherent explanation of the nature of the divine presence, of the unity of Christ's person, and of his humiliation became a pressing issue on the way to the Formula of Concord. Articles VII and VIII of the Formula of Concord demonstrate the longstanding influence of Luther's theology of the cross and of the eucharistic presence of Jesus Christ together with the Christological foundation which eventually led his theological heirs and the political rulers to reject the so-called 'Sacramentarian' account of Calvin and Zwingli in the Formula of Concord.

The specific character and profile of Lutheran theology was shaped through the debates about divine presence in correlation with the right understanding of Christ's personhood, which was in direct contrast to both Reformed and Roman Catholic thought.[14] In these debates, Lutheran theologians, in line with Luther, unanimously affirmed Christ's real and bodily presence in the Sacrament of the Altar as a consequence of the communication of divine omnipresence to the human nature of Christ in the incarnation. Additionally, in defense of Luther's doctrine, they also emphasized the unity of the personhood of Christ and developed a grammar of Christological language in the doctrines of *communio naturarum* and *communicatio idiomatum*. The challenge, however, was how to account for the reality of the humiliation during the earthly life of Jesus. On this particular issue different approaches were developed and led to intense Christological debates in the last two decades of the 16th century and in the early 17th century. The debates culminated in the so-called 'kenosis-crypsis-controversy' between theologians in Gießen and in Tübingen between 1619 and 1624.[15] Already, some contemporaries ridiculed this debate

---

[14] Cf. Nüssel 2008, 62–83.
[15] Cf. Wiedenroth 2011.

as an example of theological argumentativeness and over-sophistication. Nevertheless, it reveals the Lutheran concerns in Christology and the core idea that drove further development of Lutheran thinking and informed not only Hegel's philosophy of religion, but (as I argue here) also the account of Christ's personhood in Schleiermacher's *The Christian Faith*. In order to demonstrate this, it is necessary to have a brief look at the important points of the 'kenosis-crypsis-controversy.'

The debate started with a letter from the Gießen theologian, Balthasar Mentzer, to his Tübingen colleagues. He asked for support in a debate within his own faculty on the nature of divine omnipresence. In the internal debate in Gießen, Mentzer wanted to develop an argument against the reformed critique of ubiquity and defined omnipresence in terms of pure activity — an idea that was rather innovative in the context of the substance ontology of the time. Interestingly, the Tübingen colleagues did not respond to this first letter and only wrote back after a second request. In an astute and comprehensive reconstruction of the debate, Ulrich Wiedenroth shows that one reason for the Tübingen theologians' hesitance to respond was that they were in the process of rethinking Christology themselves. But while in Gießen the question of omnipresence was in the center, the primary theological concern of Tübingen theologians was to develop a coherent understanding of the unity of the personhood of Christ as constituted by *mutual* and *reciprocal* communication between the divine and human nature. As Wiedenroth demonstrates, it was the principle of *mutuality* and *reciprocity* that at a certain point began to motivate and trigger the development of Christological thinking in Tübingen in the early 17th century. Inspired from the reciprocal character of Luther's Christological maxims, according to which the Divine takes part in human humiliation and the human nature enjoys divine perfection in terms of almightiness and omnipresence, the Tübingen scholars aimed to give a biblically grounded and philosophically consistent account of the personhood of Christ in which reciprocal communication constituted the personhood of Jesus Christ.

It was Theodor Thumm who developed the final version of Tübingen's Christological concept and response to Gießen in two writings.[16] Thumm

---

[16] Cf. THUMM 1624.

revisits the Lutheran Christological teaching of the *communicatio idiomatum* and describes the incarnation as a communicative, reciprocal process in which the Logos makes himself present to the human nature, life, and suffering while the human nature participates in the divine almightiness, omniscience, and omnipresence. In Thumm's account, the personhood of Jesus Christ is solely constituted in mutual and reciprocal giving and taking. It is important to note that reciprocity here does not entail fully symmetrical relations, which would be impossible since in the communicative process of the incarnation, the Logos is primarily active while the human nature is receptive. The reciprocity, however, is found on the level of the propositions that explore the mutuality of the communication. In a critical and constructive reconfiguration of former Lutheran accounts, Thumm defines the *genera* of communication as the reciprocity and symmetry of the communication between the divine and human natures. Both natures are equally affected by the communication in giving and taking, but in different ways which respect the differences between the two natures.[17]

Thumm's approach involves an interpretation of the humiliation in terms of 'crypsis,' which means that Jesus did not refrain from using his power and knowledge but was almighty and omniscient already throughout his earthly life and in this way was present to the world. Thus, Jesus exercised not only his prophetic and priestly ministry in his life, but also his royal ministry, although in a hidden way. This interpretation of a permanent communication, in turn, involves a reconsideration of the divine attributes of almightiness and omnipresence that was already entailed in Luther's distinction of the modes of presence and in his theology of the cross and divine suffering.[18] Finally, Thumm's reformulation of the Christological teaching has an impact on the traditional distinction between the states of humiliation and exaltation. In his account, the two states do not simply refer to two different phases in the life of Jesus Christ but describe the activity of the Logos who assumes the human nature in a way that the life of Jesus becomes part of the divine existence of the Logos while at the same

---

[17] Cf. NÜSSEL 2017, 289–308.

[18] Schleiermacher correctly reports: "It has been believed that the capacity for suffering must be attributed even to the divine nature in Christ, partly on the ground that otherwise redemptive power would be lacking to His suffering". SCHLEIERMACHER 1999, § 97, 412.

time shares the divine power and wisdom to fulfill and exalt the human life. Thus, this account makes a significant step forward towards a dynamic understanding of the divine presence which constitutes the personhood of Jesus Christ.

Schleiermacher's revision of Lutheran Christology

Roughly two hundred years after the kenosis-krypsis-debate Friedrich Schleiermacher revisits Protestant Christology (both Lutheran and Reformed) in order to explain the character of Christ's redemptive work as the source of "a new divinely-effected corporate life, which works in opposition to the corporate life of sin and misery."[19] In his dogmatic approach he intends to reconcile the discrepancy between Lutheran and Reformed teaching. But this is only possible through a critical revision of "(t)he ecclesiastical formulae concerning the Person of Christ."[20] As a basis for this revision, Schleiermacher analyses three constitutive theorems of Protestant Christological teachings: the dogma of Chalcedon,[21] the Protestant doctrine(s) of *unitio* and *unio personalis*,[22] and the essential sinlessness and absolute perfection of Jesus Christ that distinguishes Him from all other men.[23] In his critical examination of the dogma of Chalcedon and its dogmatic reception Schleiermacher critiques both the use of the term "nature" and the distinction between different divine attributes which in his view is not appropriate to describe divine simplicity.[24] From this twofold critique it is clear that Schleiermacher can by no means adopt the Lutheran teaching of *communicatio idiomatum*. Nevertheless, this critique is not yet a sufficient reason for Schleiermacher to give up the old

---

[19] SCHLEIERMACHER 1999, § 87, 358. This "redemption is effected by Him through the communication of His sinless perfection". SCHLEIERMACHER, 1999, § 88, 361.

[20] SCHLEIERMACHER 1999, § 95, 389. Schleiermacher understands this criticism as a continual task.

[21] SCHLEIERMACHER 1999, § 96, 391–398.

[22] SCHLEIERMACHER 1999, § 97, 398–413.

[23] SCHLEIERMACHER 1999, § 98, 413–417.

[24] SCHLEIERMACHER 1999, § 97, nr. 5, 413: "Both doctrines, therefore, are equally to be rejected, since they both depend upon the false idea of a divine nature to which it is possible to ascribe a group of attributes."

dogma. In addition, he demonstrates that the dogma itself is problematic: while the communication of divine attributes to the human nature is meaningless (and does not represent "an impression from Christ"[25]), "the communication of human attributes to the divine nature" "depends ... upon wrong ideas of the work of redemption."[26] It is only on the basis of this analysis that Schleiermacher concludes "the theory of a mutual communication of the attributes of the two natures to one another ... is to be banished from the system of doctrine."[27]

In spite of this fundamental critique, Schleiermacher is anxious to say that his rejection of the theory of mutual communication by no means involves a preference for the Reformed school over the Lutheran school.[28] Rather, Schleiermacher concedes that the Lutherans were right to say that the Reformed account "of contrasted attributes of two natures in one person ... is dividing Christ."[29] The problem with the Lutheran account of mutual communication, however, is that it is "chargeable of the same division,"[30] because it is impossible to understand how the different activities of the natures could be part of the life of one and the same person. Thus, Schleiermacher shares the Lutheran concern about the real unity of the person, while also not denying the Lutheran conviction that real unity of the person of Christ involves a reciprocal communication between the human and the divine. The problem lies in the way in which this communication is exhibited in the Lutheran teaching.

With regard to his analysis of the Lutheran teaching it is remarkable that Schleiermacher, in its critical revision in the second theorem,[31] draws on a version that repeats the very structure of Thumm's account

---

[25] SCHLEIERMACHER 1999, § 97, nr. 5, 411–412.
[26] SCHLEIERMACHER 1999, § 97, nr. 5, 412.
[27] SCHLEIERMACHER 1999, § 97, nr. 5, 411.
[28] SCHLEIERMACHER 1999, § 97, nr. 5, 413.
[29] SCHLEIERMACHER 1999, § 97, nr. 5, 413.
[30] SCHLEIERMACHER 1999, § 97, nr. 5, 413.
[31] SCHLEIERMACHER 1999, § 97, 398: "The second theorem. – In the uniting of the divine nature with the human, the divine alone was active or self-imparting, and the human alone passive or in process of being assumed; but during the state of the union every activity was a common activity of both natures." See also SCHLEIERMACHER 1999, § 94, 385: "The redeemer, then, is like all men in virtue of the identity of human nature, but distinguished from them all by the constant potency of His God-consciousness, which was a veritable existence of God in Him."

of the *communicatio idiomatum*. Thumm had distinguished four *genera* to define the communication in the incarnation. The first *genus* describes the divine appropriation of the human nature by the divine nature of the Logos (*idiopoiesis*).[32] The second *genus* describes the human reception of divine attributes (*metadidosis*).[33] The third *genus* describes the joint activity of both natures (*koinopoiesis*).[34] Finally, the fourth *genus* summarizes the result of the communication process.[35] What is new in Schleiermacher's

---

[32] THUMM 1624, 412: "Idem est ordine naturali hujus generis patet. Nam *primo* dum *o logos* caro factus est, uti essentiam seu naturam humanam assumpsit, sibi intime univit & communem fecit; sic etiam omnia illius assumptae humanae naturae innoxia *pathä* non suae personae, sed suae naturae in persona tanquam in termino realissime pro modo unionis & communionis naturarum personalis & realis appropriavit, unde fluit *idiopoia*, seu appropriatio, quae primum genus communicationis Idiomatum nobis constituit." (Quote from WIEDENROTH 2011, 521, footnote 237).

[33] THUMM 1624, 412: "*Secundo o logos* assumendo, sibi uniendo & appropriando humanam naturam, eiusque innoxia *pathä*, vicissim & reciproce illi assumpto homini, vel assumptae humanae naturae, uti suam essentiam, sic & omnia sua idiomata & totam Deitatis plenitudinem vere, & realiter communicavit... per... personalem participationem, ex qua efflorescit secundum genus communicationis idiomatum, in quo de homine, seu assumpta humana natura vere enunciantur divina, quod genus appelatur a Paulo *hyperhypsosis* ad Phil.2. a Patribus Ecclesiae *beltiosis*, *metadosis*, ... hodie communicatio Maiestatis." (Quote from WIEDENROTH 2011, 521, footnote 238).

[34] THUMM 1624, 413: "Quia autem *o logos* dicto modo sibi appropriavit humana, & vicissim sua communicavit humanae assumptae naturae, ita ut jam sit reciproca (licet non idem modus reciprocationis sit...) communio non tantum inter naturas, divinam & humanam, sed & inter ipsarum attributa atque idiomata, *inde* adeo *etiam ipsae actiones* harum naturarum inter se communicant, ita ut nulla actio divina sit *amoiros* humanae, neque ulla humana sit *amoiros* divinae, sed utraque semper & ubique agat, quod sibi proprium cum communicatione alterius. Quae communicatio inde nomen sortita est, ut appelletur *koinonia* seu *koinopoiia energeion*, communication se communifactio operationum." (Quote from WIEDENROTH 2011, 521, footnote 239).

[35] THUMM 1624, 413f: "Hinc demum quarto loco ordine naturali sequitur hoc praesens praedicandi genus, in quo de tota persona... utriusque naturae proprietates in distinctis propositionibus enunciantur. Non enim quia utriusque naturae idiomata attribuuntur TOTI PERSONAE, ideo vel *logos* sibi APPROPRIAVIT humana, vel sua COMMUNICAVIT assumptae humanae naturae, & utraque agit cum alterius naturae actione, communione, *sed vice versa*, quia *o logos* APPROPRIAVIT sibi humana, & sua vicissim homini assumpto communicavit, atque exinde utraque natura agit cum alterius communicatione, *inde* adeo omnia sivi divina, sive humana TOTI personae, quae simul Deus & homo est, adscribuntur; seu non PRIUS ordine naturali TOTI personae utriusque naturae idiomata attribuntur & POSTEA demum fit appropriatio, communicatio & communifactio, sed *vice versa potius* PRIUS principio ordinis fit appropriatio, communicatio & communifactio, & TUNC demum hic, quartus praedicandi modus, secundum quem utriusque naturae proprietates de tota persona vere & realiter enunciantur." (Quote from WIEDENROTH 2011, 522, footnote 239).

presentation of the old teaching is that he emphasizes the distinction and relation between spontaneity and receptivity which is not to be equated with activity and passivity. In his view, the problem of the old doctrine and its reception in the doctrine of *communicatio idiomatum* is not "only on account of the expression 'divine nature', but, in the first place, because it makes the personality of Christ altogether dependent upon the personality of the second person in the Divine Essence."[36] This formulation is problematic because it presupposes the Trinitarian concept of personhood as a condition of Christology, which in Schleiermacher's view leads to Docetism. Schleiermacher, therefore, contends, that it is "much safer ...to establish the doctrine of Christ independently of the doctrine of the Trinity."[37] The problem of Docetism also remains if in the origin of the person of Christ the human nature is conceived to be "altogether passive, since obviously in the origin of every other human person it takes an active part, in that its body-forming power shapes itself into a new unity of human existence in the completeness of all vital functions."[38] Schleiermacher argues that the Lutheran explanation of the personhood of Christ in terms of *communicatio idiomatum* (and Schleiermacher uses the Tübingen line of explanation) is insufficient, because it reduces the activity of the human nature to "the possibility ...of being assumed into such a [personal] union with the divine, but this possibility is far from being either capacity or activity."[39] For Schleiermacher, it is essential that the human nature is "engaged in the person-forming activity"[40] and that the formation of the person of Jesus Christ is conceived as "a common *act* of the two natures."[41] In other words, the formation of the personhood of Jesus Christ must involve spontaneity and receptivity on both sides – the Divine and the human. Only if the formation of personhood is understood as a process in which the Divine and the human are mutually and reciprocally involved, one can conceive this person to be a real person. Thus, Schleiermacher critiques the Lutheran teaching because it does not

---

[36] SCHLEIERMACHER 1999, § 97, nr. 2, 399.
[37] SCHLEIERMACHER 1999, § 97, nr. 2, 400.
[38] SCHLEIERMACHER 1999, § 97, nr. 2, 400.
[39] SCHLEIERMACHER 1999, § 97, nr. 2, 400.
[40] SCHLEIERMACHER 1999, § 97, nr. 2, 400.
[41] SCHLEIERMACHER 1999, § 97, nr. 2, 400. Italics FN.

sufficiently explain the formation of personhood, but in his critique, he affirms the necessity of mutual and reciprocal relations in the constitution of the personhood of Jesus Christ that had been the theological concern in the development of Lutheran Christology in the Tübingen school building on Luther's Christological principle.

In his own account of the personhood of Jesus Christ, Schleiermacher not only leaves the language of two natures behind,[42] but explains the distinctiveness of the personhood of Jesus Christ in relation to all other human beings in a way that avoids a docetic understanding of the participation of the human nature in the formation of the person. He states that the redeemer "is like all men in virtue of the identity of human nature," but at the same time he is "distinguished from them all by the constant potency of His God-consciousness, which was a veritable existence of God in him."[43] The mutuality and reciprocity in the formation of the personhood is captured in the dialectics of the constant potency and perfection of Christ's God-consciousness and the veritable existence of God in him. The "peculiar dignity"[44] of Christ as a person consists in his perfect God-consciousness, which Schleiermacher conceives to be "implanted in the self-consciousness."[45] For Schleiermacher, "to ascribe to Christ an absolutely powerful God-consciousness" equals "to attribute to Him an existence of God in Him,"[46] which is a repeated phrase of Schleiermacher. It is not simply another phrase for the perfect God-consciousness but relates to the question of how not only the human person, but also the Divine is involved in the formation of the person, which is important for the reciprocity and dignity of his personhood.

Regarding the possibility of the existence of God in Christ, Schleiermacher states that the "expression 'the existence of God in anyone' can only express the relation of the omnipresence of God to this one."[47] That is to say, the cause of the existence or presence of God in Jesus Christ

---

[42] SCHLEIERMACHER 1999, § 96, nr. 3, 397.
[43] SCHLEIERMACHER 1999, § 94, nr. 1, 385.
[44] SCHLEIERMACHER 1999, § 94, nr. 1, 386.
[45] SCHLEIERMACHER 1999, § 94, nr. 1, 386.
[46] SCHLEIERMACHER 1999, § 94, nr. 1, 387.
[47] SCHLEIERMACHER 1999, § 94, nr. 1, 387.

is divine omnipresence.[48] However, "since God's existence can only be apprehended as pure activity, while every individualized existence is merely an intermingling of activity and passivity – the activity being always found apportioned to this passivity in every other individualized existence – there is, so far, no existence of God in any individual, but only an existence of God in the world."[49] While this seems to exclude divine omnipresence in the individual person of Jesus Christ, Schleiermacher holds that a presence of the divine *is* possible if and only if the passive conditions on the part of the individual "are not purely passive, but mediated through vital receptivity" and if "this receptivity confronts the totality of finite existence."[50] The point in Schleiermacher's Christology is to argue that this is the case with Jesus. In his case, one "can say of the individual as a living creature that, in virtue of the universal reciprocity, it in itself represents the world."[51] The argument entails two steps. First, he excludes the possibility that other human beings were ever able to portray the Divine in such a way that those representations could be taken as "an existence of God in us."[52] Second, Schleiermacher claims that this only became possible for human beings in relation to Christ, i.e. "only in so far as we bring Christ with us in thought and relate it to Him."[53] In this description Schleiermacher speaks explicitly of a human activity in which "we posit the God-consciousness in His self-consciousness as continually and exclusively determining every moment, and consequently also this perfect indwelling of the Supreme Being as His peculiar being and His inmost self."[54] Thus, this could be

---

[48] Cf. SCHLEIERMACHER 1999, § 96, nr. 3, 397: "the existence of God in the Redeemer is posited as the innermost fundamental power within Him, from which every activity proceeds and which holds every element together; everything human (in Him) forms only the organism for this fundamental power, and is related to it as the system which both receives and represents it, just as in us all other powers are related to the intelligence."

[49] SCHLEIERMACHER 1999, § 94, nr. 1, 387.

[50] SCHLEIERMACHER 1999, § 94, nr. 1, 387.

[51] SCHLEIERMACHER 1999, § 94, nr. 1, 387.

[52] SCHLEIERMACHER 1999, § 94, nr. 1, 387. Schleiermacher says that such a claim would not be adequate with regard to the history of religions human beings in which God-consciousness was not pure and "always dominated by the sensuous self-consciousness." Moreover, human beings were "not able to portray God purely and with real adequacy in thought, nor yet to exhibit itself as pure activity."

[53] SCHLEIERMACHER 1999, § 94, nr. 1, 387.

[54] SCHLEIERMACHER 1999, § 94, nr. 1, 388.

taken as if he understood the "existence of God in Him" as a product of the human mind. However, Schleiermacher continues:

> Indeed, working backwards we must say, if it is only through Him that the human God-consciousness becomes an existence of God in human nature, and only through the rational nature that the totality of finite powers can become an existence of God in the world, that in truth He alone mediates all existence of God in the world and all revelation of God through the world, in so far as He bears within Himself the whole new creation which contains and develops the potency of the God consciousness.[55]

Thus, the cause of the possibility to recognize Jesus Christ as the individual living creature who is "distinguished from them all by the constant potency of His God-consciousness, which was a veritable existence of God in him"[56] is a decree of the Divine. This decree is Schleiermacher's proposal to account for "a special divine activity in the origin of the Person of Christ."[57] To overcome the problem of "entangling the Eternal in temporality" on the one hand, and "to leave room all the more assuredly for an immediate divine activity" on the other, Schleiermacher suggests "that the uniting divine activity is also an eternal activity." Although, for Schleiermacher, in God "there is no distinction between resolve and activity, this eternal activity means for us simply a divine decree, identical as such with the decree to create man and included therein."[58] Thus, with respect to the question of the origin and cause of human recognition of the distinguished personhood of Christ, one can say, that such a recognition was only possible because of the appearance of Christ as the living individual creature who made it possible to perceive "the existence of God in Him." While Schleiermacher, in his own approach, skips the doctrine of *communicatio idiomatum*, he still "attempts to define the mutual relations of the divine and the human in the Redeemer."[59]

---

[55] SCHLEIERMACHER 1999, § 94, nr. 1, 388.
[56] SCHLEIERMACHER 1999, § 94, nr. 1, 385.
[57] SCHLEIERMACHER 1999, § 97, nr. 2, 401.
[58] SCHLEIERMACHER 1999, § 97, nr. 2, 401.
[59] SCHLEIERMACHER 1999, § 96, nr. 3, 397.

Concluding remarks

Risto Saarinen, in his profound historical and systematic study *Recognition and Religion*, analyzed Schleiermacher's contribution to the development of the modern notion of recognition (*Anerkennung*), which is to be found in his doctrine of justification as based on his Christology.[60] The innovative move in Schleiermacher is that he explains the adoption of believers in terms of recognition of their faith.[61] While analytic understanding of justification has been frequently critiqued as falling into synergism, Saarinen demonstrates the performative and creative dimension of justification as recognition. In this way, his analysis of the role of recognition in Schleiermacher helps to identify the soteriological impact of Lutheran Christological thinking in Schleiermacher even more clearly. For Luther and Schleiermacher faith is caused by way of communication of the Gospel of Jesus Christ alone. Faith involves to recognize Christ as the Redeemer in his very personhood. While Luther conceives the mutual communication between the Divine and the human to constitute Christ's personhood, Schleiermacher's Christology allows to understand how this very dynamic concretely determines Christ's personhood on the level of his self-consciousness. Thus, Schleiermacher's Christology unfolds the reason why and in what sense recognition in justification can be understood as a gift mediated through Christ himself. With regard to the line between Schleiermacher and Luther one might say that Schleiermacher not only takes up the discovery of reciprocity in Luther and the Lutheran tradition. He also translates it in such a way that the reciprocity that constitutes the formation of Christ's personhood can be understood as the reason for a mutuality in the relationship between Christ and believers and among believers.

In addition to this, Saarinen's overall analysis of the three paradigms of recognition in the development of the recognition-concept (conversion, the promise of self-preservation and existential attachment) allows to highlight another dimension of the theological development between Luther and Schleiermacher. According to Saarinen's analysis the second paradigm of religious recognition emerging in medieval constellations

---

[60] SAARINEN 2016, 141–151.
[61] SAARINEN 2016, 146.

involves a transformation of the recognizing person.[62] In Schleiermacher's account, God communicates recognition through Jesus Christ as the mediator and redeemer. While the redemption process is initiated by God through his divine eternal decree, Schleiermacher does not allow for the idea of a responsive divine transformation through a recognizing activity. On the part of the Divine, recognition does not transform the recognizer. Although Schleiermacher adopts the principal of mutuality and reciprocity in his account of Christ's personhood, he does not touch on the traditional claims of divine immutability and impassibility as Luther did. Thus, in light of Schleiermacher's contribution to the development of the concept of recognition we may discover more profoundly both the achievements and the limitations of his reception of Lutheran Christology

Bibliography

EBELING, Gerhard
1984   Schleiermacher und Luther. – *Internationaler Schleiermacher-Kongress*. Ed. Kurt-Victor Selge. Berlin: de Gruyter. 21–38.

Formula of Concord
    Solida Declaratio 1577: http://bookofconcord.org/sd-supper.php = FC SD and nr.

LUTHER, Martin
1909   *Vom Abendmahl Christi, Bekenntnis 1528*. – D. Martin Luthers Werke. Kritische Gesamtausgabe. Vol. 26. Weimar. 241–509.
1914   *Von den Konziliis und Kirchen*. – D. Martin Luthers Werke. Kritische Gesamtausgabe. Vol. 50. Weimar. 509–653.
1966   *On the Councils and the Church*. – Luther's Works. Vol. 41: Church and Ministry III. Ed. by Eric W. Gritsch. Philadelphia: Fortress Press.

NÜSSEL, Friederike
2008   Das Konkordienbuch und die Genese einer lutherischen Tradition. – *Gebundene Freiheit? Bekenntnisbildung und theologische Lehre im Luthertum*. Hrsg. Peter Gemeinhardt & Bernd Oberdorfer, LKGG 25. Gütersloh: Gerd Mohn. 62–83.
2017   "... wo du mir Gott hinsetzest, da mustu mir die menscheit mit hin setzen." Zum christologischen Profil lutherischer Theologie und seiner ekklesiologischen Aktualität. – *Schuld und Vergebung. Festschrift für Michael Beintker*. Hrsg. Hans-Peter Grosshans, Hermann J. Selderhuis, Alexander Dölecke & Matthias Schleiff. Tübingen: Mohr Siebeck. 289–308.

---

[62] SAARINEN 2016, 205–208.

SAARINEN, Risto
2016   *Recognition and Religion. A Historical and Systematic Study.* Oxford: Oxford University Press.

SCHLEIERMACHER, Friedrich
1999   *The Christian Faith.* Eds. H. R. Mackintosh and J. S. Stewart. London/New York: T&T Clark Ltd.

THUMM, Theodor
1624   *Sanae de maiestate Christi theanthropou doctrinae repetition.* Tübingen.

WIEDENROTH, Ulrich
2011   *Krypsis und Kenosis. Studien zu Thema und Genese der Tübinger Christologie im 17. Jahrhundert.* Tübingen: Mohr Siebeck.

"With Love for the Truth, with Charity, with humility":[1]
Attitudes and Ecumenical Recognition

MINNA HIETAMÄKI

Introduction

Ecumenical efforts are motivated by a conflict between the belief in the unity of the church and the observed reality of division. Ecumenical efforts are in various ways directed towards overcoming this separation and contributing to the church being the "one, holy, catholic and apostolic" church of the creeds.

This article examines movements towards church unity as processes of recognition. "Recognition" has during recent years become one of the main concepts in social philosophy to conceptualise how diverse societies function.[2] The phenomenon of recognition is not alien to theological discourse, either, even though the language of recognition might not have been so frequently used.[3] In ecumenism the idea of recognition has been present from the beginning of the modern ecumenical movement, while the concept of recognition has not drawn that much attention.[4]

The general aim of this article is to investigate the phenomenon of recognition in ecumenical contexts with the help of contemporary theories of recognition. The article focuses specifically on one of the core aspects recognition, namingly, what the recognition theories call the appropriate attitudes associated with acts of recognition. The three attitudes identified in recognition theories as the motivational background for recognition are

---

[1] *Unitatis Redintegratio*, para. 11.
[2] Often cited seminal works include TAYLOR 1994, 25–73; HONNETH 1995; FRASER 2000, 107–20.
[3] For a general description of recognition theory, see, e.g., ISER 2013.
[4] KELLY 1996; LIM 2014; HELLER 2018; HIETAMÄKI 2014, 454–72.

love, respect and esteem. Of these three, love has specific relevance, since it lies in the core of what is called "recognition proper", i.e. recognition as person. Love is one of the aspects of recognition that resonates strongly with both theological and ecumenical imagination. In ecumenical contexts love is often paired with truth as essential aspects of dialogue.[5] In ecumenism, love in general terms is something that orients towards the other and motivates to move forward despite obstacles. Jiménes speaks of "will-to-friendship"[6] and Tveit of "values of fellowship"[7]. Various formulations of "ecumenical hospitality"[8], "spiritual ecumenism"[9] and "receptive ecumenism"[10] have also emphasised elements that in the language of recognition theories could be called attitudes.

Thus far the language of recognition appears quite promising for a more detailed analysis of ecumenical processes. Critics have noted that some of the seemingly beneficial aspects of recognition mask essential flaws.[11] For some, the strive towards respectful and appreciative just communities where individuals flourish, the pursuit of recognition appears as a pathological struggle for superiority and oppression. This critique might itself make recognition unsuitable as a medium of ecumenical efforts. On top of the philosophical critique of recognition there are theological and specifically ecumenical questions having to do with how persons are perceived to relate to each other and God that might render the idea of recognition unhelpful for ecumenical pursuits. I will discuss these towards the end of this text.

Recognition: describing the phenomenon

To pinpoint aspects of the concept of recognition relevant for specifically ecumenical recognition I will start with Heikki Ikäheimo's mapping of recognition's "conceptual and theoretical landscape".[12]

---

[5] KASPER 2000, 274.
[6] JIMÉNEZ 2018, 416–29.
[7] TVEIT 2007, 160.
[8] See e.g. KESSLER 2012, 376–85.
[9] KASPER 2007.
[10] MURRAY 2007, 279–301.
[11] See e.g. MARKELL 2001.
[12] Discussion around "identity politics" arose with Charles Taylor's seminal essay in 1994.

"Recognition" in general may be understood in three different senses. The first sense is synonymous with "identification" and means recognizing things as the particular things they are, as having certain qualitative features or generically as belonging to this or that genus or species. Issues attached to identification relate to the identity and identifying individuals and groups and are often discussed under "identity politics".[13]

The second sense of "recognition" comes close to acknowledgement, acceptance or admitting. This sense of recognition may be applied to normative entities, i.e. entities or issues that may be valued, evaluated or taken responsibility for. This sense of recognition is relevant for demonstrating how institutions, norms and values are accepted and how normative descriptions of individuals and groups are created. Ecumenical dialogues have traditionally concentrated on this aspect of recognition and questions relating to the toleration of differences.[14]

The third sense of recognition is what is often perceived as recognition proper, i.e. the recognition of persons. It is in this sense of recognition where attitudes, play a central role. It is here that also love as an attitude enters the discussion.[15]

Before going into details on attitudes, it is useful to distinguish between two different directions or axis of recognition, a vertical and a horizontal one. Vertical recognition takes place between two different levels, a higher one (e.g. social institutions, God) and a lower one (persons, groups) and may be directed either upward or downward. Horizontal recognition takes place on one level, although some forms or horizontal recognition may be mediated by a form of vertical recognition (e.g. recognition of another person as a bearer of rights according to acknowledged

---

Matters of identity are significant because they address the qualities that make identities and the power to discern which qualities matter. See IKÄHEIMO 2017, 567. Questions of identity are highly relevant for ecumenical encounters as well and have been discussed since the beginning of the modern ecumenical movement. See e.g. HIETAMÄKI 2015, 204–19. This topics falls outside the scope of this article and should be discussed elsewhere.

[13] Issues of identification and identity are central recognition and ecumenical recognition. A wealth of research already exists on the aspect of recognition dealing with identities and "identity politics". E.g. TAYLOR 1994. Some discussion on identity politics and ecumenical recognition can be found in HIETAMÄKI 2015. Further discussion on identity politics and ecumenism falls outside the range of this article.

[14] HIETAMÄKI 2018, 232–43.

[15] IKÄHEIMO and LAITINEN 2004, 33–56.

institutions). For purposes that become clearer later it is important to note that the horizontal recognition mediated by vertical recognition or acknowledgement of (institutionalized) social norms can be conceptualized as the aforementioned vertical recognition. In other words, the recognition of a person as a bearer of rights may appears as the acknowledgement of the rights and the consequent appropriate action.[16]

The purely interpersonal horizontal recognition and horizontal recognitions mediated by norms differ on the conceptual level in one important aspect. Whereas the validity of the purely interpersonal recognition is judged by the attitudes that constitute the recognition (affirmative attitudes), the evaluation of recognition mediated by norms is based on the appropriateness of recognitive actions.[17] This differentiation will be later used to clarify some of the complexities and to explain some frustrations, disappointments and critiques of ecumenical relations. Giving and receiving recognition involves relations of power. In the recognitive relationship of A recognizing B (as x), "A" is usually taken as the subject (of the act of recognition) and "B" the object (of the act of recognition). A as subject performs an act of recognition, whereas B as object remains a passive recipient of recognition. The act of recognition is mostly perceived to affect B in that recognition is seen to advance the development of healthy personality, the flourishing of particular identities or equal access to the society for B. Recognition is generally perceived as something positive; B is recognized as they are or are allowed to become what they truly should be. Consequently, non-recognition and misrecognition are considered harmful towards B. Less attention has been paid to what happens to "A" as the recognizer.[18] Both the idea that correct recognition is always something positive and the disregard for effects of recognition towards "A" will be challenged later.

In the event of recognition "A" holds a position of power, because "A" may choose whether to recognize "B" or not. A also has relative authority in evaluating the appropriateness of the recognition. B may request, or even struggle, for recognition but to recognise or not is ultimately in the power of A. Ikäheimo notes that an act of recognition may be performed

---

[16] Ikäheimo 2017, 569–70.
[17] Ikäheimo 2017, 570.
[18] The main critique of Markell 2003, 9–38.

either unconditionally or conditionally. While unconditional acts of recognition are performed without any instrumental value, conditional acts are performed to the degree that one is forced to or finds useful to perform them. The distinction is significant in analysing the use of power in recognition. Even when being in the position of A, a person might not be free to refuse an act of recognition. The act might also be tainted by an ulterior motive that takes the place of B in recognition.[19] In the discussion of ecumenical recognition one is led to ask whether only unconditional acts of recognition, i.e. an unconditional care for the other, unconditional respect for their authority on some issue or gratitude on their contribution may be considered true recognitions and to what degree do these kinds of unconditional acts exist?

Theology and recognition

Theological approaches of recognition respond, very generally, to the question what happens to a person in an encounter with God?[20] Risto Saarinen has shown that in the history of Christian theological thought "recognition" appears basically in three ways that he calls paradigms. These are the paradigms of (i) conversion, (ii) promise of self-preservation and (iii) existential attachment.[21]

In conversion paradigm person attaches her life to the object of knowledge and by this attachment her identity is transformed. Conversion paradigm puts emphasis on what happens in the act of recognition to a person on an ontological level. The object of recognition is the truth (*agnitio veritatis*), that, in the Christian discourse, is not something non-personal, but the divine Christ. In the conversion encounter the object of recognition (Christ) is the cause of changes that take place in the recognizer who may receive a new identity "in Christ". The recognition of truths/Christ is an act that deeply changes the recognizer.[22]

---

[19] IKÄHEIMO 2017.
[20] I follow Veronika Hoffman's proposal, that the "specifically theological content" of recognition is justification. HOFFMAN 2018.
[21] SAARINEN 2016, 201–14.
[22] SAARINEN 2016, 201–14.

Compared to general recognition theories the theological "conversion paradigm" demonstrates a significant reversal of roles between the recognizer (A) and the recognized (B). While A is still the one who recognizes, it is B (Truth/Christ) who is the initiator and/or cause of recognition. B has an active role whereas A experiences the effects of recognition. Recognition in the conversion paradigm is vertical in the sense that the subject and object are not on the same level. Recognition is also interpersonal; it is not a set of propositions or norms but a person (Christ) that is recognized. The effects on A are on a personal level even though the language of "sinner" or "justified" refer also to status. It is not uncommon that a faith-relation between God and a Christian is described by the attitudes of love, respect and gratitude, attitudes Ikäheimo uses to designate an unconditional form of interpersonal recognition.[23] Theological opinions differ as to what degree it is possible for a person (A) to have unconditional attitudes toward God or other people. God's relation towards persons is generally understood to be unconditional. Theological opinions also differ in what emphasis they put on the conversion of an individual and to what degree the encounter is mediated by the church as a sacramental communion. The relationship between individual recognitions and communal recognitions is essential for understanding ecumenical recognition..

The second paradigm, promise of self-preservation contains a variety of religious expectations defined by recognitive response to promises of protection, benefit and fidelity. This paradigm manifests strongly the hierarchical relationship between the promise-making "lord" and the promise-receiving "servant" and thus a strong heteronomy of the "servant" who recognises the promise. The focus in the second paradigm of theological recognition is in how persons are gifted with faith in the one promising their being and their future. Also in this approach, what is significant is what happens to the one who recognizes (A); the appropriate attitudes of the recognizer could be described as faith, love or obedience.[24]

Recognition in the second paradigm is explicitly hierarchical and vertical. More than the first paradigm, the second paradigm focuses on normative statuses and the rights or powers attached to them.

---

[23] IKÄHEIMO 2017, 571.
[24] SAARINEN 2016, 201–14.

"Recognition" is about submitting oneself in the protection of the "lord" and becoming a part of an institution of lords and servants with assigned rights and responsibilities. By recognizing the lordship of the lord, a person is gifted with faith in the promises of the lord. In this model recognition is mediated by an institutional structure of lords and servants. One could ask to what degree such a recognition may be unconditional, if at the very foundation of the recognition lies an institutionalized structure of power imbalance. Recognition becomes synonymous with surrender and faith with submission. In this paradigm "love" is perceived quite compatible with hierarchical inferiority.

The paradigm of existential attachment speaks to the epistemological or cognitive horizons that become available via the attachment of the recognizer. In contrast to the two other theological paradigms in the third paradigm the object of recognition does not participate in the making of the recognizer. Instead, through the act of recognition the object becomes available to the recognizer. What changes in the recognizer is their cognitive/epistemic status, not their being.[25] In Ikäheimo's terms this form of recognition would mostly qualify as a kind of acknowledgement. It deals first and foremost with access to normative evaluations, not so much a relationship between persons.[26]

In sum, theological recognition, historically observed, appears to differ from contemporary perceptions of recognition in some essential points. Theological recognition emphasises more what happens to the person recognizing ("A") in contrast to the what/who is recognized ("B"). Saarinen proposes that theological recognition is more about "promise" or "service" that entails change in the recognizer than something that happens to the object of recognition. Theological accounts of recognition tend to reverse the direction of effect making the recognizer ("A") both the subject of recognition and the object of the effects of recognition. A is also paradoxically considered both an active recognizer and a passive recipient of the consequences of recognition.[27]

---

[25] SAARINEN 2016, 201–14.
[26] SAARINEN 2016, 236.
[27] SAARINEN 2016, 196–200. These views probably differ slightly in view of how much a theological tradition emphasises the passivity of the person in the salvific encounter with God.

Veronika Hoffmann has offered a contemporary theological conceptualisation of recognition in the language of justification. Hoffmann argues that theology of justification is in the core of any genuine theological accounts of recognition. For Hoffmann, essential to justification as recognition is the paradox of coinciding accurate and inaccurate identification. God is the only one who knows the depths of any person, yet in recognizing a person God creatively misrecognizes them not as sinners but as justified. In Hoffmann's account God is the recognizer (A) who in the act of recognition takes a person (B) as something they are not (justified) and by this misrecognition creates the reality of justification. This interpretation is noteworthy for several reasons. Firstly, in contrast to majority of recognition theories Hoffmann sees that it is precisely *misrecognition*, not recognition, that leads to positive results for the person. In facing God persons should not struggle to be recognized as they are (sinners) but as God has promised to see and take them (justified). Hoffmann emphasises the creative power of this misrecognition, i.e. that the misrecognition itself creates the misrecognized reality. Hoffmann centres on immediate God-person relations instead of formal or institutional recognition. "We are not", Hoffmann says, "first and foremost members of a church".[28] At the same time, we are also members of various churches. Recognition has more aspects than the strictly interpersonal one.[29]

What learnings can one take from the discussion over theological recognition to the discussion of ecumenical recognition? Ecumenical recognition appears not to be a straight forward process but more like a complex bundle of various recognitions not always in sync. Following Hoffmann, we can distinguish three categories of recognition that may help to understand ecumenical recognition. These categories are (i) recognition of facts, values and beliefs, (ii) formal recognition and (iii) interpersonal recognition. One of the main learnings from this categorization is that recognitions in these different categories work differently and do not necessarily converge. According to Hoffmann this means that it is very possible e.g. for a person to recognize someone's right to hold a belief (ii) without recognizing the belief as such (i) or to recognize someone as

---

[28] HOFFMAN 2018, 87.
[29] HOFFMAN 2018, 93–5.

a person (iii) and a holder of a specific status or qualification (ii) without agreeing on a subject matter (i).

Ecumenical recognition

In order to analyse the role of attitudes in ecumenical recognition it is beneficial first to identify what kinds of recognitive relations (institutional/interpersonal) exist in ecumenism. It has already been established that attitudes are critical to interpersonal recognition (recognition proper) and also that in theological terms the distinction between interpersonal and institutional recognition is ambiguous. Various parties to ecumenical encounters may evaluate the success of the "recognition" in the encounter differently, based on their different interpretations of the kind of recognition that should take place. Opinions also differ on whether one should, in theological terms, rather speak of reception than recognition. I will address this question first.

Recognition vs. reception

There are broadly two uses for the word "reception" in ecumenical theology. In the first use reception is associated with the specific method of official ecumenical dialogues that consist of discussion, the drafting of agreed documents based on the discussion and the receiving of the documents by the participating churches. The authority of the produced texts varies. Some dialogue documents are theological studies, others at some point result in joint agreements, signed by the authorized representatives of the churches. Because of their official status, agreed documents are often privileged in ecumenical research. As a consequence, ecumenical dialogues of relevance are perceived to take place "on paper", or in the intellectual sphere of arguments and counter arguments.[30] Reception becomes central, because it connects the intellectual dialogue and the reality of churches. "Reception"

---

[30] Jelle Creemer's book on Pentecostal dialogues is a welcome exception to this tradition as it explores also the processes of discerning the composition of the dialogue commission as an explication of theology. See CREEMERS 2015.

means that "consequences are drawn" from the agreed text. Churches take the results as their own and modify their being accordingly.³¹

Reception processes differ from ecclesial tradition to ecclesial tradition, because traditions understand "drawing conclusions" or authoritative discernment, in different ways. Some churches, like the Catholic church and Orthodox churches generally identify authoritative teaching power first with magisterium, the teaching office, whereas in churches that do not have such an understanding of the authority of the ordained ministry the reception process is structurally more diverse. To complicate matters in some traditions the receiving or reaffirming of official documents is also called "recognition".³²

Churches speak of reception also outside ecumenical dialogues. E.g. accepting of a person or a church into communion with other churches is called "reception". The ordering of recognition and reception may differ. Some perceive reception the ultimate goal that follows recognition, other conceptualize the final goal of ecumenical pursuits as recognition that may be preceded by reception.³³

The conceptual lines between "reception" and "recognition" are blurry. To get hold of instances of "recognition" in various context Risto Saarinen has proposed to use a pragmatic diagnostic tool consisting of three basic features. These are the cognitive, socially binding and relational features.³⁴ The cognitive feature relates to an activity where the knowing person connects the perceived object with something that is already known. According to Saarinen this can also be called identification in a broad sense of the word.³⁵ The second feature, attachment, implies that a social bond is created between the recognizer and the recognized. Saarinen relates attachment with some form of normative evaluation and agency that has also emotional and instinctive features on top of cognitive. Availability,

---

³¹ Heller 2014, 262–75.
³² Heller 2018; Saarinen 2016, 172.
³³ Rusch 2007, 87.
³⁴ Saarinen 2016, 168–72.
³⁵ In a broad sense means here using the concept of identification without taking a stance on whether the identification creates or merely reacts to an existing object or to what degree the object of identification can be called "identity". Saarinen 2016, 27–28, 184.

in Saarinen's words points to the context that allows recognition to take place.[36]

Conceptionalised like this, many instances of "ecumenical reception" could also be perceived as recognition. The first report of ARCIC can serve as an example: "By 'reception' we mean the fact that the people of God *acknowledge* such a decision or statement because they *recognize* in it the apostolic faith. They *accept* it because they discern a harmony between what is proposed to them and the *sensus fidelium* of the whole church".[37] (emphasis added) Acknowledgement, acceptance and identification (in the quotation: "recognition") are key meanings attached to recognition.[38] In this article I assume that the notion of recognition is more appropriate for a comprehensive discussion on ecumenical relations. It comprises both the aspect of normative comparison and acceptance or refusal of arguments but also the performative behaviour of "receiving" others in the sense of accepting their normative status (e.g. a citizens or as "Christians").[39]

Institutional ecumenical recognition

Churches are relevant recognition giving instances is several ways. Church as an institutional has the power and capacity to define a person's status within the community by imposing sanctions or limiting interaction. Withholding a status form a person, especially a status that deeply affects the self-image and self-worth of a person like "being a Christian", "being saved" or "justified" can have a powerful effect on a person. Some Christian

---

[36] Saarinen tends to interpret religious recognition as in one way or another always as a recognition of persons. This is because recognition discourse tends to personify also non-personal objects and/or because in the Christian context often times religious recognition is mediated by Christ as a person thus making recognition happen between persons, at least in a mediated way. SAARINEN 2016, 27.

[37] ARCIC I/Authority in the Church: Elucidation, para. 3. See also TILLARD (1982): "What is meant by reception? Simply the approach by which an ecclesial body, judging that it *recognizes* there its own faith, makes its own a rule of faith, a specific doctrinal point, a norm which an authority of the Church has determined. It is not a matter of acquiescence, pure and simple, but of the welcoming that justifies the harmony between this which is proposed and that which one 'knows' of the faith." Quoted in RUSCH 2017, 59.

[38] SAARINEN 2017, 192.

[39] I acknowledge the ecumenical challenge that the language of "reception" is in many ways preferred by the Orthodox theological tradition.

traditions exercise this status defining power actively as a form of ecclesial discipline. Withdrawing status may mean temporarily denying a member of the congregation full access to the church or the community (e.g. to the Eucharist) or to some of the communities rites (e.g. baptism, marriage), removing a person's status in the church as a whole (excommunication) or limiting or denying all forms of human interaction (shunning). Church's withholding of recognition can be presented and/or perceived as God's denial of recognition. God's denial of recognition and a belief in God's unconditional love and good will towards the human kind may be deeply disturbing for person's religious and human existence. It is notable, in ecumenical contexts, that the status giving power of a church may reach beyond its institutional boundaries when a church does not recognise the status of a person who does hold that status within another church.

The success of ecumenical recognition is generally measured by the level of churches' ability as institutions to recognise, or practise approval of each other. Alongside institutional recognition exists a wealth of recognitive praxis on the individual level. Here, on the level of individuals, attitudes and corresponding affirmative actions play a central role. Ecumenical recognition encompasses these two aspects or levels, the institutional and the individual.[40]

The two aspects of institutional and individual level recognition are enveloped or mediated by a set of religious beliefs attached to the status of persons in the eyes of God and their corresponding shared life of faith as a congregation of believers, or church. Church as an institution is a complex of authoritative claims, norms, principles and rules that manifest the church's normative rights and responsibilities. Both religious institutions and authoritative, institutionalized patterns of behaviour within them (e.g. ministry, sacraments, marriage) are justified by theological claims that may vary in different churches. An institution-to-institution ecumenical recognition, i.e. recognition by churches of churches, is mostly concerned with the aspect of recognition referred to as normative acknowledgement, or validity. Churches as institutions may acknowledge the validity or

---

[40] This may be seen e.g. in the description of the first World Conference of Faith and Order on the goal of ecumenical pursuits: "Whatever the way to the goal, complete unity will require that the Churches be so transformed that there may be full recognition of one another by members of all communions." Quoted in BELL 1955, 179.

correctness of beliefs, the effectiveness of certain practises, such as the institution of baptism, or recognize the status of individual person or groups of persons.

Churches are not perceived only as religious institutions but also as mediators of God's recognition and as God's presence in the world. The church is the Body whose head is Christ. In the acts of recognition, the personal and the institutional intertwine and become hard to distinguish. Not only does institutional recognition mediate personal recognition but at times institutional becomes personal. The attachment of person-like features to churches' recognitive praxis invites an interpretation of attitudes behind the institutional level of recognition. The church, or God, may be perceived to "reject", "embrace", "hate" or "love" those that the church recognizes. Because the institutional and personal subject of recognition become hard to distinguish, evaluation of the validity or appropriateness of institutional recognition starts to focus on the assumed (personal) attitudes, not the praxis that adequately communicates or makes the recognition tangible.[41]

For the purposes of this article the interface between individual attitudes and any forms of collectives is particularly interesting. Even though it can be argued that the recognitive actions of institutions are not motivated by attitudes, the institutions themselves may be taken as instantiations of collective attitudes and collectives as intentional agents.[42] This interface between individual, collective and institutional merits further study.

Person-to-person ecumenical recognition

Ecumenical recognition is mediated also when it takes place vertically between persons. In person-to-person ecumenical encounters individuals

---

[41] E.g. one can hold that "all persons are equal in the church" and still claim that "equality" does to need to be manifested in equal treatment. This is because emphasis is on the God's recognitive attitude which is not required to result is equal treatment of every person. If one would look at the church as merely an institution one could point to differences in recognitive praxis by gender, orientation, race or social status and claim that not all are equal in the church.

[42] List uses an enlightening conceptualisation of collective attitudes as either "aggregate", "common" or "corporate attitudes". Of these, especially common attitudes as attitudes believed to be held by also others in the community and corporate attitudes as attitudes held by a collective as an intentional agent might prove interesting for further study. See LIST 2014, 1601–22.

identify, acknowledge and have each other as objects of their recognitive attitudes. How person-to-person recognitions are mediated may vary; some rely on the official teaching of the church, some on their reading of authoritative Biblical texts, some justify their praxis by shared spiritual experience, and so forth. The quality of interpersonal recognition is measured by the attitudes that constitute recognition.

In what follows I will focus on two attitudes that contribute to the success of ecumenical recognition. These two attitudes, trust and love, relate differently to recognition. Trust is an attitude that addresses the context in which recognition takes place whereas love is more seen as a motivating force.

Trust and risk

Trust is one of the main attitudes in personal ecumenical encounters. In theological discourse trust is most often associated with faith and/or certitude. Trust is faith as *fiducia* or certitude as knowledge (*agnitio*). Trust describes the faith-relationship between a person and God or person and the content of faith (Christ/Scriptures/doctrine).

Recognition assumes some measure of trust. Two examples can be given. In Saarinen's theological paradigm of "promise of self-preservation" recognition encompasses the heteronomous relationship between the promise-giving lord and the promise-receiving servant. Servant, in recognizing the lord, is gifted with trusting faith to the promise of their own future.[43] In this paradigm, trust is a gift of recognition.

In the context of ecumenical relations trust appears both as a horizontal and as a vertical phenomenon. As a vertical phenomenon "trust" is about faithful trust in God, God's guiding Spirit in the community of believers and the presence of the Spirit in ecumenical processes.[44] This vertical aspect of trust often overcomes the horizontal aspect between persons in the community. Dietrich Ritschl has proposed a rehabilitation of "horizontal

---

[43] SAARINEN 2016, 211.

[44] In a theological sense the sociological phenomenon of trust may is a consequence of faith, but the specific character of that faith is not in question here. URBANIAK 2014, 1–9. For an example in ecumenical context see e.g. the World Council of Churches document *The Church: Towards a Common Vision*, para. 13.

trust" in ecumenical relations. This would challenge ecumenical dialogues to reform their perception of doctrine, doctrinal language and the pursuit of doctrinal consensus as the criterion of ecumenical recognition. Ritschl's point is that "horizontal" does not mean "sociological"; horizontal trust is fundamentally Christological. The horizontal and vertical aspects are not set up against each other. They are both subsumed by the presence of God as Christ in the community. Horizontal trust is trust in the presence of Christ in other communities.[45] This is in general the way in which the World Council of Churches has described the goal of ecumenism; as the ability to recognize that the church of the creeds is present in other Christian communities.[46] Trust is also not only a medium for ecumenical advance, it is not merely something one needs in order to advance towards more profound ecumenical achievements such as Eucharistic hospitality or formal recognition of ministry. Trust has a face value; it is about being a community.

Trust also has a forward-looking aspect. Trust is about betting on others to respect the trust that has been invested or a unilateral prior investment without certainty about the result. Trusting is risky. It makes one vulnerable to the attitudes and behaviour of the other. Conceptually overlapping with recognition trust has also been described as a gift. The gift-aspect of trust emphasises the voluntary character of trust. Trust cannot be forced and it is always given with conviction. One important character of trust is that it is not naive but informed. Misplaced trust is dangerous. Rudolf von Sinner asserts that it is trust that allows persons to live together in a way that could be described as "assumed neighbourliness" or conviviality. In order for trust to be a strength in a community, it needs to be a collectively promoted attitude. Trust is only effective as a mutual attitude.[47]

Mutuality is central to the effectiveness of ecumenical recognition. "Mutuality" does not mean that each recognize the other as the same as oneself (symmetrical recognition). It describes a relation between the recongniser and the recognised where neither ultimately has more power over the other in the act of recognition. Understandings on the necessity of mutuality of recognition vary. Some hold that in order for recognition

---

[45] RITSCHL 2005, 57, 179.
[46] *The Church: Towards a Common Vision*, para. 9.
[47] VON SINNER 2004, 328–32.

to be "full", recognition must be symmetrical. In reality, forms of mutual recognition are rarely completely symmetrical. Even asymmetrical relations of recognition may still be pragmatically useful for future engagement with the other, especially when practised in an atmosphere of trust. In a trusting relationship there is less need to show power or to be suspicious of one's rights not being respected. There is trust that misrecognitions will be corrected, recognition will be received and that no one will be forcefully assimilated to the other by something like "coerced recognition". This could be described as trust in the integrity of identities in ecumenical encounters.

An informed atmosphere of trust makes it possible to counteract some of the features of recognition considered pathological. One of the central pathologies of recognition is the use of oppressive power inherent in the act of recognition. E.g. Kelly Oliver has claimed that "recognition" is pathologically oriented towards the oppression of those seeking to be recognized by the group (or culture) that has colonized them and possesses the power to give and withdraw recognition. Those in a dominant position are the agents of recognition, also for the oppressed. Even if one would argue with the Hegelian imagery on the mutual dependency of the master (recognition-giver) and the salve (recognition-receiver), recognition for Oliver remains a "life and death struggle with another self-consciousness". As long as the struggle for power remains, also the pathology of oppression remains. Kelly also points out that in real-life slavery, the master and the slave are not equal subjects in the struggle. The slave has internalized their position as recognition-receiver. What the slave ultimately desires, is not to fulfil their position in the oppressive struggle for recognition, but to become an agent of their own recognition.[48]

A way out of the pathology of oppression may for Kelly take place by moving from a self-centred to other-centred love. For Kelly, "other-centred love" as an affect, i.e. as a movement towards the other, generates agency among the oppressed. A pathological recognitive relation is a struggle for superiority against inferiority. An affective relation is open and welcoming of the other.[49] Kelly is not alone suggesting that love should be first and foremost perceived as a relationship that entails a complex of attitudes.

---

[48] Oliver 2001, 26–27.
[49] Oliver 2001, 28, 42–43.

Instead of self- and other-centeredness, e.g. Brümmer speaks of impersonal and personal relationships. Impersonal relationships are characterised by one person objectifying the other, rather than relating them as a person. An impersonal relationship is manipulative, because one party of the relationship is in control. The objectified party of the relationship has no agency and cannot either bring about or prevent the relationship from taking place.[50] Brümmer's impersonal relationship represents a case of pathological recognition. Irrespective of whether the attitude of the recogniser is benevolent or not, the one being recognised has lost their agency, which is an essential part of their personhood.

Personal relationships retain the agency of everyone involved. For Brümmer the riskiest form of relationship is a "fellowship", a relationship that involves both parties entirely as a person. In an impersonal, manipulative or even in a personal, contractual relationship one of the parties either has the full control of the relationship or participates in it as an evaluator of the other's usefulness. A fellowship, Brümmer argues, involves the bestowal of personal value and commitment to actions and attitudes towards the other in the future.[51] Following Brümmer one could say that love as a characteristic of personal relationship both creates commitments, that foster trust, but involve risky personal investments that create insecurities.

Love and recognition

Recognition theories show an integral relationship between person-to-person recognition and a complex of recognitive attitudes. Following Honneth, these attitudes most often include love, respect and esteem. They may be present in various degrees and constellations and they may function differently in different contexts, but in one way or another they all contribute to what is called "taking someone as a person". They also are how the "taking as a person" happens. For Honneth, love is the primary form of recognition. "Love" encompasses several kinds interactions from intimate relations and friendship to family relations. Intimate love relations are constituted by "strong emotional attachments among a small number

---

[50] BRÜMMER 1993, 158.
[51] BRÜMMER 1993, 169–70.

of people"⁵². Recognition as love becomes real when persons mutually confirm each other in regards to their needs and thus recognize each other as needing creatures. Ikäheimo qualifies Honneth's attitude complex even further. He introduces a distinction between "purely intersubjective" or immediately interpersonal and a "mediated interpersonal" recognition, both of which fall under the category of "recognition proper". Both the purely intersubjective and mediated interpersonal recognition may appear in two variants, a conditional one and an unconditional one. What Honneth calls "love" is in Ikäheimo's view an attitude that is not mediated by institutions or norms, that is unconditional and is characterised by a concern for the life, wellbeing or happiness of the other person.⁵³

Honneth argues that love, or adequate experiences of love, are essential parts of one's psychological development. It is necessary to experience love to become a healthy and functioning individual. This, in turn, is foundational to further social and political forms of recognition. While it is not difficult to agree with Honneth on the fundamental psychological relevance of loving care, Honneth's critics dislike perceiving recognition fundamentally as a service to individual's self-realization.⁵⁴ The psychological undertone of Honneth's recognition theory brings love to the fore, but both remains confined within intimate relations and runs the risk of instrumentalising others in service of one's personal development.

Love in theology

In recognition theories love is primarily perceived as an attitude motivating recognition and strongly connected to the idea of self-worth. As a theological topic love is much discussed. It is not possible to offer an extensive presentation of historical discussions on the theology of love within this text. It suffices to say that in theology, love appears in various forms reaching from the erotic to the desire to union with God and from the charitable to the particular love in intimate relations and to the general

---

⁵² HONNETH 1995, 95.
⁵³ IKÄHEIMO 2017, 570.
⁵⁴ E.g. McBride argues that "recognition" is fundamentally not a psychological but normative phenomenon dealing with "our capacity to evaluate ourselves in light of variety of normative standards. See MCBRIDE 2013, 67.

demand to "love your neighbour". "Love" is one of the cardinal virtues, some have promoted a theory where love is detached from the body as a spiritual reality whereas others perceive love always as embodied. The perceived relationship between love and self and love and community has been differently conceptualised and love has been referred to as the ultimate motive by conflicting parties in church (and society).[55] It has to be recognised that taking love primarily as an attitude does not do full justice to the rich and complex treatment of love in theology. Love as an attitude is taken as a starting point due to its prominence in recognition theories and the wider theological discussion on love is used to offer examples on how theological approaches may expand or even necessitate additional viewpoints.

The conceptual analysis of recognition in contemporary discussions has shown that the attitude of love appears in two kinds of interpersonal relations of recognition; in the horizontal relationship between persons and the vertical relationship between human persons and God. Christian theology of love proceeds from a conviction that God is Love (1 John 4:8,16) and that divine love is the only criterion for human love. Especially protestant theological tradition has distinguished between the divine and human manifestations of love and questioned the capacity or possibility for human beings to properly love at all. Some theologies have proposed that while genuine love originates from God, one could find potential in the human capacity to love within the complex of human and divine love.[56] In Luther, Christ gives himself in faith to the believer who participates in God's love and becomes, in faith, Christ to others. In contradiction to a natural or human orientation to love what is desirable, Christ in the believer turns towards the sinner and makes it possible for the believer to love the unlovable.[57] In Tillich, love is specifically the potential to reunite what is experienced as separate. Love creates a new transformative community of love. Rahner gives priority to the love of God as the source of proper neighbourly love and self-love. Both Tillich and Rahner assume the presence of creative desire in human love.[58]

---

[55] JEANROND 2010, 6–10.
[56] JEANROND 2010, 105–6.
[57] KÄRKKÄINEN 2004, 109.
[58] JEANROND 2010, 170.

From this very brief sketch of love in theology one can already observe that in theological discussion the horizontal and vertical recognition relations often intertwine. Whether created or gifted, human love is of God's love. Love is also, in the words of Werner Jeanrond, an ambiguous vocation; pure love belongs to God's realm, not to the contextualized life on earth, even to the degree that some theological interpretations of love have been deemed unsuitable for building human communities.[59] Even with the re-introduction of human desire as an accepted part of love, the theological analysis of love ends with the paradox of the unattainability of love. It does not follow from this that that love might not be a medium of recognition, it merely means that love as an aspect of recognition is qualified by the very fragile human capacity to love.

A second noteworthy aspect of theologies of love is that on top of the subjective aspect of love, love also has aspects that relate to social contexts and conventions.[60] Against the idea that "love" is only an aspect of intersubjective recognition, love is often contextualized in friendships, partnerships and other institutions of love that organise desire and *eros* for both individuals and the collective bodies of selves. Love is never detached from the social praxis of communicating love. Brümmer goes as far as to suggest that love has been mistakenly taken as an attitude when in his view it should be understood as a relation.[61] While for the purposes of love as a motivation for recognition it is useful to conceptualize it as an attitude, also as such there is integral connection between the attitude, the orientation towards the other and the conventional institutional forms through which love is conveyed.

Friendship and love

Friendship, as a dimension or manifestation of love has been considered as a nexus between personal and public realms of life. Unlike some other aspects of love, friendship seems to be less theologically laden. Friendship-love is not restricted to the religious realm but may be experienced in all spheres of society. According to Jeanrond friendship is "a summary term

---

[59] JEANROND 2010, 64. Jeanrond is referencing Hanna ARENDT (1929).
[60] JEANROND 2010, 174.
[61] BRÜMMER 1993, 33.

for forms of free relationships built on respect, trust, honesty, obligation and mutuality".[62] Friendship not only encompasses several aspects of recognition, classically e.g. Aristotle considers friendship as one of the possible outcomes of recognition.[63] Against Honneth's idea of love as intensive, intimate and uncontrollable affect, friendship-love appears more practical, and reliable. It is a complex that emerges out of respect, trust, honesty, obligation and mutuality. The demand to love one's neighbour prevalent in biblical and Christian discourses seems to point more to this kind of love that is not first and foremost a spontaneous, intimate, affect but an attitude or virtue that one can train and develop.

Describing the attitude of love in terms of friendship might seem to downplay or dilute love into something less divine. Quite the contrary, friendship is one of the New Testament ways of describing the elevated status of Jesus' followers. The followers of Jesus are called friends, not servants. Between Jesus and his followers, there is no relationship of servitude but of friendship, because Jesus' followers have been made to know everything that also Jesus knows about God. Jesus' followers have also been given the commandment to love just as God has loved them; by laying their life for others. And "no one has greater love than this". (John 15:12-17) They have been appointed so that they may go and bear fruit and they have been given commandments so that they may love one another.[64]

The role of love in ecumenical recognition

In ecumenical theology "love" has been a contested attitude because it has been associated with "false ireinism", a willingness to compromise truth for peace. Behind the criticism is an understanding of Christian community as a normative community with distinct limits. Discerning between the insiders and the outsiders is a question of truthfulness, and no one should be counted as an insider based merely on warm feelings. Proponents of this view might not be against ecumenism as such, but for them that ecumenical pursuits align with the goal of distinguishing between insiders

---

[62] JEANROND 2010, 205–6.
[63] ARISTOTLE, *Poetics*, 1452a30-32 in KASSELL 1965.
[64] SUMMERS 2009, 9.

and outsiders against receiving "just anybody".[65] Love is understood not as the motivation for recognition but as a failure of discernment.

A response to this criticism starts with a reiteration of the two previously mentioned orientations that rob recognition of its desired goal. These two orientations are the orientation to dominate and the orientation to separate from the other. In the orientation to dominate the subject (of recognition) considers itself to contain, by itself, the power to discern, the power to define and the power to be unmoved by its own decisions. Within the truth vs. love discourse this self-contained subject either uses their power to exclude or they fail to exercise discernment (i.e. "love"). In conjunction with this orientation to dominate is the orientation to separate from the other. In the act of discerning recognition the recognizer remains unaffected by the acts of recognition. The view contrasting love and truth focuses mostly on the end result of recognition. Those recognized have passed the test and are now within accepted boundaries. The problem with this view is that it concentrates solely on the knowledge that the recognizing subject has on the object. The other-centred approach suggested above, especially in the mediated way in which it manifests in the praxis of Christian communities, is less focused on knowledge than the behaviour or new practical situation based on knowledge.[66]

Within the framework of recognition, love is not "lack of discernment" but something along the side of discernment. In the course of ecumenical recognition love is not only the critical attitude of recognition, it is also to the Truth that is the ultimate source of recognition. In a theological sense recognition changes, not only the status of the other person or community recognized, but also, and perhaps most importantly, the one giving recognition. In love, there is also receptivity.[67] As religious recognition, ecumenical recognition is ultimately initiated by God's initiative towards humans. Recognition of the "other" is recognition of the God's truth. In

---

[65] The description of "membership organisations" comes from Stevens, see STEVENS, 1999.

[66] Patchen Markell points out this difference in focusing either on knowledge or on "what we do in the presence of the other." Markell uses this distinction, originally from Cavell (CAVELL, 1977) to point out the shortcomings of the concept of recognition and to promote the use of "acknowledgement" instead. For Markell the concept of recognition fails to encompass changes in the recognizing subject in relation to the knowledge acquired. MARKELL 2003, 34–35.

[67] This receptivity has been especially emphasised in the "receptive ecumenism" approach. See MURRAY and MURRAY 2012, 79–94.

facing Truth, ecumenical advancement often includes some metanoia or repentance and turning back to God.[68]

From a theological point of view church is the central institution of love. The praxis of love is always somehow mediated by the body of the faithful that is the Body of Christ. Neither salvation nor ecumenical advancement is a solitary project. Both are about the emergence of the body of Christ as God's creative and healing activity. This communal context of Christian love puts emphasis on the mediators of love/recognition. Love is not an abstract unconditional unmediated concern for the life, wellbeing and happiness of the other but the variety of mediating norms and institutions where attitudes emerge as appropriate actions. It is based on truth, it manifests in charity and is carried out in humility.[69] Love as an attitude is other-centred, hospitable praxis that brings forth ecumenical recognition.

Bibliography

ARENDT, Hanna
1929 *Die Liebesbegriff Bei Augustin: Vesuch Einer Philoshphischen Interpretation*. Berlin: Julius Springer.

BELL, G.K.A., ed.
1955 The Unity of the Christendom and the Relation Thereto of Existing Churches. – *Documents on Christian Unity 1920–30*, 174–80. London-New York-Toronto: Oxford University Press.

BRÜMMER, Vincent
1993 *The Model of Love : A Study in Philosophical Theology*. Cambridge: Cambridge University Press.

CAVELL, Stanley
1977 Othello and the Stake of the Other. – *Disowning Knowledge in Six Plays of Shakespeare*. Cambridge: Cambridge University Press.

CREEMERS, Jelle
2015 *Theological Dialogue with Classical Pentecostals : Challenges and Opportunities*. Bloomsbury.

---

[68] For an example of how conversion has become a method of ecumenical dialogue see e.g. Lutheran World Federation and Pontifical Council for Promoting Christian Unity, *From Conflict to Communion. Lutheran-Catholic Common Commemoration of the Reformation in 2017* (2013).

[69] See *Unitatis Redintegratio*, para. 11.

Fraser, Nancy
2000 Rethinking Recognition. – *New Left Review* 3, no. May-June. 107–20.

Heller, Dagmar
2014 Anerkennung-Dimensionen Eines Schlüsselbegriffs Der Ökumene. – *Ökumene-Überdacht. Reflexionen Und Realitäten Im Umbruch*, edited by Thomas Bremer and Maria Wernsmann, 262–75. Quaestiones Disputatae. Freiburg-Basel-Wien: Herder.
2018 Receive What You Recognize – Recognize What You Receive: Reception and Recognition – Two Key Terms in the Ecumenical Discourse. – In *Just Do It?!*

Hietamäki, Minna
2014 Recognition and Ecumenical Recognition – Distinguishing the Idea of Recognition in Modern Ecumenism. – *Neue Zeitschrift Für Systematische Theologie Und Religionsphilosophie* 19, no. 4. 454–72.
2015 'Ecumenical Recognition' in the Faith and Order Movement. – *Open Theology* 1, no. 1. 204–19.
2015 Hyväksyvä Tunnustaminen Ekumenian Metodina Ja Teologisena Kysymyksenä. – *Uskonto Ja Identiteettipolitiikka*, edited by Elina Hellqvist, Minna. Hietamäki, and Panu Pihkala, 103–20. Suomalaisen Teologisen Kirjallisuusseuran Julkaisuja. Helsinki: STKS.
2018 Ecumenical Recognition and the Toleration of Otherness. – *Origins of Religion: Perpectives from Philosophy, Theology and Religious Studies*, edited by Dan-Johan Eklund, 232–43. Helsinki: Luther-Agricola-Society.

Hoffman, Veronika
2018 Vielfältige Anerkennungsprozesse Und Die Frage Nach Ihrer Theologischen Basis. – *Just Do It?!*, edited by Dagmar Heller and Minna Hietamäki. Evangelische Verlagsanstalt-Bonifatius. 85–96.

Honneth, Axel
1995 *The Struggle for Recognition: The Moral Grammar of Social Conflicts*. Cambridge: Polity.

Ikäheimo, Heikki
2017 Recognition, Identity and Subjectivity. – *The Palgrave Handbook of Critical Theory*. 567–85.

Ikäheimo, Heikki & Laitinen, Arto
2004 Analyzing Recognition: Identification, Acknowledgement and Recognitive Attitudes Towards Persons. – *Recognition and Power Axel Honneth and the Tradition of Critical Social Theory*, edited by Bert van den Brink and David Owen, 33–56. Cambridge: Cambridge University Press.

Iser, Mathias
2010   Recognition. – *Stanford Encyclopedia of Philosophy*, edited by Edward N. Zalta, Fall 2013. Metaphysics Research Lab, Stanford University.

Jeanrond, Werner G.
2010   *Theology of Love*. London: Bloomsbury.

Jiménez, Leonel Iván Jiménez
2018   Ecumenism and the Will-for-Friendship: A Contribution from Latin America. – *Ecumenical Review* 70, no. 3. 416–29.

Kärkkäinen, Veli-Matti
2004   'The Christian as Christ to the Neighbour': On Luther's Theology of Love. – *International Journal of Systematic Theology* 6, no. 2. 101–17.

Kasper, Walter Cardinal
2000   The Nature and Purpose of Ecumenical Daiogue. – *Ecumenical Review* 52, no. 3.
2007   *A Handbook of Spiritual Ecumenism*. New City Press.

Kassell, Rudolfus
1965   *Aristotelis de Arte Poetica Liber*. Oxford: Oxford University Press.

Kelly, Gerard
1996   *Recognition: Advancing Ecumenical Thinking*. Theology and Religion. New York: Peter Lang.

Kessler, Diane C.
2012   'Receive One Another...': Honoring the Relationship between Hospitality and Christian Unity – *Journal of Ecumenical Studies* 47. 376–8.

Lim, Timothy T. N.
2014   *Ecclesial Recognition: An Interdisciplinary Propos*al. Diss. Regent University, Virginia Beach.

List, Christian
2014   Three Kinds of Collective Attitudes. – *Erkenntnis* 79. 1601–22.

Lutheran World Federation and Pontifical Council for Promoting Christian Unity
2013   *From Conflict to Communion. Lutheran-Catholic Common Commemoration of the Reformation in 2017*. Leipzig-Paderborn: Evangelische Verlagsanstalt-Bonifatius.

Markell, Patchen
2003   *Bound by Recognition*. Princeton, NJ: Princeton University Press.

McBride, Cillian
2013 Recognition. Cambridge: Polity.

Murray, Paul D.
2007 Receptive Ecumenism and Catholic Learning: Establishing the Agenda. – International Journal for the Study of the Christian Church 7, no. 4. 279–301.

Murray, Paul D., & Murray, Andrea L.
2012 The Roots, Range, and Reach of Receptive Ecumenism. – Unity in Process: Reflections on Receptive Ecumenism, edited by Clive Barrett, 79–94. London: Darton, Longman & Todd, 2012.

Oliver, Kelly
2001 Witnessing. Beyond Recognition. Minneapolis - London: University of Minnesota Press.

Ritschl, Dietrich
2005 Theorie Und Konkretion in Der Ökumenischen Theologie: Kann Es Eine Hermeneutik Des Vertauens Inmitten Differierenden Semiotischer Systeme Geben? Münster: LIT Verlag.

Rusch, William G.
2007 Ecumenical Reception: Its Challenge and Opportunity. Grand Rapids, Michigan: William B. Eerdmans Publishing House.

Saarinen, Risto
2016 Recognition and Religion: A Historical and Systematic Study. Oxford: Oxford University Press.

Sinner, Rudolf von
2004 Trust and Convivencia. Contributions to a Hermeneutics of Trust in Communal Interaction Rudolf von Sinner. – The Ecumenical Review. 322–42.

Stevens, Jaqueline
1999 Reproducin the State. Princeton, NJ: Princeton University Press.

Summers, S.
2009 Friendship : Exploring Its Implications for the Church in Postmodernity. Ecclesiological Investigations. London ; New York: Continuum.

Tanner, Norma P., ed.
1990 Unitatis Redintegratio. Decree on Ecumenism. – Decrees of the Ecumenical Councils, 908–20. Washington, DC: Georgetown University Press.

Taylor, Charles
1994 The Politics of Recognition. – Multiculturalism: Examining the Politics of Recognition, edited by Amy Gutman, 25–73. Princeton: Princeton University Press.

TVEIT, Olav Fykse
2007   Ecumenical Attitudes as Criteria for Ecumenical Relations. – *International Journal for the Study of the Christian Church* 4, no. 2. 157–71.

URBANIAK, Jakub
2014   Freed by Trust, to Believe Together: Pursuing Global Ecumenism with Küng and Tracy. – *HTS Teologiese Studies / Theological Studies* 70, no. 1. 1–9.

WORLD COUNCIL OF CHURCHES
2013   *The Church: Towards a Common Vision.* Faith and Order Paper. Geneva: WCC Publications.

The Love of God as Foundation for Christian Charity in Vatican II and in the Teaching of Pope Benedict and Pope Francis

Peter De Mey

In this contribution I argue for the ecumenical significance of the Catholic teaching on the theological virtue of love since it testifies to the priority of God's love for us as revealed in the incarnation and saving death of Christ. In the first two sections of my contribution the focus will be on the two documents of the Second Vatican Council dealing with the Church, the Dogmatic Constitution *Lumen Gentium* and the Pastoral Constitution *Gaudium et Spes*. In the third and fourth section I will explore whether the encyclicals of Pope Benedict XVI – *Deus Caritas Est* (2005), *Spe Salvi* (2007) and *Caritas in Veritate* (2009) – and three longer texts by Pope Francis – *Evangelii Gaudium* (2013), *Amoris Laetita* (2016) and *Gaudete et Exsultate* (2018) – reflect the same strong focus on charity as the human response to God's love for us.

The universal call to holiness in Lumen Gentium

In chapter 5 of *Lumen Gentium* charity is presented as the proper way to answer the universal call to holiness. The opening lines of LG 42 make it clear that *caritas* is first of all the identity of the Triune God himself and, in second instance, prior to our human answer, God's "gift" to us mediated through the Holy Spirit:

> 'God is love (*Deus caritas est*), and whoever abides in love (*in caritate*) abides in God, and God abides in him' (1 Jn 4,16). God has poured out his love (*caritatem suam*) in our hearts by the holy Spirit who has been given to us (see Rm 5,5). Therefore the first and most necessary gift is that charity (*caritas*) by which we love God above all things and our neighbour for God's sake. (LG 42)

These words sound so much self-evident to us, but a brief look at the redaction history of this chapter makes it immediately clear that considering charity as the starting point of moral theology was far from evident in the Catholic Church in those years.[1] Some of the proposals sent to Rome before the Council dealt already with the notion of charity, sometimes to describe the Church's relationship *ad extra* – her social action in the world – and sometimes to argue that morality should no longer be motivated in an extrinsic way, but in an intrinsic way.[2] An interesting appeal was made by the then archbishop Wojtyla of Krakow: "The command of charity implies and at the same time surpasses everything which is asked by commutative justice and social justice."[3] The Holy Office, however, still assuming that the Council would have to condemn a number of dangers, included in its list a warning against "privileging charity while despising other virtues and laws."[4] The schema *De ordine morali* which the Preparatory Theological Commission had prepared by the start of the Council dealt in § 15 with "the false presentation of love as the unique criterion of morality," which, according to the drafters of this text is often defended with an appeal to the famous dictum of Augustine, *Ama et fac quod vis*.[5] After the end of the first session one worked hard to compose a new draft of the Dogmatic constitution on the Church. The fourth and last chapter presented to the Council during the second session of the Council was entitled: 'The call to holiness in the Church'. Of this chapter, the first part dealt with the call to holiness addressed to all members of the Church and the second part spoke about different states of perfection in the Church. On the basis

---

[1] The historical information I offer here is largely based on TRAUTMANN 2012.
[2] TRAUTMANN 2012, 285.
[3] TRAUTMANN 2012, 290, n. 491: "Praeceptum caritatis implicat et simul exsuperat ea omnia, quae ab iustitia communativa et sociali postulantur."
[4] TRAUTMANN 2012, 297, n. 504: "Proponitur *caritas* in despectum aliarum virtutum ac legum."
[5] TRAUTMANN 2012, 335.

of their baptism and confirmation all Catholics have to strive to "perfect charity" by following Christ and his command to honor God and love their neighbor. (§ 29) Even if during the plenary discussions on *De Ecclesia* in October 1963 the other chapters received much more attention, some Council fathers reacted to this chapter in a critical way as well. One of them was the head of the Secretariat for Promoting Christian Unity, Cardinal Bea, who argued that "one had to better define holiness, not in a moralistic and static way, but as a gift of God, an objective characteristic of the people of God, which will reach its fullness only in heaven."[6]

Maybe Cardinal Bea's reaction was influenced by the rather negative reactions which the observers had expressed concerning this chapter during their weekly encounters with the members of the Secretariat.[7] The American Presbyterian Robert McAfee Brown was of the opinion "that chapter IV deals too exclusively with the sanctification of men without showing that this sanctification is at all times based on the free justification offered by God to the sinner. Sanctification remains a sheer gift, and our holiness is never an initiative but always a response to God acting in us."[8] Lutheran observer Kristen Skydsgaard explained why he has great problems with this chapter, especially as the concluding chapter of a dogmatic constitution on the Church. Apart from criticising "that it is not biblical", he especially deplores that its style "is too moralistic": "It lacks the radicalism of the Kingdom of God – and thus remains within a certain 'supernatural moralism', and therefore it seems to me, that it also lacks real joy. There is more of a lifted forefinger in it than of the freedom of the children of God, there is more morality than faith."[9]

Because the formulation of the paragraph on charity (LG 42) had changed substantially, among others by making use of ideas of St. Thomas Aquinas, it is worth paying attention to both the final version and the *relatio*:

---

[6] TRAUTMANN 2012, 352, with a reference to *Acta Synodalia* II/3, p. 640.
[7] The following input on the observers is based on DE MEY 2013, 162–165.
[8] See the report of the meeting of the observers with the Secretariat for Christian Unity on November 5, 1963, as contained in the archives of Gérard Philips, KU Leuven, Centre for the Study of the Second Vatican Council; FPHILIPS 1055, 1.
[9] FPHILIPS, 1055 1–2. [my translation].

> Charity, as the bond of perfection and fullness of the law (see Col 3,14; Rm 13,10), directs all the means of sanctification, gives them their form and brings them to their goal (*omnia sanctificationis media regit, informat ad finemque perducit*). (LG 42)

The Belgian cardinal Suenens explained these lines in his *relatio*:

> Charity is the primordial and necessary way, in which all other ways are included. The text starts from the previous redaction, but with a different order and some modifications so that it would appear clearly that charity is an infused virtue (*virtus infusa*) – and for that reason it is a divine gift – and a commandment – for this reason charity urges to love God and one's neighbor through the exercise of all other virtues and means.[10]

Other numbers in this smallest chapter of *Lumen Gentium* deserve to be mentioned as well.[11] According to moral theologian Bernard Häring the Council was very much aware that "God alone is holy."[12] In his opinion, "article 39, introducing the entire chapter on the universal call to holiness, is as pneumatological as it is Christocentric"[13]:

> For Christ, the Son of God, who with the Father and the Spirit 'alone is holy', loved the church as his bride and delivered himself up for it that he might sanctify it (see Eph 5,25-26), and he joined it to himself as his body and bestowed on it the gift of the holy Spirit to the glory of God. (LG 39)

Häring insists: "The obligation of leading a holy life in the service of one's brethren for the glory of God comes above all from the fact that holiness is a gift."[14]

"Justification in a broader horizon": Gaudium et Spes

Under the title "Justification in a broader horizon" Jared Wicks S.J, a former member of the Lutheran-Roman Catholic international dialogue,

---

[10] *Acta Synodalia* III/1, p. 306.
[11] Häring 1966, 250–257. On this chapter see also DE LA SOUJEOLE 2008, 37–53; DIRIART 2015, 251–269.
[12] Häring 1966, 251.
[13] Häring 1966, 255.
[14] Häring 1966, 252.

wrote a very fine article which analyses the first part of *Gaudium et Spes* in a way which shows the convergences between Catholics and Protestants in developing a common theological basis of ethical action.[15] This theological basis is especially found in the Christological paragraphs at the end of the introduction (GS 10) and of the four chapters of the first part of the constitution.

Whereas the social teaching prior to Vatican II was often based on analyses based on natural law, "Vatican II opts to treat the same areas in the light of revelation in Jesus Christ."[16] Jared Wicks considers the concluding paragraph of chapter 1 as "the truly formative teaching on the *humanum*" and he appreciates that the paragraph is "thoroughly Christological"[17]:

> In fact, it is only in the mystery of the Word incarnate that light is shed on the mystery of humankind. For Adam, the first human being, was a representation of the future, namely, of Christ the Lord. It is Christ, the last Adam, who fully discloses humankind to itself and unfolds its noble calling by revealing the mystery of the Father and the Father's love. It is not therefore to be wondered that it is in Christ that the truths stated here find their source and reach their fulfilment. (GS 22)

The second chapter of *Gaudium et Spes* deals with 'The Human Community' (GS 23–32). According to Wicks this is highly relevant for the understanding of justification in the Catholic Church:

---

[15] WICKS, 2003, 473–491. A more critical Protestant reading of this conciliar document is found in LEXUTT 2015, 181–190. The report of the fourth phase of the Catholic-Reformed International Dialogue (2011–2017), to which an earlier version of this paper has served as an introduction, builds the new consensus on always linking justification and sanctification on the Christological emphasis present in both traditions. Cf. "Justification and Sacramentality: The Christian Community as an Agent for Justice," *Information Service* n° 150 (2017/II) 72–93, p. 77 (§ 25): "The affirmations of the Second Vatican Council that Christ is the 'focal point and goal' of human life and that in him alone is revealed the mystery of human dignity, community, and action address to some extent the Christological concerns expressed in the Reformation slogan *solus Christus*."

[16] WICKS 2003, 484.

[17] WICKS 2003, 484. See also the words of praise in LADARIA 1988, 393: "There is every good reason for insisting on the importance of GS 22. In Jesus, we find our true identity. From Christ alone Christian anthropology receives its definitive illumination." Cf. also DE DHAEM 2014, 5–21.

> The gospel of God's grace in Christ is a community-forming message. The grace it conveys, while forgiving and sanctifying, reverses egotism and empowers believers for service. Such grace stirs joyful praise of the loving and saving God. Those being justified and saved depend on others, on Jesus and his death pre-eminently, but also on the apostles and subsequent bearers of the evangelical message. The gospel of forgiveness and renewal calls them into mutual service in an ecclesial family. But ecclesial solidarity ad intra is not an end in itself, for it is a microcosm of the universal vocation of human beings to live out and promote solidarity and grateful praise of God. Such considerations can give new vitality to discourse on justification, showing the human solidarity that justification entails and orients our witness to society in a manner relevant to the whole human family.[18]

The final paragraph of this chapter, therefore, starts with a quote from LG 9 stating that it "pleased God not to sanctify and save them individually, without mutual relationships, but to make them into a people which would recognize God in truth and serve God in holiness." (GS 32) Jesus is then introduced as the one fulfilling our imperfect attempts to build communities: "This community characteristic is being perfected and completed by the work of Jesus Christ. For the incarnate Word chose to share in human society." (GS 32)

At the end of the third chapter on 'Human Activity throughout the World' (GS 33–39) a Christological paragraph (GS 38) is followed by one dealing with eschatology (GS 39). Christ is introduced both as the one revealing that "God is love" (1 Jn 4,8) and as the teacher of "the new command of love" (GS 38):

> He gives those who believe in divine love (*qui divinae credunt caritati*) the conviction that the way of love (*viam dilectionis*) is open to all people and that the attempt to establish worldwide fellowship is not a delusion. At the same time he enjoins that this love (*hanc caritatem*) is to be pursued not just in great matters but above all in the ordinary circumstances of life. (GS 38)

The eschatological paragraph makes it not only clear that "love and the work of love will abide (*manente caritate eiusque opere*)" (GS 39) but also clarifies the relationship between Church and kingdom: "Here on earth that kingdom is already mysteriously present; at the Lord's coming it will be consummated." (GS 39)

---

[18] Wicks 2003, 486–487.

To Protestant readers of this paragraph who may dislike the emphasis on human activity Jared Wicks explains that this emphasis can be interpreted as the outcome of a sound theology of justification:

> A present-day account of justification can well express its immediate finality, forgiveness and personal renewal, as a freeing of humans from egotism, precisely so that they may become active for creation's maintenance and development. Justified by grace, one is purified to contribute to promoting a more human life on earth. Being made heirs of eternal life, those now righteous in Christ do look at the coming of the kingdom that is God's work, but they do not wait passively, for the Spirit 'quickens, purifies, and strengthens' them to improve their created milieu and embody in it values that will pass over into the final kingdom.[19]

The fourth chapter (GS 40–45) deals with 'The Church's Task in Today's World'. The novelty of the Christological paragraph this time consists in the presentation of Christ as the one in whom everything will eschatologically be subsumed:

> For the Word of God, through whom all things were made, was made flesh so that as perfectly human he would save all human beings and sum up all things. (…) He it was whom the Father raised from the dead, exalted and placed at his right hand, making him judge of the living and the dead. It is as given life and united in his Spirit that we make our pilgrimage towards the climax of human history which is in full accord with the design of his love, 'to unite all things in him, things in heaven and things on earth' (Eph 1,10). (GS 45)

What is the conclusion of Trautmann after comparing the reflections on charity in *Lumen Gentium* and *Gaudium et Spes*?

> While looking at it from different angles, one starting from the Church and another one starting from the world, the Council succeeds in clarifying charity in a fruitful way. The conclusion is not that there would exist two types of charity, one for the Church which would only be valid for Christians and a 'mundane' one for the other people. By not isolating *Gaudium et Spes* from *Lumen Gentium*, the Council avoids that one would again have difficulties to understand the meaning of charity: the double commandment of love allows all people to answer their human and Christian vocation, following their states of life and a variety of modalities while contributing to the transformation of the world.[20]

---

[19] WICKS 2003, 488.
[20] TRAUTMANN 2012, 390–391.

The love of God as foundation for human solidarity in the encyclicals of pope Benedict XVI

Being not a specialist in the social doctrine of the Church I am not qualified to take position in the debate on the significance of pope Benedict's contributions for Catholic social thought.[21] My modest contribution will only consist in highlighting how the two central insights in our analysis of the first part of *Gaudium et Spes* – the strong focus on Christology and on charity as the human response to God's love for us – find a profound echo in Pope Benedict's three encyclicals: *Deus Caritas Est* (2005), *Spe Salvi* (2007) and *Caritas in Veritate* (2009).

The encyclical *Deus Caritas Est* (2005) starts with a quotation from 1 John 4:16: "God is love, and he who abides in love abides in God, and God abides in him", which we also encountered in LG 42 and GS 38. Since Scripture teaches us that "God has first loved us, love is now no longer a mere 'command'; it is the response to the gift of love with which God draws near to us." (§ 1) Very soon the Pope turns the attention to Christ. Before human beings can "give love" they must first "receive love as a gift" and this we owe to "Jesus Christ, from whose pierced heart flows the love of God (cf. Jn 19:34)." (§ 7) Even if the Pope is also attentive to those biblical passages which characterize God's love as "a passion (*eros*) for his people", its most obvious characteristic is *agape*, "because it is love which forgives." (§ 10) The self-giving of Christ on the cross "in order to raise man up and save him" is "love in its most radical form." (§ 12)

In line with *Gaudium et Spes* Pope Benedict insists that God's love creates community: "Union with Christ is also union with all those to whom he

---

[21] Among Catholic theologians differing views are found regarding the question whether the social teaching of Pope Benedict XVI is in continuity or discontinuity with *Gaudium et Spes*. VERSTRAETEN 2011, 322, emphasizes the "shift from the world-oriented theology of *Gaudium et Spes* to the doctrinal distinctiveness of the teaching of Pope Benedict XVI." While admitting that the pope changed his view in *Caritas in Veritate* (2009), he particularly deplores the separation of justice and charity in *Deus Caritas Est* (2005). BENESTAD 2008, 150, is convinced that *Deus Caritas Est* "further clarifies the text of *Gaudium et Spes* on the mission of the Church in the world by discussing her contribution to justice."

gives himself."²² (§ 14) This idea is repeated in the summary of part I, 'The Unity of Love in Creation and Salvation History':

> Love is 'divine' because it comes from God and unites us to God; through this unifying process it makes us a 'we' which transcends our divisions and makes us one, until in the end God is 'all in all' (*1 Cor* 15:28). (§ 18)

Part II of *Deus Caritas Est* is entitled: 'Caritas: The Practice of Love by the Church as a Community of Love.' The pope does not immediately focus on human love but starts with a section on 'The Church's charitable activity as a manifestation of Trinitarian love'. Whereas the first part of his encyclical had a strong Christological focus, Pope Benedict now has chosen to highlight the role of the Spirit: "The Spirit is the energy which transforms the heart of the ecclesial community, so that it becomes a witness before the world to the love of the Father, who wishes to make humanity a single family in his Son." (§ 19)

For the Pope the practice of charity is one of the "essential activities" of the Church, "along with the administration of the sacraments and the proclamation of the word." (§ 22) "The Church cannot neglect the service of charity any more than she can neglect the Sacraments and the Word." (ibid.) He explains this further with an appeal to the traditional vocabulary of *martyria – leitourgia – diakonia*:

> The Church's deepest nature is expressed in her three-fold responsibility: of proclaiming the word of God (*kerygma-martyria*), celebrating the sacraments (*leitourgia*), and exercising the ministry of charity (*diakonia*). These duties presuppose each other and are inseparable. For the Church, charity is not a kind of welfare activity which could equally well be left to others, but is a part of her nature, an indispensable expression of her very being. (§ 25)

In response to the Marxist claim that "we do not need charity, but justice" (§ 26) he makes the distinction between the pursuit of justice which he believes to be the primordial responsibility of the State (§ 28), and the

---

[22] At the end of a very positive review of the encyclical the German Lutheran theologian Eberhard Jüngel asks, "wann es an der Zeit ist, eine von Jesus Christus selbst initiierte und eben deshalb schon präsente ökumenische φιλία auch amtlich wahrzunehmen und dann daraus die ekklesiologischen Konsequenzen zu ziehen." Cf. JÜNGEL 2009, 500.

work of charity, being an essential responsibility of the Church.[23] Since the Catholic Church understands it to be the "direct duty" of the laity "to work for a just ordering of society"(§ 29), however, she does not and should not "remain on the sidelines in the fight for justice." (§ 28)

Also in his second encyclical *Spe Salvi* Pope Benedict XVI stresses that faith is always a divine gift.[24] The Pope develops his theology of the 'kingdom of God' in sharp contrast to the secular project of the 'kingdom of man' which has been defended in Western philosophy since Francis Bacon. (§§ 16–23) 'The true shape of Christian hope' for Pope Benedict consists in the truth that "it is not science that redeems man: man is redeemed by love." (§ 26) At this point the Pope turns to the doctrine of justification:

> Jesus Christ has 'redeemed' us. Through him we have become certain of God, a God who is not a remote 'first cause' of the world, because his only-begotten Son has become man and of him everyone can say: 'I live by faith in the Son of God, who loved me and gave himself for me' (Gal 2:20). (§ 26.)

The objection whether we are "not in this way falling back once again into an individualistic understanding of salvation" (§ 28) is countered by the Pope by referring to the social implications of the Christian faith: "Christ died for all. To live for him means allowing oneself to be drawn into his *being for others.*" (§ 28)

A healthy theology of the kingdom of God on one hand stresses that it is not a mere future reality: "[God's] Kingdom is not an imaginary hereafter, situated in a future that will never arrive; his Kingdom is present wherever he is loved and wherever his love reaches us."[25] (§ 31) On the other hand

---

[23] See also MURPHY 2007, 274–286.

[24] See DOYLE 2010, 350–379.

[25] It is not impossible that the Pope here as well envisages the kingdom-centred and thereby in his eyes relativist theology of the so-called religious pluralists. They were the addressees of the following lines in *Dominus Iesus*: "If the kingdom is separated from Jesus, it is no longer the kingdom of God which he revealed. The result is a distortion of the meaning of the kingdom, which runs the risk of being transformed into a purely human or ideological goal and a distortion of the identity of Christ, who no longer appears as the Lord to whom everything must one day be subjected (cf. 1 Cor 15:27). Likewise, one may not separate the kingdom from the Church. It is true that the Church is not an end unto herself, since she is ordered toward the kingdom of God, of which she is the seed, sign and instrument. Yet, while remaining distinct from Christ and the kingdom, the Church is indissolubly united to both." (§ 18)

the Pope also emphasizes that the kingdom always remains God's gift as well:

> Certainly we cannot 'build' the Kingdom of God by our own efforts – what we build will always be the kingdom of man with all the limitations proper to our human nature. The Kingdom of God is a gift, and precisely because of this, it is great and beautiful, and constitutes the response to our hope. And we cannot – to use the classical expression – 'merit' heaven through our works. Heaven is always more than we could merit, just as being loved is never something 'merited', but always a gift. (§ 35)

I conclude with one final quote from *Spe Salvi* in which it becomes clear that for the Pope eschatology and Christology are profoundly related:

> The judgement of God is hope, both because it is justice and because it is grace. If it were merely grace, making all earthly things cease to matter, God would still owe us an answer to the question about justice – the crucial question that we ask of history and of God. If it were merely justice, in the end it could bring only fear to us all. The incarnation of God in Christ has so closely linked the two together – judgement and grace – that justice is firmly established. (§ 47)

The most thorough contribution of Pope Benedict in the field of the social teaching of the Church is offered in his third encyclical *Caritas in Veritate*.[26] For our purposes however we only pay attention to the introduction in which the Pope speaks about the Trinity as the origin of the Church's work of *caritas* "in the field of justice and peace." (§ 1) Already the opening line of the encyclical reminds its readers that "Jesus Christ bore witness to charity and truth by his earthly life and especially by his death and resurrection." The Pope's most developed account of the Trinitarian origin of *caritas* is found in § 5:

> Charity is love received and given. It is 'grace' (*cháris*). Its source is the wellspring of the Father's love for the Son, in the Holy Spirit. Love comes down to us from the Son. It is creative love, through which we have our being; it is redemptive love, through which we are recreated. Love is revealed and made present by Christ (cf. Jn 13:1) and 'poured into our hearts through the Holy Spirit' (Rom 5:5). As the objects of God's love, men and women become subjects of charity, they are called to make themselves instruments of grace, so as to pour forth God's charity and

---

[26] See a.o. RENCZES 2010, 273–290; BENESTAD 2009, 411–428.

to weave networks of charity. This dynamic of charity received and given is what gives rise to the Church's social teaching, which is *caritas in veritate in re sociali*: the proclamation of the truth of Christ's love in society.

Pope Francis: holiness as the Christian response to God's mercy as expressed in Christ

In the first longer text by Pope Francis, the apostolic exhortation *Evangelii Gaudium* (2013), one encounters a similar attention to the priority of God's love for us and on charity as the peculiar form of Catholic social action.

The opening paragraph introduces the topic of the exhortation. The joy of the Gospel is presented as the fruit of our being saved in Christ:

> The joy of the Gospel fills the hearts and lives of all who encounter Jesus. Those who accept his offer of salvation are set free from sin, sorrow, inner emptiness and loneliness. With Christ joy is born constantly anew. (§ 1)

Both in the introduction (§§ 1–18) and in chapter one (§§ 19–49), dealing with 'The Church's Missionary Transformation', the primacy of God's love for us is emphasized with an appeal to 1 John 4:19.

> The life of the Church should always reveal clearly that God takes the initiative, that 'he has loved us first' (1 Jn 4:19) and that he alone 'gives the growth' (1 Cor 3:7). (§ 12)

> An evangelizing community knows that the Lord has taken the initiative, he has loved us first (cf. 1 Jn 4:19), and therefore we can move forward, boldly take the initiative, go out to others, seek those who have fallen away, stand at the crossroads and welcome the outcast. (§ 24)

In response to God's love the Church should give priority to the work of charity:

> Before all else, the Gospel invites us to respond to the God of love who saves us, to see God in others and to go forth from ourselves to seek the good of others. Under no circumstance can this invitation be obscured! (…) If this invitation does not radiate forcefully and attractively, the edifice of the Church's moral teaching risks becoming a house of cards, and this is our greatest risk. It would mean that it is not the Gospel which is being preached, but certain doctrinal or moral points based on specific ideological options. (§ 39)

After the description of the context in which evangelization has to take place (§§ 50–109) in chapter two, Pope Francis focuses in chapter three on 'The Proclamation of the Gospel' (§§ 110–175). At the outset of this chapter he deems it necessary to offer his readers a summary of his ecclesiological convictions. Whereas in contemporary ecclesiology mostly the complementarity of the images for the Church in *Lumen Gentium* is stressed, the Pope seems to give priority to understanding the Church as the people of God:

> The Church, as the agent of evangelization, is more than an organic and hierarchical institution; she is first and foremost a people advancing on its pilgrim way towards God. She is certainly a mystery rooted in the Trinity, yet she exists concretely in history as a people of pilgrims and evangelizers, transcending any institutional expression, however necessary. I would like to dwell briefly on this way of understanding the Church, whose ultimate foundation is in the free and gracious initiative of God. (§ 111)

The paragraph that follows illustrates that not only the Church, but also its moral action is affected by the "primacy of grace."[27]

> The salvation which God offers us is the work of his mercy. No human efforts, however good they may be, can enable us to merit so great a gift. God, by his sheer grace, draws us to himself and makes us one with him. He sends his Spirit into our hearts to make us his children, transforming us and enabling us to respond to his love by our lives. The Church is sent by Jesus Christ as the sacrament of the salvation offered by God. (§ 112)

In the chapter on 'The Social Dimension of Evangelization' (§§ 176–258) it becomes clear that Pope Francis prefers to speak about the social doctrine of the Church in terms of charity, but in a more critical mode, rejecting "charity à la carte":

> The kerygma has a clear social content: at the very heart of the Gospel is life in community and engagement with others. The content of the first proclamation has an immediate moral implication centred on charity. (§ 177)

---

[27] Rovati 2017, 52. In his article the author defends the thesis that "Pope Francis's pontificate represents a new, powerful invitation for us moral theologians to better appreciate and embody the council's Christological focus." (p. 57). Cf. Rovati 2017, 53: "In fact, without God's gratuitous initiative the call to conversion and sainthood intrinsic to moral theology would be void, and it would amount to an unreachable ideal (LG 39-42)." In making such claims Pope Francis is, according to Rovati, in profound harmony with the teaching of his predecessor.

> Reading the Scriptures also makes it clear that the Gospel is not merely about our personal relationship with God. Nor should our loving response to God be seen simply as an accumulation of small personal gestures to individuals in need, a kind of 'charity à la carte' or a series of acts aimed solely at easing our conscience. The Gospel is about the kingdom of God (cf. Lk 4:43); it is about loving God who reigns in our world. To the extent that he reigns within us, the life of society will be a setting for universal fraternity, justice, peace and dignity. (§ 180)

From the exhortation *Amoris Laetitia*, 'On love in the family' (2016) which is the fruit of two synods dealing with the family, I comment on just a few passages from chapter 8, dealing with 'Accompanying, discerning and integrating weakness' (§§ 291–312). In one of the most debated passages of the exhortation the pope bases his recommendation of a more welcoming pastoral attitude towards e.g. remarried divorced Catholics again on the basis of the primacy of God's grace:

> Because of forms of conditioning and mitigating factors, it is possible that in an objective situation of sin – which may not be subjectively culpable, or fully such – a person can be living in God's grace, can love and can also grow in the life of grace and charity, while receiving the Church's help to this end. Discernment must help to find possible ways of responding to God and growing in the midst of limits. By thinking that everything is black and white, we sometimes close off the way of grace and growth, and discourage paths of sanctification which give glory to God.[28] (§ 305)

The consequences for moral theology are given a few paragraphs later:

> [A]lthough it is quite true that concern must be shown for the integrity of the Church's moral teaching, special care should always be shown to emphasize and encourage the highest and most central values of the Gospel, particularly the primacy of charity as a response to the completely gratuitous offer of God's love. At times we find it hard to make room for God's unconditional love in our pastoral activity.[29] (§ 311)

---

[28] DELICATA 2017, 74–86, sees in this passage an excellent example of the "robust hamartiology" in chapter 8 of *Amoris Laetitia*, "whose heart is the human response to God's merciful call." (p. 80).

[29] See also the section on *Amoris Laetitia* in ROVATI, 2017, 63–69. Cf. ROVATI 2017, 63: "While the discussion about this document has been mostly focused on the parts concerning the pastoral care of the baptized who are divorced and remarried, for the purpose of this article, it would be good to take a step back from the heated polemics and appreciate the depth and breadth

In the opening chapter of *Gaudete et Exsultate*, 'The Call to Holiness in Today's World' (2018), Pope Francis makes it clear that his theology of holiness is rooted in the Second Vatican Council. In view of his sympathy for chapter two of *Lumen Gentium* he prefers to quote from LG 11 instead of basing his reflection on chapter 5:

> Strengthened by so many and such great means of salvation, all the faithful, whatever their condition or state, are called by the Lord – each in his or her own way – to that perfect holiness by which the Father himself is perfect. (§ 10)

The function of the subsection 'Your mission in Christ' is to repeat the Christological foundation of Christian ethics, even if the role of the Spirit is not forgotten:

> The Father's plan is Christ, and ourselves in him. In the end, it is Christ who loves in us, for 'holiness is nothing other than charity lived to the full'. (…) Every saint is a message which the Holy Spirit takes from the riches of Jesus Christ and gives to his people.[30] (§ 21)

Before interpreting the Beatitudes as a call to holiness in chapter three, chapter two is an exhortation not to fall in the trap of 'Two subtle enemies of holiness'. The first one, 'Contemporary gnosticism' (§§ 36-46) assumes that orthodoxy is for Catholic faithful more important than "the depth of their charity." (§ 37) The second one, 'Contemporary pelagianism' (§§ 47–59) gets even more attention and consists in the assumption that everything depends on personal effort in the Catholic Church.[31] It results from forgetting that God "first loved us" (§ 48, in reference to 1 Jn 4:19). Sometimes Catholics refer to grace in their words but their acts do not reflect this. (§ 49) This disease seems omnipresent according to the Pope

---

of Francis's proposal. Above all, I want to focus on an invitation that emerges time and again in Francis's *Amoris Laetitia*, namely, to put Christ at the center of our living and thinking."

[30] Reference is made to a catechesis of Pope Benedict during the General Audience of April 13, 2011.

[31] These two dangers have been criticized already in *Evangelii Gaudium* (§ 94). His request to the Congregation for the Doctrine of the Faith to study them led to the letter *Placuit Deo*, 'On certain aspects of Christian Salvation' (February 22, 2018) of which the Pope quotes the key idea in his exhortation: "Both neo-Pelagian individualism and the neo-Gnostic disregard of the body deface the confession of faith in Christ, the one, universal Saviour." (§ 33).

and can receive many unconnected forms[32] with devastating results: "Once we believe that everything depends on human effort as channelled by ecclesial rules and structures, we unconsciously complicate the Gospel and become enslaved to a blueprint that leaves few openings for the working of grace." (§ 59) As a corrective the Pope not only refers back to the teaching of the Second Synod of Orange and the Council of Trent[33] (§ 53) but also points to the existence of "a hierarchy of virtues": "The primacy belongs to the theological virtues, which have God as their object and motive. At the centre is charity." (§ 60)

Conclusion

My highly esteemed colleague Risto Saarinen reflected a lot on this theme in his 2005 book *God and the Gift: An Ecumenical Theology of Giving*. At the outset of the book Saarinen is aware that the idea "that the vertical gift from God to humans is a prerequisite of horizontal sharing among human beings" "is common in theology and ecumenism."[34] The line in *Lumen Gentium* speaking about the gift exchange among the local churches that form part of the universal Church (LG 13) is even cited in the first and last chapter.[35] Saarinen, however, distinguishes between a "receiver-oriented" perspective, which concentrates mostly on what receivers of the gift can and need to do and which is typical for much of "post-Augustinian theology," and a "giver-oriented" perspective.[36] Especially in the chapter on 'Sacrifice and Thanksgiving' it becomes clear that he still notices the differences "between Catholic anthropocentrism and Protestant theocentrism," since

---

[32] Cf. § 57: "…an obsession with the law, an absorption with social and political advantages, a punctilious concern for the Church's liturgy, doctrine and prestige, a vanity about the ability to manage practical matters, and an excessive concern with programmes of self-help and personal fulfilment."

[33] One year after the intensive participation by the Catholic Church in the common commemoration of the Reformation it is a pity that no reference was made to Luther's theology of justification and its insistence on the primacy of grace.

[34] SAARINEN 2005, 2.
[35] SAARINEN 2005, 1, 137–139.
[36] SAARINEN 2005, 4–5.

"the Catholic priest is an agent or a giver in a much stronger sense than his Protestant colleague."[37]

Throughout his book, he therefore praises Martin Luther for having developed "a consistent theology of theocentric giving."[38] He insists that the "Johannine perspective of love" is not absent from Luther's theology of the cross.[39] A Lutheran theology of love does not deny the importance of "the spiritual service of neighbourly love", but realizes that "its character is *a posteriori*, after the salvific event of Jesus Christ."[40] Such a theology, Saarinen knows, is continuously attentive not to fall in the Pelagian trap: "If we are to love our neighbour according to this model of divine love, we are not to look at our own gifts but at our neighbour's needs."[41] Hopefully, this article has convinced my colleague of the similar attention to this point in the Catholic teaching on *caritas* in recent documents by the Catholic magisterium, which emphasizes that Catholics ought to engage in a "service of charity" (*Deus Caritas Est* 22) and have to be "instruments of grace" (*Caritas in Veritate* 5), but cannot "merit heaven through their works" (*Spe Salvi* 5; *Evangelii Gaudium* 112), even if they have to be continuously warned against the pitfall of "contemporary Pelagianism" (*Gaudete et Exsultate* 47–59).

Bibliography

BENESTAD, Brian
2008   Doctrinal Perspectives on the Church in the Modern World. – *Vatican II: Renewal within Tradition*. Ed. Matthew L. Lamb & Matthew Levering. Oxford: Oxford University Press. 147–164.

2009   Pope Benedict XVI's *Caritas in veritate*. – *Josephinum Journal of Theology* 16. 411–428.

---

[37] SAARINEN 2005, 97.
[38] SAARINEN 2005, 134.
[39] SAARINEN 2005, 51. Interestingly, however, Saarinen finds the biblical base for a giver-oriented theology of the gift in the fourth Gospel, whereas the Catholic key-texts on the relation between God's love and human *caritas* (LG, GS, *Deus Caritas est* and *Evangelii Gaudium*) all refer to 1 John 4.
[40] SAARINEN 2005, 100–101: "Christ gave himself as a gift, but in addition to this gift he also gave a model of Christian love."
[41] SAARINEN 2005, 139.

CATHOLIC-REFORMED INTERNATIONAL DIALOGUE
2017   Justification and Sacramentality: The Christian Community as an Agent for Justice. – *Information Service* N° 150. 72–93.

DE DHAEM, Amaury Begasse S.J.,
2014   Christologie et sotériologie de *Gaudium et spes* 22. Un modèle de théologie unifiée. – *Gregorianum* 95. 5–21.

DE LA SOUJEOLE, Benoît-Dominique
2008   The Universal Call to Holiness. – *Vatican II: Renewal within Tradition*. Ed. Matthew L. Lamb & Matthew Levering. Oxford: Oxford University Press. 37–53.

DELICATA, Nadia
2017   Sin, Repentance and Conversion in *Amoris Laetitia*. – *A Point of No Return? Amoris Laetitia on Marriage, Divorce and Remarriage*. Ed. Thomas Knieps-Port le Roi. Münster: Lit. 74–86.

DE MEY, Peter
2013   Vatican II comme style oecuménique? *De Ecclesia* et *De Oecumenismo* évalués par des théologiens non catholiques. – *Vatican II comme style théologique: L'herméneutique théologique du Concile*. Ed. Joseph Famerée. Unam Sanctam. Nouvelle série. Paris: Cerf. 149–186.

DIRIART, Alexandra
2015   La vocation universelle à la sainteté: dynamisme et caractéristique fondamentale de l'ecclésiologie de *Lumen Gentium*. – *Nova & Vetera* 90. 251–269.

DOYLE, Dominic
2010   *Spe salvi* on Eschatological and Secular Hope: A Thomistic Critique of an Augustinian Encyclical. – *Theological Studies* 71. 350–379.

HÄRING, Bernard
1966   Holiness in the Church. – *Vatican II: An Interfaith Appraisal*. Ed. John H. Miller. Notre Dame – London: University of Notre Dame Press. 250–257.

JÜNGEL, Eberhard
2009   Durch Glaube geformte Liebe (*Caritas fide formata*). Die erste Enzyklika Benedikt XVI. *Deus Caritas est* – gelesen mit den Augen eines evangelischen Christenmenschen. – *Geist, Eros und Agape: Untersuchungen zu Liebesdarstellungen in Philosophie, Religion und Kunst*. Ed. Edith Düsung & Hans D. Klein. Würzburg: Königshausen u. Neumann, 2009. 481–500.

LADARIA, Luis
1988   Humanity in the Light of Christ in the Second Vatican Council. – *Vatican II. Assessment and Perspectives. Twenty-Five Years After (1962–1987)*. Vol. 2. New York: Paulist Press. 386–401.

LEXUTT, Athina
2015 Die Kirche in der Welt von heute – gaudium et spes? Ein protestantischer Blick aus einer 50 Jahre späteren Welt. – *Diakonia* 46. 181–190.

MURPHY, Charles M.
2007 Charity, not Justice, as Constitutive of the Church's Mission. – *Theological Studies* 68. 274–286.

RENCZES, Philipp Gabriel S.J.
2010 Grace Reloaded: *Caritas in Veritate*'s Theological Anthropology. – *Theological Studies* 71. 273–290.

ROVATI, Alessandro
2017 Mercy Is a Person: Pope Francis and the Christological Turn in Moral Theology. – *Journal of Moral Theology* 6. 48–69.

SAARINEN, Risto
2015 *God and the Gift: An Ecumenical Theology of Giving.* Collegeville, MI: Liturgical Press.

TRAUTMANN, Frédéric
2012 *La notion de charité au Concile Vatican II.* Perpignan: Artège.

VERSTRAETEN, Johan
2011 Towards Interpreting Signs of the Times, Conversation with the World and Inclusion of the Poor: Three Challenges for Catholic Social Teaching. – *International Journal of Public Theology* 5. 314–330.

WICKS, Jared
2003 Justification in a Broader Horizon. – *Pro Ecclesia* 12. 473–491.

The Individual Theologian and Ecumenical Engagement:
Case Studies on Being, Grace, and Love

Michael Root

Ecumenical theology faces an important and delicate moment of transition. The pace of ecumenical dialogues has slackened. Dialogue texts have become steadily longer and, as a result, take longer to produce and appear less frequently. The progress of the 1980s and 1990s toward agreement on issues related to salvation and its mediation, culminating in 1999 with the signing of the *Joint Declaration on Justification*, has stalled as the dialogues have turned to concrete issues of the Christian life in this world, including, most intractably, the Church and, of increasing difficulty, ethics. An ecumenism addicted to a steady diet of progress and breakthroughs is now going through withdrawal.

I have elsewhere sought to analyze the present ecumenical situation.[1] Drawing on analyses of the punctuational nature of large-scale change put forward by Niles Eldredge, Stephen Jay Gould, and Thomas Kuhn (and adapting the terminology of the latter), I argued that, after a period of 'revolutionary ecumenism' in which ecclesial attitudes, beliefs, and behaviors about church unity and division were transformed, we are now entering a period of 'normal ecumenism' in which change should be expected to be incremental, even if still significant.[2] The question for the ecumenist is what form ecumenical work should take in the context of this 'new normal.' This question is particularly acute for the Catholic theologian,

---

[1] Root 2019.
[2] An example of a highly significant but incremental rather than revolutionary development would be the discovery of the double helix structure of DNA in the early 1950s. See Bird 2013.

such as myself, since John Paul II stated in his encyclical *Ut unum sint* that the Catholic Church's commitment to ecumenism is "irrevocable."[3]

An important aspect of such a normal ecumenism, I argued, must be the cross-confessional engagement of theological institutions and individual theologians with ecumenically significant topics. I deliberately use here the term 'cross-confessional' rather than 'ecumenical' to avoid certain overtones that might attach to the latter term. A limiting factor in the work of ecumenical dialogues is often the structural pressure exerted within them toward some sort of common statement that manifests a movement toward greater consensus. Dialogues of this sort may need to continue, but if they are not be isolated from the wider enterprise of theology, they need to be surrounded by an unofficial engagement among others. Such an engagement may at times fruitfully be undertaken not out of an interest to pursue unity nor out of a polemical interest, but out of an interest in better grasping the theological issue under discussion. A Protestant utterly committed to an understanding of *sola scriptura* and convinced that such an understanding is incompatible with a Catholic commitment to the authority of tradition may still profit from an engagement with Catholic critiques of *sola scriptura*. Problems can be highlighted in new ways and potential misunderstandings uncovered. If ecumenism is not to devolve into a niche activity of specialists, theologians need to be convinced that cross-confessional reading and discussion is an important and useful part of theological reflection.

The 'research question' that guides this essay is a large and abstract one and inevitably extends beyond the reach of any one essay: what are the particular strengths and problems that need to be considered in an ecumenism more focused on the individual cross-confessional work of particular theologians who may or may not give a high priority to the pursuit of ecclesial agreement? The methods, concerns, and limits of the work of individual theologians are inevitably different from those of an official dialogue commission. A clearer sense of those differences should be an aid both in carrying out and in assessing ecumenically such work. The question will be pursued here by looking at three examples of such individual cross-confessional engagement: recent discussion in the USA between Thomists

---

[3] JOHN PAUL II, *Ut unum sint: On Commitment to Ecumenism*, para. 3.

and Barthians, the mid-twentieth-century exchange between Hans Urs von Balthasar and Karl Barth, and the late-twentieth-century work on love by Tuomo Mannermaa which flowed from his participation in dialogue with Orthodox theology. These three examples are test cases, exploratory test drillings, examined to provide a preliminary answer to the question posed. The cases were selected because of their structural diversity, representing different kinds of individual work, and because of the way their concerns overlap, creating a larger pattern. In a sense, the three cases comes together as a single example of theologians cross-confessionally engaging an interrelated nexus of questions surrounding being, grace, and love. The wisdom of the selection, however, can only be shown in the result; the proof the pudding is in the eating. A full consideration of each case is not attempted. Many details of each case will not be taken up in order to remain on focus. After the test cases are explored, some brief conclusions will be drawn. Such conclusions must at this stage be tentative and can serve as pointers toward further work.

First example: Barthians and Thomists in the United States

The first example to examined is the recent discussion between Thomists and Barthians in the United States. In relation to our topic, it is useful to note how unusual this discussion is, especially on the Catholic side. To a great extent, Catholic theology in the US has often talked the ecumenical talk but not walked the ecumenical walk. Protestant theology is largely ignored. In the particular case of Barth, a search of the Catholic Periodical and Literature Index of the American Theological Library Association for journal articles containing the word 'Barth' published between 2007 and 2017 yields only nine essays in identifiably Catholic, English-language journals.[4]

This lack of interest is not a function of a possible more conservative turn among Catholic theologians of the John Paul/Benedict era. The

---

[4] Four appeared in the *Heythrop Journal*, which might lead one to believe that there is greater interest in Barth among British Catholics, but it turns out that the four authors of these essays include two Americans, an Australian, and only one Briton. In addition, two of these four authors are not Catholic, but one Anglican and one Reformed.

Catholic Theological Society of America has certainly resisted any such conservative shift. Nevertheless, a search of the Proceedings of the CTSA going back to at least 1965 finds one presentation or session with the word 'Pannenberg' in the title, but no presentations or sessions with the words Luther, Calvin, Schleiermacher, Barth, Tillich, Niebuhr, Jüngel, Lindbeck, or Jenson in the title. By comparison, forty presentations or sessions had the word 'Rahner' in the title (inflated, I must admit, by meetings of the Rahner Society within the CTSA) and thirteen with the words 'Lonergan' or 'Thomas Aquinas.'

The American discussions in recent years between Thomists and Barthians has been primarily due to the efforts of the Dominican Thomas Joseph White, formerly of the Dominican House of Studies in Washington, DC and now at the Pontifical University of St Thomas (the Angelicum) in Rome. It was Fr. White who organized in 2008 a conference on "The Analogy of Being: Invention of the Antichrist or the Wisdom of God?," in which Barth's theology inevitably played a major role, since it was Barth who stated that the analogy of being was an invention of the Antichrist.[5] The Dominican House and the Center for Barth Studies at Princeton Seminary went on to sponsor conferences on Barth and Aquinas[6] and on Barth and Vatican II.[7]

Only a brief discussion can here by offered of the contents of these discussions. Three interrelated clusters of issues formed the foci—epistemological issues related to a knowledge of God not derived from God's revelation in Christ (what would usually be called 'natural theology'); ontological (or simply logical) issues related to an analogy of being between God and created reality; and more straightforwardly theological issues related to God's eternal election of Jesus Christ. The interrelation of the first two is fairly obvious: an alleged ontological reality—an aspect of reality bound up with a relation between God and creation—tends to correlate with a certain sort of knowledge of God. The ontological reality either is itself the content of this knowledge (for example, a knowledge of

---

[5] Barth's comment is in BARTH, *Church Dogmatics*, I/1, xiii (hereafter cited as *CD*, with indication of volume and page); German original: BARTH, *Kirchliche Dogmatik*, I/I, VIII (hereafter cited as *KD*, with an indication of volume and page).

[6] *Thomas Aquinas and Karl Barth: An Unofficial Catholic-Protestant Dialogue.*

[7] The papers from this conference were not published.

God as being itself, on which created being depends) or this ontological reality is the basis for some distinct knowledge of God (for example, of God as omnipotent or simple or some other transcendent quality). The connection of these issues with the eternal election of Christ comes through the prominent presence in the discussions of Bruce McCormack, who has argued vigorously that implicit in Barth's theology of election and its grounding in his understanding of the Trinity is a radical critique and reformulation of traditional epistemological and ontological commitments widely shared by pre-nineteenth century Protestant and Catholic theology.[8]

What do these discussions suggest about such a project of ecumenical discussion centered on two giants of the Catholic and Protestant traditions? The discussion proceeds as a conversation between the comprehensive theological schemes proposed by Aquinas and Barth, each elaborated by a tradition of interpretation (an obviously much longer tradition in the case of Aquinas). The conversation is not easy. The clusters of issues are embedded for each in a distinctive conversation, seen most prominently in the discussion of the analogy of being. For the Catholic theologian, the debate on the analogy of being usually centers on metaphysics or more narrowly on the logic of analogical predication.[9] For a Protestant inspired by Barth, the issues are focused differently. Bruce McCormack comments on Barth's famous description of the analogy of being as a creation of the Antichrist: "The protest that is expressed in these pointed words is directed not at Roman Catholicism per se but to a liberal Protestantism that shared with Roman Catholicism a commitment to a natural knowledge of God—a natural knowledge that the so-called German Christians were already using to defend the proposition that there existed a 'deep religious significance in the intoxication of Nordic blood and their political Führer.'"[10] The concerns that have shaped the discussion in the two schools has been quite different. Despite such a potential for misunderstanding, the discussions were driven by a sense that each of the two theological schemes finds its most challenging and potentially fruitful conversation partner in the

---

[8] For McCormack's interpretation of Barth, see Part 3 of *Orthodox and Modern: Studies in the Theology of Karl Barth*.
[9] See, e.g., MCINERNY 1996; MONTAGNES 2004.
[10] MCCORMACK 2011, 106.

other. White and McCormack, the guiding figures in these conversations, both see the question of the role of metaphysics in theology as a pressing contemporary question.[11]

But is ecumenism simply or even primarily about the encounter of different theological schemes or is it also and perhaps more fundamentally about the pursuit of a greater lived unity in Christ among different churches? The latter enterprise cannot ignore theology. Theology seeks to understand the gospel and the gospel is the foundation of the church's existence and the content of its proclamation. The ecumenical desideratum in the area of theology is sufficient agreement in theology to live a common life in Christ and to pursue in unity the evangelical mission given to the Church.[12] Put differently, the ecumenical task is doctrinal rather than theological—it concerns the normative theological assertions that help to preserve Christian identity and mission rather than the various detailed elaborations of the gospel by inevitably diverse theological schemes. At various moments in history, sharp theological differences have been judged to be compatible with full communion in the one church (perhaps the most notable case is the Catholic *de auxiliis* controversy of the late-sixteenth and early-seventeenth centuries[13]). The idea of the goal of ecumenical dialogue as a differentiated consensus turns precisely on this distinction between a conflict of theological schemes that is compatible with a fully shared ecclesial life and a conflict that is incompatible with such a shared life.[14]

Does the difference over the role of metaphysics in theology that comes to light in the recent Barth-Aquinas discussions constitute a genuinely *doctrinal* and not merely theological difference, a difference that threatens ecclesial communion? White states that the difference over the analogy of being is the "single most important ecumenical controversy of the twentieth century."[15] Where has this controversy, however, found doctrinal expression in formal statements by the churches? The First Vatican Council dogmatically binds Catholic theologians to an affirmation of the possibility

---

[11] For McCormack, see chapter 7 of MCCORMACK 2008, 201–33; for White, see WHITE 2016. White states that the most important difference between Thomas and Barth is the role of metaphysics in theology; see WHITE 2013, 31.
[12] For an argument for these assertions, see ROOT 1990, 165–90.
[13] A useful summary of these debates can be found in chapter 16 of RONDET 1967.
[14] MEYER 1996, 213–25.
[15] WHITE 2013, 1.

of a natural knowledge of God,[16] but that it requires any particular metaphysical scheme is dubious. Whether the Barmen Declaration,[17] the Protestant doctrinal statement that comes closest to rejecting what might be called 'natural theology,' in fact rejects what Vatican 1 asserts is even more dubious. To show that these theological differences over epistemology and metaphysics are significant ecumenical differences in the sense of affecting church communion, one would need to show that these differences affects the possibility of a common life and common mission.

The argument that differences on such questions as epistemology and metaphysics might be ecclesially significant often turn on a particular construction of the implicit structure of the doctrinal commitments of an ecclesial tradition, often but not exclusively one's own tradition, e.g., Barth's understanding of the inner logic of the Reformation and of Catholicism.[18] One might call this construction a *confessional construal*, a imaginative sense of what makes a particular tradition a structured whole and not just a collection of individual unrelated commitments, a sketch of what is fundamental in a particular tradition and how the less-fundamental relates to the fundamental.[19] Within such a construal, some seemingly recondite epistemological or metaphysical commitments might come to appear fundamental and determinative of much that is more obviously central to a tradition. Systematic theologians can see it as their task to show how a tradition comes together around certain fundamental assertions and principles, which then shape and explain other aspects of the tradition. Ecumenical encounter with another tradition can then become an encounter between a confessional construal of one tradition

---

[16] First Vatican Council, Dogmatic Constitution on the Catholic Faith, Canon 1 on Revelation; in *Decrees of the Ecumenical Councils*, 810.

[17] *Creeds & Confessions of Faith in the Christian Tradition*, 3, 504–8.

[18] Thus, Barth's sharp conclusion: "I can see no third alternative between that exploitation of the analogia entis which is legitimate only on the basis of Roman Catholicism . . . and a Protestant theology that draws from its own source. . . . I believe that because of it [the analogia entis] it is impossible to ever become a Roman Catholic, all other reasons for not doing so being to my mind short-sighted and trivial." BARTH, *CD*, I/1, xiii; *KD*, I/1, viii. The "invention of the Antichrist" phrase comes in the second ellipsis.

[19] Such a confessional construal would be analogous to what David Kelsey calls a canonical construal, a theologian's sense of how the canon of scripture hangs together, of what is authoritative and central and what is peripheral in scripture, which any theologian implicitly utilizes if she is to use scripture coherently. See KELSEY 1975.

(say, a Barthian construal of Protestantism) and a confessional construal of another tradition (say, a Thomist construal of Catholicism).

Such confessional construals, as useful as they are for careful and creative thought, also have their ecumenical limitations. A tradition may be doctrinally committed to some of its assertions being more fundamental than others,[20] but rarely is a tradition doctrinally committed to any particular confessional construal of its own nature. That a Catholic rejects some fundamental tenet of a Barthian understanding of the Reformed tradition does not automatically imply that he or she has rejected a fundamental tenet of the Reformed tradition itself. A particular confessional construal can in fact become an ecumenical hindrance. By seeing a tradition as a tightly interwoven, systematic whole, minor differences can come to appear major—the confessional construal connects the minor difference to some underlying, more fundamental difference which must not be compromised.[21] The connection drawn, however, may have more to do with the idiosyncratic vision of the tradition held by a theologian or school and less to do with the normative assertions of the tradition as a whole.

A particular confessional construal can also occlude certain aspects of a tradition and thus conceal some paths of ecumenical discussion. The index to the volume of Catholic and Protestant essays on the analogy of being noted above contains no entry to John Duns Scotus, anathema to many Thomists, whose understanding of the analogy of being, especially in some recent interpretations which see his proposal as more logical than ontological, might prove ecumenically helpful.[22]

---

[20] A central issue in the discussion leading up to and around the *Joint Declaration on the Doctrine of Justification* was the structural role of the doctrine of justification as a criterion within the Church's thought and practice. See *Joint Declaration on the Doctrine of Justification*, para. 18.

[21] A striking example of such an inflation of difference by means of a confessional construal can be seen in Eilert Herms' vigorous critique of the Ministry section of the World Council of Churches' text *Baptism, Eucharist and Ministry*, BEM (HERMS 1985, 65–96). First, Reformation theology is seen as a whole deriving from a single systematic principle ("Es ist darauf zu insistieren, dass alle Einzelsätze der reformatorischen Theologie sich analytisch als Implikate eines Grundsatzes müssen verstehen lassen," HERMS 1985, 69). Individual differences are then not allowed, for an individual difference must imply a rejection of the *Grundsatz* to which it is logically tied. To accept BEM's sacramental understanding of ordination is to give up the Reformation concept of sacrament, and thereby the Reformation concept of grace, and thereby the Reformation concept of revelation, and thereby the Reformation's characteristic impulse and specific point (HERMS 1985, 93–94).

[22] WILLIAMS 2005, 575–85.

The engagement of different confessional construals of the sort exemplified by the Barth-Thomas discussions does provide an invaluable ecumenical resource. If ecumenical dialogue is to serve the reconciliation of actual churches, it cannot limit itself to checking off one by one a series of controversial topics. It must engage the viewpoints of the traditions as comprehensive, if far from systematic, wholes. How a tradition understands itself as a structured whole, however, is not set in historical stone, but a matter of ongoing discussion and argument. Ecumenism can be furthered by theologians beyond the official dialogues bringing their particular understanding of their own traditions into an engagement across confessional lines with the particular self-understandings of groups in other traditions.

Second example: Balthasar and Barth on grace

The second exploratory test drilling is of a quite different nature. Rather than two theological schools staging an unofficial dialogue, this test case here is a cross-confessional critique of a theologian from one tradition (the Reformed Karl Barth) by a theologian of another (the Catholic Hans Urs von Balthasar), along with the response by the criticized theologian. In addition, while the Barthian-Thomist discussions focused on issues of ontology and epistemology at some conceptual distance from what are usually seen as the central church-dividing differences that emerged during the Reformation, the Balthasar-Barth discussion now to be discussed dealt with what has consistently been understood as a, perhaps the, central issue of the Reformation debates, the nature of grace and how grace operates in the justified person.[23] What can this rather different example tell us about the ecumenical role of the work of individual theologians?

---

[23] I believe this topic does not get the attention it merits in Stephen Long's recent study of Balthasar's preoccupation with Barth (LONG 2014). Long does not adequately bring out the way Balthasar's concern for a concept of nature as distinct from grace and his concern for the understanding of analogy he finds bound up with that concept of nature is closely related to Balthasar's concern for a Catholic understanding of grace, one Barth and the Reformation rejected.

Balthasar's 1951 book on Barth, *The Theology of Karl Barth: Exposition and Interpretation*,[24] is a far-reaching examination of many issues. Here, in line with this essay's focus, only one specific topic can be taken up, but one important to both theologians. In his book, Balthasar accused Barth's theology of a certain 'constriction' [*Engführung*].[25] Just what is doing the constricting and what is being excluded by such constriction varies within his study, but an important aspect of Balthasar's critique is that this constriction leads to a limitation in the way we understand God's grace.[26]

For Balthasar (as for Catholic theology in general, since the point is stated dogmatically by the Council of Trent[27]), grace is always a gift, but grace is the gift of an agency, that of Christ and the Spirit, which engages and elevates the human agent so that the human agent then plays an active role within the economy of grace. Put tersely in the terms of Aquinas and Trent, justification is pure gift—it is never merited, a return to justification if one has fallen is never merited, perseverance in justification is never merited—but within grace, the self is so moved that its actions are truly meritorious, meritorious even of eternal life.[28]

Balthasar presses this Catholic understanding of grace toward the end of his Barth study in the discussion of the Christian as *simul justus et peccator*. Whatever that formula may mean, Balthasar says, it must not exclude "a process of real sanctification. . . . One must actively allow God to act in us [*ein aktives Mitwirkendürfen*] that we may become coworkers, not only reflecting but actively radiating the real light given to us. The gift of grace should become such an intimate part of ourselves that we can bring forth its fruit as if it were our own."[29] (In the 1961 Afterword to a later edition of his Barth book, Balthasar contrasts this understanding

---

[24] VON BALTHASAR 1992; German original: VON BALTHASAR 1962.

[25] Balthasar himself identifies 'constriction' as the catchword of his criticism; VON BALTHASAR 1992, 393; German, ii.

[26] While I believe the structure of Balthasar's argument indicates that this limitation on grace is an example of the constriction of which he complains, Balthasar does not actually use the term 'constriction/*Engführung* in this precise context. As will be noted, however, Barth clearly did understand the accusation of 'constriction' to be at the heart of Balthasar's critique of his understanding of grace.

[27] See in particular chapters 6–7 and 16 of Trent's *Decree on Justification*; in *Decrees of the Ecumenical Councils*, 673–4, 677–8.

[28] On this point, see ROOT 2004, 5–22.

[29] VON BALTHASAR 1992, 373; German, 381–2.

with Barth's picture of a mere reflective power among the justified.³⁰) Two pages later, this theme is taken up in Balthasar's assertion that, just as there is a social solidarity in sin, so, in Christ, the justified can bear the sins of each other, in a strong sense of 'bear.' "The just man, to the extent that he shares an active portion in the holiness of the Redeemer, also receives a more active portion in the task of bearing a guilt not his own, thereby sharing in the very work of redemption."³¹ This is, one might say, strong beer. I am not sure all Catholics would use just such a form of words. Nevertheless, Balthasar is here getting at an essential Catholic assertion about the grace-moved agency of the justified in their salvation. It is this assertion that Balthasar finds excluded by Barth's constriction.

In Barth's response to Balthasar's book in *Church Dogamtics*, IV/1, it is just this Balthasarian move from Jesus to the saints who live out this *aktives Mitwirkendürfen* which is noted. Barth thinks he gets an inkling of what Balthasar means by a cooperation that might be excluded by a christological constriction when he reads Balthasar's writings on Thérèse of Lisieux, Elizabeth of Dijon, and Reinhold Schneider.³² Balthasar "sees from that center [Christ] which he has grasped so clearly and finely a whole field of possible and actual representations of the history of Jesus Christ, the repetitions or re-enactments of His being and activity by the saints or by those who achieve some measure of sanctity."³³ Barth then poses, as he puts it, a counterquestion to Balthasar's "mild rebuke" about christological constriction: "whether in all the spiritual splendor of the saints who are supposed to represent and repeat Him Jesus Christ has not ceased—not in theory but in practice—to be the object and origin of Christian faith." The comment about "not in theory but in practice" might suggest that Barth is only concerned with relative emphasis. This suggestion is strengthened by his last words in the paragraph: "If only we were agreed . . . that the ultimate and the penultimate things, the redemptive act of God and that which passes for our response to it, are not the same. Everything is jeopardized if there is confusion in this respect." One might think that all

---

³⁰ VON BALTHASAR 1992, 393; German, iii.
³¹ VON BALTHASAR 1992, 375; German, 384.
³² VON BALTHASAR 1992b; VON BALTHASAR, 1997.
³³ BARTH, *CD*, IV/1, 768; *KD*, IV/1, 858–9. The further quotations from Barth on Balthasar in this and the next paragraph are all to this page.

Barth is asking is for the Catholic to talk a bit more about Jesus and a bit less about the saints.

Barth's objections, however, are more systematic. He notes in his response to Balthasar that his worry that justification in Catholic theology "is absorbed into sanctification—understood as the pious work of self-sanctification which man can undertake and accomplish in his own strength" is increased by the "unshaken" character of the Catholic doctrine of the sacrifice of the mass. Seven hundred pages earlier in *CD* IV/1, Barth had addressed the Catholic understanding of grace (or, more specifically, the version of that understanding put forward by Bernhard Bartmann, a Catholic theologian of a scholastic sort who had written a good deal on Catholic and Protestant doctrines of grace and justification[34]). Barth judges that the Evangelical and Catholic understandings of grace "have diverged widely."[35] The problem is that, for Catholic theology, the grace which is "always God's grace to man" is, "effected and empowered by grace, . . . also our grace," a reality within the human self.[36] Barth's objections to this view are multiple: Christians would then depend on something within themselves and not on Christ; grace would cease to be new each day; grace seems to be only a stirring up of our native powers. He strenuously objects to the notion of a grace-empowered *mitwirken* of the sort important to Balthasar. "On what basis is there ever a *cooperari* in the relationship between the gracious God and sinful man which is not also and as such

---

[34] The English translation of BARTH (*CD*, IV/1, 84) unhelpfully cites the book of Bartmann which Barth discusses as *Dogm. Handb.* The precise title, given in the original German, is *Lehrbuch der Dogmatik* (BARTH, *KD*, IV/1, 89).

[35] BARTH, *CD*, IV/1, 84; Barth, *KD*, IV/1, 89.

[36] It is important to note again the reality of the same assertion being framed by different argumentative contexts in different traditions. The Catholic insistence that grace is a reality within us is shaped by the critical discussion and general rejection of Peter Lombard's assertion in the *Sentences*, Bk 1, Dist 17, that grace is simply the indwelling of the Holy Spirit and not a reality that indwelling brings about in us (PETRUS LOMBARDUS, *Sententiae in IV Libris Distinctae*, 1, 144). The Catholic position was elaborated as Lombard's contention was discussed over and over again in commentaries on the Sentences, not in the controversy with a Protestant understanding of grace. Thus, the first topic Aquinas takes up when he discusses the essence of grace in the *Summa theologiae* is whether grace 'places something' [ponat aliquid] in the human soul (*ST,* I–II, q. 110, a. 1). He is responding to Lombard. To understand such theologies of grace one must first relate them to the discussion of Lombard before turning to their relation to Reformation concerns.

a pure *operari*? How do the work of God and man ever come to stand on the same level, so that they can mutually limit and condition each other?"[37] Barth's objection to Balthasar cannot thus be overcome simply by a shift in emphasis; the problem is deeper.

The natural Catholic response, I think, to Barth's objection is that he has not grasped the Catholic point. Some Catholics, sometimes, perhaps have said what he is rejecting, but not the better Catholic theologians and not Catholic dogma. For example, the Catholic scholar of Aquinas Joseph Wawrykow responds that Barth's criticisms may touch Bartmann, but they do not apply to Aquinas.[38] Wawrykow shows some ways Aquinas differs from Bartmann as presented by Barth. I am fairly confident, however, that Barth would not be mollified by Wawrykow's elaborations. Wawrykow states, along lines I have sketched, that for Aquinas: "God so re-creates the justified that they are able to contribute, according to God's intention for them and as led by God, to their own salvation."[39] This is just what Barth objects to in Balthasar and will not allow, nor, as far as I can tell, would any of the Protestant Reformers.

The Catholic might go on to argue that the consequences Barth draws from a Catholic understanding of grace do not follow. There is, for the Catholic, no "pious work of self-sanctification which man can undertake and accomplish in his own strength" nor is there a *cooperari* in which God and the sinner are placed on the same level, mutually conditioning one another. It is not that Christ gives us a push and then we pedal; the relation is not that sort of efficient causality. Christ (or the Spirit) are present in our pedaling; our pedaling is ours, but even more it is Christ and his grace at work within us. There is no shared or divided agency on a common level, but a participation of the creature in the divine work, empowered and moved at each moment by Spirit. This cooperation is no limit on God; it is a witness to God's utter omnipotence.[40] It is not a compromise of grace, but a sign of God's overflowing liberality, which, always by grace, grace in a sense new every day, includes the recipient in its action, a grace that gives

---

[37] BARTH, *CD*, IV/1, 85; *KD*, IV/1, 90.
[38] WAWRYKOW 2013, 207.
[39] WAWRYKOW 2013, 201.
[40] For a full elaboration of such an understanding of divine and human agency, see LONERGAN 1971.

us, as the Catholic members of the US Lutheran-Catholic dialogue on justification put it, "the crowning gift of a merited destiny."[41]

In the context of this essay, the question must again be posed: what does this example tell us about the way the work of individual theologians contributes to ecumenical understanding? Some of the limitations noted in relation to the first test case apply again. Neither Barth nor Balthasar fully embody their respective traditions. In this case, however, focused on questions on which the traditions have taken more detailed doctrinal stands, we can be more confident that they adequately represent their traditions.

More positively, the Barth-Balthasar exchange shows not just the way the discussion of a traditional controversial issue can be deepened, but also something about how such a deepening can most fruitfully be carried out. The exchange relates particular points of Catholic-Protestant difference (e.g., on the merit of the saints) to more general questions of divine and human agency and their interaction. In ways, this discussion makes connection with some of the ontological issues from the first example above.[42]

As can be seen in the connection Barth draws between his concerns with Catholic ways of understanding justification and sanctification and his concerns with Catholic assertions about the sacrifice of the mass, the Barth-Balthasar exchange illuminates the way various points of difference between Catholic and Protestant understandings fall into larger patterns. A Catholic understanding of the sacrificial aspect of the mass can be seen as a concrete example of the sort of human-agency-within-divine-agency that Balthasar finds so important. In the mass, so the Catholic Church teaches, the Church, in Christ, offers Christ. A similar pattern holds in the Catholic understanding of the authority of Church teaching. With the aid of the Holy Spirit, the Church can, with divine authority, discern what is and is not the Christian message. In all of these examples, a similar pattern

---

[41] *Justification by Faith: Lutherans and Catholics in Dialogue 7*, sect. 112.

[42] Charles Morerod, focusing more on Luther than Barth, sees fundamental metaphysical issues involved in the sort of difference on agency that arises in the Barth-Balthasar exchange. He contends that these metaphysical issues play a causal role in the differences on agency (MOREROD 2005). I have argued that Morerod, while he has a point, exaggerates the significance of these metaphysical issues for the shape of Luther's theology. See ROOT 2008, 505–8.

emerges: human agency is taken into God's work in a particular kind of way, sharing in the divine work. The Catholic understanding of grace fits with a larger pattern of piety, practice, and institutional life, just as the Protestant understanding fits with a different pattern of piety, practice, and institutional life. As was noted in relation to the first example, only if such wider patterns of difference and how they relate to the comprehensive outlook embodied within a particular tradition are taken up can the individual differences be addressed in a satisfactory manner.

The Barth-Balthasar exchange shows also, however, how this deepening of the discussion needs to occur to be ecumenically fruitful. This exchange worked from specific, historically church-dividing differences toward a more general pattern. The Thomist-Barth discussion worked from the opposite conceptual direction, from broad philosophical differences toward more specific issues that might (or might not) be relevant to the divisions of the churches. Whether that latter discussion reached such issues was uncertain. The Barth-Balthasar discussion points to the kind of connections that need to be made to show the ecumenical relevance of the sort of discussions exemplified by the American Barthian-Thomist conversations.

Third example: Mannermaa on love

The third test case will, again, be structurally different. It involves a single theologian, the Finnish interpreter of Luther Tuomo Mannermaa and his writings on love. These texts came out of his engagement with Orthodox theology in the context of dialogues with the Finnish and Russian Orthodox churches. Again, a comprehensive treatment is not possible; the focus will need to be restricted for the sake of this essay's specific interests.[43]

---

[43] Two considerations in the treatment of Mannermaa should be noted. First, Mannermaa discusses love in the context of his interpretation of Luther. As with many other Luther interpreters (e.g., Paul Althaus and Oswald Bayer), Mannermaa presents his interpretation of Luther as a theological proposal and not merely as a reading of a significant figure of the past. Nevertheless, to avoid an overly simple identification of Mannermaa's personal views with those of his construction of Luther, one might gloss the term 'Mannermaa' as 'Mannermaa's Luther' in this presentation. Second, while the English translations cited above of German authors have been compared with the German originals, my Finnish is limited to "En puhu suomea." I have compared the English translations of Mannermaa cited with the German versions of these essays as a limited control on problems that might exist in the English.

The title of Mannermaa's detailed discussion of love, *Two Kinds of Love*, already indicates that a contrast between differing understandings of love lies at the center of his conception. Mannermaa differentiates these two kinds of love in various ways: love for what is and love for what is not, self-seeking love and other-oriented love, etc. One way the two kinds of love are contrasted, however, points to the same nexus of issues that appeared in the Balthasar-Barth exchange. One understanding of love is embedded in a Catholic understanding of grace, for which grace engages and elevates human agency, and the other, the one Mannermaa sees as truly Christian, rejects such involvement of the human agent. Thus he says: "When the relationship with God is understood within the framework of God's Love, however, the active agent and subject is God, not the human being."[44] He does not say that God is the primary agent, in whose action the human agent participates in some secondary or derivative way, but rather simply that God is the agent and the human self not an agent. This assertion is not isolated in Mannermaa's work. He says elsewhere in relation to justification: "The 'old self' of the Christian dies and is *replaced by* the person of Christ."[45]

Human agency comes into the picture when the subject is not the self's relation to God, but the self's relation to the neighbor: "In Luther's theology, the 'passivity' of faith—that is, receiving from God that which is good—and the 'activity' of love, that is, giving to one's neighbor that which is good—belong together; the glue between the two is in the idea of the presence of Christ and divinization."[46] The last phrase, however, indicates a limit to human agency. Mannermaa immediately follows this statement with a quotation from Luther, in which Christian love of neighbor becomes "a vessel or channel through which the spring of divine goods follows into other people without interruption."[47] The human agent seems to disappear, becoming only a channel for the one true agent here, God.

---

[44] MANNERMAA 2010, 45; German of this and the following reference both in MANNERMAA 1989. Here, Mannermaa 1989, 146.
[45] MANNERMAA 2005, 39.; German, 48. Emphasis added.
[46] MANNERMAA 2010, 65; German, 164.
[47] MANNERMAA 2010, 66; German, 164. The Luther citation is from the *Kirchenpostille*, WA 10/1, 100–101.

This limitation can be contrasted with the description of love by the Catholic philosopher Joseph Pieper: "In turning to another person with love, man is *not* a 'channel' and 'conduit.' Then if ever he is truly subject and person. And in 'supernatural' love also, whether it is called *caritas* or 'agape,' and although it draws its force from 'grace'—in that kind of love, too, the lovers are we ourselves."[48]

The difference between Mannermaa and Pieper fits easily into the pattern already noted. Again, divine and human agency and their relation to grace stands in the foreground. The issues related to metaphysics that arose in the first test case above also appear here. For Mannermaa, the false view of love is grounded in an Aristotelian understanding of God as pure being, toward which created beings tend as their fulfillment.[49] For Pieper, the "nucleus and beginning in all our loving . . . is simply the elemental dynamics of our being itself, set in motion by the act that created us."[50]

What does the example of Mannermaa tell us about the ecumenical role of the individual theologian? In answering that question, comparing Mannermaa's treatment of love with his treatment of justification might be useful.

In his ground-breaking interpretation of justification, Mannermaa questioned influential aspects of his own tradition by an enterprise of *ressourcement*, a reclaiming of elements in the Lutheran tradition that had been neglected because they did not fit well with the interpretations put forward either by Lutheran Scholasticism or by the generally Kantian outlook that shaped much twentieth-century Lutheran theology, especially in leading figures of the Luther Renaissance.[51] Mannermaa did just what the individual theologian is particularly fit to do: call into question presuppositions that have come to shape and limit received opinion. One can ask whether in relation to the topic of love he needed to go further in his questioning. He distances himself from the influential but widely criticized interpretation of love in Anders Nygren's *Agape and Eros*[52] because

---

[48] PIEPER 1997, 220. Pieper is here reacting to Anders Nygren's *Agape and Eros*, further discussed below.
[49] MANNERMAA 2010, 19–22.
[50] PIEPER 1997, 222.
[51] See here especially MANNERMAA 2005, 1–9.; German, 12–21.
[52] NYGREN 1953.

of its failure to see in love a *vis unitiva* that unites the Christian to God.[53] Mannermaa's interpretation of love in terms of various exclusive binary distinctions, however, remains a continuity between his interpretation and that of Nygren, as does the suspicion of any connection of love to the nature of being, two aspects of Nygren's understanding particularly open to critique.[54]

Might Mannermaa's own method of seeking unexplored resources within his own tradition have opened up other possibilities? A Catholic might be permitted to point out two such resources. One of the two figures Mannermaa cites as anticipating his views of Luther on theosis, the Danish mid-twentieth-century theologian Regin Prenter,[55] in a neglected essay on "Luthers 'Synergismus'?" challenged the conclusion that Luther simply excludes human agency from justification and explicitly extends that conclusion to the topic of love.[56] The side of Luther Prenter brings to the light may not by itself resolve Catholic-Lutheran differences over agency, love, and justification, but, as with Luther's comments on theosis that Mannermaa brought to the surface, it may help to break up conceptual logjams. A second resource are the often reviled but seldom read works of the Lutheran Scholastics. As noted, Mannermaa associates a false understanding of love with a metaphysics that roots love in a teleological orientation of all things toward God, *ens subsistens* and *summum bonum*, an orientation inherent in the nature of each thing. Such a metaphysics is ruled out of court for a truly evangelical theology. Nevertheless, John Gerhard, perhaps the greatest of the Lutheran scholastics, operated with a variant of such a metaphysics, as did others of his time.[57] To what degree is the continued Protestant suspicion of anything that smacks of Aristotelian metaphysics an aspect of a Ritschlian inheritance that needs to be reconsidered, with the seventeenth-century Scholastics as aids in that reassessment? Again, such a reconsideration may not by itself prove ecumenically decisive, but it might open new lines of investigation.

---

[53] MANNERMAA 1989, 195.
[54] For a critique of Nygren, drawing on both Catholic and Protestant sources, see WERPEHOWSKI 2005, 438–45.
[55] MANNERMAA 2005, 7; German, 18. Mannermaa also cites Georg Kretschmar.
[56] PRENTER 1977, 222–46; on love, see 236–7.
[57] For a helpful discussion of these matters, see SCHARLEMANN 1964, 57–59.

Mannermaa on love is thus a complex example in our series of test cases. In his work on theosis and justification, he brought into prominence aspects of his tradition that had been neglected, rearranging presupposed patterns and oppositions. In the aspects of his work on love here taken up, however, he worked within a widely accepted pattern of analysis, a pattern of analysis that, I would argue, is questionable. Would Mannermaa's work on love have been more forceful if he had been more willing to call into question such received patterns? In an essay of this length, the question can only be raised, not answered.

Some tentative conclusions

This essay opened with a suggestion. In light of the emergence of a relatively stable 'new normal' in the ecumenical relations among the churches in which ecumenical breakthroughs to significantly greater levels of communion becomes ever less likely, greater attention and support should be given to the cross-confessional engagement of individual theologians, especially in settings not structured by a need to produce common statements which press the envelope of agreement. The series of test cases were examined to bring to light strengths and problems of such an ecumenical approach. Inevitably, each case had to be treated briefly and many assertions have been made that require further support and elaboration. Nevertheless, some tentative conclusions can be drawn.

Ecumenical dialogue inevitably works topic by topic, with a focus more on doctrine than theology. Dialogue statements, produced by committees, are aimed to overcome difference and to maximize consensus. Creativity is important, but at the service of the pursuit of agreement. Dialogue statements are not works of systematic theology. Outlining the complex interconnection of topics is not an end in itself for such texts; in fact, a concern for progress on the matter at hand may militate against such a systematic concern.

Individual systematic theologians proceed differently. The inner logic and structure of the faith is a primary concern. The provocative and controversial might not only attract attention, but also spur discussion toward deeper insights. Interesting disagreement might be preferred to a boring consensus.

Each sort of work has its contribution. Official dialogue focuses attention on the specific needs of a communal life in Christ. For example, just what do the churches need to affirm together about the Eucharist to share in eucharistic communion? More individual work can explore the ways the assertions of each church fit into comprehensive wholes and the ways differences with another church also form coherent patterns. The examples related to being, grace, and love pointed to the way a range of issues in Catholic-Protestant discussions form a loose, but definite whole, ranging from abstract questions of the analogy of being to concrete questions of the sacrifice of the mass.

A consciousness of such larger patterns can attune the dialogue working on a specific issue to the connotations and connections that form the context for the topic at hand. As noted, however, the individual theologian can overestimate the significance of such connections, asserting relations of direct implication between ideas or propositions when the relation of implication is in fact dependent on that theologian' particular interpretive structure or confessional construal. Traditions are not systems and the systematic theologian must not turn them into such.

A final point should be made. If we have reached the end of a period of revolutionary ecumenism and cannot expect further breakthroughs to greater levels of agreement or communion, does cross-confessional theological engagement lose its point? Has such engagement been for the sake of furthering ecumenical progress, so that when such progress seems unlikely, further engagement is no longer to be sought? Or is cross-confessional theological engagement something the theologian is called to even if there is little short-term promise of agreement? An irrevocable commitment to ecumenism might mean, among other things, a commitment to be in conversation with those beyond one's tradition to show forth the unity that does exist, to examine one's own tradition from a different angle, to shine a different sort of light on the shared faith. Whatever the precise shape of the ecumenical future, some such commitment from a range of individual theologians is needed as one aspect of the church's vocation to unity.

Bibliography

VON BALTHASAR, Hans Urs
1962 *Karl Barth: Darstellung und Deutung seiner Theologie*. Cologne: Jakob Hegner.
1992 *The Theology of Karl Barth: Exposition and Interpretation*. Translated by Edward T. Oakes. San Francisco: Ignatius Press.
1997 *Tragedy Under Grace: Reinhold Schneider on the Experience of the West*. Translated by Brian McNeil. San Francisco: Ignatius Press.
1992 *Two Sisters in the Spirit: Thérèse of Lisieux & Elizabeth of the Trinity*. San Francisco: Ignatius Press.

BARTH, Karl
1956–75 *Church Dogmatics*. Edinburgh: T. & T. Clark.
1932–65 *Kirchliche Dogmatik*. Zürich: Evangelischer Verlag.

BIRD, Alexander
2013 Thomas Kuhn. – *The Stanford Encyclopedia of Philosophy (Fall 2013 Edition)*. Ed. Edward N. Zalta, https://plato.stanford.edu/archives/fall2013/entries/thomas-kuhn/.

Creeds & Confessions of Faith in the Christian Tradition
2003 Ed. Pelikan, Jaroslav, and Valerie Hotchkiss.. New Haven: Yale University Press.

HERMS, Eilert
1985 Stellungnahme zum dritten Teil des Lima-Dokumentes 'Amt'. – *Kerygma und Dogma* 31. 65–96.

JOHN PAUL II
1995 *Ut unum sint: On Commitment to Ecumenism*. Vatican City: Libreria Editrice Vaticana.

Justification by Faith
1985 *Lutherans and Catholics in Dialogue 7*. Ed. Anderson, H. George, T. Austin Murphy, and Joseph Burgess. Minneapolis: Augsburg.

KELSEY, David H.
1975 *The Uses of Scripture in Recent Theology*. Philadelphia: Fortress Press.

LONERGAN, Bernard J. F.
1971 *Grace and Freedom: Operative Grace in the Thought of St. Thomas Aquinas*. Ed. J. Patout Burns. London: Darton, Longman & Todd.

LONG, D. Stephen
2014 *Saving Karl Barth: Hans Urs von Balthasar's Preoccupation*. Minneapolis: Fortress Press.

THE LUTHERAN WORLD FEDERATION AND THE ROMAN CATHOLIC CHURCH
Joint Declaration on the Doctrine of Justification. Grand Rapids, MI: Eerdmans, 2000.

MANNERMAA, Tuomo
2005   *Christ Present in Faith: Luther's View of Justification.* Ed. Kirsi Stjerna. Minneapolis: Fortress Press.
1989a   Grundlagenforschung der Theologie Martin Luthers und die Ökumene. – *Der im Glauben gegenwärtige Christus: Rechtfertigung und Vergottung: Zum ökumenischen Dialog.* Arbeiten zur Geschichte und Theologie des Luthertums, vol. 8. Hannover: Lutherisches Verlagshaus. 183–200.
1989b   *Der im Glauben gegenwärtige Christus: Rechtfertigung und Vergottung: Zum ökumenischen Dialog.* Arbeiten Zur Geschichte und Theologie Des Luthertums, vol. 8. Hannover: Lutherisches Verlagshaus.
2010   *Two Kinds of Love: Martin Luther's Religious World.* Translated by Kirsi I. Stjerna. Minneapolis: Fortress Press.

MCCORMACK, Bruce L.
2011   Karl Barth's Version of an 'Analogy of Being': A Dialectical No and Yes to Roman Catholicism. – *The Analogy of Being: Invention of the Antichrist or the Wisdom of God?* Ed. Thomas Joseph White. Grand Rapids, Mich.: W.B. Eerdmans Pub. Co.. 88–144.
2008   *Orthodox and Modern: Studies in the Theology of Karl Barth.* Grand Rapids, MI: Baker Academic.

MCINERNY, Ralph
1996   *Aquinas and Analogy.* Washington, DC: Catholic University of America Press.

MEYER, Harding
1996   Ecumenical Consensus: Our Quest For and the Emerging Structures of Consensus. – *Gregorianum* 77. 213–25.

MONTAGNES, Bernard
2004   *The Doctrine of the Analogy of Being According to Thomas Aquinas.* Translated by E. M. Macierowski. Milwaukee: Marquette University Press.

MOREROD, Charles
2005   *Ecumenism and Philosophy: Philosophical Questions for a Renewal of Dialogue.* Ann Arbor, MI: Sapientia Press.

NYGREN, Anders
1953   *Agape and Eros.* Translated by Philip S. Watson. Philadelphia: Westminster Press.

PETRUS LOMBARDUS
        Sententiae in IV Libris Distinctae. 3rd. Grottaferrata: Editiones Collegii S. Bonaventurae Ad Claras Aquas, 1981.

PIEPER, Josef
1997   *Faith, Hope, Love.* San Francisco: Ignatius Press.

PRENTER, Regin
1977   Luthers 'Synergismus'? – *Theologie und Gottesdienst: Gesammelte Aufsätze,* . Aarhus: Forlaget Aros. 222–46.

RONDET, Henri
1967   *The Grace of Christ: A Brief History of the Theology of Grace.* Translated by Tad W. Guzie. Westminster, MD: Newman Press.

ROOT, Michael
1990   Identity and Difference: The Ecumenical Problem. – *Theology and Dialogue: Essays in Conversation with George Lindbeck,* edited by Bruce Marshall. Notre Dame, Indiana: University of Notre Dame Press. 165–90.
2004   Aquinas, Merit, and Reformation Theology After the *Joint Declaration on the Doctrine of Justification.* – *Modern Theology* 20. 5–22.
2008   Review of *Ecumenism and Philosophy: Philosophical Questions for a Renewal of Dialogue,* by Charles Morerod. – *Modern Theology* 24 (2008): 505–8.
2019   Normal Ecumenism: Ecumenism for the Long Haul. – *Pro Ecclesia* 28, no. 1. 60–77.

SCHARLEMANN, Robert P.
1964   *Thomas Aquinas and John Gerhard.* New Haven: Yale University Press.

Decrees of the Ecumenical Councils. TANNER, Norman P., ed. London: Sheed & Ward, 1990.

Thomas Aquinas and Karl Barth: An Unofficial Catholic-Protestant Dialogue
2013   Ed. McCormack, Bruce L., and Thomas Joseph White. Grand Rapids, Mich.: W.B. Eerdmans Pub. Co.

WAWRYKOW, Joseph P.
2013   Aquinas and Barth on Grace. – *Thomas Aquinas and Karl Barth: An Unofficial Catholic-Protestant Dialogue.* Ed. Bruce L. McCormack and Thomas Joseph White. Grand Rapids, Mich.: W.B. Eerdmans Pub. Co. 193–211.

WERPEHOWSKI, William
2005   Anders Nygren's *Agape and Eros.* – *The Oxford Handbook of Theological Ethics.* Ed. Gilbert Meilaender and William Werpehowski. Oxford: Oxford University Press. 433–48.

WHITE, Thomas Joseph
2011   Ed. *The Analogy of Being: Invention of the Antichrist or the Wisdom of God?* Grand Rapids, Mich.: W.B. Eerdmans Pub. Co.

2013 Introduction: Thomas Aquinas and Karl Barth: An Unofficial Catholic-Protestant Dialogue. – *Thomas Aquinas and Karl Barth: An Unofficial Catholic-Protestant Dialogue.* Ed. Bruce L. McCormack and Thomas Joseph White. 1–39.
2016 *Wisdom in the Face of Modernity: A Study in Thomistic Natural Theology.* Ave Maria, Florida: Sapientia Press of Ave Maria University.

WILLIAMS, Thomas
2005 The Doctrine of Univocity is True and Salutary. – *Modern Theology* 21. 575–85.

Compassion in Medieval Philosophy and Theology

Simo Knuuttila

Medieval Latin authors employed the word *compassio* for the emotion of feeling sorrow for the misfortune of others. Christian writers introduced this non-classical term to refer to the same emotion as did the more common word *misericordia*, the difference being that the latter had other uses as well, particularly in theology. Traditional English renderings for these terms are "pity" or "mercy". From the point of view of historical semantics, both these words have a core meaning similar to those of medieval terms, but they are also associated with later connotations. Servais Pinkaers, a noted moral theologian, comments on their use as follows: "On one hand, we reprove those who lack pity and show no mercy to others. But on the other hand, we do not feel the need for others to show us mercy, and we especially do not want to be pitied". Pinckaers adds that these terms have a disdainful tone and are consequently outmoded.[1] Disdain is not wholly irrelevant in the medieval use of these terms, but it is not usual in this context. I shall abstract from the contemporary uses of the terms and keep to their historical meanings.

The notions of compassion and mercy were widely discussed and explained in early medieval works. An anonymous fourth-century author, later mixed up with Ambrose, held that *misericordia* and *pietas*, used as approximate synonyms, could be taken to spell out the sum of Christian discipline.[2] This slogan would have been congenial to Gregory the Great, the

---

[1] Pinkaers 2015, 21.
[2] This characterization occurs in the influential twelfth-century collection of brief explanations on Bible texts; see Biblia latina cum glossa ordinaria (Strasbourg 1480/81), on I Tim. 4:8. The formulation is derived from the anonymous fourth-century commentary on the letters of Paul often referred to as a work of "Ambrosiaster", Anonymous (Ambrosiaster), *In epistulas S. Pauli*, Patrologia Latina 17, 474B.

powerful sixth-century church leader and spiritual authority, who employed compassion and mercy as central notions in his works, which came to be used for hundreds of years in early medieval times and later.³ In section 1, I shall describe the evaluation of the emotion of pity or compassion in Augustine and others who defended it against the Stoic reproach. Section 2 addresses the medieval accounts of the structure of this emotion, attending particularly to how the inner feeling involved with compassion was understood. In section 3, I add some remarks on theological formulations of God's mercy and their relation to the psychology of compassion.

One might ask why the love of neighbours is basically understood in terms of compassion in this tradition, as a readiness to feel sorrow for the miseries of others – why not in a more positive way? The recommendation to rejoice with those who rejoice and to mourn with those who mourn is often mentioned because it was advised by St Paul (Romans 12:15), but the notion of compassion did not refer to co-feeling, whether pleasant or unpleasant, as the Greek term *sympatheia* might have suggested.⁴ The lack of indiscriminate co-emotion terminology separates the medieval approach from later theories of sympathy in Hume, Smith and others.⁵

The reason for the central role of sorrowful compassion in medieval treatises on love as charity seems to be theological. The doctrine of salvation was understood with respect to fallen humankind and theologically relevant positive emotions were eschatological and associated with regulated religious practice rather than everyday life outside the monasteries or holy orders. Sorrows and miseries for their part were something people were supposed to be universally acquainted with in the post-lapsarian world, and these emotions consequently had a more definite theological status – even Christ had freely chosen to become susceptible to human suffering and weakness. This relatively dark picture of human life is found in early medieval literature in which the theology of mercy and compassion was

---

³ Gregory writes in an often quoted passage that we take up our cross in following Jesus in two ways, through abstinence and through compassion for our neighbours; see *XL homiliarum in Evangelia libri duo*, 1277. See also STRAW 2013, 178–179, STRAW 2014.

⁴ The term "sympathy" as referring to an emotion was not very common in ancient literature; it was more usually applied to physical and cosmological connections. For some discussions, see KONSTAN 2006, 213–215; MIRGUET 2017.

⁵ For sympathy in Hume and Smith, see SAYRE MCCORD 2015.

developed under the influence of Augustine and Gregory the Great. In thirteenth-century theology, Aristotle's optimistic ethics changed the theological landscape to some extent, but this did not affect the high status of sorrowful mercy. Thomas Aquinas regards it as the highest Christian other-regarding virtue.[6] Medieval theologians who believed in divine goodness and providence did not see problems in the central role of sorrow associated with their account of virtue. This was in sharp contrast to the ideal of the Stoic-inspired philosopher in Peter Abelard's dialogue between a Philosopher, a Jew and a Christian:

> Finally, whatever may happen, it is a mark of weakness rather than one of virtue to submit the mind to sorrow – a mark of misery rather than happiness, and of a disturbed rather than a quiet mind. For since God disposes all things in the best way, what happens at which a just person should be sad and grieve and thus, so far as he can, go against God's best provision, as if he considered it is in need of correction?[7]

1. Discussions of human compassion from Augustine to Aquinas

There was a well-known ancient controversy about emotions between those who argued for moderating emotions and those who stood for their radical extirpation. The former position was held by Aristotle and others, who regarded pity (*eleos*) as a spontaneous sorrow people feel toward those who are suffering for no fault of their own. They are pitied, Aristotle specifies, for misfortunes that the pitying subjects regard as possible for themselves as well. Pity is a sorrow that is somehow akin to the feeling of those who are thought to suffer, but it is not the same emotion. It is not felt toward those who are very different and not toward those who are very close because then the sorrow includes all together. Neither is pity felt toward those whose suffering is extraordinary – this calls for another emotion (*Rhetoric* II.8, *Poetics* 14).[8] Aristotle thought that because of the social nature of human beings, they have some friendly feelings toward other humans and are

---

[6] THOMAS AQUINAS, *Summa theologiae* II-2.30.4.
[7] PETER ABELARD, *Collationes*, 128.
[8] For pity in Aristotle and other ancient authors, see KONSTAN 2006, 201–216; see also KONSTAN 2001.

inclined to show fellow-feeling toward them (*Nicomachean Ethics* VIII.1, 1055a16-22).⁹ This inclination is required for the assumption that pity is a common human emotion.¹⁰ Aristotle includes pity in the list of emotions which may be learned to be felt well and thus become virtuous dispositions (*Nicomachean Ethics* II.5). He regards it as sorrow for the unmerited evil of others and related to other-regarding sorrow for unmerited prosperity (indignation), both of these belonging to a good character (*Rhetoric* II.9). These are opposite emotions because of their opposite objects. Envy is another sorrow for the prosperity of others, but it differs from indignation because it is directed to any prosperity of neighbours and is morally refutable.

While Aristotle had a positive view of educated emotions in the fabric of character, the Stoics taught that a good person was free from emotions and, consequently, they did not have anything good to say about feeling pity. Seneca wrote:

> All good men will display clemency and mildness but avoid pity; for it is the fault of a paltry spirit that collapses at the impression of other people's <woes>. Accordingly, it's most familiar to all the worst people: old and foolish women whom even the most noxious types move with their tears. (*On Mercy* II.5.5)

If a wise man felt pity, he would not be tranquil and thus not represent the Stoic ideal of following the reason calmly, without inner disturbances.¹¹ Cicero similarly states that there cannot be pity in the Stoic sage because they have no sorrow and consequently no pity.¹² Epictetus writes that one should express pity on some social occasions, but never feel it inwardly.¹³ In their rationalist construction of psychology, the Stoics held that pity and

---

⁹ Aristotle takes this emotional disposition for granted. He says that we prize "the friends of humanity" which seems to imply that a philanthropic attitude based on this emotion is a valuable character feature although Aristotle does include it in his discussions of virtues. In his ethics, he is interested in a much more limited notion of friendship and particularly in the mutual love between them in shared life. For friendship in Aristotle, see COOPER 1999, 312–335.

¹⁰ Aristotle writes that pity is felt for the sufferings of others who are close to us and less, if at all, for what happened a hundred centuries ago or will happen a hundred centuries hereafter. He seems to assume that the disposition of pity typically has a relatively broad scope with varying intensity (*Rhetoric* II.8, 1386a29–32).

¹¹ SENECA, *On Mercy* II.6.1–2.
¹² CICERO, *Tusculan Disputations* III.21.
¹³ EPICTETUS, *Encheiridion*, 16.

compassion were based on mistaken affective judgements that prevented the right use of reason in agency. Participating in Stoic therapy, people could learn to keep a distance from these wide-spread sicknesses of the soul. Their anti-emotional program notwithstanding, the Stoics were not against benevolence or philanthropy, but sharply separated these attitudes from emotions.[14]

In the part on compassion of her *Upheavals of Thought: The Intelligence of Emotions*, Martha Nussbaum moves directly from ancient discussion to eighteenth-century authors such as Smith, Rousseau and Kant.[15] Some readers have found this a problematic jump over the long medieval and renaissance tradition of analysing the notions of pity and compassion. Nussbaum does not especially explain her choice because she does not aim at an overview of the history of ideas, but a strong thesis for neglecting medieval discussion is formulated by Victor Nell: "The view that compassion is a human universal has ancient origins, but in the history of Western sensibility felt compassion was until the end of the 18th century no warrant for action".[16] This is a not very happy formulation: historians of medieval thought, literature and art consider this period as particularly rich in sources for investigating compassion in the past.[17]

Among the influential sources for medieval discussions of the Stoic view is Augustine's comment on Aulus Gellius's report of a Stoic philosopher who argued, in a pitching boat on a stormy sea, that his becoming pale was not a sign of emotion. Augustine's first point is that the reaction of the Stoic was a passion of fear, contrary to what he claimed, but independently of this, Augustine asks why the alleged *apatheia* would be of any great value:

> The Stoics, indeed, are wont to reproach even pity (*misericordia*). But how much more honourable it would have been if the Stoic [in Aulus Gellius's story] had been disturbed by pity for fellow humans, in order to comfort them, rather than by fear of shipwreck. Far better and more humane and more in keeping with religious feeling are the words of Cicero in praise of Caesar: "None of your virtues is more admirable or welcome than your pity". (*City of God* IX.5)[18]

---

[14] For Stoic therapy, see NUSSBAUM 1994; SORABJI 2000.
[15] NUSSBAUM 2001; for criticism, see COOLMAN 2008, 556.
[16] See NELL 2004, 193.
[17] For some general studies, see FULTON 2002; MERTENS FLEURY 2006; COOLMAN 2008; MCNAMER 2010.
[18] Cf. CICERO, *Pro Ligario* 37 in *Orationes* II.

Augustine thought that the Stoic criticism of emotions was based on a misguided understanding of the condition of human beings. He held, like all ancient moderators of emotions, that people are essentially emotional and the idea of extirpating emotions is wrong. While he thought that because of the general sinful deprivation of the humankind, their basic attitudes were mostly ego-centric and the suggestions of uncontrolled emotions should not be trusted, the Stoic *apatheia* is an exaggerated and wrong ideal, even as a utopian educational program. In Augustine's view, social inclinations between sinful people contribute to their communal life and have good effects when controlled by reason. It is particularly this network of fellow feeling which Augustine regards as valuable and which was eliminated from the Stoic ideal.[19] Before Augustine, this criticism of the Stoic lack of compassion was more vigorously put forward by Lactantius who argued that in leaving no room for compassion for others, the Stoics were inhumanely detached from ordinary human concerns. He associated the naturally implanted emotional concern of the suffering of others (*misericordia, pietas*) with humanity (*humanitas*), from which the Stoics irrationally separated themselves. Lactantius argued that proposing their inhumane principle was counter-effective for Stoic thinkers who spoke for active participation in human society. The notion of humanity in this connection was derived from Roman authors who used it as a translation of the Stoic notion of philanthropy. Lactantius wanted to give a new twist to it by stressing the compassionate link between humans as "the greatest bond between people".[20]

---

[19] AUGUSTINE, *City of God* XIV.9; XIX.7; according to Augustine, we are the most social species by nature, but also the "most quarrelsome by perversion" (XII.28); see also WEITHMAN 2014, 237.

[20] Lactantius writes in *Divine Institutes*, VI.10: "The first work of justice is to be joined with God and the second with human beings. The first is called religion; the second is named pity or humanity ... God gave human beings, in addition, the emotion of piety, so that humans would protect, love and cherish other humans and receive and give help against all dangers. Therefore, the greatest bond between people is humanity ... On this matter there are no precepts of philosophers, for being deceived by a false appearance of virtue, they have removed pity from human beings, and while they wish to cure vices, they increase them. And though they often agree that the union of human society is to be retained, they separate themselves from it by the rigor of their inhumane virtue." For the influence of Lactantius in the Middle Ages, see GALYNINA 2017.

In elaborating the Stoic criticism of emotions, Augustine gives a definition of mercy or compassion which was often repeated in medieval times:

> What is pity (*misericordia*) but a kind of compassion (*compassio*) in our hearts for the misery of others which compels us to help them if we can? This emotion is the servant of reason when compassion is displayed in such a way as to preserve justice, as when alms are given to the needy or pardon to the repentant. (*City of God* IX.5)

It was the position of Augustine rather than the Stoic reproach of compassion that was accepted by medieval Latin thinkers, which was understandable because of the frequency of the word "pity" and related expressions in the Bible. As mentioned above, Gregory the Great contributed greatly to the habit of combining the notion of human compassion (*compassio*) with the more traditional notion of pity (*misericordia*) and making this vocabulary central to the discussion of the main virtue of charity and therefore expressive of the hallmark of the Christian way of life.[21]

A terminological remark is in order here. *Misericordia* was a Latin translation of the term *eleos* used in Greek philosophy and literature. In the Vulgate translation of the Bible, the term *misericordia* is used of divine mercy as well as of a human emotion of sorrow for the misery of another. The term *compassio*, which literally translated the Greek term *sympatheia*, was not a Classical Latin word, but it came to be employed by Patristic authors and then increasingly used. The reason for this innovative terminology was apparently the need for an unambiguous word that would apply to the human part of the meaning of *misericordia* which continued to be used as a term with divine and human references. It was usually assumed that God

---

[21] In his *Collationes*, Peter Abelard lets the eclectic philosopher, one of the speakers, represent the criticism of pity in a way influenced by the Stoic view: "Pity (*misericordia*), however, which takes its name from those who are wretched (*miseri*), was described by our ancestors as a vice and a type of weakness of the mind, rather than a virtue. Pity is that by which we desire as a result of compassion (*compassio*) to help others simply because they are suffering affliction. By contrast, clemency goes, as a result of reasonable affect, to the aid of some people, and it is not considered whether they are suffering affliction but whether they are suffering affliction unjustly ... By pity we try to come to the aid of those who are afflicted even if they are guilty, moved by a certain bodily affect, not a rational one, and we thereby go against justice rather than further it" (128). In other works, Abelard distances himself from this approach and defends the position closer to that of Lactantius and Augustine. See MARENBON 1997, 308–310.

has no emotional sorrow or pity.²² This is the background of Augustine's use of the term *compassio*. In his *City of God*, Augustine takes this word to mean a human emotion, and he uses the term *misericordia* when speaking about a morally good compassion. Augustine states in the same place that Cicero also refers to *misericordia* as a virtue of Caesar. Seneca uses the term *clementia* of the same non-emotional political virtue applied to Roman emperors. Both epithets were also used of the God of Christians.²³

Augustine regards compassion (*compassio*) or human pity (*misericordia*) as co-suffering with those who suffer. It is a spontaneous other-concerning emotion of the psycho-somatic lower part of the soul in Augustine's Platonic psychology, and it is good or evil depending on how it is embedded in the voluntary attitudes of the subject.²⁴ In the text quoted above, pity is said to be good when it is in conformity with the requirements of justice. This was a traditional proviso also mentioned by Aristotle. In *Rhetoric* II, Aristotle does not mention the behavioural suggestion as part of pity as Augustine does above, but he discusses it when dealing with sharing the distress of a friend in *Nicomachean Ethics* IX, 11 (1171a30). Augustine thought that pity usually included an impulse to express sympathy and to help, but it may also be felt without this tendency.²⁵ Thus an Augustinian account of occurrent compassionate emotion involves an awareness of somebody as suffering, feeling sorrow for this person, and a suggestion to help, which may be strong, weak or absent.

Gregory the Great employs the term *compassio* for the emotional reaction of sorrow for the misery and suffering of others, provided that these are not just punishments, and the accompanying consoling attitude and readiness to help. He regarded humble compassion as an essential part of spiritual perfection and a balancing factor with respect to contemplation.²⁶ Gregory's understanding of compassion is similar to that of Augustine, and he treats it as a Christian sentiment which is included in the virtue of charity. Like Augustine, Gregory writes that Christ's human compassion is a model for

---

[22] KONSTAN 2001, 106. For some discussions, see also WESSEL 2017; MIRGUET 2017.
[23] RASPANTI 2009.
[24] AUGUSTINE, *City of God* XIV.8.
[25] In his *Confessions*, Augustine writes that when people go to theatre, they want to feel pity for the miseries of actors and enjoy the experience of this emotion, without an impulse to help; *Confessions*, III.2.
[26] STRAW 1988, 255–256; STRAW 2014.

believers who are imitating him in their lives. *Misericordia* is also used in this way, but this term further refers to non-emotional mercy as a divine attribute. It is part of God's charity which is imitated by believers except that their attitude to others includes emotional compassion.[27]

The same Christian terminology is employed by Hugh of St Victor in his explanation of the compassion of Christ in his *On the Fourfold Will in Christ* (c. 1135).[28] Hugh distinguishes between three forms of compassion: vicious, natural, and virtuous. Natural compassion means the natural emotion which can become vicious or virtuous depending on whether the object of compassion is deserving or not.[29] Following the tradition of Lactantius, Augustine, and Gregory, he regards humans as naturally compassionate and, like Lactantius, sees this emotion and its cultivation as the basis of humanity, rather than the Stoic apathetic philanthropy. He also calls the virtuous compassion *pietas* as Lactantius did.[30]

This corresponds to Aquinas's account of the notions of *compassio* and *misericordia* in his *Summa theologiae* (II-2.30). Quoting Augustine's definition from *De civitate Dei* IX.5, Aquinas explains that compassion is an emotion which as such is ethically neutral. When it is connected with charity love, it becomes an affective part of *misericordia* (mercy), a virtuous active concern for the miseries of others. The emotion of compassion is a necessary condition of this virtue. Aquinas writes (*Summa theologiae* II-2.45.6, ad 3) that a person should be compassionate in affect (*compatiatur*

---

[27] See Augustine, *Sermones*, 1213, 3; STRAW 2013, 190–192; STRAW 2014.

[28] For Hugh of St Victor, see COOLMAN 2008.

[29] "Compassion is threefold – from vice, from nature, or from virtue. Compassion is from vice when the emotion is aroused by a reprehensible sorrow there where it was earlier held fast by an illicit love. Compassion is from nature when the soul, owing to its implanted emotion of piety, feels sorrow for the distress of others, as often as it sees them oppressed or afflicted against the measure of pity or humanity. Compassion is from virtue when we feel sorrow for the distress of another for the sake of God. Compassion from the vice is culpable, compassion from nature is not reprehensible, and compassion from virtue is praiseworthy." (HUGH OF ST VICTOR, *On the Four Wills in Christ*, 841.) Cf. the translation in COOLMAN, 541; the same text occurs in Hugh's *On the Threefold Compassion*, 577.

[30] "This piety (*pietas*) is called humanity, and those are called humane who are pious and readily have compassion for the miseries of others. For it belongs to humanity to compassionate and to be moved with piety for the misery of others. A beast can suffer, but to compassionate belongs to humanity. The will of piety is called the will of humanity because it is of a human being to be moved with piety" (HUGH OF ST VICTOR, *On the Four Wills in Christ*, 842.)

in affectu) and helpful in effect (*subveniat in effectu*).[31] Aquinas's analysis came to be an influential conceptual model in Dominican moral theology, but less so in Franciscan voluntarism. Some of Aquinas's formulations are quoted (without reference) in a treatise on compassion by Agostino Nifo, a widely-known Renaissance writer.[32]

2. *The elements of compassion*

Augustine followed the philosophical program of moderating emotions rather than eliminating them and, in line with the standard conceptual background of the moderation approach, he understood occurrent emotions in accordance with the Aristotelian compositional analysis of emotions. An Aristotelian emotion involves (1) a cognitive aspect, which is an evaluation of the representation of a particular object as good or evil to the subject, (2) a pleasant or unpleasant feeling about being affected by this object, (3) a spontaneous behavioural suggestion with respect to the object, and (4) a physiological change caused by encountering this object.[33] This is the general framework of the discussion of the emotion of compassion from Augustine to Aquinas. The virtue of mercy has this emotion as part of it.

Let us turn to some medieval specialities in the interpretation of compassion against this background. I shall address medieval philosophical answers to three questions: first, what is the moral value of this feeling, second, how may expressing compassion lessen the sorrow, and third, what is the reason for having compassion in a particular occasion? These questions had already been formulated by ancient philosophers, but some new ideas were included in the medieval answers. Let us first consider the value question. In his *Tusculan Disputations*, Cicero presents a Stoic argument against emotions to the effect that all what one could achieve by an allegedly emotion-based act could be achieved better without an

---

[31] See also MINER 2015.
[32] See for example the quotation of the summary of Aquinas's *Summa theologiae* II-2.30.2 in THOMAS AQUINAS, *Opuscula moralia et politica* I, 5: *De misericordia* (Paris, 1645), 202.
[33] See KNUUTTILA 2004.

emotion, that is, without the feeling component.[34] Lactantius's answer to this claim is that pity as a moderated emotion represents the personal concern element of social relations. It is based on a natural inclination which qualifies human practice. Eliminating this commitment through philosophical therapy would make social life hard and poor by depriving it of emotionally displayed solidarity in misfortune. Since it was possible to help people without emotions as well, the special value of pity was taken to be precisely in the disposition to feel sorrow for the miseries of others. Lactantius thought that this social sensitivity contributed to a friendly network between people, as is seen in his amending the Stoic apathetic conception of humanity or philanthropy with an emotional formulation of these principles. "Humanity" means here "fellow-feeling" between vulnerable rational beings, not angels or beasts.[35]

According to the Stoic view, there is no sorrow in the tranquillity of virtuous persons because they do not form mistaken emotional evaluations of allegedly evil things and consequently have no reason for sorrow. Physical pain and other disadvantages are non-preferred, but not an excuse for an emotional judgement.[36] Augustine thought that this philosophically based insensitivity makes people unable to understand the human experience of sorrow and so to remain outside of shared humanity.[37] These seem to be the philosophical considerations about the positive value of compassion: the culture of compassion cultivates social solidarity and mitigates the subjective experience of distress; understanding the language and practices of compassion requires participation in them. Following Augustine, medieval authors held that the emotion of compassion inclines to help suffering others. Compassion was generically directed to the miseries of others, but virtuous persons learned to feel it differently on various occasions. Compassionate impulse to remove suffering was not appropriate with respect to just punishment, except for involuntary aspects of wrong

---

[34] CICERO, *Tusculan Disputations* IV.55.

[35] LACTANTIUS, *Divine institutes* VI.10.11; VI.15.2; see also Hugh of St Victor (note 30 above), THOMAS AQUINAS, *Summa theologiae* II-2.30.3.

[36] According to the Stoics, there are no self-regarding evils except the lack of virtue which, to be sure, is not relevant with respect to the Stoic wise; see KNUUTTILA 2004, 56–59.

[37] AUGUSTINE, *City of God* XIV.9. See also *On the Catholic and the Manichaean Ways of Life* I.27 (1333). In order to avoid misunderstandings, Augustine later explained that he did not defend the possibility *apatheia* in this paragraph (*Retractationes* I.7 (593)).

action. It was simply wrong with respect the eternal suffering of the justly damned.[38]

Two other questions mentioned above had an Aristotelian background. Aristotle writes in *Nicomachean Ethics* IX.11 that the presence of friends is pleasant both in good fortune and in bad – in bad since distress is lightened when friends sorrow with us. In explaining why this happens, he asks whether the friends share our burden as it were or whether the pleasantness of their presence and the thought that they are sorrowing with us makes our distress less. The question of whether it is for these or some other reasons that our distress is lightened is left open, but "what we have described appears to take place". This passage is explained by Aquinas in the article "Whether pain and sorrow are assuaged by the compassion of friends" (*Summa theologiae* II-1.38.3). He states that the latter alternative is more to the point. The former explanation assumes that the suffering subject imagines that the burden is divided and the consoling friend takes part of it, which makes the sorrow feel lighter. Aquinas apparently thought that affective imaginations of this kind may be helpful, but they do not provide a general explanation of why consolation makes sorrow less. A better answer is embedded in Aristotle's second suggestion. One's recognition that a friend feels sorrow for his or her sorrow is a pleasant experience in itself. This positive feeling will be mixed with sorrow and reduce its intensity. Aquinas characterizes the pleasant experience as an awareness of being loved, which causes an awareness of one's value and makes the sorrow less intense. This is based on Aristotle's explanation in *Rhetoric* I.11 (1371a19–20) that the awareness of being loved is pleasant because it is associated with the notion of oneself as a valuable person.

Aquinas mentions as a possible problem that perceiving the co-sorrow of the friend may arouse sorrow for the friend's sorrow, which increases one's feeling of sorrow instead of assuaging it. This is based on Aristotle's remark in *Nicomachean Ethics* IX.9, where he adds that better people do not want their friends to show their sorrow very much while women and effeminate men enjoy people wailing with them. Aquinas explains that even though compassion for the consoling friend's sorrow may add to the

---

[38] THOMAS AQUINAS, *Summa theologiae* II-2.30.1; *Suppl.* 94.2; see also HUGH OF ST VICTOR, *On the Four Wills in Christ*, 843–844.

original sorrow, the delight of the awareness of being loved by the friend is stronger than the new sorrow, and therefore the friend's compassion helps to mitigate the sorrow (*Summa theologiae* II-1, 38.3, ad 2).

Aquinas's explanation in *Summa theologiae* is based on his discussion in the commentary on *The Nicomachean Ethics* (IX.11). The same text was commented on similarly by other medieval commentators such as Albert the Great, Averroes, Walter Burley and John Buridan.[39] They found the first suggestion of divided sorrow artificial and unattractive. Buridan formulated the standard critical point by stating that sorrow is an act of the soul which cannot partially be transferred into another soul. The commentators regarded the second explanation as correct, usually repeating Aristotle's advice for proper consolation and his criticism of co-wailing men. Aristotle's discussion of co-sorrow pertains to the relation between friends who in his approach are educated and relatively equal people having much to do with each other and being close through shared experiences. Aquinas refers elsewhere to this text as an example of compassion which is based on human love as a natural attitude not restricted to equal friends.[40]

As for explanation of compassion, Aquinas puts forward the question of how it is possible that one feels sorrow for other people's miseries (*Summa theologiae* II-2.30.2). He thinks that this might be considered as a problem because the emotion of sorrow is felt for one's own evil. Aquinas writes that physical pain is an unpleasant sensory awareness of something repugnant to one's body and sorrow or distress is an unpleasant awareness of something happening to oneself contrary to one's preferences.[41] He explains the other-regarding sorrow first in terms of the union of affect (*unio affectus*) and then in terms of real union (*unio realis*).[42]

---

[39] AVERROES, *In Moralia Nicomachia expositio* in *Aristotelis Opera cum Averrois commentariis* (Venice 1562); ALBERT THE GREAT, *Super Ethica*, ed. W. Kübel (Münster: Aschendorf, 1951); WALTER BURLEY, *Super libros Ethycorum Aristotelis scriptum* (Venice 1481); JOHN BURIDAN, *Quaestiones super decem libros Ethicorum* (Paris 1513).

[40] THOMAS AQUINAS, *Summa theologiae* II-2.30.2; 31.1.

[41] THOMAS AQUINAS, *Summa theologiae* II-1.35.7.

[42] "Since pity is compassion for another's misery, as was said before, it follows that when someone feels pity, he is sorry about another's misery. And since distress or sorrow is about one's own evil, one feels distress or sorrow for another's misery in so far as one regards another's misery as his own. This may happen in two ways. First, this happens because of a union of affect, which is the effect of love, for since he who loves another regards his friend as if himself, he counts his friend's evil as if his own evil, so that he is sorry about his friend's evil as if it were his own...

The affective union is constituted by one's loving attitude to others. This love is formally similar to one's loving attitude to oneself, being the extension of the self-regarding attitude to those who are similar to oneself. Aquinas assumes in an Aristotelian manner that self-love is the basic form of human love as love of a human being in oneself and the foundation of the love of human beings in general.[43] Because of one's love of others, one is inclined to feel sorrow over their evil as if over one's own. In Aquinas's analysis, *the union of affect* is constituted by a representation of one's neighbours as similar to oneself as proper objects of the same emotional attention as one has to oneself, although there is an order of intensity based on the degree of closeness.[44]

Aquinas discusses compassionate sorrow in abstract terms with respect to intentional objects of the love of one's neighbour. He says elsewhere that because of the extensive scope of *the union of affect*, sorrow for the miseries of others may be directed to absent and past people as well.[45] While this is a psychological account of the inclination to compassion, Aquinas adds a brief remark on its actualization in terms of *the real union*. In this case, another's sorrow influences the affective part of the compassionate person to the effect that the emotion of the sorrow transits (*transeat*) from one to another. This metaphorical term is meant to underline the change in the analysis from potentiality to actuality.[46] Why is the inclination to

---

Second, this happens because of a real union, for instance when the evil of others comes near to us and passes from them to us. Hence the Philosopher says (*Rhetoric* II.8) that men pity such as are akin to them, and the like, because it makes them realize that the same may happen to themselves... Accordingly a defect is always the reason for feeling pity, either because one regards another's defect as one's own on account of the union of love, or else on account of the possibility of suffering similar evils." (THOMAS AQUINAS, *Summa theologiae* II-2.30.2)

[43] THOMAS AQUINAS, *Summa theologiae* II-1.27.3; for some problems in this approach with respect to the virtue of charity, see FUCHS 2013, 203-219.

[44] Bonaventure says, like Aquinas, that compassionate *misericordia* for the evil of others includes a conception of conformity in nature and the similitude of the species between people. He adds that *pietas* attends to the image of God in man. See BONAVENTURE, *In tertium librum Sententiarum*, 35.6 (378b).

[45] THOMAS AQUINAS, *Scriptum super libros Sententiarum*, III.32.1.3, ad 4.

[46] MINER (2015) offers a different interpretation about these unions: the union of affect refers to a close relationship between people who regard each other as other selves like in Aristotle's ideal friendship and the real union, without the union of affect, to perceiving one's "real commonality with others". My reading is based on what Aquinas says about the union of affect in *Summa theologiae* II-1.25.2, ad 2 and 27.3.

compassion based on the union of affect actualized as real compassion? Aquinas thinks that the awareness of the suffering of another may be associated with fear that something similar might happen to oneself. If there is no such fear, the inclination to compassion remains unrealized or is only weakly felt. He refers to Aristotle's remark on various groups of people who are slow to actual pity because of their lack of fear such as people who are happy and think that they are sufficiently powerful against the threats of evil. Weak and fearful people are different in this respect as are old and wise people because of their experience and understanding of what might happen. Aquinas seems to understand this as an experience of joint vulnerability.

3. Theological discussions of God's mercy

All medieval masters of theology commented on the conception of God's mercy (*misericordia Dei*). It was a biblical epithet of God who expressed love and mercy to humankind in spite of their fall and sinful condition which as such called for punishment by God's justice. Catholic doctrine was that believers should understand themselves as hoping for salvation on the basis of God's mercy, which was particularly demonstrated by the salvific history of Jesus Christ. Divine love known through revelation and represented by the holy institutions and the sacraments, gave rise to the virtues of faith, hope and charity in the souls of believers with the help of the supernatural influence of grace. According to the standard formula, saving faith was informed by love (*fides caritate informata*). Charity, the highest virtue of Christian perfection, included the vertical love of God as its centre and the horizontal love of neighbours as a consequent. The horizontal charity was understood in terms of a compassionate attitude, which in some way imitated God's mercy.[47]

In late medieval theology of atonement, divine mercy was often associated with the doctrine of the gracious covenant created by God as the basis of salvation. This theological model developed the concept of mercy somewhat differently from Aquinas's more Aristotelian model. According

---

[47] For imitating God's mercy, see THOMAS AQUINAS, *Summa theologiae* II-2.30.4, ad 3.

to the covenant of grace, God mercifully rewards those who love God and their neighbours and thus prepare themselves for the promised salvation by doing their part (*facere quod in se est*). Because of the covenant, God does not deny his grace to those who do their best. He accepts their acts as merits on the basis of grace rather than as grace-informed acts worthy of divine love as in Aquinas.[48] Because of the religious import of these doctrinal considerations, the anti-Pelagian notion of divine mercy, *misericordia Dei*, was among theological key terms in this context.[49]

The question of how the divine attributes of justice and mercy stand to each other was continuously addressed in theological discussions of the doctrine of the forgiveness of sins or, as it was increasingly called in Reformation theology, the doctrine of justification. It was thought that divine justice demanded the punishment of humankind as a whole as well as of all individual sins. Mercy is the source of God's saving activity through which repentant sinners are offered grace, which makes them pleasing to God and restores their original status before the fall. Mercy is here understood analogously to the impulse towards help, an element of the human emotion of compassion, although without sorrow about the miseries of others. It is a loving response to the miseries, but differs from human compassion as being directed to the self-caused misery of humankind.

Many followed Augustine in arguing for divine simplicity to the effect that divine attributes do not constitute any real distinction in the essence of God. In this sense there is no distinction between justice and mercy. While Augustine and his followers admitted that this may not be understandable to human intellect, they held that theologically speaking these attributes are indistinguishable.[50] Apart from this often-repeated onto-theological thesis, it was usually thought that the humanly understandable semantics

---

[48] The presence of God's grace and auxiliary activities made the acts of a virtuous believer sufficiently meritorious for an eternal reward by divine justice in Aquinas. Covenant theologians preferred to speak about the merciful acceptance of merits even when based on habitual grace. See WAWRYKOW 1995; OBERMAN 2001.

[49] See STEINMETZ 1968; SAARINEN 2007.

[50] See AUGUSTINE, *De Trinitate* XV.5.7; ANSELM OF CANTERBURY, *Proslogion*, 9. For the formal distinction in this context, see JOHN DUNS SCOTUS, *Quaestiones in librum quartum Sententiarum*, IV.46.3.

of these terms were not identical although they represented simultaneous aspects of divine action.

Aquinas thinks that divine justice should be understood in terms of Aristotle's distributive justice. Through God's creative and conservative action, all things receive what they need in their proper place in the metaphysical order of things.[51] This is how divine justice works, but Aquinas says that it also shows mercy because all divine acts express justice and mercy. His explanation is that when things actualize their nature in accordance with justice, the notion of mercy in the sense of removing misery or a defect applies to the order of things counterfactually in that their relative perfection due to their fair and just creator saves them from defects which otherwise could have been imagined belonging to them. He particularly argues that all acts of divine justice presuppose the conservation of things which removes the defect of non-being.[52] This sounds like a problematic attempt to explain why the created order exemplifies justice and mercy together by applying the notion of removing a defect to existing things and also to non-existing things. Duns Scotus did not agree with Aquinas's conception of metaphysical justice and criticized it from the point of view of his voluntarist theory of the contingency in the created order.[53] Dropping the extensive notion of justice and its link to

---

[51] Aquinas explains God's *suum cuique* justice as follows: "We may discern two ways in which the notion of due pertains to divine action: in respect of what is due to himself, and in respect of what is due to a creature. In either way, God renders what is due. It is due to God that created things should fulfil whatever his wisdom and his will ordains, and that they should manifest his goodness. God's justice upholds his decency in this respect, rendering to himself what is due to himself. It is also due to each creature that it should have what is ordained for it. It is due to a man that he should have a hand, and that other animals should serve him. Herein also God acts with justice, giving to each thing what is due according to its nature and condition, although this is due only because each thing is entitled to what God's wisdom has ordained for it in the first place." (THOMAS AQUINAS, *Summa theologiae* I.21.1, ad 3.)

[52] THOMAS AQUINAS, *Summa theologiae* I.21.4. According to him, God's act of creation shows mercy in the sense that things are moved from non-being to being (ad 4).

[53] "God does not owe anything in an unqualified sense except to love his own goodness. But he owes something to creatures in virtue of his goodness, namely, that he communicates to them what their nature demands; this demand is identified as something just in them, as a secondary object of God's justice. But in truth nothing outside God is determinately just except in a certain respect, namely, with the qualification "as far as it concerns a creature". Only what is referred to the first justice, in that it is actually willed by the divine will, is just in an unqualified sense." (DUNS SCOTUS, *In Sent.* IV, 46.1, trans. in Williams 2017).

mercy in Aquinas, Scotus argues that these attributes are formally distinct and mercy does not pertain to created connections representing justice in Aquinas.[54] He remarks that the notion of mercy properly pertains to alleviating or removing deficiencies that cause unhappiness.[55] However, his own account of divine mercy is also rather speculative and counterfactual.[56] Scotus argued that mercy is active wherever more or less thinkable miseries are not included in the actual course of events. This shows goodness and "liberating" or "mitigating" mercy.[57] In the approaches of Aquinas and Scotus, the counterfactual possible defects are imaginary deviations from the actual course of things. Metaphysical mercy is goodness in comparison with worse alternatives.

A more concrete question was the role of justice and mercy in commutative and retributive contexts. According to the standard view about divine punishment and reward, also repeated by Aquinas and Scotus, punishments are merciful in the sense that when they retributively correspond to crimes, the scale of punishment is moderated by mercy.[58] This is roughly how Seneca and Cicero understand the virtue of *clementia* in their political philosophy. As for the reward of merits, ultimately the eternal happiness, many authors addressed the question of how this could

---

[54] "Justice and mercy are not formally the same, since justice has as its first object the divine goodness, whereas mercy attends to something in a creature, excluding what can be just in a creature in the sense of exigency, for there is no mercy in God with respect to that which is just in that sense." (DUNS SCOTUS, *In Sent.* IV.46.3 (446–447.)

[55] DUNS SCOTUS, *In Sent.* IV.46.4 (454).

[56] "Mercy is a habit or (however you want to put it) a form by which we will-against another's misery. It first inclines us to an act of willing-against the misery of another, whether future, which one prevents if one can, or present, which one alleviates if one can ... after this activity it disposes to an emotion, namely displeasure over impending or present misery. Mercy is not in God according to the second aspect, that is, as mercy inclines to this emotion ... But in terms of the activity of willing-against evil, whether present or impending, mercy is properly in God. It is proved that this is true in the case of impending misery as follows: Just as no good things come about unless God wills it, so too nothing is prevented unless God wills-against it. Now many possible instances of misery are prevented from coming about. Therefore, God wills-against them. And it is similarly proved in the case of present misery: No misery is prevented unless God wills-against it, and it frequently happens that miseries are prevented." (DUNS SCOTUS, *In Sent.* IV, 46.2 (442); cf. the translation in WILLIAMS 2017)

[57] DUNS SCOTUS, *In Sent.* IV.46.2 (443).

[58] See THOMAS AQUINAS, *Summa theologiae* I.21, ad 1; DUNS SCOTUS, *In Sent.* IV.46.4 (480).

be regarded as just. Thinking how hard the final eternal punishment was thought to be, at least for some people, it is somewhat surprising that it could be worse without merciful moderation. As for duration, no moderation seems to be available. The predestination idea that the general punishment of humankind is mitigated through the merciful salvation of those who are eternally elected was not helpful at all for those who remain under punishment. Medieval and reformation theologians did not find any satisfactory intellectual answer to the question of hell and mercy as is witnessed by the inconclusiveness of the discussions in philosophical theology then and later. Eternal reward is also problematically extreme; in order to avoid Pelagianism, reformation theologians prefer to speak here about a gift.[59] If this gift is given to freely chosen group of people, not necessarily better than those moving towards eternal punishment, the problem is that there seems to be no understandable link to justice. Even though divine mercy was a central theme of spiritual literature, the more theoretical attempts to tell how it always occurred together with justice remained weak.

Primary sources

ALBERT THE GREAT
Super Ethica. Ed. Wilhelm Kübel. Opera omnia XIV.2. Münster: Aschendorf, 1951.

ANONYMOUS (AMBROSIASTER)
In epistulas S. Pauli. Patrologia Latina 17. Paris 1879, 47–536.

ANSELM OF CANTERBURY
Proslogion. Ed. Franciscus Salesius Schmitt. Opera omnia I. Stuttgart-Bad Canstatt: Frommann, 1968.

ARISTOTLE
Ars rhetorica. Ed. William David Ross. Oxford: Clarendon Press, 1959.
Ethica Nicomachea. Ed. Ingram Bywater. Oxford: Clarendon Press, 1988.

---

[59] Cf. SAARINEN 2017.

AUGUSTINE
Confessionum libri XIII. Ed. Luc Verheijen. Corpus Christianorum Series Latina 27. Turnhout: Brepols, 1981.

De civitate Dei. Ed. Bernhard Dombart and Alphons Kalb. Corpus Christianorum Series Latina 47–48. Turnhout: Brepols, 1955.

De moribus ecclesiae catholicae et de moribus Manichaeorum. Patrologia Latina 32. Paris 1841, 1309–1378.

De Trinitate. Eds. William John Mountain and François Glorie. Corpus Christianorum Series Latina 50. Turnhout: Brepols, 1968.

Retractationes. Patrologia Latina 32. Paris 1841, 583–656.

Sermones. Patrologia Latina 38. Paris 1865.

AVERROES
In Moralia Nicomachia expositio in *Aristotelis Opera cum Averrois commentariis*. Venice 1562.

BIBLIA LATINA CUM GLOSSA ORDINARIA
Reprint of the editio princeps (Adolph Rusch, Stasbourg 1480/81). Turnhout: Brepols, 1998.

BONAVENTURE
In tertium librum Sententiarum. Quaracchi: Collegium S. Bonaventurae, 1887.

CICERO
Tusculanae disputations. Ed. Max Pohlenz. Leibniz: Teubner, 1918.

Orationes II. Ed. Albert Curtis Clark. Oxford: Oxford University Press, 1918.

DUNS SCOTUS, John
Quaestiones in librum quartum Sententiarum. Opera omnia 20, Paris: Vivès, 1894. *Selected Writings on Ethics*. Trans. Thomas Williams. New York: Oxford University Press, 2017.

EPICTETUS
Encheiridion. Ed. Jean Schweighäuser, Stuttgart: Teubner, 1965.

GREGORY THE GREAT
XL homiliarum in Evangelia libri duo. Patrologia Latina 76. Paris 1857.

HUGH OF ST VICTOR
De quatuor voluntatibus in Christo. Patrologia Latina 176. Paris 1854, 841–846.

De triplici compassione. Patrologia Latina 177. Paris 1854, 577–579.

JOHN BURIDAN
Quaestiones super decem libros Ethicorum. Paris 1513.

LACTANTIUS
Institutiones divinae. Ed. Samuel Brandt. Corpus Scriptorum Ecclasiasticorum Latinorum 19. Vienna: F. Tempsky; Leipzig: G. Freytag, 1890.

NIFO, Agostino
Opuscula moralia et politica I, 5: *De misericordia.* Paris 1645.

PETER ABELARD
Collationes. Ed. and trans. John Marenbon and Giovanni Orlandi. Oxford: Clarendon Press, 2001.

SENECA
Anger, Mercy, Revenge. Trans. Robert A. Kastner and Martha Nussbaum. Chicago and London: The University of Chicago Press, 2010.

THOMAS AQUINAS
In decem libros Ethicorum Aristotelis ad Nicomachum expositio. Ed. Raimondo M. Spiazzi. Turin: Marietti, 1964.
Scriptum super libros Sententiarum III. Ed. Maria Fabianus Moos. Paris: Léthielleux, 1933.
Summa theologiae, ed. Petrus Caramello. Turin: Marietti, 1948–1950.

WALTER BURLEY
Super libros Ethycorum Aristotelis scriptum. Venice 1481.

Secondary sources

COOLMAN, Boyd Tailor
2008 Hugh of St. Victor on 'Jesus wept': Compassion as Ideal Humanitas – *Theological Studies* 69. 528–556.

COOPER, John
1999 *Reason and Emotion: Essays on Ancient Moral Psychology and Ethical Theory.* Princeton: Princeton University Press.

FUCHS, Marko
2013 *Philia* and *Caritas*: Some Aspects of Aquinas's Reception of Aristotle's Theory of Friendship – *Aquinas and the Nicomachean Ethics.* Eds. Tobias Hoffmann, Jörn Müller, Matthias Perkamps. Cambridge: Cambridge University Press. 203–219.

FULTON, Rachel
2002 *From Judgment to Passion: Devotion to Christ and the Virgin Mary, 800–1200.* New York: Columbia University Press.

GALYNINA, Irina
2017 *Accessus ad Lactantium?* Zur handschriftlichen Überlieferung der Werke des Lactanz und zur Exzerptmethode im Mittelalter – *Revue d'histoire des textes* 12. 161–214.

KNUUTTILA, Simo
2004   *Emotions in Ancient and Medieval Philosophy.* Oxford: Clarendon Press.

KONSTAN, David
2001   *Pity transformed.* London: Duckworth.
2006   *The Emotions of the Ancient Greeks: Studies in Aristotle and Greek Literature.* Toronto: Toronto University Press.

MARENBON, John
1997   *The Philosophy of Peter Abelard.* Cambridge: Cambridge University Press.

MCNAMER, Sarah
2010   *Affective Meditation and the Invention of Medieval Compassion.* Philadelphia: University of Pennsylvania Press.

MERTENS FLEURY, Katharina
2006   *Leiden Lesen. Bedeutungen von* compassio *um 1200 und die Poetik des Mit-Leidens im 'Parzival' Wolframs von Eschenbach.* Berlin: de Gruyter.

MINER, Robert
2015   The Difficulties of Mercy: Reading Thomas Aquinas on Misericordia – *Studies in Christian Ethics* 28. 70–85.

MIRGUET, Françoise
2017   *An Early History of Compassion: Emotion and Imagination in Hellenistic Judaism.* Cambridge: Cambridge University Press.

NELL, Victor
2004   Compassion – *The Oxford Companion to the Mind.* Ed. Richard L. Gregory. Oxford: Oxford University Press. 193–195.

NUSSBAUM, Martha
1994   *The Therapy of Desire: Theory and Practice in Hellenistic Ethics.* Princeton: Princeton University Press.
2001   *Upheavals of Thought: The Intelligence of the Emotions.* Cambridge: Cambridge University Press.

OBERMAN, Heiko
2001   *The Harvest of Medieval Theology: Gabriel Biel and Late Medieval Nominalism.* Grand Rapids: Baker.

PINKAERS, Servais (OP)
2015   *Passions and Virtue.* Trans. Benedict Guevin (OSB). Washington DC: The Catholic University of America Press.

RASPANTI, Giacomo
2009   *Clementissimus Imperator*: Power, Religion, and Philosophy in Ambrose's *De obitu Theodosii* and Seneca's *De clementia* – *The Power of Religion in Late Antiquity.* Ed. Andrew Cain and Noel Lenski. London: Routledge. 45–56.

SAARINEN, Risto
2007   *In sinu Patris*: The Merciful Trinity in Luther's Exposition of John 1 – *Trinitarian Theology in the West*. Ed. P. Kärkkäinen. Schriften der Luther-Agricola-Gesellschaft 61. Helsinki: Luther-Agricola-Gesellschaft. 280–298.
2017   *Luther and the Gift*. Tübingen: Mohr Siebeck.

SAYRE-MCCORD, Geoffrey
2015   Hume and Smith on Sympathy, Approbation, and Moral Judgment – *Sympathy: A History*. Ed. Eric Schliesser. New York: Oxford University Press, 208–246.

SORABJI, Richard
2000   *Emotions and the Peace of Mind: From Stoic Agitation to Christian Temptation*. Oxford: Oxford University Press.

STEINMETZ, David
1968   *Misericordia Dei: The Theology of Johannes von Staupitz in Its Late Medieval Setting*. Leiden: Brill.

STRAW, Carole
1988   *Gregory the Great: Perfection in Imperfection*. Berkeley, Los Angeles, London: University of California Press.
2013   Gregory's Moral Theology – *Brill's Companion to Gregory the Great*. Eds. Bronwen Neil and Matthew Dal Santo. Leiden: Brill. 177–203.
2014   Gregory and Tradition: The Example of Compassion – *Gregorio Magno e le origini dell'Europa*. Ed. Claudio Leonardi. Firenze: Sismel-Edizioni del Galluzzo. 23–62.

WAWRYKOW, Joseph
1995   *God's Grace and Human Action: "Merit" in the Theology of Thomas Aquinas*. Notre Dame: University of Notre Dame Press.

WEITHMAN, Paul
2014   Augustine's Political Philosophy – *The Companion to Augustine*. Eds. David Meconi and Eleonore Stump. Cambridge: Cambridge University Press. 231–250.

WESSEL, Susan
2016   *Passion and Compassion in Early Christianity*. Cambridge: Cambridge University Press.

Luther on Christian Unanimity in Faith and Love

Antti Raunio

The problem of consent and diversity in the church

The need for unanimity or consensus between Christians in a church and between churches as well as questions concerning its presuppositions and possibilities are constantly current issues. They are important for inward concord in churches and for the ecumenical search for the unity of the Church. The problems of the conceptual content of unanimity or consensus and its presuppositions have been discussed, particularly in ecumenical theology. It has become clear that the concept of consensus may be used in different meanings.[1] According to Minna Hietamäki, the recent criticisms of the 'consensus ecumenism' point out that the pursuit of consensus implies that the unity of the Church is primarily about cognitive agreement on propositional beliefs and that this approach fails to recognise the real pluriformity, which is essential to the nature of the Church.[2] For example, the Lutheran churches have tried to take this into account by supporting and developing a model of unity in reconciled diversity, which presupposes unanimity in certain issues, also allows room for different views and traditions. The starting point of the Lutheran model is the 7th article of the Augsburg Confession (1530), which states certain sufficient conditions for the unity of the Church: "And to the true unity of the Church it is enough to agree concerning the doctrine of the Gospel and the administration of the Sacraments. Nor is it necessary that human traditions,

---

[1] Hietamäki 2010, 11–14.
[2] Hietamäki 2008, 203.

that is, rites or ceremonies, instituted by men, should be everywhere alike."³ As Risto Saarinen states, the CA VII has gained new actuality because it seems to provide a flexible set of criteria, which leave room for variation and even plurality. The degree of the flexibility has, however, remained a topic of debate.⁴ The model of reconciled diversity and the so-called *satis est* dictum do not inevitably solve the problem between unanimity and pluriformity, because they leave open the questions of what is central and what is peripheral and how this should be decided. We are not going to present the modern discussion on this topic here but refer only to some aspects of it.⁵ The main task of this paper is to ask what Martin Luther's contribution to the question of the relation between unanimity and diversity in the Christian communion could be, and how he understands the relation between faith and love in the unanimity.⁶

Unanimity in love

In recent discussion, some prominent theologians have criticised the idea of consensus as an ecumenical aim or denied the possibility of a 'differentiated consensus'. A common emphasis has been the disapproval of a propositional conception of consensus. Christian unity is not based on a set of cognitive propositions that have to be agreed on. This view emphasises something other than the propositional nature of unity and unanimity but it does not inevitably deny all propositional content of the Christian belief.⁷ For Luther, the unanimity, consensus or concord

---

³ BSELK, 61: "Et ad veram unitatem ecclesiae satis est consentire de doctrina evangelii et de administratione sacramentorum. Nec necesse est ubique similes esse traditiones humanas se uritus aut ceremonias ab hominibus institutas..." On this theme, see also Kenneth Appold's article in this same volume.

⁴ SAARINEN 2010, 172.

⁵ For the Finnish research and discussion concerning the *unity in reconciled diversity*, see, e.g., WIKSTRÖM 1982, 263–267; GRÖNVIK 1993; SAARINEN 1994, 116–117; TYÖRINOJA 1994, 219–225.

⁶ I have dealt with these questions earlier from the point of view of the relations between doctrine, ethics and practice. See RAUNIO 2016.

⁷ HIETAMÄKI 2010, 7–8, 198–209. The contemporary discussion concerning the nature of the doctrinal formulations is initiated by George Lindbeck's study 'The Nature of Doctrine',

between Christians is a significant theme.[8] We may well ask, however, if he understands it as an aim, which the Christians should search for or could it be defined more accurately in some other way. As for the second theme of the recent discussion, the criticism of cognitive and propositional understanding of consensus, Luther certainly has something in common with the critics. For him, Christian unanimity is not just a propositional cognitive agreement on the Christian doctrine, but neither does he reject the doctrine's propositional content.

Luther makes important conceptual differentiations concerning the question of Christian unanimity. First, he differentiates between 'unanimity in faith' and 'unanimity in love'.[9] Both concepts occur of course in theology before Luther, and he uses certain traditional elements in his own thought. Second, Luther also differentiates between the philosophical and theological senses of these concepts, especially when he deals with the unanimity in love. The difference between these two senses is important for Luther's thought in many other contexts as well. He treats the question of the unanimity of love in a sermon on Romans 15.[10] There, the conceptual difference between philosophy and theology is not expressed directly but in connection with elucidating the meaning of 'knowing or understanding the same'.[11] In the philosophical sense, unanimity means that people agree on or share a common view of something. We may well call this philosophical understanding of unanimity 'cognitive' and 'propositional'. In theology, however, 'unanimity' refers to something that the 'God of patience and consolation' gives to the humans so that they will unanimously honour God and the Lord Christ's Father.[12] We will later see why Luther calls God here purposely 'the God of patience and consolation' and 'our Lord Christ's Father'. Furthermore, he sees the Christian unanimity as the most intimate movement of the human heart, that is, an affect or emotion.

---

where the author introduces the idea of doctrine as grammar of religious language. LINDBECK 1984. For the recent discussion, see SAARINEN 2012 or SAARINEN 2017, 276–297.

[8] The terms 'unanimity,' 'consensus,' 'concord' and 'consent' will be used here as synonyms.
[9] WA 38, 276, 16–17: "Alia est enim concordia fidei, alia Charitatis."
[10] WA 7, 480–487.
[11] WA 7, 480, 12–15: "Deus autem patientiae et solatii det vobis idipsum sapere in alterutrum secundum Ihesum Christum, ut unanimes uno ore honorificetis deum et patrem domini nostri Ihesu Christi."
[12] See the footnote 2.

This intimate movement that honours God, orientates itself simultaneously towards the neighbour and searches after his/her good, not after one's own. Accordingly, when one dissents with one's neighbour in theological sense, his/her intimate affect is directed against the other and his/her good.[13] This emotive description of unanimity goes well with Luther's idea of Christian love of neighbour. Unanimity as mutual searching for the neighbour's good is an aspect of the effect of Christian love. In this matter, Luther clearly adheres to the Augustinian tradition, where Christian unanimity and unity is connected especially with love (*caritas*).[14] Nevertheless, he not only follows Augustine or later Augustinian theology, but applies the tradition originally. In this context, his own contribution is the emphasis of the emotive sense of 'knowing the same', setting oneself in the neighbour's position and searching for his/her good.

According to Luther, God, the creator of patience and consolation, gives people something that they do not have by themselves: the mutual knowing of the same. This means that when everyone understands the same as the other, they are influenced, moved and oriented by the same objects, and the same things please them. This happens so that the weak understand the same as the strong and the strong take the difficulties of the weak as if they were their own. They do so because they would wish the same for themselves if they were in the position of the weak. Luther emphasises that 'understanding the same' does not mean seeking one's own but looking for what is good for the others.[15] Luther thus defines the theological sense of unanimity in love with the same words as he speaks about love of neighbour. Understanding the same with another presupposes setting oneself in the other's place and dealing with his or her weakness or distress as if they were

---

[13] WA 7, 484, 5–19: "Scriptura quidem docet, sed gratia donat quod illa docet. 'Deus', inquit, 'autor et largitor pacientiae et solacii, det vobis, quia non habetis ex vobis, idipsum sapere in alterutrum', hoc est, ut unusquisque sentiat idem quod alter, hoc est, eisdem afficiamini, moveamini, teneamini, eadem omnibus placeant. Quo modo? Scilicet ut infirmi sapiant ea quae firmi, rursus firmi non secus habeant infirmorum incommoda ac sua propria, ut, sicut sibi vellent fieri, si in loco infirmorum essent, ita faciant et ipsi eisdem. Hoc enim est idem sapere, non sua quaerere [Eph. 5, 15 f., Phil. 2, 4., 1. Cor. 10, 24.] sed quae aliorum, ut Ephe. 5. docet… Unde 'sapere' hoc loco non usu philosophico sed Christiano significat affectum esse seu, ut vulgo dicunt, habere sentimentum, videre, opinionem, inclinationem et similia, Intimum scilicet cordis illum motum in proximum vel contra proximum."

[14] HENDRIX 1974, 20–23, 72–74.

[15] WA 7, 484, 6–13.

one's own.¹⁶ And one should acknowledge the other's strength as well. So, a weak person may participate in a strong one's strength and a strong person in a weak one's disadvantage. For Luther, this spiritual effect, which is also called 'Unity of the Spirit', is the strength of the whole of Christianity, without which it would not stand.¹⁷ In the *Large Commentary of the Galatians*, Luther stresses that love does not mean goodwill for another but bearing their burdens. Love is sweet, kind and patient, not in receiving but in giving. It must ignore many things and bear several burdens. In the same context, Luther implicitly refers to the difference between unanimity in love and unanimity in faith. He sets one qualification for the bearing of the burdens of others: Christ and his kingdom shall not be offended. This would mean insulting the word, the faith and the Spirit, which maintain Christ's kingdom.¹⁸

As becomes clear from Luther's own words, this spiritual effect of unanimity also contains the aspect of understanding, so it does not occur without some cognitive content. In other words, the Christian communion is based on the intimate movement of mutual understanding of and quest for another's good. *Augustine* also speaks partly in similar way. He interprets the exhortation to carry another's burdens so that the other's sin also becomes one's own and those who live in love bear others' burdens. But he does not connect this with unanimity in love.¹⁹ In some texts, he looks at the Christian community from the point of view of one who may participate in another's good and strengths. These statements lack the aspect of sharing the sins and weaknesses as well as helping another with one's own virtues and strength.²⁰ Comparably, Richard of St. Victor writes about love that unites the Christians with their neighbours so that

---

¹⁶ Luther emphasises setting oneself in the neighbour's position in order to know his/her real needs as the demand of the commandment of the love of neighbour or the golden rule. See Raunio 2001 and Raunio 2017.

¹⁷ WA 7, 484, 13–16: "Hic enim affectus spiritualis est nervus totius Christianae religionis, sine quo subsistere nequeat, quem alibi [Eph. 4, 3.] vocat unitatem spiritus: 'solliciti', inquit, 'servare unitatem spiritus in vinculo pacis'."

¹⁸ WA 40 II, 144, 20–145, 25 [Dr.].

¹⁹ St. Augustine, In Psalmum XLI enarratio. Sermo ad plebem, cap 4. PL 37.

²⁰ Augustine's texts about Christian unity as the body of Christ are cited in Althaus 1929, 11. See St. Augustine, De gratia Novi Testamenti liber, seu epistola CXL, cap. XXVI, 63, PL 33; Sermo CXLIX, cap. X., 11. PL 38; Ad Marcellinum de civitate Dei contrapaganos, liber decimus, caput VI. De vero perfectoque sacrificio. PL 41

everything becomes shared as well 'in tribulation as in the reign', as he says referring to the Revelation 1:9. According to him, the believers have one heart and one mind and neither diversity of wills nor possession of different things divide their souls, since love combines them firmly, and keeps them in the unity of the spirit and in the pond of peace. Like Augustine, Richard stresses participation in each other's virtues and assets in the one body where love unites the believers.[21] Thomas Aquinas sees Gal. 6:2 as an admonition to the Christians to support one another and so to fulfil the law of Christ, that is, charity. For him this must be done in three ways: in one way by patiently enduring the bodily or spiritual defects of another; in a second way by coming to one another's aid in their needs, and in a third way by making satisfaction through prayers and work for the punishment one has incurred. The obstacle to bearing another's burdens is pride. Thomas writes that if any man thinks himself to be something, that is to say, through pride judge in his own mind that he is greater than a sinner, whereas he is nothing by himself, he deceives himself, cutting himself off from the truth, because whatever we are it is from the grace of God. The way to avoid such a failing is to consider one's own faults, for it is because one considers the faults of others and not one's own that one appears to oneself as 'something' in comparison to others in whom one observes defects. When one does not consider one's own faults, one has a feeling of pride. But when one diligently examines one's own work, both inwardly and outwardly, one will find in one's infirmities that one's glory will be in the power of Christ and in God who dwells in him.[22] Thus, Thomas' focus is on tolerating the faults of another and helping in his/her needs, but he neither discusses the unanimity in love nor suggests setting oneself in the situation of another. *Johannes Tauler*, whom Luther appreciated, describes the Christian community using the human body with its different members as an example. None of the members work for themselves, but for the others and for the whole body. Accordingly, all the members of the community are there for one member and one for all the others. Tauler understands this reciprocal being there for others

---

[21] RICHARD OF ST. VICTOR, Tractatus de gradibus charitatis, cap. IV. De amoris inseparabilitate, 1204–1205.

[22] ST. THOMAS AQUINAS, Super Epistolam B. Pauli ad Galatas lectura/Commentary on Saint Paul's Epistle to the Galatians, Chapter 6, Lecture 1.

as consensus (*Eintracht*). In unanimity, a Christian rejoices about Christ's love of his/her neighbour even more than his love of him/herself. Then all the neighbour's virtues will also be one's own – and if one loves them in oneself more that in the neighbour, they belong to one even more than to the neighbour.[23] In Tauler's version of the Augustinian emphasis of the participation in the neighbour's virtues, the criterion of owning them is the amount of love of them.

So, even though Luther has some views common to the Augustinian tradition concerning the unity and unanimity of the Christian communion or the Body of Christ, his concept of love differs from the preceding ideas. He accentuates the reciprocal setting in the other's position and the sharing of everything, as well as the good and the bad, and sees this as unanimity in love. For him, such unanimity also leads to reciprocal helping and serving. All this presupposes his understanding of Christian love, which is not directed towards good objects but makes its objects good.[24]

Unanimity in faith

Unanimity in love is not all that Luther has to say about the Christian consent. He also speaks about unanimity in faith. The relationship between the two consents can be revealed by investigating how Christian unanimity began. So far, we have stated that unanimity is something that God gives, but no definite answer to the question of how this takes place has yet been given. The Christian concord is something that God gives through his word or, as Luther says, "the Scripture teaches and the grace gives what it teaches." In such giving, God's grace uses both the Scripture and the Sacraments. Luther combines the common faith and doctrine with the Holy Communion, which unites the Christian with Christ and other Christians. The Holy Communion unites Christians as one in a real spiritual body where they have one head, Christ, and they all are each other's members.

---

[23] Hoffmann 1961, 237–240. Tauler 1979, 301–302.

[24] In the texts where Luther considers unanimity in love, he does not mention Aristotle explicitly. It is, however, clear that he simultaneously criticises the Aristotelian view of love that was applied to Christian theology in the Middle Ages. For a thorough analysis of Luther's critique of the Aristotelian view of love, see Dieter 2001, 64–130.

In this communion, a Christian has the same faith, doctrine and sacrament as the other. Likewise, they have the same weakness, foolishness, infirmity and poverty. Accordingly, if a Christian's neighbour is naked, the Christian is as well and he/she will not cease until the neighbour is clothed. And when a Christian is thirsty or hungry, his/her hunger and thirst are also the others', so the Christian acts as if his/her neighbour's need were her own. Likewise, sins become common: if one Christian is a sinner, so are all the others.[25] Their task is then to help the sinner as if the sins were their own.[26] Among Christians, there is no division between the sinful and the sinless. Especially in the doctrine of the Holy Communion, we see how unanimity in faith and unanimity in love belong together and how everything becomes shared between Christians.

The communion between human beings becomes reality when they receive the Sacrament of Altar.[27] When partaking in the Sacrament, the believers also receive Christ himself and become united with him and he unites himself with them. The sinners come to Christ, leave their sins to him, and get from him faith, righteousness, eternal life and the will to obey God's will. When the faith renews the Christians this way, they let others 'eat and drink' them. The mutual eating and drinking fulfils the call to bear each other's burdens. When taking care of one's neighbour, one serves the other both spiritually and materially, both by faith and love, so the neighbour may hear the Gospel, experience consolation, and receive what he/she needs for daily living.[28] In a Christian community based on receiving Christ by faith, people serve each other reciprocally in this way through the Gospel and good deeds. Consequently, there is no division between the givers and the receivers but all belong to both groups simultaneously.

So, in the communion of the saints, everything good that one member has is every believer's own, and one member's iniquities are everyone's iniquities. This means, for example, that if one member of the community suffers, all its members, that is, Christ and all Christians, suffer with him/her and if one is glorified all the members rejoice with him/her. All

---

[25] WA 30 I, 26, 22–27, 5.
[26] RAUNIO 2001, 343–354, especially 352.
[27] WA 30 I, 27, 16–18.
[28] WA 30 I, 27, 6–16; 19–21. About Luther's view of mutual eating and drinking, see RAUNIO 2001, 352–354.

the members carry everyone's burdens and all strengths are also shared. The nobler members of the community cover, serve, and honour their dishonourable neighbours. Therefore, Luther says, echoing the traditional Augustinian and especially Tauler's view, that one may boast of others' virtues as if they were one's own, and when one congratulates others and rejoices with them, their virtues are also one's own. By such love of others, one not only owns their virtues and assets but also the others themselves. In and with them, one gets everything that one needs. One needs not be desperate because of one's own sins, because one does not have to carry them alone but gets help from all the saints and from Christ himself.[29]

Unanimity in the Christian communion

According to Luther, in the communion where everything is shared, Christians are of the same mind or, more exactly, they have one common mind. In the condition of being of the same mind, faith and love are intertwined.[30] Being of the same mind includes a common knowledge of the most important article of faith in Christ, but also unanimity, for example about weakness, foolishness and poverty. Common knowledge of the faith means, above all, consent about salvation in Christ.[31] The minds of Christians become united to the utmost concord by teaching and knowing the 'healthy doctrine',[32] and in the real Church the unity of faith, word, doctrine and opinion remains with the most different gifts.[33] For Luther the doctrine is principally the revealed doctrine about God who has manifested himself in Christ. The doctrine tells that God is available in

---

[29] WA 6, 131, 7–29.
[30] See also RAUNIO 2016, 122.
[31] WA 40 II, 603, 23–28: "Omnes enim, quantumcunque diversi sint in donis, tamen sunt unanimes et consencientes in summo articulo, quod fide in Christum fiant salvi et nulla alia re. Sic ego, si sum Doctor Euangelii, idem facio, quod Paulus et Petrus faciunt. Sic pastor Antiochenae Ecclesiae idem facit quod Prophetae. Omnes sequuntur unum Christum, nihil volunt scire, sapere, predicare praeter Christum crucifixum".
[32] WA 40 I, 626,13–16: "Ea est natura et fructus sanae doctrinae, quod bene docta et cognita coniungit mentes summa concordia. Ubi vero homines neglecta pietatis doctrina amplectuntur errores, scinditur ista animorum concordia."
[33] WA 40 II, 603, 31–33: "Hic autem in vera Ecclesia manet unitas fidei, verbi, doctrinae, opinionis inter differentissima dona."

Christ, and it also gives the incarnated God to the believers.[34] This is the case because the divine revelation not only refers to God but God himself is present in it. The doctrine therefore gives to Christians Christ's whole person and work and, in them, the Triune God.[35] This is for Luther the reason for the importance of unanimity in faith, which receives Christ and with him the Triune God.

The concord of the faith in Christ is simultaneously the foundation of the unanimity in love.[36] Luther states that Christ alone must govern human reason and heart. Without that, the heart inwardly hates the law of God, but Christ dwells and reigns in a person who hears and believes that Christ has suffered because of him and has fulfilled the law. Then the humans' own works cease and they – as Luther says – "give themselves to the grace". The Holy Spirit comes and fills their hearts and leads them. For Luther, this is the same as experiencing Christ who does everything in the heart.[37] So, before everything else, Christians know what they have from Christ. They understand that they have received the redemption freely and without price, so that they have enjoyed the abundance of Christ and need not to do anything for their own salvation. Therefore, their task is to promote their neighbours' salvation. If, however, they arrogantly oppose this, they

---

[34] Nüssel 2017 summarises Luther's concept of doctrine as follows: "…the core topic of Christian doctrine is Christ's redemption through his proclamation, his death on the cross, and his resurrection by which God in the power of his spirit graciously offers justification by faith alone. By representing God's gracious revelation in the incarnation and redemptive and salvific activity of his son, Christian doctrine communicates the presence of the loving and justifying God who evokes faith and trust through his word. While Christian doctrine grants knowledge about God's triune activity, it is not only informative, but communicates God's promise efficiently."

[35] About Luther's concept of doctrine, which refers to God as an actually present object and donates its content to the believer, see Martikainen 1992 and Nüssel 2017.

[36] WA 40 II, 137, 11–14: "Caterum cum his, qui Christum diligunt et verbum ipsius pie docent et credunt, offerimus nos non solum servaturos pacem et concordiam, sed etiam laturos eorum infirmitates et peccata et eos lapsos instauraturos nos, iuxta hoc praeceptum Pauli, spiritu mansueto."

[37] WA 11, 74, 17–26: "Ratio et cor non potest regi nisi per Christum. Quanquam legem servemus ad literam, tamen nobis molesta est, quia intus odio habet legem cor, dicit semper 'velim legem me non habere', donec discipuli veniant iussu domini et ferant pullum, ut Christus insideat. Hoc fit, quando apostoli veniunt et praedicant, hi faciunt, ut Christus insideat, hoc est: quando audio Christum omnia passum pro me, quando eum esse qui legem impleat, audiunt, tum a suis operibus cessabunt seque dabunt in gratiam meam. Tum veniet spiritus sanctus et implebit cor eorum, ut iam non suo, sed spiritus ductu regantur. Illud equitare nihil aliud est quam Christum sentiri in corde nostro, quod omnia faciat."

speak according to their own mind and end up with disagreement.[38] Consequently, seeking what is good for a neighbour presupposes consensus about what Christ has done for human beings and given to them. This common understanding is the propositional aspect of Christian unanimity.

Unanimity and diversity

Luther's view of the reality concerning the concord of the Gospel of Christ has some common features with recent emphases on discussion about consensus. For him, the Gospel is preached to everyone but only a few receive it. Humans have the words of the Gospel, but still they divide into sects, that is, they do not have the same mind. People interpret the Gospel in different ways so that countless sects are born. The reason for this is that people are sinful and receive the Gospel in a carnal way. In fact, according to Luther there is no hope of a full concord between Christians. Nevertheless, the proclamation of the Gospel must be continued in order to reach greater unanimity. "If you cannot serve all fishes and your net tears, serve those who you can," says Luther. Anyway, the preaching of the Gospel aims at the formation of one mind among Christians.[39] He may say even more strongly that, under the reign of the Devil, there will be no peace and concord about the doctrine. Then there is only one way,

---

[38] WA 11, 74, 31–36: "Videte, quid sit charitas, ante omnia, quandoquidem Christiani sitis: scitis enim, quid a Christo habeatis, nempe redemptionem frey umb sonst, ut satis habeatis a Christo, hin furt non opus est, ut ordinetur, quid agatis in vestram salutem, sed proximi, et greifft er an den dunckel, estque pessimum vitium, quando homo auff sein synn geredt, tum fit discordia."

[39] WA 11, 74, 37–75, 12: "Euangelium omnibus praedicatur, sed pauci accipiunt: qui non recipiunt, habent quidem verba, sed sectas incipiunt, quod et ego iam experior. Et videtis, quando Euangelium in populum spargetur, ille sic, alius aliter interpretabitur, et innumerae sectae exorientur, quia carnales sumus et verbum intrat in veterem utrem. Ego praedicare debeo Euangelium et omnibus annunciare, Et pauci sunt qui recte accipiunt, quin et damnum nobis facient, quid faciemus? non est spes habenda, quod una futura sit concordia, sed potius cum Euangelium auditur, fit dissensus. Haec est art et dispositio verbi, quando venit unter das volck, quia carnaliter accipimus illud. 2. tamen nit abzulassen ist et treiben debemus, ut fiant unius sensus. Si omnes pisces non servantur et rumpitur rethe, serventur tamen, qui possunt. Ita nobis faciendum, ut Paulus ut [Phil. 2, 2, Hos. 10, 2] 'unus sit sensus in nobis'"

which is patience in the love of Christ.⁴⁰ Even though Luther saw no hope of concord between Lutherans and Catholics, he presented patient love as the way forward.

Actually, in Luther's view believers may have one mind in faith even though they are divided in orders and groups with different understandings of faith. The Christians serve faith and love purely when the condition of the others pleases them, and they also ask the others to be pleased about their condition.⁴¹ This indicates that even unanimity in faith may allow some kinds of differences. If this holds true, simultaneity of unanimity and certain differences concerning the understanding of the Gospel are possible, but how should we understand this kind of unanimity?

Luther stresses that we should try to serve pure faith and love, and then refers to consent as the best and ultimate example of love. This consent includes faith in Christ, even though Luther does not mention it explicitly. The love about which he is speaking here is God's love of humanity, which is shown in Christ's kenosis, his self-emptying of the divine attributes. The biblical teaching of kenosis is combined with an exhortation to a certain kind of unanimity. All Christians are invited to have the mind, which Christ had when he emptied himself. He, who was God and could have treated humans like a God, has lived as if he were not any God. He took the 'form of a slave' incarnated, and accepted our similarity. Among the weak, he became equally weak and among the poor, he was poor.⁴² For Luther, Apostle Paul means that Christ's example should allow Christians to feel likewise. If this example does not move them, they will not do anything

---

⁴⁰ WA 38, 279, 3–4. The context of this statement is Luther's disagreement with Erasmus of Rotterdam and the pope.

⁴¹ WA 11, 75, 37–36, 4: "…in fide unum sensum habebimus, sed erit nobiscum, sicut factum est cum monachis immeritis, praedicatoribus, carthusianis, Caelestinis. Christianus dicit 'mihi placet tuus status, placeat tibi et meus'. Hoc ergo conandum, ut fides et charitas pura serventur…"

⁴² WA 11, 76, 3–13: "Hoc ergo conandum, ut fides et charitas pura serventur, optimum et extremum charitatis exemplum [Phil. 2, 6] est consensus. Et Christum pro exemplo proponet dicens 'Cum esset in forma dei' &c.. quid hoc? Christus erat verus deus, ambulavit in terris et potuisset nobiscum agere ut deus, et dicere, 'es dunck mich ita bonum, ut occidatis mihi ad genua', sed non fecit, sed dicit Paulus 'formas dei abiecit et ita se gestelt, tanquam non esset deus', 'formam servi' i. e. incarnatus est, non ita intelligas, non de humanitate Christi loquitur, sed in vita sua non se gestelt ut deum, sed servum. 'In similitudinem hominum', hoc est: ubi fuerunt infirmi, fuit infirmus, ubi pauperes ipsi, pauper, pauperes cum pauperibus conveniunt &c."

good that they are commanded and urged to do,[43] so unanimity or being of the same mind is created by faith in Christ's incarnation. By giving himself in this way, Christ is realising the divine love towards human race. But humans, who receive Christ through faith, must be unanimous with him, in order to share the same mind with Christ and between each other. Only then will they be able to love each other as Christ loves them.

Unanimity with Christ presumes that only Christ's righteousness is valid, not our own rectitude. When humans trust in their own righteousness they inevitably disagree, but peace and concord follow when they all become sinners and desire grace. The agreement on everyone's own sinfulness collects together those who have disagreed about justice. They are now like each other and no one can place him- or herself above the others.[44] Consequently, the unanimity presupposes not only shared acquaintance with Christ and his righteousness but also the other side of the same knowledge, that is common understanding of humans themselves as sinners.

In his *Large Commentary of the Galatians*, Luther emphasises the pure doctrine and the need of doctrinal consent. This emphasis is so strong that at least occasionally love appears inferior in comparison with faith. Nevertheless, the impression of love's subordination to faith can be explained in that faith gives to the believer Christ and unanimity in him, whereas unanimity in love presupposes unity in faith and in Christ. We need to receive Christ through the common faith, in which every topic concerning him is important. He points out that if there is no consent about Christ, love does not help at all, so he stresses the right succession of things but does not make love unimportant or secondary. Doctrine comes first because if one denies some topic of the Christian faith – Luther speaks

---

[43] WA 11, 76, 21–25: "Quid vult Paulus? nempe hoc: cum ita Christus ergo vos se exhibuit, ita et vos sentire, illud exemplum Christi vos moneat, nihil faciemus, quodcunque praescribatur nobis et urgeamur, si hoc exemplum nos non moverit, si nos humiliemus, nihil boni faciemus, sed wir seins schuldig, ipse Christus immeritus hoc fecit et nobis exemplum fecit."

[44] WA 25, 134, 22–28: "'Non nocebunt.' Erit summa pax in Ecclesia, erit concordia, quae etiam discordes congreget. 'Quia repleta est terra scientia.' Haec est causa pulcherrimae concordiae, quod scilicet abundabunt cognitione Christi. Quando enim meum et tuum tollitur, hoc est, quod nec mea nec tua iusticia valeat sed solius Christi, tum necessario pax sequitur, quia pariter omnes sumus peccatores et indigemus gratia. Sic omnia in Christo sunt unum nec est, quod unus alteri se praeponat."

here especially about the doctrine of the Eucharist – he or she denies Christ and therefore loses him.[45] But when people teach and proclaim Christ unanimously and not their own opinions, they will give the honour to Christ and through him to the Father.[46] Unanimity in faith is required for receiving Christ and honouring God as well as for loving one's neighbour.

Luther stresses that the content of faith or the doctrine is something that belongs to God, so Christians are not competent to make any changes in the doctrine. He compares the doctrine with the 'mathematical point'. Similarly the doctrine cannot be divided into pieces, nothing can be removed from it, and nothing can be added to it.[47] The Christian doctrine must be like one continuous and perfect golden ring without any joint.[48] Luther also accentuates the unity of the doctrine by saying that if people – in this case the so-called "sacramentarians" – believed that the word is God's word, they would respect it highly and adopt it by faith, without debating or doubting it. They would also know that one word of God is all the words and all words are one and similarly that one article of the doctrine contains all its articles. So, if one is neglected or disregarded, all will be neglected little by little.[49] Even though Luther does not handle the topic of Christ as the Word of God[50] explicitly when he speaks about Christian unanimity, he very likely presupposes it. His assertions about God's words become understandable if he intends that Christ and in him the Triune God is present in every word.

For Luther the doctrine is one because God cannot be divided between many articles of faith. If one denies God in one article, one will deny him in all of them. The content of all articles is contained in every single article

---

[45] WA 40 II, 136, 29: "… nos praedicare debemus concordiam doctrinae et fidei. Quam si nobis integram relinquunt, tum amplificabimus una cum ipsis etiam charitatis concordiam, quae longe postponenda est concordiae fidei seu Spiritus. Nam si hanc amiseris, Christum amisisti; illo amisso nihil proderit tibi charitas."

[46] WA 40 II, 136, 20–25.

[47] WA 40 II, 46, 16–28.

[48] WA 40 II, 47, 17–19.

[49] WA 40 II, 47, 30–34: "Quod si crederent esse verbum Dei, non ita cum eo luderent, sed summo honore afficerent et sine ulla disputatione aut dubitatione fidem ei adhiberent scirentque unum verbum Dei esse omnia, omnia esse unum, Item, scirent unum articulum esse omnes, omnes esse unum et uno omisso omnes paulatim amitti; cohaerent enim et quodam communi vinculo continentur."

[50] See, for example, Nüssel 2017.

and the subject matter of every distinct article is in all of them. Luther's words may also be understood in the sense that God is wholly in every single article and that one and the same God is in all articles.[51] As was stated earlier, the same could also be said about Christ.

The love of Christ unites him and Christians with each other so that faith, love and everything good and evil become shared. This means that the Church and its members are obliged to nurture the common faith. On the other hand, not all errors or mistakes in the doctrine are reasons for breaking the communion. Luther appears to think that even though the doctrine is one with its content, Christ, given in faith, humans are not able to grasp it as such. There is no church without weakness, sin and even heresy. God has hidden the true church and the real Christians under the cross. When one errs, but not knowingly or voluntarily, one will be forgiven. So, an error or difference in doctrine does not inevitably lead to a disagreement, which breaks the communion.[52] The love that endures the errors and seeks the good of the neighbour, keeps all those together who receive one and the same Christ and honour the same Father through faith. Christians' unanimity in love that shares everything good and bad, and seeks what is good for the others, albeit imperfectly, sustains even though the Christians were not able to formulate full unanimity in faith. Nevertheless, for Luther the common expression of Christian unanimity, which is given in Christ through faith, is an aim to be pursued.

Bibliography

Sources

WA 6	Tessaradecas consolatoria pro laborantibus et oneratis.	WA 6, 104–134.
WA 7	Epistola dominicae secundae adventus Ro. XV.	WA 7, 480–487.
WA 11	In die Palmarum.	WA 11, 73–77.
WA 25	In Esaiam Scholia ex D. Mart. Lutheri praelectionibus collecta.	WA 25, 89–401.
WA 30 I	Die erste Reihe der Katechismuspredigten.	WA 30 I, 2–27.

---

[51] WA 40 II, 48, 22–24: "Quare si Deum in uno articulo negas, in omnibus negasti, quia Deus non dividitur in multos articulos, sed est omnia in singulis et unus in omnibus articulis."

[52] WA 40 II, 106, 19–107, 21.

WA 38   Vorrede zu Antonius Corvinus, Quatenus expediat aeditam
recens Erasmi de sarcienda Ecclesiae concordia Rationem sequi. WA 38, 276–279.
WA 40 I   Commentarius in Epistolam ad Galatas.   WA 40 I, 33–688.
WA 40 II Commentarius in Epistolam ad Galatas.   WA 40 II, 1–184.

Literature

ALTHAUS, Paul
1929   *Communio Sanctorum. Die Gemeinde im lutherischen Kirchengedanken I. Luther.* Forschungen zur Geschichte und Lehre des Protestantismus. Erste Reihe, Bd. I. München: Chr. Kaiser Verlag.

ST. AUGUSTINE
PL 33   De gratia Novi Testamenti liber, seu epistola CXL.
PL 37   In Psalmum XLI Enarratio. Sermo ad Plebem.
PL 38   Sermo CXLIX
PL 41   De vero perfectoque sacrificio.

DIETER, Theodor
2001   *Der junge Luther und Aristoteles. Eine historisch–systematische Untersuchung zum Verhältnis von Theologie und Philosophie.* Theologische Bibliothek Töpelmann, Band 105. Berlin, New York: Walter de Gruyter.

HENDRIX, Scott H.
1974   *Ecclesia in via. Ecclesiological Developments in the Medieval Psalms Exegesis and the Dictata Super Psalterium of Martin Luther.* Studies in Medieval and Reformation Thought, Vol. VIII. Leiden: E. J. Brill.

HIETAMÄKI, Minna
2010   *Agreeable Agreement. An Examination of the Quest for Consensus in Ecumenical Dialogue.* Ecclesiological Investigations Vol. 8. London, New York: T&T Clark.

HOFFMANN, Adolf OP
1961   Taulers Lehre von der Kirche. – *Johannes Tauler. Ein deutscher Mystiker.* Gedenkschrift zum 600. Todestag. Hrsg.E. Filthaut OP. Essen: Hans Driewer Verlag. 232–240.

LINDBECK, George A.
1984   *The Nature of Doctrine. Religion and Theology in a Postliberal Age.* Louisville, Kentucky: Westminister John Knox Press.

MARTIKAINEN, Eeva
1992   *Doctrina. Studien zu Luthers Begriff der Lehre.* Schriften der Luther-Agricola-Gesellschaft 26. Helsinki: Luther-Agricola-Gesellschaft.

NÜSSEL, Friederike
2017   Martin Luther's Concept of Doctrine. – *The Oxford Research Encyclopaedia of Martin Luther.* Ed. Derek R. Nelson et al. Oxford: Oxford University Press.

RAUNIO, Antti
2001   Summe des christlichen Lebens. Die „Goldene Regel" als Gesetz der Liebe in der Theologie Martin Luthers von 1510 bis 1527. Veröffentlichungen des Instituts für Europäische Geschichte Mainz. Abteilung für abendländische Religionsgeschichte, Bd. 160. Mainz: Philipp von Zabern/Vandenhoek & Ruprecht.
2016   Doctrine, Ethics, and Practice in Luther and Lutheran Theology. –*Towards Closer Unity. Communion of the Porvoo Churches 20 Years.* Eds. B. Fagerli, L. Nathaniel and T. Karttunen. Helsinki: Porvoo Communion of Churches. 114–126.
2017   Love. – *The Oxford Research Encyclopaedia of Martin Luther.* Eds. Derek R. Nelson et al. Oxford: Oxford University Press.

RICHARD OF SAINT VICTOR
PL 179 Tractatus de gradibus charitatis.

SAARINEN, Risto
1994   *Johdatus ekumeniikkaan.* Helsinki: Kirjaneliö.
2010   Lutheran Ecclesiology. – *The Routledge Companion to the Christian Church.* Eds. G. Mannion & L. S. Mudge. New York and London: Routledge. 170–186.
2012   *Reclaiming the sentences: A linguistic loci approach to doctrine.* – Neue Zeitschrift für systematische Theologie und Religionsphilosophie 54, 1–22.
2017   *Luther and the Gift.* Tübingen: Mohr Siebeck.

TAULER, Johannes
1979   *Predigten. Band I–II.* Vollständige Ausgabe. Hrsg. Von Georg Hofmann. Einsiedeln: Johannes Verlag.

ST. THOMAS AQUINAS
1966   *Super Epistolam B. Pauli ad Galatas lectura/Commentary on Saint Paul's Epistle to the Galatians.* Albany, N.Y.: Magi Books, Inc.

TYÖRINOJA, Pirjo
1994   *Ad veram unitatem: Luterilainen identiteetti Luterilaisen maailmanliiton ja roomalaiskatolisen kirkon välisissä oppikeskusteluissa vuosina 1967–1984.* Studia missiologica et oecumenica Fennica 58. Helsinki: Luther-Agricola-Seura.

WIKSTRÖM, Iris
1982   *Fundamentalkonsensus i dialogen mellan romersk-katoliker och lutheraner?* Meddelanden från Stiftelsens för Åbo Akademi forskningsinstitut Nr 73. Åbo.

Luther, Seneca, and Benevolence in both Creation and Government

Bo Kristian Holm

Luther was not a political theorist like Machiavelli.[1] He was, however, a political advisor, and in this function he was almost incomparable with any contemporary figure. In his ideas of government, he combined theologically revolutionary ideas with political conservatism. The political imaginaries of Luther involved both the ideal of a "harmonisierties Gemeinwesen"[2] and an anthropology emphasising human sinfulness and need for discipline. Care and order became the two keywords for the temporal authority, not only having a theological background but also having societal consequences. The ideal of a harmonious society was closely linked to an increasing emphasis on God as the good creator, culminating in the promissional creation theology of his *Lectures in Genesis*.[3] His emphasis on monarchical authority was intimately connected to his anthropology as it represented the necessary order and framework for human sociality. In both cases Luther, and to a great extent Melanchthon as well, became an important bridge for ancient Roman ideas of the ideal monarchical supremacy, especially emphasised by Seneca, into the early modern era, as seen e.g. in Luther's *Fürstenspiegel*. But this bridge was founded in a new variation of the emphasis on divine presence in creation based on the long tradition of correlating the Christian doctrine of creation with ancient Roman ideas, as they can be found in Seneca. The reformers continued a tradition of combining important aspects of the stoic idea of a natural

---

[1] I must thank my anonymous peers for valuable comments, especially for references to the patristic tradition for emphasising divine giving through creation.
[2] Cf. Gutmann 1991, 212–226.
[3] Cf. Asendorf 1998, 20, 29, who speaks of an universalisation of the *promissio* in Luther's Lectures on Genesis.

deity giving benefits through nature with biblical material and used it in an increased emphasis on the creator giving himself through the created world.

Luther and Seneca

In his work, Risto Saarinen has pointed at the importance of ideas presented by ancient Roman philosophers like Cicero and Seneca, widely read in Renaissance humanism, for Luther's, and Melanchthon's theologies. Like others, Saarinen distinguishes here between classroom philosophy and philosophy as a way of life, understanding the latter more as a common cultural heritage than a specific therapeutic practice.[4] This distinction is important, since the parallels between Seneca and the reformers are not those of philosophical convergences, lying instead in the "social imaginaries" forming the life of people.[5] Moreover, it is in particular this way of thinking about life that had an impact on the reformers, who in the Roman philosophers could find authors who (based on natural law) dealt rationally with how to form life in the worldly realm, without attempting to draw theological conclusions. Therefore, the Humanist reception of Cicero and Seneca played a role in the formative years of the Lutheran Reformation.[6]

In his critique of medieval theories of action, Luther was, according to Saarinen, motivated by the distinction between gifts and sales and presents "a theological view of gifts, favours and passivity", creating a "non-Pelagian alternative to this economic theory of meritorious action".[7] In doing so, Saarinen highlights, Luther "employs views that are prominent in the classical Humanist way of speaking about giving and receiving." A mere

---

[4] SAARINEN 2017, 17–37, with reference to HADOT 1995.
[5] The reference to "social imaginaries" lies in continuation of Charles Taylor, who underlines the importance of the "imaginary" for analysing the impact of religion. The understanding of the "social imaginary" of the Reformation differs, however, from Taylor. See TAYLOR 2012, 171–172. For an introduction to the focus on "social imaginaries", see HOLM & KOEFOED 2018, 17–18.
[6] SAARINEN 2017, 37. On the role of natural law in Luther's political theology, see ANDERSEN 2010, 59–65.
[7] SAARINEN 2017, 31–32.

reference to the crucial verbs in Cicero, Seneca and the Vulgate version of the Bible underlines this: they are *dare* and *accipere*.[8]

Both Cicero and Seneca discuss the proper receiving of favours and both emphasise the voluntary nature of favours, but Saarinen notices an important difference. While Cicero focuses on active reciprocity and mutual duties,[9] Seneca grants that a passive reception of favours is possible, regarding only the clear intention of the giver as constitutive of favours or benefits. According to Seneca, the giver "must act for the sake of the person who is the intended recipient, and …judge him worthy and give willingly, deriving joy from [his] gift".[10] In the ideal case, the recipient reacts to such proper giving with gratitude, manifesting that he is worthy.[11] This places emphasis on the continuous giving of the benefactor, rather than on the capacities of the recipient.

The present chapter is an attempt to dig a little deeper into the relation between the Humanist reception of Senecan ideas[12] and Lutheran theology by considering something that was only dealt with briefly by Saarinen: Luther's theology of creation.[13] Two related notions will also attract our attention: the idea of the benevolent creator, and the ideal of the benevolent prince.

---

[8] Cf. SAARINEN 2017, 32.
[9] CICERO 1913, 1, 47–48.
[10] SENECA 2011, 104–105. See Seneca 1930, 4, 29, 3: "Deinde hoc, quod potentissimum est, oportet accedat, ut eius causa faciam, ad quem volam pervenire beneficium, dignumque eum iudicem et libens id tribuam percipiensque ex munere meo gaudiam." Cf. SAARINEN 2017, 32.
[11] SAARINEN 2017, 32.
[12] As pointed out by Saarinen, the reformers may not always have been aware of the Senecan provenience of some of the ideas, which is why this study focuses on "Senecan ideas" instead of trying to prove any direct line between Seneca's own texts and Luther's and Melanchthon's writings.
[13] Cf. SAARINEN 2017, 52: "The texts give a stable picture in which beneficia remains the central interpretative concept of God's work in both creation and redemption. A more extensive and exhaustive study would, however, be necessary in order to confirm or to rule out possible differences between the younger and the older Luther." Although an exhaustive study is not possible within this rather limited study, it is possible to draw some conclusions regarding possible developments in Luther's theology.

Seneca and the Lutheran theology of creation in the early writings

Theologically, the most important influence of Senecan thinking upon Luther's theology may be his understanding of the character of benefits or favours and his idea that real benefits depend on the will of the giver rather than on the gift itself. Despite important differences between stoicism as a philosophy and Lutheran theology, this idea creates the background for Luther's distinction between *donum* and *gratia/favor dei* in his writing *Against Latomus*, as shown by Saarinen.[14] Remarkable convergences exist between Luther and Seneca's understanding of the benevolent God of nature with regard to creation, too.[15]

In Luther's first lecture, *Dictata super Psalterium*, he dealt quite extensively with God as a giver and with divine favours. His understanding of God's *beneficia* is quite comprehensive and related to daily life. God's favours appear in the form of both natural and spiritual gifts and include life, being, feeling, mind, food, clothing and the service of the sun, as well as the service of the sun of righteousness, of heaven and earth and of all the benefits of the church.[16]

At the same time, for Luther this reminder of the continuous flow of divine favours is a reminder of human ingratitude and lack of proper thanksgiving, which again emphasises the difference between the God giving good for evil,[17] and the human beings who cannot do anything but receive either with gratitude or ingratitude. The whole sequence of examples of divine favours follows, therefore, after an admonition to consider one's omissions, first in natural things, then in the sacraments and gifts of the

---

[14] SAARINEN 2017, 38–57.
[15] SAARINEN 2017, 53–57.
[16] Cf. WA 55 II: 401, 508–525: "Primo in naturalibus, Quia Vide an per singulos dies et horas in tota vita tua Deum laudaueris et gratias egeris, ad hoc enim teneris stricto precepto et Iure naturali. Nam cum singulis diebus et horis beneficia Dei acceperis, scil. vitam, esse, sensum, intellectum, Insuper victum et amictum et ministerium solis, celi et terre et omnium elementorum multis nimis varietatibus, manifestum est quod accepsti gratias debes. Sed quis hic non videat infinitas omissiones et ingratitudines suas? Quis enim pro vna die satis gratias egit? Secundo in gratuitis perceptis, scil. sacramentis et bonis Ecclesie, Que non minus tibi ministrat, quam totus mundus, cum ipsa sit mundus quidam intellectualis." Cf SAARINEN 2017, 41.
[17] WA 55 II: 883,100: "Sed hoc est esse Deum: non accipere bona, Sed dare, ergo pro malis Bona retribuere."

Church.[18] Luther's list of favours is clearly inspired by Psalm 104,[19] and the emphasis on the lack of gratitude by Rom 1:20f, but the rhetoric follows Seneca's in *De beneficiis*.

The parallel between biblical notions and certain aspects of stoic philosophy is not in itself new in Reformation theology. New Testament scholar Troels Engberg-Pedersen dates it back to Paul himself when using the Roman ideas of gift-giving in his translation of Jewish covenant thinking for a non-Jewish audience.[20] The notion became widespread in patristic theology and can be found (for instance) in the works of Philo of Alexandria, in Basil of Caesarea's numerous homilies on power and wealth, in Ambrose of Milan's *De officiis* and *De Nabuthe*, and in John Chrysostom's *De eleemosyna*. To illustrate the link, Basil's homily on Julitta's martyrdom is sufficient:

> He has called us into being out of nothing; he has endowed us with reason, bestowed on us skills to help us preserve life; he has caused food to grow from the ground and has made the beasts subject to us. For our sake it rains, the sun shines, there are mountains and plains, and he has prepared for us places of shelter in the mountains even up to the highest peaks. The rivers flow for our use, springs bubble up, the sea is open to us for trade, the mines for treasures. All that we enjoy, bestowed on us in all creation, we have around us through the rich and marvellous good of the creator.[21]

The formulaic tone in Basil's homily, as in many other patristic writings, is reminiscent of formulations in Seneca's *De beneficiis*, indicating the closeness of the biblical notion of creation to the idea of the benevolent creator in Seneca. In *De beneficiis*, the author counters the reader's argument:

> "God does not confer benefits." What, in that case, is the source of the things that you possess, that you give, that you refuse, that you store, that you grab. What is the source of the countless things that delight your eyes, your ears, your mind? ... Not only are necessities provided for us; we are loved to the point of being spoiled. What is the source of all those trees with their varied yield of fruit, all those healing plants, all the varieties of food distributed throughout the year, so many that earth provides even those who make no effort with random sustenance? What is the

---

[18] WA 55 II: 401,508: "Primo itaque Consydera omissiones tuas et hoc multipliciter."
[19] Cf. SAARINEN 2017, 41.
[20] ENGBERG-PEDERSEN 2008, 22–25. To this see also HOLM 2013, 173–183.
[21] BASIL, PG 31, 253.

source of animals of every species, some born on dry ground, others in water, others coming down from the sky, so that every part of nature pays some tribute to us? ... If someone had given you a few acres of ground, you would say you had received a benefit. Do you deny that the immeasurable extent of land stretching out before you is a benefit? ...do you deny that you have received a gift? And though you attach great value to what you have, do you behave like an ingrate and claim that you are not indebted to anyone? What is the source of the breath that you draw?... "It is nature," someone objects, "that provides these things for me." Do you not grasp that when you say this, you are merely giving god a different name? What else is nature but god and the divine reason which permeated the whole world and all its parts?[22]

For Seneca a benefit is an "act of benevolence bestowing joy and deriving joy from bestowing it, with an inclination and spontaneous readiness to do so".[23] According to Griffin, "Seneca's *beneficium* is construed as a *benevola actio*, which is a good in stoic terms, and is contrasted with the thing given, which is an indifferent: it has attitude as its essential element."[24] The distinction between the things given and the attitude or intention of the giver is radicalised beyond the stoic position in Luther's understanding that only God's promise can unambiguously show that divine gifts are merciful. While the indifference of the external good remains a problem for a full theory of benevolence and material aid, as argued by Martha Nussbaum,[25]

---

[22] SENECA 2011, 97–89. Cf. SENECA, 1935, 4, 5, 1–4, 7, 1: "'Non dat deus beneficia.' Unde ergo ista, quae possides, quae das, quae negas, quae servas, quae rapis? Unde haec innumerabilia oculos, aures, animum mulcentia? ...(neque enim necessitatibus tantummodo nostris provisum est; usque in delicias amamur)? Tot arbusta non uno modo frugifera, tot harbae salutares, tot varietates ciborum per totum annum digestae, ut inerti quoque fortuita terrae alimenta praeberent? Iam Animalia omnis generis, alia in sicco solidoque, alia in umido nascentia, alia persublima demissa, ut omnis rerum naturae pars tributum aliquod nobis conferret? ... Si pauca quis tibi donasset iugera, accepisse te diceres beneficium; immensa terrarum late patentium spatial negas esse beneficium? ... negas te ullum munus accepisse? Et cum ista, quae habes, magno aestimes, quod est ingrate homines, nulli debere te iudicas? Unde tibi istum, quem trahis, spiritum? ... 'Natura,' inquit, 'haec mihi praestat.' Non intelligis te, cum hoc dicis, mutare nomen deo? Quid enim aliud est natura quam deus et divina ratio toti mundo partibusque eius inserta? See also SAARINEN 2017, 53–57.
[23] SENECA 1935, 1, 6, 1: "benevolentia actio tribuens gaudium capiensque tribuendo in id quod facit, prona et sponte sua parata." (Eng. translation from SENECA 2011).
[24] GRIFFIN 2013, 106.
[25] NUSSBAUM 2001, 9–15. I also have to thank my peers for this precise reference to Nussbaum. However, a thorough discussion of the relation between benevolence and material aid goes far beyond the limits of this minor study.

Luther is preoccupied far more than Seneca with the relation between the divine benevolent giver and ungrateful human recipients, who are unable to receive divine gifts in good faith themselves. A lack of confidence keeps divine giving ambiguous in Luther. Divine benefits are dependent not only on the *benevola actio*, but also on the recipient's belief. Materiality and intentionality are therefore combined in a rather un-stoic fashion in Luther's theology, finding their climax in Luther's emphasis on incarnation and divine self-giving, and their results in the emphasis on the prince's social responsibility. There is, however, a clear resemblance between the view of *De beneficiis* that God continues to give to ungrateful receivers, hoping they will learn to acknowledge him as a giver, and God in Luther's *Dictata*, who acts in a similar way by reciprocating good for evil.[26]

Elements of creation theology in the early Luther

It is quite clear that the creation theology of the mature Luther after 1528 is much richer than the creation theology we find in his early works. This does not mean that creation theology is totally lacking before 1528. Luther has remarkable things to say about creation already in the *Dictata*, as we have seen. In this first series of lectures, we also find formulations that later become crucial for his understanding of creation. Here Luther writes that every creature is a word of God, because God has spoken and it has happened,[27] which anticipates Luther saying that creatures are divine words in the divine grammar in his last lectures on Genesis.[28] A theology combining creation and words, as Luther does, and which emphasises divine presence in the created world based on the Psalms, is relatively open to the integration of certain stoic elements.

In Luther's *Lectures on Romans* we also find elements that point towards his later creation theology. For instance in the thought that a gift is of no

---

[26] See footnote 17.
[27] WA 55 II: 536, 37–39: "Omnisque creatura Dei verbum Dei est: 'Quia ipse dixit, et facta sunt.' Ergo Creaturas inspicere oprtet tanquam locutions Dei".
[28] WA 42: 37, 6–7: "Quaelibet igitur avis, piscis quilibet sunt nihil nisi nomina divinae Grammaticae, per quam grammaticam, quae sunt impossibilia, fiunt facillima, et quae plane sunt pugnantia, fiunt simillima, et econtra."

use when it is not related to the presence of the giver.²⁹ However, Luther's interpretation of Romans 5:5 is related to the idea that human love has to be directed towards God without any interest in either punishment or reward. Only the "empty" love of God himself and his will alone should be the object of the pure love of human beings, not God's gifts.³⁰ On the one hand, this idea anticipates to some extent Luther's later emphasis on divine presence in the created world. On the other hand, Luther's interpretation of Romans 5:5 clearly directs human love away from the gifts towards the giver alone and makes no direct link between divine presence and the continuous creation of the necessities of daily life, which we find later in Luther's works.

Luther's theology of giving

Luther's theology focuses on God as the giver, and humans as receivers. So it is possible to reformulate Luther's theology and to highlight its inner structure using the concepts of gift and giving. In the work of prominent scholars such as Oswald Bayer, Martin Seils, Hans-Martin Gutmann and Martin Wendte – not forgetting Risto Saarinen – we can find attempts to make such interpretations, although with different emphasis.³¹

The definition of divine being in *Dictata* ("giving goods") makes it possible to reformulate Luther's understanding of human beings by emphasising that human beings receive their existence – connecting on the one hand human beings to the rest of creation. On the other hand, this is precisely a vital aspect of their special status among creatures: As *animal rationale*, the human being has the possibility of recognising this gift and praising and thanking the giver – but also of refusing to recognise the giver. This is what lies in thesis 17 in the disputation against scholastic

---

[29] WA 56: 308, 26–28: "Quia non satis est habere donum, nisi sit et donator presens." Cf. SAARINEN 2017, 2.

[30] WA 56: 307, 30–33: "Sic enim Deum super omnia estimare est eum preciosa dilectione i. e. Charitate diligere. Diligere autem eum propter dona et propter comodum Est vilissima dilectione i. e. concupiscentia eum diligere."

[31] BAYER 1981; 1999, 1–18, 118–122; 2001; SEILS 1985; GUTMANN 1991; WENDTE 2013; SAARINEN 2005; 2017.

theology: "Man is by nature unable to want God to be God. Indeed, he himself wants to be God, and does not want God to be God."³² Without altering the content of this sentence, one can reformulate it by replacing the predicative use of God as with the word Giver: "Man is by nature unable to want God to be the Giver. Indeed, he himself wants to be the Giver, and does not want God to be Giver." The ambivalence of the gift, related to the ambivalence of power, is recognised just as much by Martin Luther as by Marcel Mauss. Gifts are good, but only in an absolute or fulfilled way when you are able to trust the giver. Without trust, God becomes a Devil, according to Luther.

The role of trust in gift-giving relations becomes clear when we contrast the early radical negative formulation from 1516 with a positive and well-known equivalent found in Luther's famous interpretation of Gal 3:6 in the *Large Commentary on Galatians* from 1531/35. Here Luther describes faith as the creator of divinity: *Fides est creatrix divinitatis, sed non in substantia/ persona sua sed in nobis* (Faith is the creator of the deity, however not in his substance/person, but in us).³³ Without a major loss of content, this sentence can also be reformulated using gift language: *Fides est creatrix donatoris, sed non in substantia sua sed in nobis.* (Faith is the creator for the giver, however not in his substance but in us).

The reception of a gift in confidence is what fulfils the gift relation and makes the giver a giver in the full sense. However, this is also precisely what makes a gift ambiguous. Without trust in the giver's good intentions, the gift becomes a token of power and a cause for anxiety.³⁴ This emphasis upon confidence in the giver's mercy or benevolence could be the distinguishing factor when comparing the young Luther's understanding of creation with the older Luther. This aspect of faith as trust in God's true mercy is missing

---

³² WA 1: 225, 1–2: "Non potest homo naturaliter velle deum esse deum, Immo vellet se esse deum et deum non esse deum."

³³ WA 40 I: 360, 5–6 [Hs]. Cf. WA 40 I: 360, 24–25.

³⁴ At this point I have to skip a major argument against Derrida and others who insist that gifts can only be gifts if they remain uncontaminated by gift economy, and that the only way gifts can be true gifts is if they are invisible. Luther's critique of the Roman Church was an attack on specific practices of reciprocal giving, not of mutual giving in general. For this argument, see HOLM 2009. See also SAARINEN 2017, 17–37, who emphasises that the distinction between gift relationships and economic exchange is important for understanding Luther's use of gift terminology in theology.

in Saarinen's linguistic analysis of the word "give,"[35] probably because concepts of trust and confidence are receptive attitudes not explicitly detectable through a pure linguistic analysis.

Justification and creation in Melanchthon and Luther

The role of confidence or trust in the giver's intention is crucial for gift-giving relations if some kind of acknowledgement of the giver is intended. It is the lack of confidence in the benevolence or intention of the giver that makes gifts ambiguous. In Luther, it is the lack of trust in the giver's benevolence that characterises the feeling of the wrath of God, which in Luther's eyes makes God indistinguishable from the Devil. To trust the giving God, one needs a point of unambiguity.[36] From 1520, this unambiguous God is to be found in his promise.[37] Melanchthon shares this fundamental idea, and it is in his work that we find the first clear connection between the promise of God revealed in the Gospel and the recognition of the goodness of the creator.

In dealing with Lutheran creation theology, scholars have focused on works of the old Luther from *On the Lord's Supper* and the *Catechisms* onwards.[38] Very few have included Melanchthon in their study. Consequently, none of these scholars have paid attention to his role in the development of a Lutheran creation theology. In 1521 the 24-year-old Melanchthon wrote the first textbook in Lutheran theology, the *Loci communes*. Most scholars

---

[35] It is noteworthy that in SAARINEN 2017 there are no entries for "confidence" or "promise" and only four for "trust" in the index of subjects, thereby downplaying the reformer's emphasis on faith as *fiducia*. Cf. e.g. SAARINEN 2017, 271–275. Saarinen seems only to find inspiration in Bayer's concept of categorical giving and his emphasis on the doctrine of the three estates, not in his understanding of the importance of *promissio*, which within a *beneficia*-oriented approach could be understood as the very element revealing the good intention of the giver.

[36] This fundamental part of Luther's theology has been investigated extensively by Oswald Bayer, who has used Jacob's fight at Jabbok as an illustrative metaphor for every human's fight with the giver of both good and evil. Cf. BAYER 2007, 181–186.

[37] As shown by Oswald Bayer. See BAYER 2007, 41–61.

[38] See e.g. the recent and impressive work of Anne KÄFER (2010). There are good reasons for focusing on the older Luther, but this does not mean that the young Luther is of any less value. On the contrary, developments in the creation theology of the young Luther might be crucial for the later more elaborated creation theology found in Luther's *Lectures on Genesis*, for instance.

argue that Melanchthon did not pay any attention to creation. He focused on the benefits of Christ, not of creation, and we do not find any *locus* on either creation or the Creator. However, a closer look reveals another story.

To find creation theology in Melanchthon's *Loci communes*, one needs to go to the most central *locus* of the book, the paragraph on justification and faith, rather than merely concentrating on his introduction, which seems to give creation an insignificant position.[39] Firstly, Melanchthon defines justifying faith as *non aliud nisi fiducia misericordiae divinae promissiae in Christo,* as nothing else than confidence in divine mercy promised in Christ.[40] A few pages later he continues: "Do not come in doubt in your confidence that you now no longer have a judge in Heaven, but a father that cares for you, in no other way than human parents care for their children."[41] Melanchthon learned that faith primarily must be understood as confidence from Luther.[42] What should draw our attention here is the way he uses this basic element of Reformation theology to open the doctrine of justification towards the doctrine of creation.

> In this way, he who due to the Spirit judges the things of creation, he sees also the power of God, the author of such great things as well as his goodness. When he feels that, he receives life from the hands of the Creator, the life, the nourishment, and the child. And leaves everything to the creator so that he can organise, govern, administer (*suppeditet*) what he wills, according to his goodness. This faith in creation is no cold opinion, but a very vivid knowledge of God's power and goodness, which flows upon all creatures, and which governs and takes care of all creatures.[43]

---

[39] Sven Grosse is one of the few scholars to have noticed the intimate relation between the doctrine of justification and creation theology in the *Loci communes*. See GROSSE 2003, 83–86.

[40] MELANCHTHON 1997, 6, 22.

[41] MELANCHTHON 1997, 6, 27: "nihil dubita, quin iam non iudicem in coelis, sed patrem habeas, cui tu sis curae non aliter atque sunt parentibus filii inter homines."

[42] See e.g. *Instructio pro confessione peccatorum* 1518, WA 1: 258, 4; *Von den guten Werken* 1520, WA 6: 209, 25–27.

[43] MELANCHTHON 1997, 6, 64f: "Ita, quo spiritu rerum conditionem aestimat, is et potentiam dei videt auctoris tantarum rerum et bonitatem, cum se omnia velut e minibus creatoris sentit accipere, vitam, victum, sobolem, et illa permittit creatori, ut temperet, regat administret, suppeditet pro sua bonitat quae libet. Haec fides ist de rerum conditione non frigida opinio, sed vivacissima cognitio tum potentiae tum bonitatis die effundentis se in omnes creatures, regentis et administrantis omnes creaturas…"

This way of introducing creation corresponds with Melanchthon's general understanding of the relation between philosophy and theology with regard to the understanding of the world, as he would later develop it. Only within the church can one rightly know creation.[44]

Melanchthon's formulation in 1521 is brief; but in relating creation to everyday life and the doctrine of justification, he anticipates Luther's well-known formulations from the Small Catechism eight years later:

> I believe that God has created me together with all that exists. God has given me and still preserves my body and soul: eyes, ears, and all limbs and senses; reason and all mental faculties. In addition, God daily and abundantly provides shoes and clothing, food and drink, house and farm, spouse and children, field, livestock, and all property – along with all the necessities and nourishment for this body and life.[45]

The correspondence with Melanchthon's link between the doctrine of creation and daily needs is obvious, as is the link between creation experience and the doctrine of justification. As Oswald Bayer has emphasised, a few sentences later Luther refers terminologically both to justification (merit) and to the sacrament of the altar (worthiness), when he writes: "And all this is done out of pure, fatherly, and divine goodness and mercy, without any merit or worthiness of mine at all."[46]

When we compare Melanchthon's formulations in 1521 with Luther's first attempt to make an Enchiridion, *Eine kurze Form* from 1520, the differences are striking. Although we find formulations in the *Dictata* that are close to the Senecan pattern, in 1520 there is no talk of the real world of

---

[44] Cf. CR 21: 615. See LINK 2017, 371. With references to Loci 1559 (CR 21: 609), Link also sees an intimate relation between the first and the second article of faith. The Creator "wird am Ort der Inkarnation, am Ort von Kreuz und Auferstehung, also durch die der Kirche anvertraute *Offenbarung* als Schöpfer der Welt erkannt." (LINK 2017, 372). See Link for a description of how Melanchthon follows the Stoa in his understanding of divine providence, but not when it comes to the stoic idea of immanent necessity (LINK 2017, 366).

[45] KOLB & WENGERT 2000, 354/BSLK 510, 33–511, 1: "Ich gläube, daß mich Gott geschaffen hat sampt allen Kreaturn, mir Leib und Seel, Augen, Ohren und alle Gelieder, Vernunft und alle Sinne gegeben hat und noch erhält, dazu Kleider und Schuch, Essen und Trinken, Haus und Hofe, Weib und Kind, Acker Viehe und alle Güter, mit aller Notdurft und Nahrung dies Leibs und Leben reichlich und täglich versorget."

[46] KOLB & WENGERT 2000, 354/BLSK 511, 3–5: "… und das alles aus lauter väterlicher, göttlicher Güte und Barmherzigkeit ohn alle mein Verdienst und Widrigkeit …" See BAYER 2007, 87–92.

lived life in Luther's explanation of the first article of faith. Instead, Luther's explanation focuses on recognising God as Creator and honouring him for it. Almost every sentence in 1520 is about the divine/human relationship. The world is of secondary relevance. It is still the monk speaking here. The world is, primarily, the Devil's kingdom, and the first article of faith is for Luther here primarily about honouring God and only trusting him and not anything human, oneself, or what one has.[47] And any confirmation of the goodness of life in the created world is only found to a very limited degree in Luther's explanation of the Lord's Prayer. Here, Luther identifies the bread with Jesus Christ, and understands the prayer for daily bread as a prayer for Christ staying in the believer and the believer in Christ, and for carrying the Christian name worthily.[48]

Later developments in Luther's theology of creation

Seneca's list of divine favours in *De beneficiis* ends in a rhetorical crescendo, culminating by stating that even what humans invent they owe to God.[49] Neither between the old nor the young Luther and Seneca are there any differences in their understanding of the totality of the human position as recipients for divine giving; and by relating creation to the very conditions for daily existence, Seneca anticipates the stress on *creatio continua* by the reformers. For Melanchthon and Luther, creation is about the present life and about the present world received as a divine gift. This is a fundamental insight from the very beginning, but in 1520 Luther's understanding of creation was still being developed. In his Catechisms, Luther's approach is completely in line with Melanchthon's in 1521.

A year before the Catechisms, Luther developed his theology of creation to a hitherto unseen level in the concluding confession in *On the Lord's Supper*, when he understands the triune God as triune self-giving. It is not only Christ and the Sprit that give themselves: the Creator also gives

---

[47] WA 7: 215, 24–216, 29.

[48] WA 7: 226, 12–14: "Und summa summarum, gib uns unßer teglich brott, das Christus in uns und wir yn yhm ewiglich bleyben, und den namen, das wir von yhm Christen heyssen, wirdiglich tragen."

[49] Cf. GRIFFIN 2013, 235. Seneca is arguing against Epicurean views on nature and God.

himself with all that he is and all that he has. This move from Christological self-giving to creational self-giving is remarkable – and new![50] It means that the giving God is present in the actual world, not only represented by his gift, but also by himself. By no coincidence, the doctrine of the three estates as the forms of social life in which God is present is given a central position in the concluding confession. Worldly authority participates in the divinely ordered world, which despite the evil that worldly authority has to fight, is one of the forms or masks in which God, as the benevolent creator, is present in the world.

This view on the created world supports a specific image of the ideal prince, which corresponds largely with the ideal emperor in Seneca's work. The understanding of the Creator as the benevolent father, present in nature, shapes Luther's understanding of political authority in two ways: 1) it underlines the positive value of order for securing human life in the world; and 2) it emphasises the ideal of benevolence for everyone holding an office. In this way, Luther clearly places himself in the anti-Machiavellian line of monarchical thinking.[51] This development parallels the development in Luther in which he moved from a tendency in his early work of "conflating the image of the earthly kingdom as the evil realm of the Devil with that of the earthly kingdom as the political realm of the magistrate" towards a more nuanced view of worldly authority.[52]

Luther's understanding of political authority

Luther wrote repeatedly on secular authority. A focus on parallels in Luther and Seneca shows how Luther builds and develops key elements

---

[50] WA 26: 505, 38-506, 12. Anne Käfer also takes her starting point in Luther's 1528 confession (KÄFER 2010). However, she does not trace the background for this important move in Luther's theology. For the relation between the Small Catechism and Luther's Confession, see BAYER 2007, 87–92.

[51] This is contrary to the position of Ernst Troeltsch, who believed that Luther's political thinking was clearly in line with Machiavellianism. Cf. TROELTSCH 1992, 2: 532–533, 858n246. For this false interpretation of Luther, see WRIGHT 2010, 26–28.

[52] WITTE 2002, 92. At the same time, Luther did little to distinguish the law of God from the law of the magistrate. "This double conflation led the early Luther dangerously close to intimating that not only the law of the magistrate but also the Law of God was part of the earthly kingdom of the Devil."

in the Western tradition of monarchical thinking. According to Quentin Skinner, "there is no doubt that the main influence of Lutheran political theory in early modern Europe lay in the direction of encouraging and legitimating the emergence of unified and absolutist monarchies".[53] In Luther's emphasis on the necessary benevolence and care of the worldly prince, we find parallels to Seneca's thinking once again.[54] In addition, Luther's understanding of the relation between household and state implies a new almost organic understanding of society and not a split, as argued by some.[55]

The notion that Luther places himself in the European tradition of *Fürstenspiegel*, of which Seneca's *De clementia* is normally regarded as the first, is commonly accepted. His interpretation of *Magnificat* is a *Fürstenspiegel* for the young Johann Friedrich of Saxony.[56] In his *De clementia* Seneca reminds Nero that the gods are the best role models for an emperor, and that it would be wise to imitate their mildness.[57] The reformers' view is very similar. The princes have a divinely ordered role to play in caring for their subjects. When Seneca compared the emperor with good parents, there is an explicit connection to Luther's understanding of worldly authority based upon the fourth commandment.[58]

Luther emphasised that princes distinguish themselves from other people because the actions of other people affect only themselves or a few others. So if God rules princes graciously, the result will be welfare for many – whereas God's disfavour with regard to princes will be the ruin

---

[53] SKINNER (1978, 113) begins his chapter on the background of constitutionalism by quoting Figgis: "Had there been no Luther there could never have been a Louis XIV." (FIGGIS 1960, 81). For a critique of Skinner, based on Luther's theology focusing on Skinner's accentuating of the unworthiness of human beings and a voluntaristic understanding of divine commands, and on his neglect of the importance of the doctrine of the three estates, see LAFFIN 2016, 9–13. For a critique of Skinner's interpretation of Luther's Two Kingdoms Doctrine, see WRIGHT 2010, 18.

[54] But also to the Christian understanding of imperial virtues in Late Antiquity continuing long-lived stoic traits. For this, see RAPP 2009, 82.

[55] E.g. CAVANAUGH 2001. For a critique of Cavanaugh for misreading Luther, see MALYSZ 2007 and LAFFIN 2016.

[56] Cf. BURGER 2007, 184–185. For no clear reason, Burger deals specifically with the character of Luther's *Magnificat* as *Fürstenspiegel* only in the last half page of his book, although it is mentioned at the very beginning (24).

[57] SENECA 1928, 1, 7.

[58] SENECA 1929, 1. 12. Cf. BSLK 596, 17–46.

of many.[59] In this way, the duties of princes are parallel to God's actions towards the world. Their role on earth is so similar to the creator's that the Bible can name them gods.[60]

Luther's anthropology distinguishes the prince from his subjects because the prince has a heightened risk of falling into presumptuousness, having no one on earth to fear.[61] This makes it even more necessary for the prince to fear God. This is the major reason for choosing the humble Mary as the ideal person to look at for a prince. Mary becomes an image of confidence in the divine grace given even to the lowliest person.[62]

Like a *Fürstenspiegel*, Luther's *Magnificat* deals primarily with the prince's own relation to God, and corresponds here with the tone in the explanation of the first article of faith in *Eine kurze Form*. This does not mean, however, that the relation to his subjects is put aside completely. In the concluding paragraph, Luther admonishes the prince that there will be a sudden end to the prince who rules without fear of God and without the kind of love for his people that ensures that the people experience an improvement of their situation.[63]

The attempt to find convergences between the idea of the ruler in Roman philosophy and Lutheran theology has some parallels in the work of Peter Stacey. In his book on the "Roman Monarchy and the Renaissance Prince", he has shed new light on what he sees as a neglected connection between Roman authors and Renaissance political thinking. According to Stacey,

> [the] process (in Roman history) produce(d) some of the monarchical and monological elements of Roman political theory which make a distinctive

---

[59] LUTHER StA 1: 314, 24–315, 1: "Die weil an eines solchenn grossen Fursten person vieler leut heil ligt, szo er yhm selb genummen, von got gnedig geregiert wirt, widderumb vieler vorterben szo er yhm selb gelassen vnd vngnedig regiert wird."

[60] LUTHER StA 1: 315, 7–10: "Aber herrnn sein nur datzu gesetzt, das sie ander leuttten schedlich oder nutzlich seynn, szo viel mehr szo viel weitter sie regieren, darumb auch die schrifft frum gottfurchtige Fursten nennet Engel gottis ia auch gotter."

[61] StA 1: 315, 12–20. See BURGER 2007, 26–27. According to Luther, it was presumptuousness among princes that caused the peasants' war. Cf. WA 18: 294 [Dr]. See ANDERSEN 2010, 29.

[62] LUTHER WA 7: 569, 10–25.

[63] LUTHER WA 7: 602, 10–14: "Wer sich denn nit hynder solch exempel legt vnd yhm die forcht gottis zu einem gutten schudt vnd wallen macht. wie mag er bleyben? denn wo ein herr vnd ubirkeit nit sein volck lieb hat vnd das lessit sein sorg allein sein, wie nit er selb gut tag habe, szondern wei seinn volck durch yhn besserung empfahe, so ists schon ausz mit yhm."

contribution to the historical formation of a post-classical European subjectivity and to the construction of a sovereign order within early-modern states.[64]

At the end of Stacey's book, he turns briefly towards the role of Seneca in the political theology of Jean Calvin: "In the 1530s, the Senecan argument about the mercy of the mighty received further attention among French humanists at the hands of the young lawyer Jean Calvin, whose first complete published work was a commentary on *De clementia*."[65] In Stacey's view, Calvin followed a major trend which was also detectable in France (Budé), Belgium (Lipsius) and Spain (Ribadeneyra), emphasising the empathy and benevolence of the absolutist ruler.[66] In Seneca we find the ideal of a benevolent ruler that Renaissance thinkers and theologians could also easily combine with other traditions, especially the biblical tradition since there was already a long tradition for doing so, with each using Senecan thoughts within their own particular context.

The fact that Luther was able to combine the tradition of Roman monarchical thinking with biblical material becomes quite clear when we look for political imaginaries in Luther's lectures on the Song of Songs in 1530 and on Genesis in 1535-1545. One major trend is detectable: Luther's view of the caring ruler mirrors his understanding of the divine care for the created world, underlined in his understanding of the prince as "Father".[67]

Luther's lectures on the Song of Songs from 1530 represent an exegetical novelty, in so far as Luther interprets it as a political treatise describing the relationship between the king and God, and between the king and his people. Luther opens with the argument that the Song of Songs is

---

[64] STACEY 2007, 3.

[65] STACEY 2007, 312.

[66] The question of whether one should rightly read Machiavelli as an ironic defender of freedom, as Stacey proposes, is here put aside. Marica COLISH's (2008) critique of Stacey for being monocular in his positive evaluation of Machiavelli as a liberal thinker, criticising the monarchicism of Seneca, does not have any major impact on this study, which focuses on the impact of Seneca on early Lutheran theology.

[67] For the relation between creation and politics, see e.g. ANDERSEN 2010, 28: "Der Status der Herrschaft als 'Vateramt' bedeutet nun, dass Herrscher wie die Eltern nicht einfach Mitmenschen oder Nächsten sind, sondern gerade als Vermittler der göttlichen Schöpfergüte für andere einen besonderen Rang einnehmen."

about politics and nothing else.⁶⁸ King Solomon describes his state using metaphors, something which a king is forced to do because the personal affairs of a king cannot be dealt with openly. Therefore, Luther interprets the Song of Songs as praise for the divine gift of government. In Luther's interpretation, God is the groom and the state is the bride. The prince naturally takes the role as the head of state, but at the same time the whole metaphor only makes it possible to see the whole state as one social being. In his book *Über Liebe und Herrschaft*, Hans-Martin Gutmann has shown that in his lectures Luther develops his understanding of the three estates so that he no longer distinguishes clearly between *oeconomia* and *politia* as in *On good works*. The political realm is characterised by features belonging to the household: a relation of mutual caring and service for the whole.⁶⁹ In Luther's interpretation, the bride is the state. This underlines the fusion of *politia* and *oeconomia*. The three estates become one organic unity in the lecture. The prince is not just the head of the state because the state is one harmonious social being (*Wesen*).⁷⁰ In Luther's social imaginary of the state, all parts of society cooperate on their own particular levels to the benefit of the common good. Beneath lies a fundamental theology of creation as the space of divine benevolent presence. The mystical union in monastic theology is turned into a strong social imaginary of the state as a whole, which is intimately related to the presence of the creator in his creation, and the state almost becomes an organism. Gutmann's interpretation makes it even more obvious that the idea of divine self-giving in creation and the doctrine of the three estates in On the Lord's Supper are naturally related. Moreover, this connection allows Luther to radically alter the traditional

---

⁶⁸ WA 31 II: 587, 30–590, 17 (Rörer). Cf. GUTMANN 1991, 195–197. See also CARTY 2017, 80. Very few scholars have taken notice of the lectures. Carty notices the lack of knowledge of the lectures explicitly, but references to Gutmann are missing in his study. So are references to Seneca's impact on Luther's view on God and government. This is also the case in CARTY 2011.

⁶⁹ GUTMANN 1991, 234.

⁷⁰ GUTMANN 1991, 241: "Die Neudefinition der drei Ordnungen, die Luther in der Hoheliedvorlesung vornimmt, läßt sich in beide Richtungen nachzeichnen: er radikalisiert die in den traditionellen Ordnungen bereits angelegte Innen-Außen-Differenzierung, und er gewichtet die interne Hierarchisierung der Ordnungen neu." Gutmann points here to the fact that the ideal of a "harmonisiertes Gemeinwesen" introduced a new focus on societal hierarchy that marginalises conflicting vernacular practices. Cf. GUTMANN 1991, 242.

interpretation of the key text of mystical theology.[71] Following Luther's confession from 1528, the crucial point here concerns the close connection between creation and justification, politics and Eucharist.[72] The sacraments are to be understood as corporal promises, revealing the benevolent heart of God in both justification and creation. In this way, sacraments are the place where each individual is identified as both sinner and justified, as passive receiver and giver of themselves, in order to live a Christian life in the social world. It is no coincidence at all that painters filled Lutheran altarpieces from the 16th century with kneeling princes receiving bread and wine from their pastors.

As far as the relation between people in the state is concerned, it becomes quite clear that regarding the political (and economic) realm the ideal form of exchange is not economic sales but mutual aid. The beneficial and even self-giving action of the ideal prince also becomes the ideal for every Christian member of the state.

We find the same understanding of the ideal prince in Luther's Lectures on Genesis, which probably give the most extensive elaborations of Luther's idea of good government. As an ordinance, the state is part of God's good creation:

> This respect toward the king is memorable, for one must conclude that the state is an ordinance of God, just as marriage and the church are from God, and whatever good is done in those stations is divine and has been obtained by God by the prayers of the godly.[73]

The state plays a vital role in taking care of the temporal world, whereas it is the task of the church to take care of the future life.

> These examples should be carefully observed, and there should be no doubt that political power is a divine arrangement ordained for the benefit of this life and also

---

[71] Cf. GUTMANN 1991, 194, although without references to *On the Lord's Supper*.

[72] Cf. LAFFIN (2016, 76), who rightly states: "In Luther's view, unlike in the view of much subsequent 'Protestantism,' the sacraments are not secondary to the preached Word, but rather as another form of the same word, the sacraments are central to the life of the church. Scripture and preaching are sacramental and the sacraments are proclamation. In particular the centrality of the Eucharist means that the worship of the church is political."

[73] LW 7: 143/WA 44: 405, 20–23: "Haec reverentia erga regem memorabilis est. Quia statuendum est politiam esse ordinationem divinam, perinde ut coniugium et Ecclesia et quicquid boni in illis ordinibus fit, divinum est et impetratum a Deo precibus piorum."

of the church, which it serves when it fosters and preserves peace, even though the church has another office, which pertains to the future life.[74]

Luther's ideal of the caring ruler finds one of its most significant expressions in his comments on Joseph's interpretation of Pharaoh's dreams. Joseph's explanation of the dream gives Luther occasion to emphasise the role of princes for the wellbeing of the people.

> For this political and necessary doctrine has been handed down in this place to princes, to whom the care of the people pertains, in order that they may take thought for the necessities of life – meat, grain, wine – especially when means of subsistence are hard to obtain.[75]

He continues by praising Elector Frederick the Wise, for storing food for the sake of his lazy (!) people:

> The example of our most illustrious Prince Frederick, Duke of Saxony, is noteworthy; he has not only provided for public barns and granaries but has also seen to it that there are trenches for the same use in the fields and has filled them with grain and the cellars with wine. But when he was censured by Staupitz and his counselors for this, he replied that he did not do this for the sake of greed or gain but because of the laziness of the citizens and peasants, who took no thought whatever for the famine that was to come but lived from hand to mouth, and that he was collecting the grain in order that the people might remain alive when means of subsistence were hard to obtain.[76]

We find here, again, almost a fusion of *oeconomia* and *politia*, household and government, in the sense that government is not just understood negatively to mean securing the safety of the people, but also positively

---

[74] LW 7: 145/WA 44: 406, 19–22: "Haec exempla diligenter observanda sunt, nec dubitandum est politicam potestatem esse rem divinam ordinatam ad utilitatem huius vitae et ecclesiae quoque, cui servit, quando colit et conservat pacem, quanquam ipsa aliam administrationem habet, quae pertinet ad futuram vitam."

[75] LW 7: 158/WA 44: 416, 31–33: "Haec enim politica et necessaria doctrina est hoc in loco tradita principibus, ad quos pertinet cura populi, ut providreant illi necessaria ad vitam, carnes, frumentum, vinum, praesertim in difficultatibus annonae."

[76] LW 7: 159/WA 44: 416, 37–417, 3: "Et memorabile est exemplum illustrissimi Principis Friderici ducis Saxoniae, qui non tantum horrea et granaria publica, sed et fossas ad eundem usum in campis paratas frumento et cellaria quoque vino repleri curavit. Cum autem a Staupitio et consiliariis ob id reprehenderetur: respondit, se non avaritiae aut quaestus studio hoc facere, sed propter ignaviam civium et rusticorum, qui nihil cogitarent de futura fame, sed in diem viverent, colligere frumentum, ut haberet populus unde viveret in difficultate annonae."

to mean securing the essentials of daily life. In Luther's description of the creation of the three estates earlier in the lectures, one can summarise his understanding of the household as the use and circulation of God's gifts, which Adam received through thanksgiving in the church. After the Fall, the primary function of the household became production; but both church and household are rooted in the uncorrupted creation, whereas it was sin that made the state necessary, in order to safeguard the church and household.[77] In this way, church and household both point backwards towards original creation and forwards towards their eschatological fulfilment; whereas the state remains a temporal (emergency) order.[78] All orders emphasise that worldly tasks are instruments of the benevolent God, who continues to give.[79] This corresponds to the general scope of the Genesis lectures: What is necessary for human beings is to recognise God as the generous giver, whether this involves providing for the basics of daily life or just one good tax collector. In both cases, God shows his wonderful governing.[80]

At the moment when government and household merge into each other (as in the lectures on the Song of Songs) in describing the duty of the prince to be benevolent towards his people, glimpses of God's eternal glory fell upon the prince, allowing him to be understood as God's vice-regent not only in his negative punishing function, but also in his positive sustaining function. The monarchical prince is a divinely ordered ruler who governs the temporal world, but also has the duty of taking care of his people showing divine fatherly benevolence.[81] It is this view of temporal

---

[77] WA 42: 79, 3–9.

[78] Cf. BAYER 2007, 296: "Die Dreiständelehre greift demgegenüber [i.e. der Zwei-Regimenten-Lehre] weiter, insofern sie in dem Grundstand, der Kirche, aber auch im zweiten Stand, der mit dem Ehestand und der Familie verbundenen Ökonomie, bereits im Paradies beginnt und dementsprechend im Eschaton nicht negiert, sondern vollendet wird." See also ASENDORF 1998, 450–483.

[79] Cf. SAARINEN 2007, 118–119: "The right way to think about the orders is in terms of receiving and accepting a gift. Household and state are not given us in order that we may think of ourselves as authors. As organs or instruments humans remain co-workers who labour as secondary causes and whose labours produce fruits but not merits."

[80] WA 44: 15, 12–26.

[81] This emphasis is parallel to a change in the reformer's view on the prince's duty to secure religious uniformity. See Ob Christliche Fürsten schuldig sind, der Wiederteuffer unchristlichen Sect mit leiblicher strafe, und mit dem schwert zu wehren, WA 50, 9–15. Cf. ANDERSEN 2010, 74.

authority that makes John Witte Jr. conclude that both metaphors (i.e. the lofty vice-regent of God and the loving father of the community) provided Luther and his followers with the core ingredients of a robust Christian republicanism and budding Christian welfare state.[82] Any attempt to follow this line further lies beyond the scope of this study. The examples show, however, that the Lutheran combination of Roman political philosophy and biblical theology was an important brick in the course of Western political thinking, giving pan-European ideas of ideal anti-Machiavellian policy a new direction and emphasis. The idea that the duty of the prince should be carried out in such a way that the prince can continue to give even to the unworthy finds parallels both in Seneca's idea of the giver who keeps giving, and in Luther's doctrine of justification that gives life to the one who does not deserve it. During the Reformation, the ancient ideals of the philanthropic ruler[83] were connected with a new emphasis on daily life in the created world.

Concluding perspectives

The conclusion of this investigation is quite simple, but important for the understanding of the role of the Reformation in the theological and political history of Western Europe. The reformers' understanding of benefices connects them to political ideals from the ancient world of both Christian and non-Christian origin, and the ideas and "social imaginaries" of benefits and favours helped them sharpen not only their understanding of justification, but also – and this may be equally important – their theology of creation. This happened through an increasing focus on the force of the divine promise. This advanced an emphasis on the government's care for the people, also known as the common good. This line of social and political development is still in need of further investigation, but we can conclude that the new emphasis on divine self-giving through creation also gave the political authority an important function as an instrument of continuous giving within a society understood almost organically. At the

---

[82] WITTE 2002, 112–113.
[83] For this, see RAPP 2009, 81–82.

same time, society in general was given an ideal of care for the common good that covered everyone.

Bibliography

ANDERSEN, Svend
2010 *Macht aus Liebe. Zur Rekonstruktion einer lutherischen politischen Ethik*. TBT 149. Berlin & New York: de Gruyter.

BASIL of Caesarea
1885 *Homilia in martyrem Julittam. Patrologia Graeca*, ed. Jacques Paul Migne, vol. 31. Paris: Migne (= PG 31), 237–261.

BAYER, Oswald
2007 *Martin Luthers Theologie*. 3rd ed. Tübingen: Mohr Siebeck.

BEKENNTNISSCHRIFTEN DER EVANGELISCH-LUTHERISCHEN KIRCHE (= BSLK)
1930ff Göttingen: Vandenhoeck & Ruprecht.

BURGER, Christoph
2007 *Marias Lied in Luther's Deutung*. SuRNR 34. Tübingen: Mohr Siebeck.

CARTY, Jarett A.
2011 Martin Luther's Political Interpretation of the Song of Songs. – *The Review of Politics* 73.
2017 *God and Government: Martin Luther's Political Thought*. MGQSHI 73. Kingston: McGill-Queen's University Press.

CAVANAUGH, William
2001 Eucharistic Sacrifice and the Social Imagination in Early Modern Europe. – *Journal of Medieval and Early Modern Studies* 31.

CICERO, Marcus Tullius
1913 *De officiis*. LCL 30. Cambridge, Mass: Harvard University Press.

COLISH, Marcia L.
2008 Review of Peter Stacey, Roman Monarchy and the Renaissance Prince. – *American Historical Review* 113.

ENGBERG-PEDERSEN, Troels
2008 Gift-Giving and Friendship: Seneca and Paul in Romans 1–8 on the Logic of God's Kharis and Its Human Response. – *Harvard Theological Review* 101.

FIGGIS, John N.
1960 *Political Thought from Gerson to Grotius*. New York: Harper & Brothers.

GRIFFIN, Miriam T.
2013   *Seneca on Society. A Guide to* De Beneficiis. Oxford: Oxford University Press.

GROSSE, Sven
2003   Die Nützlichkeit als Kriterium der Theologe. – *Melanchthon und die Neuzeit.* Ed. Günter Frank & Ulrich Köpf. Stuttgart/Bad Cannstatt: fromman holzboog. 69–93.

GUTMANN, Hans-Martin
1991   *Über Liebe und Herrschaft. Luthers Verständnis von Intimität und Autorität im Kontext des Zivilisationsprozesses.* GTA 46. Göttingen: Vandenhoeck & Ruprecht.

HADOT, Pierre
1995   *Philosophy as a Way of Life: Spiritual exercises from Socrates to Foucault.* London: Wiley-Blackwell.

HOLM, Bo Kristian
2006   *Gabe und Geben bei Luther. Das Verhältnis zwischen Reziprozität und reformatorischer Rechtfertigungslehre.* TBT 134. Berlin & New York: de Gruyter.
2013   Beyond Juxtaposing Luther and the "New Perspective on Paul": A Common Quest for the "Other" Way of Giving. – *Lutherjahrbuch* 80.

HOLM, Bo Kristian & KOFOED, Nina Javette
2018   Studying the Impact of Lutheranism on Societal Development. An Introduction. – *Lutheran Theology and the Shaping of Society: The Danish Monarchy as Example.* Ed. Bo Kristian Holm & Nina Javette Koefoed. R5AS 33. Göttingen: Vandenhoeck & Ruprecht. 9–24.

KÄFER, Anne
2010   *Inkarnation und Schöpfung. Schöpfungstheologische Voraussetzungen und Implikationen der Christologie bei Luther, Schleiermacher und Karl Barth.* TBT 151. Berlin & New York: de Gruyter.

KOLB, Robert & WENGERT, Timothy J.
2000   *The Book of Concord. The Confessions of the Evangelical Lutheran Church.* Minneapolis: Fortress Press.

LAFFIN, Michael R.
2016   *The Promises of Martin Luther's Political Theology: Freeing Luther from the Modern Political Narrative.* London et al: Bloomsbury T&T Clark.

LINK, Christian
2017   Schöpfungslehre. – *Philipp Melanchthon. Der Reformator zwischen Glauben und Wissen. Ein Handbuch.* Ed. Günter Frank. Berlin: de Gruyter, 363–376.

LUTHER, Martin
1883ff   *D. Martin Luthers Werke. Kritische Gesamtausgabe.* Weimar: Hermann Böhlaus Nachfolger (= WA).
WA 1: 224–228 Disputatio contra scholasticam theologiam, 1517.

WA 1: 258–265 Instructio pro confessione peccatorum, 1518.
WA 6: 202–276 Von den guten Werken, 1520.
WA 7: 204–229 Eine kurze Form der zehn Gebot, eine kurze Form des Glaubens, eine kurze form des Vaterunsers, 1520.
WA 7: 544–604 Das Magnificat verdeutschet und ausgelegt, 1521.
WA 26: 251–509 Vom Abendmahl Christi, Bekenntnis, 1528.
WA 40 I: 1–688 In epistolam S.Pauli ad Galatas Commentarius, 1531 [1535].
WA 42–44 Vorlesungen über 1. Mose von 1535–45.
WA 50: 9–15 Ob Christliche Fürsten schuldig sind, der Wiederteuffer unchristlichen Sect mit leiblicher strafe, und mit dem schwert zu wehren, 1536.
WA 55 II 1. Psalmenvorlesung. Scholien, 1513/16.
WA 56 Diui Pauli apostoli ad Romanos Epistola, 1515-16.
1955–1986 Luther's Works. Ed. Jaroslav Pelikan and Helmut T. Lehmann. Minneapolis & St. Louis, MO: Fortress Press & Concordia Publishing House (= LW).
LW 7 Lectures in Genesis.

MALYSZ, Piotr
2007 Exchange and Ecstacy: Luther's Eucharistic Theology in the Light of Radical Orthodoxy's Critique of Gift and Sacrifice. – *Scottish Journal of Theology* 60.

MELANCHTHON, Philipp
1997 *Loci communes 1521. Lateinisch – Deutsch.* Translated by Horst Georg Pöhlmann. Güsterloh: Gütersloher Verlagshaus.
1834ff *Corpus Reformatorum.* Ed. Karl Gottlieb Bretschneider et al. Halle (Saale): Schwetschke et filium (= CR).
CR 21: 602–1108 Loci praecipui theologici, 1559.

NUSSBAUM, Marta C.
2001 Duties of Justice, Duties of Material Aid: Cicero's Problematic Legacy. – *Nussbaum, Ethics and Political Philosophy. Lecture and Colloquium in Münster 2000*, ed. Angela Kallhoff. MVPh 4. Münster: LIT Verlag. 3–42.

RAPP, Claudia
2009 Charity and Piety as Episcopal and Imperial Virtues in Late Antiquity. – *Charity and Giving in Monotheistic Religions*, ed. Miriam Frenkel and Yaacov Lev. STIO N.F. 22. Berlin & New York: Walter de Gruyter,

SAARINEN, Risto
2017 *Luther and the Gift.* SHR 100. Tübingen: Mohr Siebeck.

SEILS, Martin
1985 Die Sache Luthers. – *Lutherjahrbuch* 52.

SENECA, Lucius Annaeus
1928 *De clementia.* – Moral Essays I. Loeb Classical Library 214. Cambridge, Mass: Harvard University Press. 356–449.
1935 *De beneficiis.* Loeb Classical Library 310. Cambridge, Mass: Harvard University Press.

2011 *On Benefits*. Translated by Mariam Griffin and Brad Inwood. Chicago & London: The University of Chicago Press.

SKINNER, Quentin
1978 *The foundations of modern political thought. Volume Two: The Age of Reformation*. Cambridge: Cambridge University Press.

STACEY, Peter
2007 *Roman Monarchy and the Renaissance Prince*. Ideas in Context 79. Cambridge: Cambridge University Press.

TAYLOR, Charles
2012 *A Secular age*. Cambridge, MA: The Belknap Press of Harvard University Press.

TROELTSCH, Ernst
1992 *The Social Teachings of the Christian Churches*. Louisville, Ky.: Westminster John Knox Press.

WENDTE, Martin
2013 *Die Gabe und das Gestell. Luthers Metaphysik des Abendmahls im technischen Zeitalter*. CM 7. Tübingen: Mohr Siebeck.

WITTE JR, John
2002 *Law and Protestantism. The Legal Teachings of the Lutheran Reformation*. Cambridge: Cambridge University Press.

WRIGHT, William J.
2010 *Martin Luther's Understanding of God's Two Kingdoms: A Response to the Challenge of Skepticism*. Text and Studies in Reformation and Post-Reformation Thought. Grand Rapids, Mich: Baker Akademic.

Shorthands

BSLK	Bekennntnisschriften der evangelisch-lutherischen Kirche
CM	Collegium Metaphysicum
GTA	Göttinger theologische Arbeiten
MGQSHI	McGill-Queen's studies in the history of Ideas
LCL	Loeb Classical Library
MVPh	Münsteraner Vorlesungen zur Philosophie
PG	Patrologia Graecae
R5AS	Refo500 Academic Series
SMR	Spätmittelalter, Humanismus, Reformation
STIO N.F.	Studien zur Geschichte und Kultur des islamischen Orients. Beihefte zur Zeitschrift "Der Islam". Neue Folge
SuRNR	Spätmittelalter und Reformation. Neue Reihe
TBT	Theologische Bibliothek Töpelmann

Is God's Grace Really a Gift?
Unraveling a Pseudo-Problem

Ted Peters

To be is to be gifted. One's very being is an unrequested gift. Sheer presence is a gift. Life is a gift. Every new possibility is a gift. The divine promise of forgiveness and resurrection is an unmerited gift of the same fundamental order.[1] Our very creation is a gift, and our justification by God's grace marks the gift of new creation.

But, theologians must ask: is this all wrong? What if there is no such thing as a gift? What if every relationship is indelibly corrupted by reciprocity, return, repayment? Does this render the gifted character of our creation and new creation null and void? Should theologians discard the idea of gift and replace it with the "art of the deal"?[2]

If it is in fact the case that all gifts come with strings attached--meaning that no pure gift exists – then we must ask: does this obliterate the doctrine by which the church stands or falls? Have the bulwarks of *Ein Feste Burg* collapsed? No. The problem of the so-called "pure gift" is a pseudo-problem. The philosophical formulation of the problem does not apply to the concrete life of the person of faith who enjoys living daily in God's grace. To apply a definition of "pure gift" to the life of faith would commit the fallacy of misplaced concreteness. The philosophical concept of "pure gift" is an abstraction, an idea, an ideal. What is concrete is the historical event of Jesus Christ combined with the indwelling of the

---

[1] "'Gabe' ist ein Urwort der Theologie," says Bayer 2009, 21. Creation understood as gift becomes the inclusive locus of Christian theology. Bayer 2009, 20: "Schöpfung durch das Wort geschiet ex nihilo (aus dem Nichts) als unverdiente, kategorische Gabe; ich bin, was mir gegeben wurde."

[2] Trump 1987, 1: "I like making deals, preferably big deals. That's how I get my kicks."

resurrected Christ in the person of faith. This concrete phenomenon is theologically described by terms such as *grace, favor, mercy, agape,* and even *gift*. Overdefining a term such as *gift* so that it no longer describes concrete actuality may be an interesting exercise in sophistry, but it ought not cause a theologian to lose sleep.

To engage in a discussion about *gift* is akin to dumping a bowl of cooked spaghetti on the table and then attempting to straighten out each strand. To the task of straightening out those strands we now turn.

The abstract question: is a gift really a gift?

Is a gift really a gift? Risto Saarinen registers doubt: "There is no free gift. If somebody offers you a gift, this person is increasing his or her social status and putting you in his or her debt. It belongs to the idea of gift that this is not said but, on the contrary, explicitly denied."[3] If Saarinen is right, then this turns a purported gift into a lie. When we give, we deny that strings are attached; yet, our reputation in the eyes of the recipient is enhanced not only by the gift itself but also by our denial of the strings attached. If we are the recipients, we contribute to the self-justification and delusion of magnanimity on the part of the gift-giver. The strings attached to a gift may be at first invisible. We do not notice them until we find ourselves entangled.[4] When we find ourselves entangled in a gift's strings, we realize that it is not a gift at all.

Does this apply to God? Recall, 1 John 4:11: "Beloved, since God loved us so much, we also ought to love one another". Are we mistaken to think of God's love for us as a gift? Should we think of our love for one another as sharing that gift? Or, should we think of God's love coming to us with strings attached, with the imperative to love one another? If we are commanded to love one another, does this make God's love a non-gift?

---

[3] SAARINEN 2005,18. MORRUS 2009, 330: "In the ecumenical movement, it is important to consider whether a proffered gift is actually a Trojan horse, i.e., an attempt to impose one's view or practice on others The model for ecumenical giving should not be an 'exchange of gifts', as Saarinen explains, but the Pauline idea of the body of Christ, where members use their gifts in service of others." It is not Saarinen's agenda to "impose" his views on ecumenical colleagues.

[4] This treatment extends two previous analyses of the concept of gift: PETERS 2015; 2015b.

Saarinen draws out the implication. "Even God giving freely to the creatures is, in terms of this interpretation, attempting to win support or exercise power over creatures through creating relationships of obligation and dependence."[5] Have we as Jesus' disciples unwittingly entangled ourselves in God's manipulative strings that have ensnared us? Should we become more suspicious of divine narcissism than we have been?

This anxious hand-wringing over the possibility or impossibility of authentic gift-giving keeps Reformation Lutherans awake at night. Have we Lutherans misled ourselves and our beloved followers by telling them that out of divine grace God is bestowing on us the gift of creation and new creation? Are we misleading when we proclaim that the forgiveness of sins, justification, and reconciliation are divine gifts apart from any human work, merit, or deserving? Are we Lutherans misleading our followers because the very idea of the gift is incoherent, impure, and corrupt? If justification is the article by which the church stands or falls (*iustificatio – articulus stantis vel cadentis ecclesiae*) then should we fear 1 Corinthians 9:16? "Woe to me if I do not proclaim the gospel" rightly!

Is Jesus Christ really God's gift to us?

Twenty-first century disciples of St. Paul and Martin Luther are so accustomed to using the friendly word, *gift*, that such skepticism comes as a shock. Was it a mistake for the *Mannermaa School* at the University of Helsinki to remind us that the very presence of Jesus Christ is given to us as a gift of divine grace in faith? After all, Luther is now remembered for emphasizing that "Christ lives in us through faith."[6] Saarinen himself adds, "Through receiving Christ by faith, we have union with Christ. The gift is given for us, but also to us."[7]

---

[5] SAARINEN 2005, 18.
[6] LUTHER 2015, 1:103 (Proofs of the Thesis Debated in the Chapter at Heidelberg 1518).
[7] SAARINEN 2005, 51. Saarinen's own position begins with the perspective of God as giver tied to the indwelling model of the Mannermaa interpretation of Luther. "If…the perspective is shifted to God as giver, the human person ceases to appear as agent and becomes the recipient of the word and Christ. In this new, seemingly passive perspective he or she reappears, again paradoxically, as vivid and animated partner." SAARINEN 2017, 202–203.

It is the gift of Christ's presence that effects justification and, at the same time, changes the ontological status of the sinful person. The presence of Christ is the gift (*donum*) itself which effects justification. Luther "does not separate the person (*persona*) of Christ and his work (*officium*) from each other. Instead, *Christ himself,* both his person and his work, *is* the Christian righteousness, that is, the 'righteousness of faith'. Christ – and therefore also *his entire person and work* – is really and truly present in the faith itself (*in ipsa fide Christus adest*)."[8] The person of faith should feel he or she is the recipient of a divine gift (*donum*) which results from a divine disposition of favor, mercy, love – that is, from the divine disposition we name, *grace.*

Mannermaa and his disciples are not the only ones to see this in Luther. Roman Catholic theologian, David Tracy, sees it this way too. "Grace though faith is both God's *favor* through the righteousness of Christ imputed to us as forgiveness and *donum* (pure gift, i.e., passive incipient righteousness, which, through the Holy Spirit can increase until the ultimate *donum* of our graced glory after this life). The righteousness we receive is Christ's own active righteousness which endows upon us passive righteousness."[9] Similarly, American Evangelical Matt Jenson reports, "Luther stresses that faith is a divine gift mediated through the Word. Faith is not a human accomplishment, something to be mustered; it is given to us by God as he nourishes us on his Word throughout our lives."[10] Even retired Pope Benedict XVI assumes Christians have come to know "the astonishing experience of gift."[11]

So, just what is wrong with this picture? It seems clear that God is gracious and loving and disposed to give good things to his creatures. One gift is his Son, Jesus Christ, who died on Calvary. A second gift is his Son, Jesus Christ again, whom the Holy Spirit makes present to us in faith. Are there any strings attached which would nullify God's graciousness in gift giving? One might observe that the sixteenth century Reformation debates regarding justification, grace, faith, hope, and love were an indirect attempt to answer these questions.

---

[8] MANNERMAA 2005, 5. Mannermaa's italics.
[9] TRACY 2015, 108.
[10] JENSON 2015, 155.
[11] Pope BENEDICT XVI 2009, 34.

Does God's grace and mercy lead to a genuine gift?

It seems reasonable to apply terms such as *love, grace, favor,* and *mercy* to God's disposition. These are traits of the divine, kataphatically speaking. *Grace* refers to God's favor, while *gift* refers to what we receive.[12] We might then ascribe *faith, hope, charity, neighbor love* (*Nächstenliebe*), and *good works* to human activity, to the human response to divine grace. Might such distinctions help us untangle the spaghetti noodles?

What does Luther think? On the one hand, Luther seems to distinguish grace from gift. "Grace must be sharply distinguished from gifts," he writes. "A righteous and faithful man doubtless has both grace and the gift. ...but the gift heals from sin and from all his corruption of body and soul. ...Everything is forgiven through grace, but as yet not everything is healed through the gift. ...for with the gift there is sin which it purges away and overcomes."[13] Because God's justification declares a person just while still in a state of sin, the person of faith begins the arduous process of overcoming that sin. The sin prior to and following justification is the same, argues Luther; but our status before God is different. Prior to justification sin warrants wrath, condemnation, death. Subsequent to justification, sin is not counted, so to speak. While we strive to purge sin from our daily life, "it is called sin, and is truly such in its nature; but now it is sin without wrath, without the law, dead sin, harmless sin, as long as one perseveres in grace and gift."[14] Note how this applies "as long as one perseveres in grace and gift."

---

[12] Grace is not a thing, a substance, an object. The term *grace* applies to God's disposition to be generous, to *divine generosity,* according to GREGERSEN 2009. For others, *grace* includes the entire divine-human interaction. LODBERG 2015, 247: "Grace is understood as the unexpected kairotic moment of change, where the future opens up to new possibilities of reconciliation in situations of conflict, war, and hatred. It is a moment you cannot plan for, but you always hope it will happen; and simply hoping for and trusting in the possibility of a gracious moment can influence your gratitude and behavior in the present."

[13] LUTHER 1955, 32: 229 (Against Latomus).

[14] LUTHER 1955, 32: 229. Gift with response seems to be the structure of grace and reconciliation in the work of Karl Rahner. RAHNER 1961, IV: 257 (*The Word and the Eucharist*): "For God's salvific action on man is not merely a forensic imputation of the justice of Christ. And it is not merely the announcement of a purely future act of God. Nor is it constituted merely by man's faith, however this is to be further interpreted. It is a true, real, creative action of God in grace, which renews man interiorly by making him participate in the divine nature--all of which, being the condition of possibility of a salutary action on the part of man, is prior, at least logically, to such *action* of man." Is the renewal a human response to the divine gift or is it the gift itself?

Yet, on the other hand, Luther elsewhere equates grace and gift. "But 'the grace of God' (*gratia Dei*) and 'the gift' (*donum*) are the same thing, namely, the very righteousness (*Iustitia*) which is freely given to us through Christ."[15] In our justification, grace and gift are the same thing, he says. It appears that Luther is not consistent on his use of terms.

Even if Luther is inconsistent, this in itself should not cause a theological problem. Whether grace and gift are identical or different is not an issue that should bother a contemporary theologian. What has become an issue, however, is the question: does the gift of grace come with strings attached? Does it necessarily imply reciprocity? Does the declaration of forgiveness in justification-by-faith necessarily imply effective transformation in the sinner? Does justification require sanctification before reconciliation?

The confusing interpretation of Oxford evangelical Alister E. McGrath illustrates the problem. He writes, "The *gift* of justification lays upon us the *obligation* to live in accordance with our new status."[16] If he would be a German, he might say the gift (*Gabe*) comes with a duty (*Aufgabe*). What McGrath fails to recognize is that Luther and his disciples would not want to say such a thing, because they believe that the gift of justification is just that, a gift, and not an obligation. Yet, we ask: can today's Lutherans get away with this? If the concept of grace (*gratia*) refers to God's disposition of mercy toward us, and if the concept of gift (*donum*) refers to what is given to us, we must ask: are there any strings attached? Conditions? Obligations? If the gift comes with obligations, as McGrath thinks, does this make it a conditional gift and, thereby, a non-gift?

For purposes of clarification as I mentioned before, I recommend that we use the term *grace* to refer to the divine disposition to give. "Grace is the favor, mercy, and gratuitous goodwill of God toward us,"[17] says Philip

---

[15] LUTHER 1955, 25: 306 (*Romans*).
[16] McGRATH 1988, 117. Because reconciliation is inclusive of both justification and sanctification for John Calvin, this Reformer looks like a better fit than Luther for a reciprocal gift exchange. BILLINGS 2005, 91, 92: "Thus, if one is searching for a theology of grace in which the reception of grace in salvation will not be severed from being reborn for a life of holiness through the Spirit, Calvin's theology is a good place to look. Rather than 'active reception', Calvin's reception of grace might be better called 'activating reception'. ...Calvin also makes extensive use of the language of a mutual, bilateral covenant, particularly when he wants to emphasize human responsibility."
[17] MELANCHTHON 1969, 88. SITTLER 1972, 24: "The fundamental meaning of grace

Melanchthon, suggesting that *grace* belongs to the divine disposition.[18] With this in mind, I also recommend that we use the term *gift* to refer to what God gives and we receive. I further recommend that we use the term *agape* to refer to gracious love – that is, love that asks for nothing reciprocal in return.

Must the obligation to reciprocity hide in every gift?

"In all societies gifts have reciprocal character," Sammeli Juntunen asserts.[19] There is no free lunch. Is every gift only a mask hiding the obligation to reciprocate?

When we turn to the phenomenology of gift giving and receiving, we find ourselves in a dilemma, an aporia. The dilemma has been pointed out by philosophers such as Jacques Derrida. The dilemma looks like this: If I give you a gift, then I look good and put you in my debt. But if this is to be a genuine gift, there must be no reciprocity, return, exchange, counter-gift, or debt.[20] The concept of the gift implies that you return nothing to

---

is the goodness and loving kindness of God and the activity of this goodness in and toward his creation." SAARINEN 2009, 84: "Die Gabe wird nicht materiell konstitutiert, sondern die Intention des Gebers bleibt für sie wesensbestimmend. Auch an diesem Punkt sind sich die Reformation mit Seneca einig." SAARINEN 2010, 293: "Seneca's discussion of divine and parental education as paradigm of *beneficia* displays similarities to Luther; the parental favour or first gift is received in a state of ignorance and even unwillingness... Only in retrospect, that is, after receiving the proper education, can the child become grateful. But the decisive life-changing *beneficium* has nevertheless been received much earlier."

[18] At the heart of Christian living is "knowing God for one self, as opposed to merely knowing or thinking *about* him... [it includes] discovering that God is gracious." WRIGHT 2009, 23. Italics in original.

[19] JUNTUNEN 2004, 55. Sociobiologists employ the concept of *reciprocal altruism* in their attempt to explain inclusive fitness in evolution. Gifting is, by definition, reciprocal even when we pretend that it is not. The giver gains through an enhanced reputation, which Harvard's E.O. Wilson calls "indirect reciprocity, by which a reputation for altruism and cooperativeness accrues to an individual, even if the actions that build it are no more than ordinary. A saying in German exemplifies the tactic: *Tue Gutes und rede darüber*. Do good and talk about it. Doors are then opened, and opportunities for friendships and alliances increased." WILSON 2012, 249.

[20] DERRIDA 1992, cited by SAARINEN 2009, 24. In *Given Time* and *The Gift of Death* (DERRIDA 1995), Derrida reinterprets the previous anthropology of Marcel MAUSS 1990, with the following result: no pure gift is possible. Every gift is corrupted by exchange. Even the reception of a gift counts as reciprocity. Death is the only gift which does not demand

me. Yet, in giving you the gift, my social standing increases; and you are required to respond with gratitude. The mere recognition of the gift by the receiver nullifies the gift as gift. Within the economy of exchange, the very condition that makes gift-giving what it is includes strings even while, by definition, it denies the strings.

If Derrida is accurate, then we must ask: does this observation regarding gift-giving in the economy of exchange apply to the gift given us in the gospel? No, says German theologian Oswald Bayer. "God's coming into the world and his existence in it is *contrary* to human experience and corresponding expectations" for reciprocity.[21] In the case of God's gracious giving, there are no strings attached.

In opposition to Bayer, Danish theologian Bo Holm sees strings when he interprets Luther's understanding of the gospel through an economic

---

reciprocity. Whereas for Mauss, gift-giving is part of human exchange, Derrida believes that a genuine gift should be an interruption in the pattern of exchange. The idea of the *pure gift* in Derrida becomes ineffable, elusive, death-obsessed, and eschatological. But, according to the interpretation of Sarah COAKLEY (2008, 226), gift for Derrida is "nonetheless endlessly alluring, a remaining token of the divine." How does *gift* illuminate our human relationship to the divine? Jean-Luc MARION (1991) critiques Derrida's notion of the impossibility of a gift, replacing it with the notion of a 'saturated phenomenon' which becomes a revelation of the divine. By 'saturated phenomenon' Marion means a gift which overwhelms the receiver, surpassing his or her concepts and expectations. In John Milbank's, "Can a Gift be Given?" (MILBANK 1995), gift-exchange gets purified from self-interest and agonistic manipulation between human parties. How? Gifting becomes a circle of delayed, but appropriate human, response to the ultimate. The divine gift is characterized by asymmetrical reciprocity and nonidentical repetition. Milbank finds the divine model for this in Augustine's account of the Trinity, where the Holy Spirit is God's gift. Milbank discredits Derrida's unavoidably corrupt gifting as a chimera or will-o'-the-wisp. In contrast to Milbank, Kathryn TANNER (2005) embraces a Calvinized notion of divine unilateralism grounded in an Augustinian Trinity. This unilateralism is just what Milbank rejects as a false, modern idea of pure gift. COAKLEY (2008, 228) contrasts the two positions: "whereas Milbank's theological vision is of a circle of divine gift and human, participatory response – thereby creating an alternative social reality to that of capitalism, Tanner's vision is of a 'unilateral' and absolutely 'unconditional' divine gift by the non-competitive 'persons' of the Trinity, which, if duly welcomed, issues forth in a 'reflected' human 'horizontal' generosity of wealth to those in need: 'The good is distributed by God, and is to be distributed by us, in imitation of God'." Is this dispute more apparent than real? This is COAKLEY's (2008, 229) question. "Are the rhetorical differences between Milbank and Tanner (between 'purified gift exchange' on the one hand and 'unilateral' gift on the other) in some respects more apparent than real?" I tend to side with Coakley, asking if this debate might be centered around a pseudo-problem.

[21] BAYER 2007, 5: 431.

lens. What is the economy of justification? It requires a component of reciprocity, mutuality, exchange. In response to God's love, we love. We participate. "Justification is the opening of reciprocity, making realized reciprocity itself the gift of grace."[22] Grace stimulates. We respond. Holm likes the sentence that connotes economic reciprocity: "*Deus dat ut dem, et do ut des* (God gives that I may give, and I give that you may give)."[23] Holm distances himself from exaggerated avoidance of all reciprocity in justification-by-faith.

On the one hand, Lutherans want to claim that God's gracious gift comes with no strings attached. On the other hand, a gift by definition has strings; a gift requires some level of reciprocity even if only in receiving it. The definition of "gift" means that even God is incapable of giving a free lunch. How can the Lutherans see their way through this aporia?

Suppose we drive a deep wedge between justification and sanctification? Suppose we deny any reciprocity to justification and attribute all human cooperative contribution to sanctification? Suppose we speak of two gifts instead of just one? Would this help clarify things?

No, argues Saarinen. There is only one divine gift at work, and this gift includes both passive reception and effective renewal. Following Seneca, God's grace is like a parent's love to a child. Whether or not the child immediately responds with gratitude or even accepts the parent's love at all does not change the fact of the parent's unconditional love. However, after the child has grown to adulthood, he or she looks back and realizes the gifted quality of those earlier years. There is only one love offered by the parents, yet it is perceived differently over time. So also with God's justifying grace.

> Thus it would be artificial to claim that 'justification is not sanctification', as the operative initial gift already contains the full reality of the divine *beneficium*, including the potential of receiving the gift (*das Empfangenkönnen der Gabe*). The prolongation of this one gift sustains this potential of receiving so that we as recipients come into picture. At the same time, the beneficial act of God does not change. Thus the change from the first to the second gift only concerns our

---

[22] HOLM 2005, 85.
[23] HOLM 2005, 86.

perspectival change while the self-giving of God in Christ remains one. It would be more adequate to say that sanctification is nothing else than the prolongation of justification.[24]

The distinction made so frequently among Luther's disciples between justification and sanctification functions well to emphasize our passivity in justification and our involvement in sanctification. Yet, it is not necessarily the case that the person of faith experiences justification one day and sanctification the next. The two come wrapped together in a single package. What is concrete is a person's single life of faith described with terms such as *justification* and *sanctification*. To split them is to make an abstract distinction that does not reflect an empirical separation. Perhaps Saarinen is right when he avers that the difference amounts to a theological perception only.

---

[24] SAARINEN 2017, 269–270. Saarinen here is disagreeing with Ingolf Dalferth who distinguishes between justification as a pre-gift with total passivity and sanctification as a gift accompanied by passive-activity (*Passivitätsaktivität*). It is my own observation that, when interpreting Luther, Dalferth offers some brilliant ontological observations such as: God's gift makes what it gives, therefore, the receiver is made into that which is given. In addition, he avers that whatever God gives is a *good* gift. DALFERTH 2009, 49: "*Alles, was Gott uns gibt, macht uns gut*--das ist die Grundregel." Dalferth's italics. Justification, by making a new creation, does not involve reciprocity, even when justification is followed by sanctification which does include human cooperation. This is reminiscent of Thomas' distinction between operative and cooperative grace. Even though Saarinen disagrees with this two-step gift giving position, Dalferth is clear on separating out the non-reciprocal character of divine justification of the sinner. So far, so good. Yet, I believe Dalferth goes too far when he nullifies the first creation to make room for the new creation, when he says that only by placing the human being in a state of nothingness, *nihil*, can the human be created anew. DALFERTH 2009, 52: "Wer *neu geschaffen wird*, ist dagegen zuvor schon so, dass dies retrospectiv als Werden vom alten Menschen zum neuen Menschen beschrieben werden kann. Das hier zu bedenkende Werden ist daher kein Wechsel von *nihil* zu *aliquis* (Schöpfung) und auch nicht von der Möglichkeit zur Wirklichkeit (Verwirklichung), sondern eher von der Unmöglichkeit zur Wirklichkeit..." SAARINEN (2017, 269) asks rhetorically, "Why does Luther speak so emphatically of God giving himself 'to us' in *The Large Catechism*, if he thinks that 'we' do not even exist at the moment of justification?" Here is my observation: the gift of reality out of impossibility is dramatic here, to be sure. Yet, the radicality of passing again through non-being prevents Dalferth from accounting for something very important in theological anthropology, namely, human fulfillment in the new creation. By reducing the old creation to nothing and starting brand new, the tie to the old would be cut and this would nullify any plan for quenching human thirsts or fulfilling human yearnings. An alternative view would be that of John Polkinghorne, according to whom the new creation is created not *ex nihilo* but rather *ex vetere*. POLKINGHORNE 1994, 167: "The first creation was *ex nihilo* while the new creation will be *ex vetere*. ...It is a new creation but, unlike the first creation, it is not *ex nihilo*. The new creation is what the Spirit of God does to the first creation."

Justification as new creation

Does the gift look different when we look through the lens of new creation rather than today's economy? Let's try this on for size.

The indwelling Christ is God's gift to us; and this amounts to a creation, a new creation. It is Christ from within the new creature who motivates our life of loving service. Luther likens the justified person to a tree that sprouts leaves. Is the tree obligated to sprout leaves? No. Sprouting leaves is natural to the tree. Similarly, Luther likens the justified person to the sun. Do we have to demand that the sun shine? No. The sun shines spontaneously. So also does the person of faith who has been given the living Christ. This person spontaneously loves the neighbor. In sum, this particular gift does not involve a reciprocal or obligatory character. This leads Juntunen to conclude: "I think that the idea of the *donum* being comparable to creation makes it clear that all reciprocity between the giver and the receiver is excluded."[25]

Does the effect of justification on the life of the sinner count as obligation, as strings attached? According to Simo Peura, the indwelling Christ leads to transformation, to effective justification, and even to deification (*theosis*). Peura believes Luther's view includes "participation, change, and deification. The aim of justification is actually a complete transformation in Christ."[26] This transformation follows from the real presence of Christ in faith. "Luther's understanding that God the Father is favorable to a sinner (*favor Dei*) and that Christ renews a sinner (*donum Dei*) is based on the idea of a *unio cum Christo*. This same idea explains why grace and gift are necessary to each other. Gift is not only a consequence of grace, as is usually emphasized in Lutheran theology, but it is in a certain sense a condition for grace as well."[27] For Peura, we now have a "condition for grace." Does this condition amount to the completion of the gift exchange, a completion that requires our response, participation, and achievement? Are these the strings?

---

[25] JUNTUNEN 2009, 61.
[26] PEURA 1998, 60. The key to the New Finnish School of Luther Research is the real presence of the indwelling Christ. "Faith means the presence of Christ and thus participation in the divine life," writes Mannermaa (2005, 39), "Christ 'is in us' and 'remains in us'. The life that the Christian now lives is, in an ontologically real manner, Christ himself."
[27] PEURA 1998, 56.

Suppose we think for a moment about a Christmas gift, wrapped in such a way that the contents are hidden. We may shake it, but in itself this shaking will not reveal precisely what the contents are. We must open it. Once it is open and we can identify it, then we will put it on or use it or in some way integrate it into our other possessions. The gift may be a stimulus, but it becomes a gift in the full sense only when we receive and respond. No giver would give an expensive gift without expecting it be enjoyed through usage. This response does not amount to reciprocity, to be sure; yet the gift giver feels a sense of accomplishment only when the gift is opened, used, and appreciated. Does gift analysis help us understand divine love and divine gift giving?

Can we think of our very existence as a gift?

Let's return for a moment from new creation back to creation. Let's turn to the phenomenological observations of philosopher Martin Heidegger and the later Heideggerians. According to Heidegger, we sort of wake up at some point in our life and realize that we are here. We are here! And your or my being-here is not the result of our own decision or action. We're just here in this time and this place. We are *Dasein,* simply being here or there, anywhere specific. This being-here has the feel of having been thrown. We feel we have been thrown from non-existence into existence. We live with a sense of thrownness, *Geworfenheit.*[28] Might we think of our basic having-been-thrown-into existence as a gift? Jean-Luc Marion considers this and remarks: *"The gift delivers Being/being."*[29]

Might the way we use language indicate something relevant here? In English, we simply say "there is" when identifying something that exists. The same in French, *il y a.* The Finnish language does not need this structure, because much of the indicating of what-is or is-happening is in the suffixes and cases or specific pronouns or subjects. The "there is" does not really work unless you want to say that "something ... is there..." quite concretely, meaning "there" = *siellä,* pointing to "over there".

---

[28] HEIDEGGER 1962.
[29] MARION 1992, 101.

But, note what happens in Heidegger's language, German: *es gibt*. To say, "there is," we literally say, "it gives." Marion comments, "No one more than Heidegger allowed the thinking of the coincidence of the gift with Being/being, by taking literally the German *es gibt*, wherein we recognize the French *il y a*, there is... we would understand the fact that there should be (of course: being) as this fact that *it gives, ça donne*. Being itself is delivered in the mode of giving."[30] *To be is to be gifted*, say philosophers such as Heidegger and Marion. *To be is to be graced*, say theologians.

The theologian will ask Heidegger: who threw us into existence? Who is the giver when we say, *es gibt*? Is our very existence best understood as a gift? And, if so, how can we pay back the giver? We can't. There is no reciprocity possible. No economy of exchange is at work. The basic gift of our existence is radical, brute, impenetrable.[31] The philosophers seem to stop with givenness. The theologian proceeds to ask: might there be a giver? Is it too soon to say the giver is God?[32]

Philosopher Eric Voegelin suggests that we are thrown into existence and then retrieved by the same source. While we exist between birth and death, we experience estrangement. If we give attention to the giftedness of our existence, we become attuned to the being – the ground of being – from which our existence is estranged. "Attunement, therefore, will be the state of existence when it hearkens to that which is lasting in being, when it maintains a tension of awareness for its partial revelations of the order of society and the world, when it listens attentively to the silent voices of conscience and grace in human existence itself. We are thrown into and

---

[30] MARION 1992, 102.

[31] Marion places both feet in the pure givenness or pure giftedness of existence without relying on the being of the giver. Thereby, Marion can think of God without being. Critics such as John Milbank want to deny this move to Marion. When you and I recognize the givenness and hence giftedness of our very existence and respond in gratitude, this counts as reciprocity. It implies a divine giver. See MILBANK 2003 and the discussion by SAARINEN 2009, 30–33.

[32] What we are looking at here is the phenomenology of human experience which raises the question of transcendence and the question of God. SMITH 1958, 103. "This realization that one's existence is completely dependent upon factors beyond one's control--factors unified by the mind's instinctive drive toward simplicity, coherence, oneness--issues in the theological concept of God's sovereignty. When it is compounded with gratitude for the goodness of this life which God's sovereignty has affected and is continuously sustaining we have the germ of the concept of grace; God's free and unstinted gifts to man which not only have made his life possible but sustain and enable it at every point along the way."

out of existence without knowing the Why or the How, but while in it we know that we are of the being to which we return."[33] As a philosopher, Voegelin uses the word *being* where a theologian might use the word *God*. Heidegger and Voegelin both tell us that if we simply stop for a moment to reflect on our throwness into existence, we will catch the first glimmer of grace in our creation. In, with, and under our very being-here is grace.

Pertinent here is the obligation to love. Our experience of being thrown into existence includes being thrown into relationship with the obligation to love our neighbor. This is the point made by two of Heidegger's disciples – Lutheran philosopher Knud Løgstrup and Jewish philosopher Emmanuel Lévinas. According to Løgstrup, "life has been given to us. We have not ourselves created it." When we wake up to realize that we have been given a life which we did not create, we further realize that we are not alone. Someone who is other is present.

We find ourselves already in relationship with other persons, persons whom we trust and to whom we owe moral responsibility. The other person is other; and our relationship is already characterized as love for the other. "Man's relationship with the other is *better* as difference than as unity: sociality is better than fusion," writes Lévinas; "The very value of love is the impossibility of reducing the other to myself." In sum, what we have been given is existence, and this is personal existence-in-relationship-to-the-other. This relational existing is basic, fundamental. It is the givenness with which we begin to understand ourselves as individuals.[34] The gift of existence has an obligation to love the other – the neighbor – built in to it.

Is our creation from a gracious God?

If we turn our gaze from new creation back to creation, does the phenomenology of brute existence give sufficient evidence of a gracious God and the gift of being here? Not for Luther. Luther would not stop here. He would go on to identify the giver, God, and prompt within us a sense of gratitude for God's gracious gifts. He opens his commentary

---

[33] VOEGELIN 1956, 1:5.
[34] See citations and discussion of Løgstrup and Lévinas on gift in RINDERS 2007.

on the creed in *the Small Catechism* with the lines, "I believe that God has created me together with all that exists. God has given me and still preserves my body and soul: eyes, ears, and all limbs and senses; reason and all mental faculties… And all this is done out of pure, fatherly, and divine goodness and mercy, without any merit or worthiness of mine at all! For all this I owe it to God to thank and praise, serve and obey him. This is most certainly true."[35]

First, note how for Luther the focus on you and me as individual persons. We are given priority over the universe and everything that exists. Your and my subjective identity and awareness come first; then everything else that objectively exists. God is personal. Our self or our soul provides the point of orientation from which we look out upon the world.

Second, God's grace in creation comes with strings attached. On the one hand, we are not responsible for our existence. We have been placed here by "divine goodness and mercy, without any merit or worthiness" of our own. On the other hand, we "owe (*schüldig*) it to God to thank and praise, serve and obey him." We are obligated to show gratitude for the gift of existence. Whether we show gratitude or not does not change the fact that God is gracious, that God is merciful and good. But, we ask: is it necessary for us to show gratitude to God if our existence is to be a gift? Is this reciprocal response necessary for this basic gift to actually be a gift?

Here is the unresolved problem left us by the reformers. On the one hand, they stressed that the gifts of God's grace are utterly independent of any merit or worthiness on our part. On the other hand, God's gifts are concrete and specific to us in our daily lives. This specificity implies participation, transformation, and soul formation. This participation implies a response on our part, an active living out of the gift. Does this amount to merit or worthiness after the fact?

Let's return for a moment to Reformation themes such as justifying faith, loving neighbors, and sinning boldly.

---

[35] LUTHER 2000, 354–355.

Must God's gift of justifying faith be received?

Can we equate the gift of being-here with justifying faith? Is the anonymous *es gibt* the model for the divine gift of justification? Are all people of all times and all places automatically justified because of some eternal divine decree?[36] Does justification come automatically with creation?

Saarinen would answer negatively. Justifying faith is personal, he contends. For any gift to be given there must be a receiver; and the receiver is a participant in the gift-giving interaction. This applies especially to the gifts of God's grace in faith. "Faith does not signalize a cooperative act, but a personal participation in the reciprocity of giving and receiving. A gift cannot be given if the receiver is not there." Saarinen teases out the implications for the means of grace, the sacraments. "At least four requirements can be read from the Lutheran Confessions: (1) that the recipient is alive, (2) is faithful, (3) is a person and (4) is not just anybody, a placeholder or a representative of a larger group, but the very person to whom the sacrament is physically given."[37] Or, to say it another way, reception makes it possible for giving to result in a gift.

If this is the case, does the very fact that a receiver is present for the gift to be a gift entail reciprocity? Not precisely. At least no reciprocity is required according to the economy of exchange where we would be obligated to pay God back for his gracious gifts. Our gratitude does not accrue directly to God's advantage; rather, our gratitude comes to expression as our love for our neighbor.

At this point we should introduce the qualities of agape love.[38] Note the multiple uses of *agape* in 1 John 4:11 cited above. Saarinen, following Luther, develops the notion of agape love in the Christian life. "In Luther's account, Christians are called to imitate the divine love in such a manner

---

[36] RITSCHL 1874, 128: "We must not think of merely isolated acts of justification. These acts are only manifestations in time of the one eternal Divine decree of the justification of men for Christ's sake."

[37] SAARINEN 2005, 11. Bo HOLM (2009, 92) places receiving a gift into the category of reciprocity. "Receiving a gift is already a way of giving back."

[38] BASTIANEL 2010, 110: "Rooted in the gift of the theological virtue, in communion with God, Christian charity is a love like that of Christ: recognized in him, made possible through him, learned from him."

that they fulfill the needs and wants of others."[39] Agape attends to the needs of the needy, not to your or my needs as the lover of the needy. "A pure love would require a person who is not seeking his own profit but would act altruistically. Giving a completely free gift would be an example of pure love and altruism."[40] Now, to be frank, I need to ask: is it possible that agape love defined this way is possible in the human economy of exchange?

I will answer no for two reasons. The first is the philosophical reason adumbrated above, namely, *all* gift-giving in the economy of exchange is a disguised form of reciprocity. There are no gifts without strings attached. Would this apply to a gift God gives us? Let's work with the hypothetical positive answer to this to see where it might lead.

My second reason has to do with theological anthropology. According to the Augustinian tradition on human nature – the tradition to which Luther belongs – the human ego cannot in this life be de-centered. Everything that we do – whether we are baptized or unbaptized – is an expression of the ego for the sake of the ego. There can be no human action which is totally selfless or ego-free. Every one of our attempts to love our neighbor with agape love is compromised if not contaminated with a self-serving motive. Even the pursuit of a transformed soul would betray a self-serving motive, thereby disqualifying what action we take as pure agape. In sum, pure agape is impossible for us.

Here is Saarinen on Luther: "Luther shares this skepticism with regard to pure love and genuine altruism. For Luther, human reason is inevitably egoistic and thus incapable of pure giving. ...Luther is always and tirelessly making the point that all human efforts to do good and to live a good life are contaminated by egoism."[41] If this skepticism obtains, then why ask us to respond to God's grace by graciously loving others? Are we being asked to do the impossible?

Trying to label every one of these spaghetti strands poses a challenge. To try to unravel it all in order to find a single strand of pure self-sacrificial love would be both tedious and unnecessary. Plunge ahead with daily life,

---

[39] SAARINEN 2005, 56.
[40] SAARINEN 2005, 52.
[41] SAARINEN 2005, 52.

Luther would say. Sin boldly![42] Don't let the spiritual spaghetti tie us up and restrict our bold attempts at loving our neighbor.

Might the idea of "pure gift" be a pseudo-problem?

We have been working to resolve a dilemma or aporia. If we define a gift as what is given without any strings attached, then, in the ordinary economy of human exchange, no pure gift-giving can practically exist. Every gift implies a gain given to the gift-giver, a gain due to the obligation of the receiver to offer thanks and to define the gift-giver as someone who is a gift-giver. To be defined as a gift-giver is to be noble, generous, and good. In short, the act of gift-giving including its reciprocal response serves the function of self-aggrandizement for the gift-giver. If this obtains, God looks less than fully gracious, because God's gift-giving becomes an expression of divine narcissism. In addition, the command for us to love God and love our neighbor with agape love – to give to God and give to neighbor – becomes a fiction, an incongruent demand. In daily life, loving and gift-giving without strings attached simply does not take place, at least in pure form.

Here is my hypothesis: this is not a real problem. It is a pseudo-problem. The difficulty arises from the fallacy of misplaced concreteness, to use the term of Alfred North Whitehead.[43] Tracy offers a variant: "though life is reflected upon through general ideas, it is always lived in the details."[44] There is a confusion at work among the philosophers of gift, a confusion between what is abstract and what is concrete, between what is general and what belongs to details. Or, to say it another way, the apparent impossibility of pure reciprocity-less gifting along with pure selfless loving confuses an

---

[42] LUTHER 1955, 48:281–282 (Letter to Philip Melanchthon, August 1, 1521): "If you are a preacher of grace, then preach a true and not a fictitious grace; if grace is true, you must bear a true and not a fictitious sin. God does not save people who are only fictitious sinners. Be a sinner and sin boldly, but believe and rejoice in Christ even more boldly, for he is victorious over sin, death, and the world. As long as we are here [in this world] we have to sin. This life is not the dwelling place of righteousness... Pray boldly — you too are a mighty sinner."

[43] WHITEHEAD 1929, 7.

[44] TRACY 1987, 70.

abstract generality with the concrete details of our daily life. It confuses the dog with the tail.[45]

Please recall how I suggested we define our terms: *grace* should refer to the divine disposition to give; *gift* should refer to what God gives and we receive; and *agape* should refer to gracious love. Each of these is an ideal definition, an abstraction, a general idea, a concept. None of these describe with precision what actually happens in your or my daily life. Nor do any of these describe with precision what actually happens in God's relationship to us. We need to begin with what actually happens – *the concrete* – and then reflect theologically – *the abstract* – on what happens. What happens is the dog; and our reflective wagging represent the tail. The tail should point us to the dog, not the reverse.

In this case the dog is the event of Jesus Christ. What does this event mean? It means that God has entered the created order, become present in our souls, forgiven us our sins, justified us by grace; and we have begun to live with faith, hope, and love. An interaction has taken place in the history of the world and in the biography of our individual lives. That's the dog, the concrete dog.

In my extended metaphor, the dog's wagging tail consists of our attempt to understand the dog abstractly by proffering theological ideas and religious descriptions about what the dog means. Theological reflection is second order discourse, one step removed from concrete experience. Our theological attempt to define terms such as *grace, gift,* and *agape* is tail wagging. Let's avoid confusing the tail with the dog, confusing the abstract descriptions from the concrete reality toward which they point.

God's interaction with the world and with our individual souls is messy. It's not neat. It's equivocal and ambiguous. On the one hand, God comes with grace and beauty and glory. God comes in light. On the other hand,

---

[45] Saarinen almost concedes that this is a pseudo-problem. He abstracts the tail from the dog. When defining "pure gift" he does not isolate an actual event of pure gift. Rather, he points to one dimension of any gift, namely, the intention of the giver. SAARINEN 2017, 235: "Purity is found in the clarity and depth of their intention and purpose." Or, purity can be "manifest" in the "unconditional attitude of the giver." SAARINEN 2017, 233. Or, the tail can be manifest in the dog, even if the dog as a whole is more than the tail alone. Here is my contention: the gift is a single event (the dog) from which we theoretically extract or abstract one aspect (the tail), namely, the intentionality of the giver. It is not the gift that is pure, according to Saarinen, it is only the intention of the giver that is pure. This, if I understand Saarinen correctly.

the world greets God with selfishness and ugliness and tragedy. The world's darkness snuffs out the light. Where we find ourselves is at the point of collision, experiencing two realities at once. To posit pure concepts such as grace, gift, or agape is to posit abstractions, to imagine ideals that simply do not exist in pure form at the collision point. Such purities do not exist either for us or for God.

When St. Paul wrote the letters to the Romans and Galatians, he tried to persuade these communities that our justification is the result of God's grace and not of our works. The Reformation took up the same mission, reiterating that we are saved by God's grace and not by any merit on our part. So far, so good. Once this point has been made, what does it add to speak of a divine gift that is so pure that it avoids contamination by reciprocity? What does it add to speak of agape love that is so pure that no ego or self is involved? Speaking this way only *adds abstractions that may become distractions*. We live everyday responding to God's love with our own love; and this takes place in a world already messy with ambiguity. This observation led Luther to throw in the towel on the purity question and simply tell us to "sin boldly."

Can we think of God as both giver and gift?

Luther stressed the graciousness of God by generously slathering the concept of gift over many theological expositions. Take the Trinity, for example. The three persons of the Trinity give themselves to one another, making each both a giver and a gift within the divine life (*ad intra*). In turn, each person gives to us, making the divine both giver and gift for us (*ad extra*). "The Father gives himself to us," writes Luther. "But," he adds, "this gift has become obscured and useless through Adam's fall. Therefore the Son himself subsequently gave himself." It does not end there. "The Holy Spirit comes and gives himself to us also, wholly and completely."[46] Saarinen comments that this amounts to a specifically Lutheran emphasis: "the trinitarian creed is rewritten from the perspective of God's self-giving."[47]

---

[46] LUTHER 1955, 37: 366.
[47] SAARINEN 2005, 46.

Similarly, the Mass or the Sacrament of the Altar must be understood as a divine gift to us and for us.[48] The reformers rejected the idea that on the church's altar a sacrifice is performed that propitiates God's wrath and renders satisfaction on our behalf. The priest at the altar cannot offer a sacrifice as a gift to God, because Christ's death on the cross has put an end to all human sacrifices. Rather, it is God who renders satisfaction in Christ and offers the benefits to us. "For the passion of Christ was an offering and satisfaction not only for original guilt but for all other remaining sins," we find in the Augsburg Confession. "Likewise, Scripture teaches that we are justified before God through faith in Christ... The Mass, therefore, was instituted so that the faith of those who use the sacrament should recall what benefits are received through Christ... For to remember Christ is to remember his benefits and realize that they are truly offered to us."[49] Every leak in the bottom of the spiritual boat is plugged by reference to God's self-giving and our receiving.

With this in mind, we must avoid seeing faith as an efficacious product of human achievement. I weep when I read Matt Jenson: "many evangelicals begin with the gospel only to settle into a toilsome life under the law."[50] Jenson's description is accurate. The tragedy is that where the gift of faith should liberate, for "many evangelicals" it incarcerates.

We must receive faith as a gift if it is to exert liberating power. Or, perhaps better said, our faith is our act of unwrapping the gift that the Holy Spirit gives, namely, the presence of Christ. The indwelling Christ is due to both the giving of Christ and Christ as gift. "Through receiving Christ by

---

[48] "It is frequently alleged that Martin Luther's doctrine of justification by grace through faith posits absolute human passivity vis-à-vis God and, on account of the past completion of Christ's sacrifice, disconnects Christians from the cross," acknowledges Piotr Malysz. So, he takes issue with this view. Specifically, he disputes "the claim that, through his doctrine of justification, Luther became an unwitting advocate of the conceptual juxtaposition of gift and exchange and thus also an ideologue of the shift from an organic to a contractual view of society. "Instead," he argues, "Luther's eucharistic theology anticipates the concerns of Radical Orthodoxy's critique of gift and sacrifice. It does so, however, in a more forceful manner, in that for Luther gift and exchange are so bound together in his doctrine of justification that the eucharist, instead of being a *mere paradigm* for social relationships (as Radical Orthodoxy would have it), radically restructures those relationships in the *all*-embracing unfolding of its participatory gratuity." See MALYSZ 2007, 294.

[49] *Augsburg Confession*, XXIV, BC, 2000, 71.

[50] JENSON 2015, 63.

faith, we have union with Christ. The gift is given for us, but also to us," says Saarinen rightly.[51]

In sum, the generous use of the language and conceptuality of gift becomes one of the ways we emphasize the priority of God's grace in our creation, redemption, and daily lives. There is no pill we need to take to relieve the intellectual constipation brought on by the philosophical debate over the nature of gift. Our employment of gift language is an attempt to explicate the significance of the gospel message; we are not trying to shave the gospel to fit a predetermined concept of gift.

Conclusion

Risto Saarinen is well aware how Martin Luther and his followers emphasize that our justification and hence our salvation is a gift from God, a gift from a gracious God. To tease out what this could mean, we have sorted through the spaghetti strands served by up philosophical discussions of gift giving. For the most part, phenomenologists find that no pure gift giving exists in the human economy because gift givers commonly receive an indirect return in the form of enhanced reputation and even adulation. In addition, for a gift to be a gift it must be received – that is, some level of the recipient's participation in the phenomenon of the gift belongs to the very definition of gift.

How should the theologian respond to this philosophical discussion? Certainly not with anxiety.

It is simply not necessary for a Reformation theologian to wring his or her hands out of fear that justification-by-faith is defective because it falls short of a "pure gift" measurement. To talk about a "pure gift" is to postulate an abstraction from the concrete history of God's gracious work in human history and in human spirituality. Pressing the very concept of "pure gift" would turn God into an untouchable and immutable monad. It would isolate God. The God we have come to know through the benefits of the gospel is relational, both internally relational as Trinity (*ad intra*) and relational to the world of creation and redemption (*ad extra*). I recommend

---

[51] SAARINEN 2005, 51.

that Reformation theologians yawn, label the sophist's wish for a pure gift a *pseudo-problem,* and then retire for a night of sound sleep.

Having said this, we do not want to rid ourselves of gift language. Gift language still helps us explicate the meaning of our fundamental biblical symbols such as Jesus' cross and Pauline affirmations of justification-by-faith. Here is the point: biblical symbols are not slaves to the gift language of the philosopher. The concept of gift illuminates God's gracious action, to be sure. But divine action comes first and our theological reflection in light of the concept of gift comes second. What we can expect from the gift of the Holy Spirit who places the living Christ in our souls is power, excitement, transformation, and vigorous activity on behalf of loving our neighbor.

Bibliography

BASTIANEL, Sergio
2010   *Morality in Social Life.* Tr. Liam Kelly. Miami FL: Convivium Press.

BAYER, Oswald
2007   Gift: Systematic Theology. – *Religion Past and Present.* Eds. Hans Dieter Betz, Don S. Browning, Bernd Janowski, and Eberhard Jüngel; English translation of *Religion in Geschichte und Gegenwart.* 14 Volumes: Leiden and Boston: Brill, 2007–2014; 5: 431.
2009   Schöpfungslehre als Rechtfertigungsontologie. – *Word – Gift – Being.* Eds. Bo Kristian Holm and Peter Widmann. Tübingen: Mohr Siebeck. 17–42.

BC
2000   *The Book of Concord: The Confessions of the Evangelical Lutheran Church.* Eds. Robert Kolb and Timothy J. Wengert. Minneapolis: Fortress Press.

BENEDICT XVI, Pope
2009   *Caritas in Veritate.* Online: http://www.vatican.va/holy_father/benedict_xvi/encyclicals/documents/hf_ben-xvi_enc_20090629_caritas-in-veritate_en.html .

BILLINGS, Todd J.
2005   John Milbank's Theology of Gift and John Calvin's Theology of Grace: A Critical Comparison. – *Modern Theology* 21:1 (January).

COAKLEY, Sarah
2008   Why Gift? Gift, gender, and Trinitarian relations in Milbank and Tanner. – *Scottish Journal of Theology* 6:2.

DALFERTH, Ingolf U.
2009 Mere Passive. Die Passivität der Gabe bei Luther. – *Word – Gift – Being*. Eds. Bo Kristian Holm and Peter Widmann. Tübingen: Mohr Siebeck. 43–72.

DERRIDA, Jacques
1992 *Given Time 1. Counterfeit Money.* Chicago: University of Chicago Press.
1995 *Given Time* and *The Gift of Death.* Chicago: University of Chicago Press.

GREGERSEN, Niels Henrik
2009 Radical generosity and the flow of grace. *Word – Gift – Being*. Eds. Bo Kristian Holm and Peter Widmann. Tübingen: Mohr Siebeck. 117–144.

HEIDEGGER, Martin
1962 *Being and Time.* Tr. John Macquarrie and Edward Robinson. New York: Harper.

HOLM, Bo
2005 Luther's "Theology of the Gift". – *The Gift of Grace: The Future of Lutheran Theology.* Eds. Niels Henrik Gregersen, Bo Holm, Ted Peters, and Peter Widman. Minneapolis: Fortress Press. 78–88.
2009 Justification and reciprocity. – *Word – Gift – Being*. Eds. Bo Kristian Holm and Peter Widmann. Tübingen: Mohr Siebeck. 87–116.

JENSON, Matt
2015 Much Ado about Nothing: The Necessary Non-Sufficiency of Faith. – *Luther Refracted: The Reformer's Ecumenical Legacy.* Eds. Piotr J. Malysz and Derek R. Nelson. Minneapolis: Fortress Press. 141–168.

JUNTUNEN, Sammeli
2004 The Notion of Gift (*donum*) in Luther's Thinking. – *Luther Between Present and Past: Studies in Luther and Lutheranism.* Eds. Ulrik Nissen, Anna Vind, Bo Holm, and Olli-Pekka Vainio. Helsinki: Luther-Agricola-Society. 53–69.

LODBERG, Peter
2015 Grace and Reconciliation as Gift. – *Dialog* 54:3 (September).

LUTHER, Martin
1955 *Luther's Works: American Edition.* Vols. 1–30. – Ed. Jaroslav Pelikan. St. Louis: Concordia Publishing Company, 1955–1967; Vols. 31–55. Ed. Helmut T. Lehmann; Minneapolis: Fortress Press, 1955-1986.
2000 *The Small Catechism.* – *The Book of Concord: The Confessions of the Evangelical Lutheran Church.* Eds. Robert Kolb and Timothy J. Wengert. Minneapolis: Fortress Press. 354–355.
2015 *The Annotated Luther.* Eds. Hans J. Hillerbrand, Kirsi I. Stjerna, Timothy J. Wengert. 5 volumes: Minneapolis MN: Fortress Press.

HOLM, Bo Kristian and WIDMANN, Peter, Ed.
2009 *Word – Gift – Being.* Tübingen: Morhr Siebeck.

MALYSZ, Piotr J.
2007 Exchange and ecstasy: Luther's eucharistic theology in light of Radical Orthodoxy's critique of gift and sacrifice. – *Scottish Journal of Theology* 60:3.

MANNERMAA, Tuomo
1998 Why is Luther So Fascinating? Modern Finnish Luther Research. – *Union with Christ: The New Finnish Interpretation of Luther.* Eds. Carl E. Braaten and Robert W. Jenson. Grand Rapids MI: William B. Eerdmans. 1–21.
2005 *Christ Present in Faith: Luther's View of Justification.* Minneapolis MN: Fortress Press.

MARION, Jean-Luc
1991 *God Without Being.* Chicago: University of Chicago Press.

MAUSS, Marcel
1990 *The Gift: The Form and Reason for Exchange in Archaic Societies.* London: Routledge.

MCGRATH, Alister E.
1988 *Justification by Faith: What It Means To Us Today.* Grand Rapids MI: Zondervan.

MILBANK, John
1995 Can a Gift be Given? – *Modern Theology* 11.
2003 *Being Reconciled, Ontology and Pardon.* London: Routledge.

MORRUS, Wilda K.W.
2009 Review of Risto Saarinen's *God and the Gift. Journal of Ecumenical Studies* 44:2.

PETERS, Ted
2015 *Sin Boldly! Justifying Faith for Fragile and Broken Souls.* Minneapolis: Fortress Press.
2015b Is Faith Really a Gift? – *Luther Refracted: The Reformer's Ecumenical Legacy.* Eds. Piotr J. Malysz and Derek R. Nelson. Minneapolis: Fortress Press. 169–192.

PEURA, Simo
1998 Christ as Favor and Gift: The Challenge of Luther's Understanding of Justification. – *Union with Christ: The New Finnish Interpretation of Luther.* Eds. Carl E. Braaten and Robert W. Jenson. Grand Rapids MI: Wm. B. Eerdmans. 42–69.

POLKINGHORNE, John
1994 *The Faith of a Physicist.* Princeton NJ: Princeton University Press.

RAHNER, Karl
1961 *Theological Investigations.* 22 Volumes. London: Darton, Longman, and Todd, 1961–1976; New York: Seabury, 1974–1976; New York: Crossroad, 1976–1988.
1978 *Foundations of Christian Faith.* Tr. William V. Dych. New York: Crossroad.

RINDERS, Hans S.
2007 Donum or Datum? K.E. Løgstrup's Religious Account of the Gift of Life. – *Concern for the Other: Perspectives on the Ethics of K. E. Løgstrup.* Eds. Svend Andersen and Kees van Kooten Niekerk. Notre Dame IN: University of Notre Dame Press. 177–206.

RITSCHL, Albrecht
1874 *The Christian Doctrine of Justification and Reconciliation.* Tr. H.R. MacKintosh and A.B. Macaulay. Clifton NJ: Reference Book Publishers.

SAARINEN, Risto
2005 *God and the Gift: An Ecumenical Theology of Giving.* Collegeville MN: Liturgical Press.
2009 Im Überschuss. Zur Theologie des Gebens. – *Word – Gift – Being.* Eds. Bo Kristian Holm and Peter Widmann. Tübingen: Mohr Siebeck. 73–86.
2010 The Language of Giving in Theology. – *Neue Zeitschrift für Systematische Theologie und Religionsphilosophie* 52:3 (January).
2017 *Luther and the Gift.* Tübingen: Mohr Siebeck.

SITTLER, Joseph
1972 *Essays on Nature and Grace.* Minneapolis: Fortress Press.

SMITH, Huston,
1958 *Religions of Man.* New York: Harper.

TANNER, Kathryn
2005 *Economy of Grace.* Minneapolis: Augsburg Fortress.

TRACY, David
1987 *Plurality and Ambiguity: Hermeneutics, Religion, Hope.* New York: Harper.
2015 Martin Luther's *Deus Theologicus.* – *Luther Refracted: The Reformer's Ecumenical Legacy.* Eds. Piotr J. Malysz and Derek R. Nelson. Minneapolis: Fortress Press. 105–140.

TRUMP, Donald and SCHWARTZ, Tony
1987 *The Art of the Deal.* New York: Ballantine.

VOEGELIN, Eric
1956 *Israel and Revelation.* – *Order and History.* 5 Volumes: Baton Rouge LA: Louisiana State University Press.

WHITEHEAD, Alfred North
1929 *Process and Reality, Corrected Edition.* Eds. David Ray Griffin and Donald W. Sherburne. New York: Macmillan Free Press.

WILSON, Edward O.
2012 *The Social Conquest of Earth.* New York: W.W. Norton.

WRIGHT, N.T.
2009 *Justification: God's Plan and Paul's Vision.* Downers Grove IL: IVP Academic.

"Companions in Shipwreck":
J. R. R. Tolkien's Female Friendships[1]

Jason Lepojärvi

A fairly perilous topic

What did J. R. R. Tolkien believe about the value, danger, or even possibility of *philia* (friendship-love) between the sexes? Did any of his relationships with the women in his life rise to the level of intimate friendship? Ironically symptomatic of the lack of concentrated attention these two questions have received is the recent study, *Perilous and Fair: Women in the Works and Life of J. R. R. Tolkien* (2015).[2] Of the fourteen articles that tackle the subject of the book, thirteen focus exclusively on Tolkien's *works* and only one is devoted to his *life*. Considering the subtitle *Works and Life*, the imbalance seems fairly misleading and potentially perilous, too. Why so?

For the purpose of this paper, I will leave aside Tolkien's celebrated works. This is not only to help, however modestly, to plug a real gap in scholarship on Tolkien. We must also be on guard against the perils of the so-called eisegetical temptation. Extracting any author's personal views from their fiction alone should only be attempted with extreme caution, if at all, lest we read into our sources opinions that the author may not have endorsed personally. This is certainly the case with Tolkien and (perhaps more so) with C. S. Lewis.

---

[1] This essay would have been much poorer were it not for Holly Ordway's infectious encouragement and stubborn pushback. For helpful exchanges and thoughtful feedback, I would also like to thank Tom Shippey, Wayne Hammond, Christina Scull, John Rateliff, Kirstin Jeffrey Johnson, Mark Scott, Monika Hilder, Gregory Bassham, and two anonymous reviewers – and for their editorial eyes, Aime Nadeau, Ashley Moyse, M. Lee Alexander, and Simon Howard.

[2] Croft and Donovan 2015.

A less hazardous and irresponsible endeavour is to try to establish their positions using more straightforward and biographical sources. In Tolkien's case, I am thinking of his personal letters, for example. While not impervious to hyperbolism, they often reveal uncensored opinions about contentious topics, ranging from male promiscuity to the quality of Belgian tap water.³ As for views on women, whereas we are hard pressed to find negative characterizations of female characters in any of Tolkien's works,⁴ he was more candid privately. Women are "companions in shipwreck not guiding stars", as he reminded his son in a remarkable letter we will revisit later.⁵

Before we dig into our two main questions above, however, we must prepare the ground and commit to some spadework. I will first give a short overview of Tolkien's interaction with women. The types of relationships he tended to have with women can be grouped under three Fs: *family*, *fandom*, and *philology*. Rising out of these – just possibly – we may later be able to add a fourth: *friendship*. We will of course require a standard against which to determine whether any of his many female acquaintances or companions can also be called close friends. For this, we will need to describe friendship-love, as distinct from ordinary companionship. But first: the spadework.

The three Fs – Tolkien's interaction with women

John Rateliff's well-researched study "The Missing Women: J. R. R. Tolkien's Lifelong Support of Women's Higher Education" is the contribution in *Perilous and Fair: Women in the Works and Life of J. R. R. Tolkien* that actually discusses women in the *life* of J. R. R. Tolkien. It is a persuasive critique of Humphrey Carpenter's influential account of Tolkien as (here

---

³ On the other hand, Tolkien could also be quite indirect (SHIPPEY 2003, xviii), as well, compounding the need for careful consultation of his letters.
⁴ See RATELIFF 2015, 67. It has been suggested (e.g. FREDERICK and MCBRIDE 2007, 36; STIMPSON 1969, 19; PARTRIDGE 1983, 191) that Shelob is an evil *female* character and thus the exception to the rule, but according to a rival school of interpretation giant spiders do not really count.
⁵ TOLKIEN 2006, 49.

paraphrased by Rateliff) "a man who, by choice, spent most of his time, most of his life, in exclusively male company".⁶ Leaning on Christina Scull and Wayne Hammond but primarily on his own explorations, Rateliff does a marvellous job of reminding us of the various female influences in Tolkien's life.

Tolkien had been orphaned at a very young age. He lost his father soon after birth and his mother at the age of eight. Mabel Tolkien (*née* Suffield, 1870–1904) had taught him to read by the age of four, and to write soon after. She tutored him in German, Latin, French, and botany (as one does).⁷ Tolkien's *family* further included five aunts, two from his mother's side and three from his father's. As a young boy he would regularly visit them and spend time with their families. He shared private languages and staged plays with his cousins Mary and Marjorie.⁸

Tolkien's aunt Jane Suffield (later Suffield Neave) taught him geometry (*Letters* 377). In fact, she was the only family member prior to Tolkien to get a university degree. As he wrote in 1961: "The professional aunt is a fairly recent development, perhaps; but I was fortunate in having an early example: one of the first women to take a science degree" (*Letters* 308). Aunt Jane had begun her career as a schoolteacher, recommenced it after her husband's death as the Warden of University Hall at St. Andrews, and (it being Scotland) ended it as a farmer.⁹

While living with Mrs Louis Faulkner and her husband in Edgbaston, near Birmingham, Tolkien fell in love with another lodger, Edith Bratt (1889–1971), three years his senior. Fearing its distractive effects on Tolkien's education, his guardian Father Francis Morgan ordered him to break off the dalliance until the age of twenty-one. Tolkien accepted, not wanting

---

⁶ RATELIFF 2015, 41. In a talk presented to the Oxford University C. S. Lewis Society, Holly Ordway, drawing from her forthcoming book *Tolkien's Modern Sources: Middle-earth Beyond the Middle Ages* (2019), diagnosed well the problem of stubborn generalisations: "Especially in the early years of scholarship on an author, a half-truth or a generalization can be taken as a whole truth, a convenient way to sum up an author in a phrase. The complexity of the man – and his work – is easily lost to sight, and it takes a great deal of time and effort to change this over-simplified perception." (ORDWAY 2016).

⁷ TOLKIEN 2006, 218, 377. See also SCULL and HAMMOND 2006b, 1118–1120; and CARPENTER 1977, 17–27.

⁸ SCULL and HAMMOND 2006b, 1108.

⁹ MORTON and HAYES 2008, 16.

to disobey, grieve, or deceive the man who, he explains, "had been a father to me, more than most fathers" (*Letters* 53). He broke off communication with Edith for years. On the night of his twenty-first birthday, he wrote to her, and five days later "went back to her, and became engaged, and informed an astonished family" (*Letters* 53). Tolkien and Edith eventually had four children: three sons (John, Michael, and Christopher) and one daughter (Priscilla).

It is easy to understand why Tolkien himself would find the Carpenterian "male-only" charge oddly misguided. In a radio interview in 1965, he described himself as "a man surrounded by children – wife, daughter, grandchildren".[10] Women who spent time with the Tolkiens would agree. In their memoirs of Tolkien, one of the family's Icelandic *au pairs* Arndis Þorbjarnardóttir and Tolkien's student-turned-colleague Simonne d'Ardenne both remember him as a "family man".[11]

Another former student Mary Challans (pen name Mary Renault) remembers how Tolkien felt "unusual for being notably sympathetic to women undergraduates".[12] That she was known to be in a lesbian relationship, and probably no sort of believer, testifies to the Catholic Tolkien's tolerance, in the true sense of the word tolerance. Challans was a published novelist herself, and she and Tolkien read each other's books. They got along well, but were not close friends. Tolkien describes an appreciative card from her as "perhaps the piece of 'Fan-mail' that gives me most pleasure" (*Letters* 376). It was but one of many: over the course of his life Tolkien received innumerable letters from a truly international female *fandom*.

Tolkien's most persistent and famous admirer, however, lived closer to home. Naomi Mitchison (1897–1999) was the daughter of the Oxford physiologist J. S. Haldane, and the sister of the equally celebrated evolutionary scientist J. B. S. Haldane (with whom C. S. Lewis debated in the 1950s). She was a prolific writer in her own right, and an ardent

---

[10] GUEROULT 1965.
[11] ÞORBJARNARDÓTTIR 1999; D'ARDENNE 1979, 34. Another Icelandic *au pair*, B. S. Benedikz's aunt Sigrid, did not like being with the Tolkiens, having been passed on to them by William Morris's daughter May (see BENEDIKZ 2008). I thank Tom Shippey for directing me to Benedikz's reminiscences.
[12] SWEETMAN 1993, 29.

feminist and political activist, so her fame was self-earned. She was even asked to write a blurb for *The Lord of the Rings*.[13] Devoted to Tolkien, she sent him gifts and wrote letters peppered with informed questions about his *legendarium*. Some of Tolkien's longest letters in this respect are responses to her inquiries. The two were friendly, but probably not intimates.

One Amy Ronald also sent Tolkien gifts. Once she sent him "4 Ports and 3 Sherries", which were accepted with gratitude (*Letters* 396). Tolkien's replies to her thereafter include some of the most endearing language found in his letters: "my dear" (397) and "poor dear" (401). He would slip in references to Edith, such as "I said to my wife" (396) or "we both like" (405). Perhaps he was deflecting a suspected romantic interest. Perhaps it was just a facet of his generosity to his wife. Tolkien took particular pains in this regard, as Edith felt so isolated in Oxford. His academic friends were seldom shared with Edith, but if she liked one at all, he would graciously speak of them as "a friend of my family" (374).[14]

Unlike the bachelor C. S. Lewis, who began his career tutoring women only in groups, the married Tolkien needed no chaperone and thus tutored women in both group and private settings throughout his career. And he was committed to the task. "Tolkien was unusual for dons of his era", says Rateliff, "in his support for women taking degrees and pursuing academic careers."[15] Examples abound, and the statistics are remarkable. As a tutor Tolkien particularly associated with four of Oxford's five all-female colleges: Lady Margaret Hall (where Lewis had also taught women[16]), St Hugh's, Somerville, and St Hilda's. St Anne's was the last to receive college status in 1952. Scull and Hammond have calculated that nearly half of the advanced degree students Tolkien supervised were women, a very high proportion for his era.[17] This support remained consistent in his personal life as evidenced when his daughter Priscilla (b. 1929) writes:

---

[13] SCULL and HAMMOND 2006b, 592–593.
[14] I thank Holly Ordway for helpful exchanges and probing observations about Tolkien's relationship with his wife and daughter in particular.
[15] RATELIFF 2015, 42.
[16] LEWIS 2017, 506.
[17] SCULL and HAMMOND 2006b, 1111.

> [My father believed completely] in higher education for girls; never at any time in my early life or since did I feel that any difference was made between me and my brothers, so far as our educational needs and opportunities were concerned. [...] It was, I think, a source of pride and pleasure for him that he had a daughter as well as sons at the University, which was his scholarly and academic home for much of his working life.[18]

Rateliff notes the "easygoing camaraderie he had with his students, male and female alike".[19] (The reader might make a note of *camaraderie*, a key concept for later.)

Tolkien's exceptionality heightens when viewed against Oxford's milieu with respect to women at the time. Despite Carpenter's oversimplifications, he is right about how "the men really preferred each other's company".[20] The effects of the university's long all-male history and hurdles in transitioning to a mixed environment should not be underrated. Bonded by an interest in literature and a love of language – or *philology* – Tolkien, however, got to know several female colleagues, not only female students.[21] Oxford University women were granted full academic rights in 1920 and were thereafter able to take degrees, but for decades it remained difficult for women to acquire tenure. Attitudes changed slowly. Tolkien's own progressive attitude is well described, again, by his daughter: "[O]f the five women's colleges in Oxford at the time [Lady Margaret Hall] was probably the one he knew best; he spoke with appreciation of his visits to the High Table in the days when Miss Grier was Principal and Miss Everett was his colleague on the language side of the English Faculty."[22] Dining at High Table would have been by personal invitation only.

Tolkien was, however, perplexed by the academic non-advancement of some of his brighter female students. "[W]hy did his male students do so much better", asks Rateliff, "after they had left his supervision, than his

---

[18] Priscilla TOLKIEN 1992, 12–13.
[19] RATELIFF 2015, 55.
[20] CARPENTER 1977, 1954. But then, this might be true on average of both sexes in every generation.
[21] I am assuming a broad sense of "philology" that includes both language and its appreciation in and as literature. For a discussion of how difficult it has been for the English Faculty at Oxford to pair them in mutually enriching ways, see SHIPPEY 1991, esp. 144.
[22] Priscilla TOLKIEN 1992, 12.

female students did?"²³ Tolkien came to believe that some of his female students' success *as students* had depended on their personal interest in him and on his work – innocent interest, to be sure, but still a sort of dependency. Rateliff believes that what Tolkien failed to consider was the glass ceiling. When few academic chairs were available to begin with, "inertia and institutional bias" worked against women.²⁴ According to Rateliff, Tolkien was "observing a very real phenomenon but completely missing the factors that caused it".²⁵

But was Tolkien really oblivious about contemporary attitudes to women in the academy or society at large? I have difficulties accepting this explanation *tout court*. There may have been other factors of which we are unaware. We should perhaps not be too quick to dismiss Tolkien's own intuition either. Whatever his possible blind spots, he really "understood and empathized with women", as Rateliff himself well demonstrates.²⁶ The "final proof" of Tolkien's empathy, Rateliff says, was that "a large percentage of Tolkien's readers have been women, who thus do not find his world unwelcoming".²⁷ It is no coincidence that the J. R. R. Tolkien Professorship of English Literature, created in 1981, has rotated between the very colleges that had spearheaded female education, twice at Lady Margaret Hall.²⁸

We have now hopefully established that Tolkien was a man who, by choice, spent much of his time, much of his life, in largely female society. His mother raised him. His aunts cared for him. As a boy he played with girl cousins. Women tutored him. He fell in love with a woman and remained committed to her for a lifetime. He raised a daughter into a woman. He corresponded prolifically with women. He mentored women throughout his career. He worked alongside women, he dined with women, he even smoked pipes with them!²⁹ But did he ever *befriend* any women? Did any

---

[23] Rateliff 2015, 60.
[24] Rateliff 2015, 62.
[25] Rateliff 2015, 62.
[26] Rateliff 2015, 64.
[27] Rateliff 2015, 64. This argument should of course work in C. S. Lewis's favour, too. But in an unfortunate move, Rateliff pairs his defence of Tolkien with a critique of Lewis – rescuing one from the cage of critics by tossing in the other. Here the evidence seems selective and the argument least persuasive (2015, 65–67).
[28] Rateliff 2015, 64.
[29] Priscilla Tolkien 1992, 12.

of his female relationships rise to the level of true friendship? This is an entirely different question.

What we need next is to establish some core characteristics of friendship itself. We need a yardstick or sorts to evaluate the questions and propose an answer. The careful reader might have noticed my earlier seemingly careless refusal to assign the name "friendship" to one or two of Tolkien's relationships. I was, in fact, operating under implicit defining criteria for friendship that must now be made explicit. We will then be in a good position to answer our two main questions: What did Tolkien think about the possibility of intimate non-romantic friendship-love between the sexes? Did any of his relationships with the women in his life rise to the level of friendship-love?

The nature of philia (friendship-love)

Lewis first met Tolkien in May 1926. How appropriate, from our point of view, that Lewis's first description of Tolkien happens to refer to gender: "He is a smooth, pale, fluent little chap [...] thinks all literature is written for the amusement of *men* between thirty and forty [...] No harm in him: only needs a smack or so."[30] They quickly become friends. Tolkien would learn to admire what he called Lewis's "great generosity and capacity for friendship" (*Letters* 362).[31] During a very bleak time in his life, for example, Tolkien wrote in his diary: "Friendship with Lewis compensates for much."[32] Lewis's death in 1963 had felt like "an axe-blow near the roots", he confided in his daughter (*Letters* 341).[33] In another letter he explained, "C. S. L. was my closest friend from about 1927 to 1940, and remained very dear to me" (*Letters* 349). Tolkien was among the few friends

---

[30] LEWIS 2017, 523–524, emphasis original. Tolkien was still relatively young, and his attitudes did change a lot over time.
[31] TOLKIEN 2006, 362: "The unpayable debt that I owe to him was not 'influence' as it is ordinarily understood, but sheer encouragement. He was for long my only audience. Only from him did I ever get the idea that my 'stuff' could be more than a private hobby."
[32] Tolkien's diary on 1 October 1933 (quoted in CARPENTER 1978, 32).
[33] TOLKIEN 2006, 341. "Very sad that we should have been so separated in the last years; but our time of close communion endured in memory for both of us."

who in November 1963 attended Lewis's funeral, his death having been overshadowed by a high-profile American assassination.

It is primarily because of Tolkien's great love of and friendship with Lewis and their fellow "Inklings" that I have chosen Lewis's *The Four Loves* as the *likeliest* source for an approximate framework for friendship that Tolkien, too, for the most part, would subscribe to. Naturally, any standard of friendship is somewhat subjective, and different standards yield different outcomes when applied to our questions.[34] Lewis's account of friendship, however, seems to provide explicit, relevant, and helpful characteristics. Especially relevant is the characteristic that made Lewis's view famous – his exploration of what gives friendship (*philia*) its unique flavour among the other loves.

Before introducing friendship proper, Lewis distinguishes it from the *camaraderie* that is "often confused with Friendship" (*TFL* 75). Friendship can *arise out* of camaraderie, he says, that is, from the "pleasures in co-operation, in talking shop, in the mutual respect and understanding of men who daily see one another tested" (77). If this was all there was to friendship, our task would be easy: we could point to such amicable relations between Tolkien and the women in his life, and call it a day. But our task is more complicated. Camaraderie or companionship, Lewis explains, "is often called Friendship, and many people when they speak of their 'friends' mean only their companions. But it is not Friendship in the sense I give to the word. By saying this I do not at all intend to disparage companionship. We do not disparage silver by distinguishing it from gold" (77).

So, what is gold then? What is friendship proper? We can single out six core characteristics. Friendship shares the first three characteristics with all other love-relationships, and these three allow Lewis to call friendship a love in the first place. The love-relationships discussed in *The Four Loves* – affection (*storge*), friendship (*philia*), and romance (*eros*) – belong to the same genus, and I believe it is this: They are in their own distinct ways *appreciative and responsive commitments to the other's flourishing*. The three

---

[34] For example, although it would be tempting, I will refrain from discussing key friendships in *The Lord of the Rings* and elsewhere in Tolkien's *legendarium*. Gleaning biography from fiction was methodologically ruled out for the purpose of this paper.

main elements or alloys in all love-relationships, then, including friendship, are *appreciation, responsiveness,* and *commitment*.[35]

1. In order for camaraderie or companionship to develop into intimate friendship-love it must be permeated by *appreciation*, what *The Four Loves* calls "Appreciative love", a basic alloy in all love metals. It is the ability to see goodness in the beloved and rejoice in it non-possessively. If a so-called friendship "is not full of mutual admiration, of Appreciative love, it is not friendship at all" (103). In a true circle of friends, each one finds "the intrinsic beauty of the rest" (104) and "counts himself to be lucky to be among them" (97). "[O]ur reliance, our respect, and our admiration blossom into an Appreciative Love of a singularly robust and well-informed kind" (84).

2. The second element is *responsiveness* or, in Lewis's terms, "Need-love". This means openness, receptivity, and even (in a highly evolved form of love) happy vulnerability. Stoic apathy and deluded self-sufficiency have no place in true love-relationships, whether friendship or affection or romance. Lewis even chastises "a great saint and a great thinker" (137) for such ideas: St Augustine's *Confessions* led him to suspect a failure to fully recover from a Stoic or Neo-Platonic "hangover" (138).[36]

3. The third element is *commitment* to the beloved's (in our case, the friend's) overall wellbeing and flourishing, insofar as possible and permissible. It is not so much duty as it is fidelity, reliability, or consistency in one's commitment to the beloved, and to the relationship. Lewis calls it "Gift-love".

If these three characteristics – appreciation, responsiveness, and commitment – are the characteristics that friendship-love shares will all forms of love, the final three characteristics are what set friendship apart: *joint interests, freedom,* and *uninquisitiveness*. The last two are perhaps disputable: freedom because it is almost superfluous, and uninquisitiveness because it may be "a projection of Lewis's own preferred way of relating to his friends",[37] and not necessarily shared by Tolkien.

4. Now the most famous of these, the one that has given Lewis's account of friendship its characteristic flavour, is *joint interests*. Or mutual passions. If

---

[35] See LEPOJÄRVI 2015, 68–71; and LEPOJÄRVI 2019.
[36] For Lewis's disagreement with Augustine, see LEPOJÄRVI 2012 and ZEPEDA 2012.
[37] BASSHAM 2012, 118.

romantic lovers stand face-to-face, friends stand shoulder-to-shoulder. True friends are "travellers on the same quest" (80) or "on the same secret road" (79). A friend is "a kindred soul" (78). Friends are bonded by a common interest, be it a religion, discipline, profession, or recreation. For this sort of friendship-love "must be *about something*, even dominoes or white mice" (79, emphasis added) or moths and butterflies. (Even lepidopterists have been known to make friends.) Friends can disagree about the answers but rarely about the questions. Tolkien and Lewis certainly had their fair share of disagreements, too.

5. The love of affection or family-love (*storge*), Lewis says, "obviously requires kinship or at least proximities which never depend on our own choice". But friendship-love is *free*, the "world of relationships freely chosen" (104). No one has a duty to be anyone's friend. Friends seek out each other's company; their bond is unforced. This might sound superfluous, however, because *all* love must in a sense be given and received "freely", even love bound by blood. (Obviously, we can befriend our relatives, too, or some of them, as Lewis did his brother Warnie.)

6. If joint interests or mutual passions are the most famous characteristic of Lewis's account of friendship-love, its supposed *uninquisitiveness* is the most infamous. This is the key passage:

> For of course we do not want to know our Friend's [personal] affairs at all. Friendship, unlike Eros, is uninquisitive. You become a man's friend without knowing or caring whether he is married or single or how he earns his living. [...] No one cares twopence about any one else's family, profession, class, income, race, or previous history. [...] This love (essentially) ignores not only our physical bodies but the whole embodiment which consists of our family, job, past and connection. [...] Eros will have naked bodies; Friendship naked personalities. (83–84)

Some of this is witty wordplay, with a dash of hyperbole. But many modern readers might be put off by it. Was Lewis not interested in his friends' personal lives, only in their ideas? How could something so unfriendly be friendship?

A more positive reading, one that I have not seen made, is that this account reflects an understanding of friendship that is – for their era and for ours – admirably and surprisingly *inclusive*. Lewis and Tolkien lauded friendship that was tolerant, non-judgemental, anti-elitist, anti-racist. One did not have to be a wealthy, well educated, upper class white man with a spotless criminal record to become their friend. Besides, Lewis never wanted his shoulder-to-shoulder metaphor pressed. "The common quest or vision which unites Friends does not absorb them in such a way that they remain ignorant or oblivious to one another. On the contrary it is *the very medium* in which their mutual love and knowledge exists. One knows nobody so well as one's 'fellow'" (84, emphasis added).[38]

The above six characteristics define the sort of friendship we are looking for. I close this section with a few additional indicators, specific to Tolkien, that do not define but might help us *recognize* Tolkien's friendships. These are not essential constituents of friendship but signposts; they do not establish Tolkien's friendships but help us notice and identify them. First, we should remain alert to times when Tolkien actually refers to women as his "friends". It is also important to flag relationships that are on first-name basis, as any transition in that era from formal cordiality to using a person's Christian name, male or female, would not have been insignificant. Finally, I am interested in non-family members whose photograph might have been reproduced for *The Tolkien Family Album* (1992), compiled and edited by Tolkien's children to commemorate the centenary of their father's birth.[39]

It goes without saying that absence of evidence does not mean evidence of absence. Tolkien may have had female friends whom he never on record addressed casually or called friends, and occasionally he may have used "friend" liberally to refer to mere companions. Also, family albums are not infallible judges of the quality of relationships. This is especially the case with *The Tolkien Family Album*, which was meant to be only a scrapbook, or sampler, from Tolkien's life. Not making the cut, so to speak, does not necessarily mean anything. But making it does mean something. These are small pieces in a very large puzzle, and when assembling a complex image for the very first time, every piece counts.

---

[38] Lewis's radio talks on love support and even bolster this more magnanimous and inclusive reading of his view. There "nationality" is included in the list of things that friendship "cares nothing about". And Lewis explicitly distinguishes between a friend's *personality* and his *ideas*, emphasizing that friendship is rooted in the former. One may enjoy a person's conversation and ideas, but he or she may still be disqualified for the title of "friend" if his or her character repels us upon closer intimacy.

[39] TOLKIEN and TOLKIEN 1992.

Friendship between the sexes: Problems and prospects

"The Inklings", explains Alister McGrath in a recent article on gender, "were a system of male planets orbiting its two suns, Lewis and Tolkien".[40] The group had, he continues, one "obvious shortcoming": "there were no female members".[41] Whether this really is a shortcoming depends on our assumptions about single-sex friendships and clubs. Do we oppose them on principle? Tolkien and Lewis did not. This is not because they objected to mixed groups, either. On the contrary, they were members of various such groups at several stages of their careers.

"The Cave", for example, was a conclave of like-minded scholars in the English School at Oxford, which formed in the early 1930s to advocate certain curricular reforms. Its members included both J. R. R. Tolkien and C. S. Lewis, possibly again in a solar capacity, with Dorothy Everett, Elaine Griffiths, Neville Coghill, Joan Blomfield, Dorothy Whitelock, Hugo Dyson, and others exerting their planetary influences. After achieving their initial goals, The Cave became "more of a social and literary club which held informal dinners or met in members' rooms".[42] Much more could be said of Lewis's enthusiastic involvement with the "Socratic Club" that was predominated by female students and scholars.[43]

In *The Four Loves*, Lewis explains that *historically* friendship between women and men had been rare, because home and work were so often segregated by gender. As a result, men and women had "nothing to be Friends about" (*TFL* 86). Circumstances have since changed, he argues contentedly, because "where they can become companions they can become Friends. Hence in a profession (like my own) where men and women work side by side, or in the mission field, or among authors and

---

[40] McGrath 2015, 82. I blame Michael Ward, the author of *Planet Narnia*, for the recent tidal wave of planetary witticisms in Lewis scholarship.

[41] McGrath 2015, 83.

[42] Scull and Hammond 2006b, 958. Lewis mentions the group at least three times in his letters to his brother, on 25 December 1931, 18 December 1939, and 17 March 1940 (Lewis 2004, 26, 306, and 365).

[43] The Socratic Club was founded in 1941 by Stella Aldwinckle (1907–1989), and Lewis was its first university representative, or "Senior Member" (Aldwinckle 1984). In Michaelmas Term 1944, out of 164 members 109 were from Oxford's all-female colleges (McGrath 2013, 252).

artists, such Friendship is common" (86).⁴⁴ Even romantic lovers, Lewis insisted, can benefit from each other's friendships with the opposite sex. "Nothing so enriches an erotic love as the discovery that the Beloved can deeply, truly and spontaneously enter into Friendship with the Friends you already had" (80).

Was Tolkien quite as optimistic?

During 6–8 March 1941, Tolkien wrote a long letter to his son, Michael, who was possibly thinking about marrying. This is the letter that in Rateliff's words includes Tolkien's "notorious" theory of his female students' excessive dependency on him that later stymied their academic careers. But Rateliff's dissatisfaction with this letter does not stop here. I agree that the letter is disconcerting, but not primarily for the reasons he suggests.

First of all, Rateliff says Tolkien's intention was to "talk his son *out* of marrying".⁴⁵ Scull and Hammond have suspected the same.⁴⁶ I am less convinced. Direct internal evidence is lacking. According to Tolkien's first grandson, also named Michael, his grandparents had "disapproved" of Michael's "hasty wartime marriage".⁴⁷ But this, of course, does not prove that Tolkien's purpose *in this letter* was to talk his son out of marrying. Despite its more peculiar points, which we will discuss presently, the letter is full of wise and balanced advice about love and marriage. It is almost a "call to arms" to take love seriously – and to take women seriously, for that matter. Women are "companions in shipwreck not guiding stars", Tolkien writes.⁴⁸ The image is at once egalitarian and responsible, aimed against the double temptation to either patronize or idolize women.

I propose an alternative hypothesis: *Were* Michael to marry, his father wanted him to enter matrimony *with both eyes open*; mindful, above all, of the indissoluble nature of Catholic marriage and of the dangers of sentimental love-idolatry. "Nearly all marriages, even happy ones, are mistakes", Tolkien writes, "in the sense that almost certainly (in a more

---

⁴⁴ But not as common as misreadings of Lewis's clear affirmation of friendship-love between the sexes. For example, both Janet SOSKICE (2007, 163–164) and Gregory BASSHAM (2012, 116) misrepresent Lewis's view on this point.

⁴⁵ RATELIFF 2015, 59.

⁴⁶ SCULL and HAMMOND 2006b, 1112: "Tolkien's purpose – to caution a son who might be marrying in haste."

⁴⁷ Michael TOLKIEN 1992, #2.

⁴⁸ TOLKIEN 2006, 49.

perfect world, or even with a little more caution in this imperfect one) both partners might have found more suitable mates. But the 'real soul-mate' is the one you are actually married to. [...] In this fallen world we have as our only guides, prudence, wisdom (rare in youth, too late in age), a clean heart, and fidelity of *will*" (*Letters* 51–52). In an unpublished follow-up letter to Michael, dated 12 March 1941, Tolkien continues this line of advice: marriage advice, in effect, rather than advice against marriage.[49]

Nor do I think the letter notorious because Tolkien suggested that "*men are polygamous; women are monogamous* (*Letters*, p. 51, emphasis added)".[50] These are actually Rateliff's own words, including the words "emphasis added", not Tolkien's. Rateliff may have accidentally italicized parts of his own paraphrase, here mistaken as a direct quotation. Tolkien's original language runs as follows:

> They [women] have, of course, still to be more careful in sexual relations, for all the contraceptives. Mistakes are damaging physically and socially (and matrimonially). But they are instinctively, when uncorrupt, monogamous. *Men are not...* No good pretending. Men just ain't, not by their animal nature. [...] Each of us could healthily beget, in our 30 odd years of full manhood, a few hundred children, and enjoy the process. (*Letters* 51)

Rateliff dismisses this as "one of the things men tell themselves in self-justification of their more reprehensible impulses".[51] This is unfair. Whether or not Tolkien here indulged in hyperbole again – and I think he did: what he really means is that on average men are *more* polygamous or promiscuous than women – he is not trying to self-justify anything.[52] A factual claim about male biology is not a moral alibi. On the contrary, the letter openly sets and embraces the higher moral standard of lifelong faithfulness in marriage for men and women alike. But Tolkien believes that this standard is "revealed" to us through Scripture and tradition more

---

[49] In this letter, Tolkien advices against using subterfuge in marriage. See the extract quoted in CARPENTER 1977, 156–7, and CARPENTER 1978, 168.
[50] RATELIFF 2015, 60.
[51] RATELIFF 2015, 60.
[52] While Scull and Hammond believe that key paragraphs were "probably exaggerated for the occasion" (SCULL and HAMMOND 2006b, 1113), they veer towards a more literal interpretation: "Considering modern *mores*, Tolkien seems to have had an unrealistic view of women as being 'instinctively, when uncorrupt, monogamous' (p. 51), unlike men" (1114).

so than through mere biology, "according to faith and not to the flesh" (*Letters* 51). One might be tempted to dismiss Rateliff's dismissal as one of those things men tell women to score easy points or to avoid the ire of combative feminists. But that would be unfair, too.

The fundamental reason why I think the letter is objectionable is this: Tolkien expresses extreme cynicism about friendship between the sexes, basing it on problematic and generalized assumptions about male motivations and the effects of sin. Let us take the safer road by examining Tolkien's words, rather than words about Tolkien's words.

> The dislocation of the sex-instinct is one of the chief symptoms of the Fall. [...] In this fallen world the "friendship" that should be possible between all human beings, is virtually impossible between man and woman. The devil is endlessly ingenious, and sex is his favourite subject. [...] Later in life when sex cools down, it may be possible. It may happen between saints. To ordinary folk it can only rarely occur: [...] The other partner will let him (or her) down, almost certainly, by "falling in love". But a young man does not really (as a rule) want "friendship", even if he says he does. There are plenty of young men (as a rule). He wants *love*: innocent, and yet irresponsible perhaps. (*Letters* 48)

Unless you are a *senior* or a *saint*, friendship between the sexes is virtually impossible. We are far from Lewis's optimism. What should be made of this?

Lewis also believed that sin has distorted the sex-instinct.[53] But he never attributes the facile propensity to fall in love unilaterally to the symptoms of sin. Rather it reflects the whimsical and playful nature of *eros* itself. Even *venus*, the sexual element in *eros*, is a "mischievous spirit, far more elf than deity, and makes game of us [...] a catch-as-catch-can" (*TFL* 115–116). One-sided and unreciprocated love may be painful and embarrassing (Lewis was no stranger to this), but it is not obvious why this should be a *moral* failure. Tolkien and Edith might have fallen in love simultaneously, in an orderly and synchronized manner, but their story is so unique that it hardly qualifies as normative.[54] Romance is generally messy, and not only for sinful reasons.

---

[53] LEWIS 1940, 57–76; also LEWIS 1952, II, 3.
[54] TOLKIEN 2006, 52: "My own history is so exceptional, so wrong and imprudent in nearly every point that it makes it difficult to counsel prudence. Yet hard cases make bad law."

It is far from "certain" that one-sided falling in love will occur in the first place. Even if it did it is not obvious why this necessarily ruins the relationship. It may or may not. And I think it silly and even irresponsible to suggest "as a rule" that young men do not want friendship with women – even if they say they do – because (this would be comical were it not serious) otherwise they would "obviously" choose a man! On what grounds? How could he possibly know this? Tolkien is, of course, not alone in his pessimism. Many authorities agree with him, including St. Augustine in *The Literal Meaning of Genesis*[55] and Harry in *When Harry Met Sally*.[56] Did Tolkien live by these beliefs?

Apart from letters to his wife and daughter, one searches *The Letters of J. R. R. Tolkien* in vain for intimate letters to female correspondents. Based on this vacuum, and in light of his letter to Michael, one might conclude that Tolkien anticipated and lived by the maxim that some Evangelical churches today know as the "Billy Graham Rule" (what I like to call the "Mike Pence Manoeuvre") and avoided intimate correspondence with women in fear of "falling in love" or creating a sex-scandal – much like the absolutist who in fear of intoxication simply abstains from wine instead of letting the virtues of moderation and charity inform its enjoyment and consumption. Except that women are not drinks. They are human persons.

We must remember, however, that *The Letters of J. R. R. Tolkien* is merely a selection. The collection's editor, Humphrey Carpenter, explained that "priority" was given to letters that discussed Tolkien's *works*, and "an enormous quantity of material was omitted".[57] Few letters from between 1918 and 1937 survive, though thereafter, thanks to Tolkien's carbon copies, the epistolary stream is more or less unbroken until his death in

---

[55] AUGUSTINE, *The Literal Meaning of Genesis* 9.5. Augustine is asking how Eve "helped" Adam in Genesis 2. I thank Iain Provan for bringing this to my attention.

[56] The young Harry, but not the mature Harry. In the movie Harry actually grows out of his youthful cynicism ("Men and women can't be friends because the sex part always gets in the way") and becomes Sally's best friend for several years, before the inevitable (it is Hollywood) transformation of *philia* into *eros*.

[57] TOLKIEN 2006, 1–2. With the assistance of Christopher Tolkien, Carpenter selected 354 letters from the thousands he had read (ANDERSON 2005, 219). For this paper I have not been privy to Tolkien's unpublished letters held in the Tolkien Papers at the Bodleian Library in Oxford. Careful analysis of these manuscripts from the concentrated perspective of Tolkien's female friendships awaits future scholars and will undoubtedly yield valuable insights.

September 1973. The vast majority of his letters remain unpublished to this day. And, even without a more comprehensive collection (such as exists of Lewis's voluminous correspondence), if we broaden our focus to include diary extracts, personal memoirs, oral histories, and other miscellaneous sources, a rather different image of Tolkien emerges.

There is reason to believe Tolkien did *not* strictly adhere to such restrictive beliefs. Perhaps his dissuading advice to his son about friendship was tailored to him only. Perhaps it did not represent his full beliefs about male-female friendships. Or perhaps Tolkien knew better than he thought he did. Life sometimes runs ahead of theory. His biography certainly reveals a different tale.

Approaching Tolkien's female friendships

Tolkien's interactions with women were grouped into three: family, fans, and philologists (students and colleagues). I propose that some of them became true friends. When I use the words *friend* or *friendship*, I invoke again the following: a relationship that is marked by (1) appreciative and responsive commitment to the other's flourishing insofar as possible, (2) with joint interests or mutual passions (as opposed to mere kinship or proximity) providing the unforced medium for affectionate mutual understanding. On this basis, Tolkien loved dozens of women (1) and befriend some of them (both 1 and 2).

In the category of female fans, there is little evidence of Tolkien befriending any. (Lewis, on the other hand, did; eventually *marrying* his most persistent one.) We are left then with Tolkien's family, students, and colleagues. Several of these seem "friendly" enough, in sense above, but I hesitate to assert that many do. What should we say, for example, about Tolkien's relationship with his wife and daughter?

We should not overlook these two relationships simply because they are family. Tolkien may have had a genuine friendship-relation with his daughter Priscilla. There are some indications of this; most notably, their father-daughter holiday in Italy in August 1955. While his wife Edith was vacationing separately with her friends, Tolkien, who could have easily taken one of his sons or male friends were they available, chose to travel with Priscilla instead, and, based on his travel diary *Giornale d'Italia*, enjoyed the two-week voyage eating, drinking, and discussing religion, history, art, and architecture in a companionable, friendly way.[58] Tolkien evidently loved and adored Edith, too, despite their marital challenges. It is not, however, easy to point to meaningful *shared interests* with her.[59] I suppose that insofar as they felt passionate about their *children*, and thrived in exchanges about them, perhaps they did share *philia* in addition to *eros*.

If I have underestimated the "friendly" aspect in either of these family relations, I am open to being corrected.[60] The same applies to the following four women, all but one of them students, a core sample of women I am tempted (but again hesitate) to call Tolkien's close friends: Katherine Farrer, Mary Salu, Helen Buckhurst, and Auvo Kurvinen.

Katherine Farrer (1911–1972) was the wife of the Oxford theologian Austin Farrer, a dear friend of C. S. Lewis. She was a published detective novelist, like Dorothy Sayers (another friend of Lewis), and she shared a range of interests with the Inklings. She translated Gabriel Marcel's *Être et avoir* (1935), published as *Being and Having* (1949).[61] The Farrers and the Tolkiens were neighbours for over three years between 1947 and 1950. This explains why Tolkien, in one of his many letters to Katherine, could say that he would "bring you round some *unique MSS.* [manuscripts] later to-day" (*Letters* 130). Though most of the letters are focussed on his works, at least one, dated 27 November 1954, betrays deeper intimacy:

> I have felt very mean indeed, since I have known that you have both been ill and troubled, and I have never written, or called, or made any offer of help (or even sympathy). Always meaning to, of course! To any *eyes* but those of your charity

---

[58] SCULL and HAMMOND 2006a, 462–474; and 2006b, 434–435. In Venice they met with Tolkien's son Christopher and his wife Faith, and the four spent some time together. A much earlier father-daughter trip had been to the Jesuit seminary Stonyhurst in Lancashire, staying at a nearby guesthouse for ten days in August 1947 (see SCULL and HAMMOND 2006b, 981).

[59] For example, CARPENTER 1977, 39: "Certainly she did not share his interest in languages."

[60] A case could also be made for Tolkien's relationship with other female relatives, such as his Aunt Jane, mentioned above, and, perhaps more surprisingly, his son Christopher's first wife, Faith (*née* Faulconbridge, b. 1928). Tolkien mourned over the breakup of that marriage. One wonders if added to the pain of what it must have meant to Tolkien as a Catholic, was personal sadness about Faith. She sculpted a bust of him for the Royal Academy, with a copy at Exeter College Chapel in Oxford. Tolkien corresponded with a number of other female relatives until his death. Wayne Hammond and Christina Scull informed me some of these letters have recently come up for sale.

[61] SCULL and HAMMOND 2006b, 295.

I shd. [should] have appeared the sort of "friend" that dumps his works on you when you are already overloaded, sucks up praise and encouragement, [...] and then departs when you begin to break down... (*Letters* 207–208)

Realizing that Katherine and her husband were in dire need of respite, Tolkien writes that "*nothing* would give me more pleasure than to [help]. I could for instance *well* spare £50 (and *more* if this rise in my wages occurs)" (*Letters* 208).[62] Notably, his letters to her were signed "Ronald Tolkien" instead of the official signature "J.R.R. Tolkien".[63]

Mary Salu was supervised by Tolkien from 1941 to 1949, a long process for a mere B.Litt degree.[64] Incidentally, she also worked for the professor, compiling indexes and glossaries, a task likely to stall anyone's progress even without a war or post-war austerity. Tolkien wrote a two-paragraph preface for her translation of *The Ancrene Riwle* (1955).[65] She would later co-edit the essay collection *J. R. R. Tolkien, Scholar and Storyteller: Essays in Memoriam* (1979). Salu's picture is not reproduced in *The Tolkien Family Album*, Scull and Hammond's *Reader* provides a mere one-paragraph biography, and nearly all mentions of her in their *Chronology* are the same flat one-liner ("Tolkien will continue to supervise B.Litt Student M. B. Salu"). Yet, for reasons that escape me, Scull and Hammond still rank her among the "close friends of Tolkien and his family".[66]

Helen Buckhurst, on the other hand, does not even receive a biographical sketch in the *Reader*. We know that she was Tolkien's former student and

---

[62] Tolkien's generosity here is astounding. According to the Office for National Statistics composite price index, £50 in 1957 had the purchasing power of around £1,200 in 2019. Tolkien's children remember him winning a literary prize for *The Hobbit* in 1938: "A somewhat poignant memory is of him opening the letter at the breakfast table and passing the enclosed cheque for fifty points – a formidable sum in those days – to Edith, so that she could pay an outstanding doctor's bill with it" (TOLKIEN and TOLKIEN 1992, 69).

[63] SCULL and HAMMOND 2006b, 625. Only intimates such as Edith received letters from "Ronald" (without "Tolkien"). Scull and Hammond refer to Katherine Farrer consistently as Tolkien's "friend" (625, 674, 710).

[64] Tom Shippey has called the Oxford B.Litt degree "strange and anomalous [...] (a Bachelor's degree, but only taken by graduate students), which [C. S.] Lewis obviously felt was a waste of time, but which even in the 1970s was regarded as one of the glories of the [English] Faculty" (SHIPPEY 1991, 147).

[65] SCULL and HAMMOND 2006b, 44–46.

[66] SCULL and HAMMOND 2006b, 1111.

also a Fellow at St Hugh's.[67] She shared Tolkien's Catholicism, like so many of his female acquaintances, and she even became Priscilla's godmother.[68] The latter suggests amicable family relations, to say the least. Were they close friends, as well? The jury seems out and I pass no definitive judgement, but Buckhurst herself certainly considered Tolkien more a friend or colleague than a tutor, as she addressed her letters to "Dear Ronald".[69]

It is similarly difficult to gauge the intimacy of Tolkien's relationship with Auvo Kurvinen (1916–1979) who, to the best of my knowledge, was his only Finnish student. (Despite a traditional *male* name, she was indeed a woman.) Auvo Kurvinen is not well known outside of Finland, and barely known inside. And yet she was academically one of Tolkien's two most successful female students. Completing both a B.Litt (1947–1949) and a D.Phil (1954–1962) under his supervision at Oxford, she had a long career at the University of Helsinki from 1955 onward, becoming full Professor of English Literature in 1972.[70] Perhaps it was Kurvinen who orchestrated Tolkien's proposed visit to Finland in 1958, eventually abandoned due to Edith's poor health.[71] He never did get to visit "*Suomi*", Tolkien explains in an unpublished letter from 1971, but the Finnish language continued to give him "great aesthetic pleasure".[72]

---

[67] SCULL and HAMMOND 2006a, 143. I have since learned that the revised edition of the *Reader's Guide* includes a biography of Helen Buckhurst, occupying most of a page. Omitting her from the first edition had been "merely an oversight" (personal correspondence with the authors, 21 March 2018).

68 SCULL and HAMMOND 2006b, 830; and 2006a, 149–150.

[69] RATELIFF 2015, 58.

[70] RATELIFF 2015, 61 n. 23. See also Professor Tauno Mustanoja's obituary of his colleague Auvo Kurvinen (MUSTANOJA 1982, 1–3).

[71] In a letter dated 26 February 1958, Tolkien explains that he cancelled tours to "Sweden, Finland, USA etc." (quoted in SCULL and HAMMOND 2006a, 520). This is all we know about his planned visit to Finland (SCULL and HAMMOND 2006a, 798).

[72] Letter to a Miss Morley dated 8 November 1971 (quoted in SCULL and HAMMOND 2006b, 463). For a review of the reception of Tolkien in Finland, see HEIKKINEN 2013.

The Fourth F – Tolkien's female friendships

Several other countries Tolkien did visit. He visited Belgium at least four times.[73] What drew him repeatedly back to Liège and Solwaster? Formally, academic conferences did, but informally, and perhaps as importantly, his very dear friend Professor Simonne d'Ardenne (1899–1986). While many of his relationships with women – his wife and daughter, Farrer, Salu, Buckhurst, and Kurvinen – approached friendship, his relationship with d'Ardenne is, I propose, the *first of three* that almost certainly reached it. Of course, his range of friendships was more a spectrum than a clearcut binary, but there is nothing ambiguous about his relationship with d'Ardenne. It was a true friendship in the full sense of the word.

When Simonne d'Ardenne arrived in Oxford to begin her B.Litt in February 1932, she was 33 years old. Eight months later in October, she moved into the Tolkien household and lived with the family for an entire year as "an unofficial aunt".[74] She was the second of Tolkien's two most successful female students. Working hard through the holidays, and with Tolkien's generous hands-on assistance, d'Ardenne graduated rapidly in 1933 and was awarded a doctorate at Liège. Though Liège requirements compelled her to exclude Tolkien's name, she later referred to her thesis as their joint work (suggesting a level of collaboration possibly frowned upon today).[75] She served as Professor of Comparative Grammar in Liège from 1938 until her retirement in 1970.

During the Second World War, the Germans occupied d'Ardenne's town and the two lost touch with each other. On 11 November 1944, having not heard from her for nearly a year, Tolkien reached out to the British Council for help in locating her.[76] In March 1945, he writes to Stanley Unwin with good news about his "lost friend Mlle. Simonne d'Ardenne, who has suddenly reappeared, having miraculously survived the German

---

[73] SCULL and HAMMOND 2006b, 82.
[74] TOLKIEN and TOLKIEN 1992, 68.
[75] SCULL and HAMMOND 2006b, 202. The thesis was dedicated to Tolkien.
[76] SCULL and HAMMOND 2006a, 283. *The Tolkien Family Album* apparently misdates the event, or it was not the first time d'Ardenne had gone missing: "We heard nothing from, or about, her [Simonne d'Ardenne] until we received a message from the International Red Cross in 1943 to say that she and her family were alive and well. The village where she lived […] had been occupied by German troops" (TOLKIEN and TOLKIEN 1992, 68).

occupation" (*Letters* 114). Later that year d'Ardenne returned to Oxford on a stipend for a couple of years, and possibly stayed with the Tolkiens again for part of it.[77] Priscilla visited her in Belgium in the summer of 1948.[78] Once, in November 1950 after a three-day conference in Liège, Tolkien spent four days with d'Ardenne in her family's old hunting lodge at Solwaster.[79] On a subsequent visit in 1957, possibly his last one in Belgium, he complained that the local "chalybeate water [impregnated with iron salts] is nearly brick-red: a bath is like being in a dye-vat; to drink is nonsense".[80]

D'Ardenne's short memoir of Tolkien, "The Man and the Scholar", published in *J. R. R. Tolkien, Scholar and Storyteller: Essays in Memoriam* (1979), expresses gratitude for "a friendship which extended over forty years".[81] The description is wholly warranted. It was visibly characterized by all the hallmarks of friendship-love: by significant joint interests, reciprocal appreciation and affection, often tangible mutual support, and formidable trust on all sides – in effect, by shared lives. Even the Tolkien-specific signposts are there. They called each other friends. They were on first-name terms. Her photograph is reproduced in *The Tolkien Family Album*.[82] She travelled to his memorial service in November 1973.[83]

The second of Tolkien's three female friends whom I wish to single out is the aforementioned Dorothy Everett (1894–1953). She was the "Miss Everett" in Priscilla Tolkien's account of her father's High Table dinner invitations, and one of the members of The Cave. Dorothy Everett had first been a Tutor at St Hugh's, and then a Lecturer at Somerville, before being elected Fellow of English at Lady Margaret Hall. Tolkien had been among

---

[77] SCULL and HAMMOND 2006a, 297.
[78] SCULL and HAMMOND 2006a, 327.
[79] SCULL and HAMMOND 2006a, 370.
[80] Early English Text Society archive (quoted in SCULL and HAMMOND 2006b, 82–83). Douglas Anderson claims Tolkien's last visit to d'Ardenne was in October 1954, when the University of Liège awarded him an honorary doctorate (see ANDERSON 2013, 118).
[81] D'ARDENNE 1979, 33. Tolkien's fatherly virtues are lauded, but his marriage goes entirely unmentioned. D'Ardenne's piece is the only one that discusses Tolkien's life. The editors must have known she was optimally placed for the task. In 1962 she had contributed to Tolkien's 70th *Festschrift*, as well (DAVIS and WRENN 1962).
[82] TOLKIEN and TOLKIEN 1992, 68. "She [Simonne d'Ardenne] entrusted to Priscilla a great bundle of letters she had received form J.R.R.T. over a period of forty years" (86).
[83] SCULL and HAMMOND 2006a, 775.

her electors. He served on various boards with her. They dined together at college. They co-examined students.[84] While we know less about Everett than we do about d'Ardenne, Priscilla in passing credits her for a most telling achievement that almost single-handedly lodges her among Tolkien's friends: "[My father's] many years of friendship with Dorothy Everett, the great beauty of the Hall's situation", Priscilla explains, "were the things that led me naturally to 'choose' Lady Margaret Hall."[85]

"I am supping with Elaine, and others", Tolkien wrote to his son Christopher on 13 April 1944 (*Letters* 71). Here we meet Elaine Griffiths (1909–1996), the last of Tolkien's three definitive female friends, and we close our study with her. She, too, was Catholic. She, too, was a member of The Cave. Griffiths started her B.Litt under Tolkien's supervision in 1933 and soon "became his *de facto* assistant".[86] She was one of the very few intimates allowed to read *The Hobbit* in typescript.[87] Tolkien's personal dedication of her copy was as humorous as it was affectionate: "To Elaine, queen of the Hobbits and my very old friend."[88] (She was tiny.) Scull and Hammond designate Griffiths "a close friend of Tolkien and his family".[89] She contributed to Tolkien's 70th *Festschrift* in 1962, and her picture is in *The Tolkien Family Album*.[90]

One spring day, having just cast their votes for the new Professor of Poetry, Elaine Griffiths invites Tolkien over to her place. They travel in her car, unchaperoned. Upon arrival his hostess asks Tolkien what he would like to drink. Had he been a overcautious Evangelical pastor, flaming red flags would have gone up by now. Instead, the reckless Catholic layman asks for a whisky! But it was 24 May 1973.[91] Tolkien would have been eighty-one years old. And Griffiths (having passed sixty) was no spring chicken, either. The venerable old man visiting his "very old friend" was, by this time, a widower, a senior, and quite possibly a saint.

---

[84] Scull and Hammond 2006a, 166, 254, 342.
[85] Priscilla Tolkien 1992, 12.
[86] Scull and Hammond 2006b, 353.
[87] Scull and Hammond 2006b, 353.
[88] Bonhams, *Printed Books and Maps* (online), 24 February 2004, lot 601 (quoted in Scull and Hammond 2006b, 354).
[89] Scull and Hammond 2006b, 353.
[90] Tolkien and Tolkien 1992, 69.
[91] Scull and Hammond 2006a, 771–772. My fellow Evangelicals will appreciate this friendly jibe.

Bibliography

ALDWINCKLE, Stella
1984   Memories of the Socratic Club. – *C. S. Lewis and His Circle: Essays and Memories from the Oxford C. S. Lewis Society*. Eds. White, Robert & Wolfe, Judith & Wolfe, Brendan N. Oxford: Oxford University Press (2015). 192–194.

ANDERSON, Douglas A.
2005   Obituary: Humphrey Carpenter. – *Tolkien Studies*. Vol. 2. 217–224.
2013   D'Ardenne, S. R. T. O (1899–1986). – *J. R. R. Tolkien Encyclopedia: Scholarship and Critical Assessment*. Ed. Michael D. C. Drout. New York: Routledge. 117–118.

AUGUSTINE
1982   *The Literal Meaning of Genesis*. 2 vols. Trans. John H. Taylor. ACW 41–42. New York: Newman.

BASSHMAN, Gregory
2012   Who Could Have Deserved It? C. S. Lewis on Friendship. – *Persona and Paradox: Issues of Identity in C. S. Lewis, His Friends and Associates*. Eds. Suzanne Bray and William Gray. Cambridge Scholars Publishing. 114–124.

BENEDIKZ, B. S.
2008   Some Family Connections with J. R. R. Tolkien. – *Amon Hen: The Tolkien Society's Journal*. Vol. 209. January 2008.

CARPENTER, Humphrey
1977   *Tolkien: A Biography*. Ed. Humphrey Carpenter. London: Allen and Unwin.
1978   *The Inklings: C. S. Lewis, J. R. R. Tolkien, Charles Williams and Their Friends*. London: HarperCollins.

CROFT, Janet Brennan & DONOVAN, Leslie A. (eds)
2015   *Perilous and Fair: Women in the Works and Life of J. R. R. Tolkien*. Mythopoeic Press.

D'ARDENNE, Simonne
1979   The Man and the Scholar. – *J. R. R. Tolkien, Scholar and Storyteller: Essays in Memoriam*. Eds. Salu, Mary & Farrell, Robert T. Ichaka and London: Cornell University Press. 33–37.

DAVIS, Norman & WRENN, Charles Leslie (eds.)
1962   *English and Medieval Studies Presented to J. R. R. Tolkien on the Occasion of his Seventieth Birthday*. London: Allen and Unwin.

FREDERIC, Candice & McBRIDE, Sam
2007   Battling the Woman Warrior: Females and Combat in Tolkien and Lewis. – *Mythlore* 25 3/4. Spring/Summer. 29–42.

GUEROULT, Denis
1965   BBC Radio Interview with J. R. R. Tolkien. Re-released by Audio-Forum. Guilford, CN. 1980.

HEIKKINEN, Kanerva
2013   Finland: Reception of Tolkien. – *J. R. R. Tolkien Encyclopedia: Scholarship and Critical Assessment.* Ed. Michael D. C. Drout. New York: Routledge. 208–209.

LEPOJÄRVI, Jason
2012   A Friend's Death: C. S. Lewis's Disagreement with Augustine. – *Sehnsucht: The C. S. Lewis Journal.* Vol. 5/6. 67–80.
2015   *God Is Love, but Love Is Not God: Studies on C. S. Lewis's Theology of Love.* Ph.D. dissertation. University of Helsinki.
2019   How Many Loves? New Light on C. S. Lewis's *The Four Loves.* – *The Undiscovered C. S. Lewis: New Thoughts and Directions in Lewis Studies.* Ed. Bruce R. Johnson. (Forthcoming.)

LEWIS, C. S.
1940   *The Problem of Pain.* London: The Centenary Press.
1952   *Mere Christianity.* London: Geoffrey Bless.
2004   *The Collected Letters of C. S. Lewis.* Vol. 2. Ed. Walter Hooper. London: HarperCollins.
2017   *All My Road Before Me: The Diary of C. S. Lewis, 1922–1927.* Ed. Walter Hooper. San Francisco, CA: HarperOne.

MCGRATH, Alister
2013   *C. S. Lewis: A Life: Eccentric Genius, Reluctant Prophet.* Carol Stream, Ill: Tyndale House Publishers.
2015   On Tolkien, the Inklings – and Lewis' blindness to gender. – *Women and C. S. Lewis.* Eds. Carolyn Curtis and Mary Pomroy Key. Oxford: Lion Books. 79–84.

MORTON, Andrew & HAYES, John
2008   *Tolkien's Gedling 1914: The Birth of a Legend.* Studley: Brewin Books.

MUSTANOJA, Tauno
1982   Auvo Kurvinen: In Memoriam. – *Neuphilologische Mitteilungen.* Vol. 83. No. 1. 1–3

ORDWAY, Holly
2016   Tolkien's Modern Sources: Middle-earth Beyond the Middle Ages. Talk delivered to the Oxford University C. S. Lewis Society. 19 January 2016.
2019   *Tolkien's Modern Sources: Middle-earth Beyond the Middle Ages.* Kent, OH: Kent State University Press. Forthcoming.

PARTRIDGE, Brenda
1983   No Sex Please – We're Hobbits: The Construction of Female Sexuality in *The Lord of the Rings.* – *J. R. R. Tolkien: This Far Land.* Ed. Robert Giddings. London: Vision. 179–197.

RATELIFF, John D.
2015   The Missing Women: J. R. R. Tolkien's Lifelong Support of Women's Higher Education. – *Perilous and Fair: Women in the Works and Life of J. R. R. Tolkien.* Eds. Janet Brennan Croft and Leslie A. Donovan. Mythopoeic Press. 41–69.

SALU, Mary & FARRELL, Robert T. (eds)
1979   *J. R. R. Tolkien, Scholar and Storyteller: Essays in Memoriam.* Ichaka and London: Cornell University Press.

SCULL, Christina & HAMMOND, Wayne G.
2006a   *The J. R. R. Tolkien Companion and Guide.* Vo. I: *Chronology.* New York: Houghton Mifflin Company.
2006b   *The J. R. R. Tolkien Companion and Guide.* Vol. II: *Reader's Guide.* New York: Houghton Mifflin Company.

SHIPPEY, Tom
1991   The Lewis Diaries. – *C. S. Lewis and His Circle: Essays and Memories from the Oxford C. S. Lewis Society.* Eds. White, Robert & Wolfe, Judith & Wolfe, Brendan N. Oxford: Oxford University Press (2015). 134–149.
2003   *The Road To Middle-earth: How J. R. R. Tolkien Created a New Mythology.* Revised and Expanded. Boston, MA: Houghton Mifflin.

SOSKICE, Janet
2007   *The Kindness of God: Metaphor, Gender, and Religious Language.* Oxford: Oxford University Press.

STIMPSON, Catherine
1969   *J. R. R. Tolkien.* New York: Columbia.

SWEETMAN, David
1993   *Mary Renault: A Biography.* London: Chatto and Windus.

TOLKIEN, John & TOLKIEN, Priscilla
1992   *The Tolkien Family Album.* London: HarperCollins.

TOLKIEN, J. R. R.
2006   *The Letters of J. R. R. Tolkien.* Ed. Humphrey Carpenter. HarperCollins.

TOLKIEN, Michael
1995   Autobiographical Essay on My Grandfather, J. R. R. Tolkien. – Essay based on a talk presented to The Leicester Writers' Club at the College of Adult Education. 19 October 1995.

TOLKIEN, Priscilla
1992   Memories of J. R. R. Tolkien in his Centenary Year. – *The Brown Book.* Lady Margaret Hall: Oxford. December.

ÞORBJARNARDÓTTIR, Arndis
1999   Barnfóstran frá Íslandi og Tolkien-fjölskyldan ("Au Pair from Iceland and the Tolkien Family") – *Morganblaðið.* 28 February.

ZEPEDA, Joseph
2012   "To whom my own glad debts are incalculable": St. Augustine and Human Loves in *The Four Loves* and *Till We Have Faces.* – *Journal of Inklings Studies.* Vol. 2. No. 2. 5–26.

The list of contributors

Kenneth Appold, James Hastings Nichols Professor of Reformation History, Princeton Theological Seminary, USA

Theo Dieter, Research Professor, The Institute for Ecumenical Research, Strasbourg, France

Jaana Hallamaa, Professor of Social Ethics, University of Helsinki, Finland

Minna Hietamäki, University Lecturer of Dogmatics, University of Helsinki, Finland

Bo Kristian Holm, Associate Professor of Systematic Theology, Aarhus University

Werner Jeanrond, Professor of Systematic Theology, University of Oslo

Sari Kivistö, Professor of Comparative Literature, University of Tampere, Finland

Simo Knuuttila, Professor Emeritus of Philosophy of Religion, University of Helsinki, Finland

Jason Lepojärvi, Assistant Professor of Religious Studies, Thorneloe University at Laurentian, Canada

Veli-Matti Kärkkäinen, Professor of Systematic Theology, Fuller Theological Seminary, USA

Peter de Mey, Professor of Systematic Theology, KU Leuven, Belgium

Friederike Nüssel, Professor of Systematic Theology, University of Heidelberg, Germany

Ted Peters, Distinguished Professor Emeritus in Systematic Theology and Ethics at Pacific Lutheran Theological Seminary and the Graduate Theological Union in Berkeley, USA

Sami Pihlström, Professor of Philosophy of Religion, University of Helsinki, Finland

Antti Raunio, Professor of Systematic Theology, University of Eastern Finland, Finland

Michael Root, Professor of Systematic Theology, Catholic University of America, Washington D.C., USA

Olli-Pekka Vainio, University Lecturer of Dogmatics, University of Helsinki, Finland

Michael Welker, Senior Professor of Systematic Theology, University of Heidelberg, Germany

www.ingramcontent.com/pod-product-compliance
Lightning Source LLC
Chambersburg PA
CBHW070010010526
44117CB00011B/1493